Lecture Notes in Artificial Intelligence   5049

Edited by R. Goebel, J. Siekmann, and W. Wahlster

Subseries of Lecture Notes in Computer Science

Danny Weyns   Sven A. Brueckner
Yves Demazeau (Eds.)

Engineering Environment-Mediated Multi-Agent Systems

International Workshop, EEMMAS 2007
Dresden, Germany, October 5, 2007
Selected Revised and Invited Papers

 Springer

Series Editors

Randy Goebel, University of Alberta, Edmonton, Canada
Jörg Siekmann, University of Saarland, Saarbrücken, Germany
Wolfgang Wahlster, DFKI and University of Saarland, Saarbrücken, Germany

Volume Editors

Danny Weyns
Katholieke Universiteit Leuven
3001 Leuven, Belgium
E-mail: danny.weyns@cs.kuleuven.be

Sven A. Brueckner
NewVectors, A Division of TechTeam Government Solutions, Inc.
Ann Arbor, MI 48105, USA
E-mail: sven.brueckner@newvectors.net

Yves Demazeau
CNRS, Laboratoire d'Informatique de Grenoble
38031 Grenoble Cedex, France
E-mail: Yves.Demazeau@imag.fr

Library of Congress Control Number: 2008931050

CR Subject Classification (1998): I.2.11, D.2

LNCS Sublibrary: SL 7 – Artificial Intelligence

ISSN   0302-9743
ISBN-10   3-540-85028-7 Springer Berlin Heidelberg New York
ISBN-13   978-3-540-85028-1 Springer Berlin Heidelberg New York

Springer is a part of Springer Science+Business Media

springer.com

© Springer-Verlag Berlin Heidelberg 2008
Printed in Germany

Typesetting: Camera-ready by author, data conversion by Scientific Publishing Services, Chennai, India
Printed on acid-free paper   SPIN: 12279692   06/3180   5 4 3 2 1 0

Preface

Software intensive systems are increasingly expected to deal with changing user needs and dynamic operating conditions at run time. Examples are the need for life reconfigurations, management of resource variability, and dealing with particular failure modes. Endowing systems with these kinds of capabilities poses severe challenges to software engineers and necessitates the development of new techniques, practices, and tools that build upon sound engineering principles. The field of multi-agent systems focuses on the foundations and engineering of systems that consists of a network of autonomous entities (agents) that interact to achieve the system goals. One line of research in multi-agent systems, inspired by biological, physical and other naturally occurring systems, concerns multi-agent systems in which agents share information and coordinate their behavior through a shared medium called an agent environment. Typical examples are gradient fields and digital pheromones that guide agents in their local context and as such facilitate the coordination of a community of agents. Since environment-mediation in multi-agent systems has shown to result in manageable solutions with very adaptable qualities, it is a promising paradigm to deal with the increasing complexity and dynamism of distributed applications.

Control in environment-mediated multi-agent systems is decentralized, i.e., none of the components has full access or control over the system. Self-organization is an approach to engineer decentralized, distributed and resource-limited systems that are capable of dynamically adapting to changing conditions and requirements without external intervention. This useful system property is often reflected in functions such as self-configuration, self-optimization, and self-healing. Engineering approaches to self-organizing systems often rely on global functionality to emerge from local and autonomous decisions of individual agents that communicate through a shared agent environment. When designing a system that is based only on local interactions in the environment and the emergent properties resulting from these interactions, it is a difficult research problem on the one hand to obtain the required global behavior of the system and on the other hand to avoid undesired global properties.

A particular issue in the design of self-organizing systems is determining the suitable complexity of the individual agents required to achieve the desired emergent functions. Typically, agents in self-organizing systems are less complex in their sensing, reasoning, and acting capabilities than agents in traditional multi-agent systems that follow a deliberate organizing approach. But, depending on the application domain, the functional requirements, and the sheer number of agents available in a particular setting, individual agent complexity may vary. As agent complexity increases, self-organization may become harder to achieve and to prove. EEMMAS addresses the approach of environment mediation among self-organizing agents that off-loads some of the agent complexity into the processes of the dynamic agent environment. Off-loading agent complexity into the agent environment simplifies agent design, implementation, and evaluation and thus increases the likelihood of a successful application development.

The papers in this volume include both selected and thoroughly revised papers from EEMMAS 2007 and invited papers. The papers show how the agent environment provides a design element that allows multi-agent system engineers to manage complexity at different stages of the development life cycle. We hope that the papers of this volume stimulate further research in environment-mediated multi-agent systems.

March 2008   Danny Weyns
                                                              Sven Brueckner
                                                             Yves Demazeau

Organization

EEMMAS 2007 was organized in conjunction with the European Conference on Complex Systems (ECCS 2007), Dresden, Germany, October 5, 2007.

Program Co-chairs

Danny Weyns · · · · · · · · · · · · · · Katholieke Universiteit Leuven, Belgium
Sven Brueckner · · · · · · · · · · · · NewVectors, Ann Arbor, USA
Yves Demazeau · · · · · · · · · · · · CNRS, Laboratoire d'Informatique de
                                       Grenoble, France

Program Committee

Flavien Balbo · · · · · · · · · · · · · · · LAMSADE, Université Paris-Dauphine, France
Tibor Bosse · · · · · · · · · · · · · · · · Vrije Universiteit Amsterdam, The Netherlands
Cristiano Castelfrachi · · · · · · · ISTC-CNR, Rome, Italy
Giovanna Di Marzo Serugendo · University of London, UK
Marco Dorigo · · · · · · · · · · · · · · Université Libre de Bruxelles, Belgium
Alexis Drogoul · · · · · · · · · · · · · · IRD/IFI/MSI, Hanoi, Vietnam
Jacques Ferber · · · · · · · · · · · · · Université de Montpellier II, LIRMM, France
Marie-Pierre Gleizes · · · · · · · · IRIT Toulouse, France
David Hales · · · · · · · · · · · · · · · University of Bologna, Italy
Tom Holvoet · · · · · · · · · · · · · · · DistriNet, K.U.Leuven, Belgium
Mark Jelasity · · · · · · · · · · · · · · Hungarian Acad. Sci. and University of Szeged,
                                          Hungary
Jeff Kephart · · · · · · · · · · · · · · · IBM, USA
Franziska Klügl · · · · · · · · · · · · University of Wurzburg, Germany
Marco Mamei · · · · · · · · · · · · · · Università di Modena e Reggio Emilia, Italy
Fabien Michel · · · · · · · · · · · · · LERI, Reims, France
James Odell · · · · · · · · · · · · · · · James Odell Associates, Ann Arbor, USA
Andrea Omicini · · · · · · · · · · · · Università di Bologna, Italy
Juan Pavón Mestras · · · · · · · · · Universidad Complutense Madrid, Spain
H. Van Dyke Parunak · · · · · · · NewVectors, Ann Arbor, USA
Alessandro Ricci · · · · · · · · · · · · Università di Bologna, Italy
Nicolas Sabouret · · · · · · · · · · · LIP6 Paris, France
John Sauter · · · · · · · · · · · · · · · NewVectors LLC, Ann Arbor, USA
Guy Théraulaz · · · · · · · · · · · · · Université Paul Sabatier, Toulouse, France
Karl Tuyls · · · · · · · · · · · · · · · · University of Eindhoven, The Netherlands
Adelinde Uhrmacher · · · · · · · · University of Rostock, Germany
Paul Valckenaers · · · · · · · · · · · PMA, Katholieke Universiteit Leuven, Belgium
Mirko Viroli · · · · · · · · · · · · · · · Università di Bologna, Italy

Daniel Yamins   Harvard University, USA
Franco Zambonelli   Università di Modena e Reggio Emilia, Italy

Website

http://www.cs.kuleuven.ac.be/~distrinet/events/eemmas/2007/

Acknowledgements

We are grateful to the ECCS organizers for hosting EEMMAS and for their financial support. A special word of appreciation goes to Peter Felten for his support with the practical organization of EEMMAS. We thank the PC members for their critical review work. Finally, we thank the Springer staff for supporting the publication of this volume.

Table of Contents

Environment-Based Support for Context and Organizations

Swarms of Self-assembling Robots

Marco Dorigo

IRIDIA, CoDE, Université Libre de Bruxelles
Avenue Franklin Roosevelt 50, CP 194/6, B-1050 Brussels - Belgium
mdorigo@ulb.ac.be

Abstract. In this talk I present recent research in swarm robotics, the discipline that studies robotic systems composed of swarms of robots tightly interacting and cooperating to reach their goals. In particular, I will present a new type of robot, called swarm-bot, and the results of a number of experiments run with it. A swarm-bot [4,7] is an artifact composed of a swarm of assembled s-bots. The s-bots are mobile robots capable of connecting to, and disconnecting from, other s-bots. In the swarm-bot form, the s-bots are attached to each other and, when needed, become a single robotic system that can move and change its shape. S-bots have relatively simple sensors and motors and limited computational capabilities. A swarm-bot can solve problems that cannot be solved by s-bots alone. In the talk, I first describe the s-bots hardware and the methodology we followed to develop algorithms for their control. Then I illustrate the capabilities of the swarm-bot robotic system by showing video recordings of some of the many experiments we performed to study coordinated movement [1], path formation [8], collective transport [5], shape formation [2,3], and other collective behaviors [6,9,10].

Keywords: swarm robotics, swarm-bot, s-bots.

Acknowledgements

This work was supported by the Swarm-bots project, funded by the Future and Emerging Technologies programme of the European Commission (grant IST-2000-31010). The information provided is the sole responsibility of the authors and does not reflect the Community's opinion. The Community is not responsible for any use that might be made of data in this publication. Marco Dorigo acknowledges support from the Belgian F.R.S.-FNRS, of which he is a Research Director.

References

[1] Baldassarre, G., Trianni, V., Bonani, M., Mondada, F., Dorigo, M., Nolfi, S.: Self-Organized Coordinated Motion in Groups of Physically Connected Robots. IEEE Transactions on Systems, Man, and Cybernetics-Part B 37(1), 224–239 (2007)
[2] Christensen, A.L., O'Grady, R., Dorigo, M.: Morphology Control in a Multirobot System. IEEE Robotics & Automation Magazine 14(4), 18–25 (2007)

D. Weyns, S.A. Brueckner, and Y. Demazeau (Eds.): EEMMAS 2007, LNAI 5049, pp. 1–2, 2008.
© Springer-Verlag Berlin Heidelberg 2008

[3] Christensen, A.L., O'Grady, R., Dorigo, M.: Morphogenesis: Shaping Swarms of Intelligent Robots. Winners of the Best Video Award. In: AAAI 2007, AAAI International Conference, Vancouver, Canada, July 23 (2007), http://www.aivideo.org/2007

[4] Dorigo, M., Trianni, V., Sahin, E., Groß, R., Labella, T.H., Baldassarre, G., Nolfi, S., Deneubourg, J.-L., Mondada, F., Floreano, D., Gambardella, L.M.: Evolving Self-Organizing Behaviors for a Swarm-bot. Autonomous Robots 17(2-3), 223–245 (2004)

[5] Groß, R., Dorigo, M.: Evolution of Solitary and Group Transport Behaviors for Autonomous Robots Capable of Self-Assembling. Adaptive Behavior (in press)

[6] Labella, T.H., Dorigo, M., Deneubourg, J.-L.: Division of Labour in a Group of Robots Inspired by Ants' Foraging Behaviour. ACM Transactions on Autonomous and Adaptive Systems 1(1), 4–25 (2006)

[7] Mondada, F., Pettinaro, G.C., Guignard, A., Kwee, I.V., Floreano, D., Deneubourg, J.-L., Nolfi, S., Gambardella, L.M., Dorigo, M.: SWARM-BOT: A New Distributed Robotic Concept. Autonomous Robots 17(2-3), 193–221 (2004)

[8] Nouyan, S., Campo, A., Dorigo, M.: Path Formation in a Robot Swarm: Self-Organized Strategies to Find Your Way Home. Swarm Intelligence 2 (in press)

[9] O'Grady, R., Groß, R., Mondada, F., Bonani, M., Dorigo, M.: Self-assembly on Demand in a Group of Physical Autonomous Mobile Robots Navigating Rough Terrain. In: Capcarrère, M.S., Freitas, A.A., Bentley, P.J., Johnson, C.G., Timmis, J. (eds.) ECAL 2005. LNCS (LNAI), vol. 3630, pp. 272–281. Springer, Heidelberg (2005)

[10] Trianni, V., Nolfi, S., Dorigo, M.: Cooperative Hole Avoidance in a Swarm-Bot. Robotics and Autonomous Systems 54(2), 97–103 (2006)

Complex Systems and Agent-Oriented Software Engineering

Juan Pavón[1], Francisco Garijo[2], and Jorge Gómez-Sanz[1]

[1] Facultad de Informática, Universidad Complutense Madrid
Ciudad Universitaria s/n, 28040 Madrid, Spain
[2] Telefónica I+D
C/ Emilio Vargas 6, 28043 Madrid, Spain
jpavon@fdi.ucm.es, fgarijo@tid.es, jjgomez@sip.ucm.es

Abstract. Although there is a huge amount of work and valuable proposals about agent oriented software engineering, it seems that the paradigm has not been yet widely adopted by software industry. Some claim that there is a need for a killer application showing clearly the benefits of multi-agent systems with respect to other techniques. Others may consider the approach as too academic to be applied in real projects. However, in our opinion, the answer may be found in the simple explanation of lessons learned while developing applications with agent-orientation, and confronting these with object and component oriented solutions, especially when faced to the development of complex systems. This paper discusses contributions of multi-agent systems from a software engineering perspective, as a way to put in value some of the properties of the agent paradigm in the development of complex software systems.

1 Introduction

The conception of software engineering methodologies should take into account both theoretical works and the experiences of lessons learned. In the first case, the scientist collects and contrasts information from different sources, which are mainly academic (e.g., journal and conference papers, books), and analyse the best ways to synthesise the work done in a coherent set of methods. Usually, the result is the definition of some new modelling language, guidelines and examples to apply it, and a process model. Other issues, such as code production and the availability of tools, are fundamental to put the methodology into practice, but they are not always taken into account. On the other hand, some experimented developers can derive, as a result of accumulation of successful practices, a set of recommendations, which are usually accompanied by tools. A good example is object-oriented design patterns. Unfortunately, application developers working in industry lack of time and motivation to write papers, and this may hinder the dissemination and systematization of their knowledge. Both approaches are complementary and need each other.

This is perhaps a simplistic view, however, the intention here is to underline several aspects that are usually underestimated, but have great relevance in software engineering. In fact, the purpose of this discussion is to review some

D. Weyns, S.A. Brueckner, and Y. Demazeau (Eds.): EEMMAS 2007, LNAI 5049, pp. 3–16, 2008.

experiences of the application of agent-oriented software engineering in the development of real systems, which involve coping with certain types of complexity. The starting point is that most agent-oriented methodologies have been defined in the academia and the impact in industry is very low. There are at least three important reasons for this failure. The first is that there is not too much reporting on agent-based developments, from a software engineering perspective. In fact, the lack of consideration of implementation issues by academics, who stay usually at analysis and design levels, broadens the gap with practitioners. Also, it should be taken into account that agent-oriented methodologies are mainly concerned with the production process (e.g., analysis, design, implementation, validation, etc., of the software product). Essential aspects in the whole life cycle such as the management process, planning and control of resources, which are equally important, are usually ignored in agent-oriented methodologies. This makes it difficult to put agent-oriented methodologies in practice as they fail in logistics. Furthermore, agent technology, although an appealing paradigm, is not alone and must coexist with other technical approaches. In concrete, there are many techniques that could be combined with agents such as service oriented architecture, software component frameworks, aspect oriented programming, model driven engineering, software product lines, etc. This integration is necessary and paves the way for the adoption of multi-agent systems (MAS) in well established frameworks.

This paper looks at several issues that, from the experience of the authors, could be of interest to software practitioners when considering agent-oriented software engineering. It starts by considering the role of MAS for the development of modern complex systems, in section 0. This motivates the need for the MAS approach, and the role of architecture in MAS as a way to organize the use of patterns, which result from experience in the development of applications. An example of a component-based architecture for MAS is described in section 0, with the purpose to show that a framework can help to enforce the reuse of patterns, as a way to improve the development process. Section 0 identifies issues to take into account from a management perspective in the software process, which are not usually covered in most agent-oriented software engineering proposals. There is also a need to measure the impact of the agent paradigm in software processes, and with this purpose section 0 presents some work on metrics for MAS developments, considering two aspects: cost estimation and the value of reusability. To conclude, section 0 summarizes relevant issues that should be addressed by agent-oriented software engineering.

2   Multi-agent Systems for Modern Complex Systems

Software engineering was born in the late sixties as a way to cope with the *software crisis*. This term denotes the problems to master the trade-off between customers' requirements and the development costs, as well as the difficulty of writing correct, understandable and verifiable computer programs as far as systems grow in complexity [23]. As Dijkstra stated, the major cause for the software crisis was the fact that *machines have become several orders of magnitude more powerful* [9]. At that time, software was usually conceived to run in single computers. Various software methodologies contributed to manage complexity of software by considering several aspects that go beyond formal methods to guarantee algorithms correctness. The definition of software processes, requirements engineering, analysis and design methods, etc., started to be applied with more or less intensity in software projects, and in some cases with a high degree of success.

However, the last decade has introduced new elements for the complexity of software systems, as a consequence of rapid and tremendous advances in networking and multi-modal interface technologies. The first implies great connectivity and communication among software entities, and the second new ways to make end-users interact with software systems. At the beginning, the development of object-oriented programming languages and methodologies has, more or less, succeed to manage the development of new systems. Objects adapt well to the client-server paradigm where interface and implementation can be clearly separated. This promotes a kind of abstraction that facilitates interoperability in heterogeneous configurations.

As far as distributed computing progresses, the environment of software entities is gaining complexity in several aspects, and this is motivating the need to review the distributed object computing paradigm. It is not merely the interaction between one entity and another, but of many to many. A software entity now is situated in a context that only knows partially. For instance, which services are available, how to access them, and with what quality of service. There are other issues in the environment that provide uncertainty, such as the availability at a certain time of required resources and services (e.g. there can be communication failures, security risks, disconnected servers, etc.) Also some new opportunities, such as the appearance in the environment of new entities that are able to provide new services, better quality of service, or a lower cost. Such changing environment motivates the need to build software that adapts continuously. And this ability to adaptation requires some degree of autonomy. The management of some of these problems has motivated the evolution of object-orientation towards component frameworks, where some services and abstractions are made possible [25].

Moving forward to add more flexibility, by providing greater degree of autonomy to components, is where the agent paradigm enters into scene. This autonomy is not only understood in terms of self-management, as it is the case of the *autonomic computing* initiative [20]. More concretely, it refers to the ability to specify agent *goals* and the *decision-making* process [1, 8]. This has implications in the analysis and design of complex software systems, where most agent-oriented methodologies focus, and it is reflected in MAS architecture, as it is explained in the following section. But it should have also impact in the management process. MAS technology takes inputs from different fields, not only computer science, such as Sociology, Biology, Psychology and Organizational studies. This may involve the participation of multi-disciplinary teams and their management. The management process has to deal with setting a work environment for the fruitful collaboration of team members and with the customer, planning of activities, provision and availability of resources on time, quality assurance procedures, risk management, etc. In this respect, agent autonomy can contribute as it facilitates separation of concerns and better organization of responsibilities among team members. This should be explicitly addressed by the corresponding methodologies.

3 Software Architectures for MAS

One of the best ways to cope with complexity is abstraction. Software engineering deals with management of different levels of abstraction along the life-cycle of software systems. For instance, requirements focus on *what* the system should provide, design is concerned on the definition of solutions, from a high level identification of system structure towards more complete specification of each component, and implementation goes to the details of code. The accumulation of developers' experiences is reflected as patterns, *ranging from idioms that shape the use of a particular programming language to mechanisms that define the collaboration among societies of objects, components, and other parts* [4]. A system architecture enforces the use of a set of patterns. This implies the establishment of behaviour principles and a system structure. Both facilitate the management of complexity by a separation of concerns. In this way, the system architecture guides the developer in the identification of relevant system features and the application of patterns. This means that system architecture represents the link between the result of experience in the development of complex systems and the intention to reuse well-proven solutions.

Traditionally, proposals for agent architectures are categorized as reactive, cognitive, or hybrid. They are useful for building particular agents with specific abilities (e.g., reasoning, learning, real-time responsiveness). For complex systems, we need to consider also architectures with a wider scope, at the MAS level. In this sense, there is a growing number of proposals, which can be found in most agent-related conferences, for particular applications. Here we present a MAS architecture, the ICARO-T framework by Telefónica I+D (TID), which can be applied for a wide scope of agent-based applications. This MAS framework provides a component-based architecture for MAS to work at MAS organizational level and individual agent level. It is the result from the cumulative experience in the development of agent-based applications in the last eight years. Therefore, the architecture has been elaborated, refined and validated through the realization of several agent-based applications. The first system discovered patterns for building reactive and cognitive agents. It was a cooperative working system [11], which was refined with the development of a project management system for the creation of intelligent network services [14]. Scalability of the cognitive agent model was considered in a context with thousands of users, in a MAS that supported personalization of web sites [13], and the reuse of this solution in an online discussion and decision making system [22] and a prototype to validate the MESSAGE methodology [6]. Refinements where applied to several services with voice recognition at Telefónica [10].

An application in the ICARO-T framework is modeled as an *organization* made up of controller components, which are *agents*, and *resources*. Therefore, there are two layers in the organization: the control layer, which is made up of controller components, and the resource layer, made up of the components that supply information or provide some support functionality to the agents to achieve their goals. The service's organization is shown in Figure 1.

The Control Layer contains two categories of controller components: *managers* and *specialists*. Their interfaces and internal structure are similar; however, they play

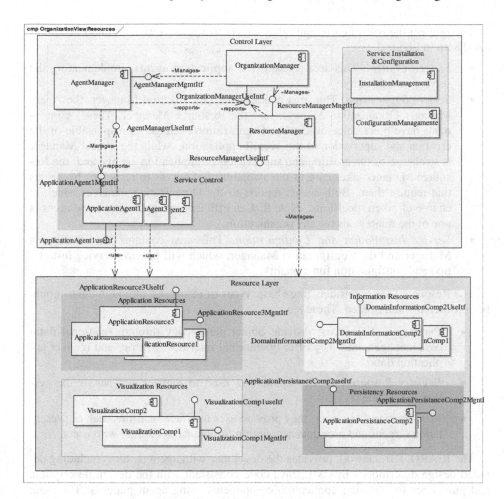

Fig. 1. ICARO-T framework architecture

different roles. Manager components are responsible for the management aspects of the service such as installation, configuration, activation, monitoring and exception handling. Specialist components are in charge of achieving the functionality of the service. Managers and specialists collaborate to accomplish their tasks during the whole service life cycle. It is important to note here the relevance of management components, as this is an issue normally underestimated in most agent prototypes. In this way the framework provides well-proved patterns to cope with common problems associated with installation, initialization, monitoring and reconfiguration of agents and resources in the system. Following these patterns, developers are forced to be aware of the basic management functionality that new components (agents or resources) have to provide to be manageable. And the framework will take care of them.

To highlight the role of each controller, the control layer is divided into three areas (as shown in Figure 1):

- *Service Control.* This area contains the application agents implementing the service functionality.
- *Service Supervision.* This area contains the Organization Manager, the Agent Manager Organization Manager and the Resource Manager. These components have hierarchical roles. The Organization Manager is responsible of the creation and supervision of the overall application, while the Agent Manager is in charge of the creation and supervision of application agents, and the Resource Manager takes care of the availability of access to resources by agents that require them. Both agents reports to the Organization manager which in charge of taken decisions. Note that an efficient management of resources is one of the main goals for any organization.
- *Service Installation and Configuration.* This area contains the Installation Manager and the Configuration Manager, which will provide service installation and configuration functionality.

The Resource Layer considers three basic types of resources, although others could be considered when needed. These are:

- *Persistency Resources:* provide object persistency through relational database management. They offer operational interfaces to store and recover application data.

- *Registry Resource:* this component is used to register and access the system's available services.

- *Visualization Resources:* they provide user interface facilities such as presentation screens and user data acquisition for agents to interact with users.

The ICARO-T framework provides the developer with agent patterns including detailed design descriptions in UML, Java code consistent with the design description, and guidelines for creating application components using agent patterns. The main advantage of the ICARO-T framework is that it provides to engineers not only concepts and models, but also architectural patterns and flexible components. The ICARO-T framework focus on providing an agent component fully compatible with software engineering standards, while in other agent based platforms, such as FIPA, the focus is on communication standards. In this sense both are complementary, but FIPA is more limited in scope as it provide engineers with communication infrastructure but nothing about the communicating entities, which are the agents. In concrete, it provides two agent patterns, one for reactive agents and other for cognitive agents. The structure of components for building a cognitive agent is shown in Figure 2. This shows that a cognitive agent also follows the management pattern by providing a manager interface. The pattern shows that an agent has a perception and a knowledge processor component. This is usually the most complex part, and the architecture facilitates its implementation by structuring it in several components: a cognitive control component, and inference engine, a set of basic entities to represent agent mental state, and a task manager. The architecture provides the way these components interrelate from both structural and dynamic points of view. For this reason it is important to represent dynamics. For this case, Figure 3 shows how a cognitive agent processes events from its environment (from applications, messages from other agents, or the result of tasks). These are taken by the Perception component, which filters events and decides which are considered by the agent to generate evidences in agent's knowledge base. Evidences are put in a queue for processing by the inference engine, which takes into account the goals of the agent. Thus, with evidences, the rule engine will be able to determine goal resolution, task execution, or changing the focus of the agent.

Observe that the cognitive agent architecture facilitates the work of the developer by providing the mechanisms for agent perception and reasoning. The developer has to concentrate on the definition of agent goals, the identification of agent perceptions and how they are represented in agent mental state, and the definition of tasks that the agent can execute. There is also flexibility to change some components. For instance, the rule engine has been changed from Jess [http://herzberg.ca.sandia.gov/] to ILOG Jrules [http://www.ilog.com/products/rules/], and recently to Drools [http://labs.jboss.com/ drools/].

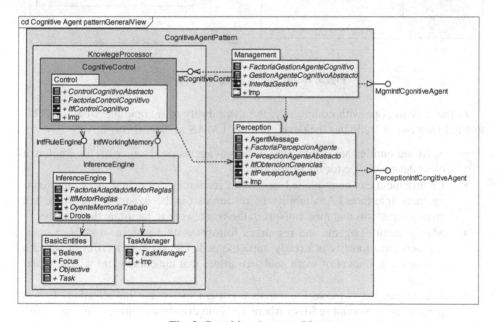

Fig. 2. Cognitive Agent architecture

In addition to agents, there are also other kind of patterns:

- Organisations patterns modelling agent based applications.
- Resource patterns encapsulating computing entities providing services to agents. These services include message oriented middleware, transaction monitors, security and authentication services, information services, databases, visualization, speech recognition and generation, etc.
- Basic components, which model components for building new agent and resource models. This category includes abstract data types, specialized libraries, domain ontologies, rule processors, buffers, etc.

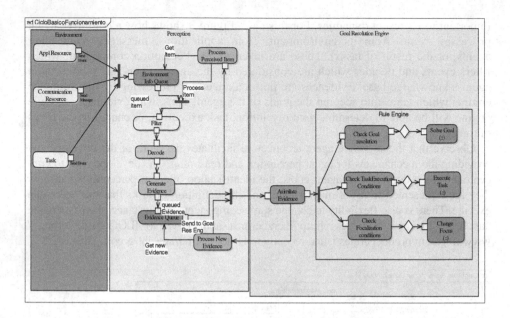

Fig. 3. Behaviour of a cognitive agent

In the way to cope with complexity, the availability of a component-based architectural framework facilitates the development of MAS in several ways:

- Software entities are categorized either as agents or resources. This implies a clear design choice for the developer.
- Environment can be modelled as a set of resources, with clear usage and management interfaces. Availability of resources can be dynamic. But there are standard patterns and mechanisms in the framework to facilitate their access.
- Management of agents and resources follows certain patterns and most management functionality is already implemented. This relieves the developer of a considerable amount of work, and guarantees that the component will be under control.
- In concrete, the framework enforces a pattern for system initialization. This is particularly important in MAS where multiple distributed entities have to be initialized consistently and this turns out to be a complex issue in many systems.
- Agents work as autonomous entities and encapsulate their behaviour (reactive, cognitive, hybrid) behind their interfaces.
- Interactions can be defined at an application level, independently of the underlying middleware (remote objects, web services, FIPA, etc.)

4   AOSE and Process Management

The ICARO-T framework shows the relevance of management in any application. This is in fact one of the common functionality that is supported by component-based frameworks. But management has to be considered also from the perspective of the software process, and this is a weak point in most agent-oriented methodologies. MAS-Common KADS [16], one of the first agent-oriented methodologies but now inactive, is probably the only to have addressed this issue, as it takes this from more classic software engineering approaches.

Most agent-oriented applications now are mostly prototypes and do not involve teams of more than half a dozen persons. But there are several issues that agent-oriented applications development will have to face. It is common to consider in software engineer three basic elements, the three P: Persons, Process, and Product. The product has been the focus by now, as it has been stated before, but there are issues to consider about the first two: Persons and Process.

Persons are the most important factor for success of a software project. We have also mentioned that in the future we can expect more and more interdisciplinary teams, and as far as MAS are applied in more ambitious applications, MAS development teams will increase in number of persons considerably. In order to manage persons, several issues have to be taken into account, such as:

- Difference in skills of the team members.
- Variability of the composition of the team members. In academia it is common to have grant holders for specific periods of time. In industry, there is not a periodicity, but rather unexpected changes in the team composition (people that moves from one project or company to other).
- Organization structure. This involves the identification of responsibilities of the team members, and the role of the team in its institution, i.e., how the team can get access to resources in its organization.
- Corporate culture.
- Development strategies and tactics.

A way to cope with some of these issues is to have clear organizational norms but also that the architecture of a complex system can be structured into flexible and independent parts which may be assigned to specific members of the team according to their personal profiles.

Generally, the process is quite short in agent-oriented methodologies. It is usually defined as a set of some simple steps. The particularities of the development process when agent technology is involved needs a deeper study. The question is not trivial and requires a huge effort, since every argument needs weeks or months or work to test each development process instance. For instance, what are differences between a waterfall process model and a spiral process model for a specific problem domain when using the agent paradigm? These models have concrete features. The waterfall model is visible (its internal state is easy to be known even though many people may be involved), it is easy to comprehend (just a sequence of activities ordered lineally in time), it is very sensible to changes in the requirements (it hardly allows to go back and reconsider previous decisions easily), and it takes a long time until seeing some software running (software is elaborated at implementation stage, by the end). A spiral process is not visible, it is not easy to comprehend (it includes the concept of development iteration, increment, or risk management among others), it permits to react on unexpected changes in the requirements (it is possible because cycles of development are shorter), and it produces software almost from the beginning of the project (it proceeds incrementally focusing on concrete features step by step). Most works in agent oriented software engineering follow a waterfall model or a kind of customary evolutionary model (spiral model is a kind of evolutionary process model) that, in any case, are customized to the concrete specification language. The description of their activities is rather short and limited, in most cases, to the generation of concrete diagrams. To realize the gap between agent-oriented software engineering process models and previous processes, it is clarifying to look at the descriptions of many of existing process models. They require more than a sequence of steps in one page.

4.1 Risk Management

A software project manager faces a large list of issues. It is just illustrative to look up the list of risks identified by the Software Engineering Institute [7]. These risks can be managed in different ways, but in general they have to be identified, analyzed, monitored, and solving/alleviating/contingency plans have to be devised. The relevance of these risks in an agent-oriented methodology is high in some aspects. For instance, there is a risk in [7] referring to the design area and the difficulty attribute. This risk is characterized by the existence of unrealistic client requirements; requirements whose design may pose a challenge and for which there is no trivial solution. This risk, and others that can be found in more recent risk management works [3], is supposed to be evaluated by a team of workers against current client requirements list. The team is assumed to determine what to do to attenuate the difficulty of these requirements, for instance, by locating similar developments; to avoid the risk, for instance finding a satisfactory solution to the requirement; or to deal with the negative impact of the risk if it cannot be avoided, for instance, contacting experts in the concrete problem and dedicating extra time in the development for studying the problem.

4.2 Software Quality Assurance

Another problem in academy developments is the quality of the generated products. In an industrial project, Software Quality Assurance activities are relevant since they ensure the product will meet client expectations as well as the criteria of a professional practice of software development [17]. The IEEE Glossary [26] provides two meanings for quality. The first refers to the extent to which a system, component, or process meets specified requirements. The second refers to the degree a system, component, or process meets customer or user needs or expectations. The relevance of these aspects for an agent development is clear but has been considered slightly in the agent literature. For instance, from the perspective of the professional practice of software engineering, there are no guidelines for documenting a MAS. There are meta-models but these are not sufficient if the complete behaviour of the MAS is to be captured. Another example from the generic perspective of the specification satisfaction, there is little concern about the definition of specialized activities for the analysis of the specification elaborated so far. Some initial concerns about quality start to appear in works like [27], where a MAS architecture is developed pursuing some quality attributes, namely performance, configurability, flexibility, and openness.

Testing activities are starting to be explored in the context of MAS. The more complex the problem, the more difficult the definition of tests that ensure the satisfaction of initial requirements. The agent community is starting to realise these problems and developing testing strategies integrated into agent oriented methodologies (see, for instance, the ACLAnalyser tool [5]).

5 MAS Metrics

Measuring the products and activities of software engineering is an important task. Metrics determine the degree to which an attribute is present in the measured element. Activities responsible of applying different metrics can be enacted during the development or at the end. When executed during the development, they provide valuable information about the current state of the project. When used at the end, they permit to measure the effectiveness (productivity, reusability, defect detection rate) of the development team as well as the development process. Results from the different measurements in a software project are stored in what is called a *baseline*. This baseline contains historical data about the developments and it is a key element towards predicting performance aspects of future projects.

In an agent-oriented development, metrics are relevant as well. They provide objective arguments that support the claims of the agent community about the benefits of an agent oriented development. Therefore, it is an important task of the community to collect statistical data about the different agent oriented developments. In this line, we have already given preliminary steps, one about cost estimation [15] and other studying reusability of code in an agent oriented development [10]. Although these aspects are quite related to implementation, metrics benefit from the application of good architectures and design practices. In this sense, the availability of a MAS architecture has an impact on cost estimation and reusability.

5.1 Cost Estimation

Providing adjusted cost estimation values in a project is not trivial at all. Trying to translate traditional software engineering cost estimation techniques to the agent domain, we prepared a simple baseline made up of three projects with the participation of industry [15]. This baseline contained statistical data about the lines of code of each terminated product as well as an account of the average lines of code required to represent each logical component (event, goal, rule, state machine, or task) of the agents. Using this base line and well-known software engineering cost estimation techniques based on lines of code, concretely COCOMO II, it was possible to estimate with a reasonable precision the real cost of each project.

The reliability of these estimations depends greatly on the number of projects belonging to the baseline. In principle, the more projects are recorded, the more reliable is the prediction. Nevertheless, accurate predictions depend as well of more factors, like the problem domain, the experience of the development team, or the complexity of the problem.

5.2 Reusability

Reusing agent software across projects should start to be a common practice. To illustrate the benefits of reuse, Garijo et al. [10] introduce some measurements showing important savings in the development of spoken dialog systems using a library of agent based components, BOGAR_LN, a precedent of the ICARO-T framework. Metrics were established to determine the percentage of reuse of library components, and the time and effort required for design and implementation of application components and subsystems.

In the design phase, metrics parameters focus on the number of classes and diagrams carried out. Metrics parameters for cognitive agent components also include the number of objectives, tasks and classes in the re-used domain. For reactive agents, the metrics parameters only consider the complexity of the control automaton (status, types of event and transitions). In the implementation phase, the metrics parameters consider the number of code lines corresponding to the implementation of classes. The number of rules for cognitive agents, and the number of states of the Finite State Automata of reactive agents, are also considered.

Experience gathered during the development of the CITA2 project (a mixed-initiative spoken dialog system for appointment management over the telephone), have shown that using the components allows substantial reduction in development time and effort, concretely 65% less. Cost reduction was achieved without minimising or skipping activities like design, documentation and testing. The number of errors in the testing phase, and error detection/correction cycle duration, also decrease. The testing period for CITA2, was one third of those spent for previous services in BOGAR, and the amount of errors was 60% smaller.

6   Conclusions

Today, most works in the agent community focus on concrete isolated problems. The need of producing more pragmatic results has been already stated. Wooldridge et al. [19] point at the need of more applications, and for that goal, more tools that enable an agent oriented development. Luck et al. [21] continue this line, pointing at the lack of proper development methods as the reason for slow penetration of the agent technology in the industry.

Various agent-oriented methodologies are contributing with agent-oriented modelling languages and tools to manage complexity of MAS development [1]. They have shown that the agent paradigm is a valid technical solution for developing software in an heterogeneous and changing environment. But they should look also at the logistics for the production process and for the management process of the system. As it has been mentioned, agent-oriented software engineering approaches are addressing mainly the production process. How the agent concept can contribute to the management process as a unit for work distribution, the role of the MAS and agents in the planning of the development activities, the definition of quality assurance procedures for agent-based applications, are pending issues. In this respect, the agent concept is still underestimated.

Given the degree of maturity in the development of agent-based applications, we can start to consider some agent-based frameworks that enforce the use of certain patterns, from system architecture to implementation, as the one shown in this paper. The availability of agent-based frameworks, supported by agent-oriented methodologies that address the whole software process, will make MAS complexity manageable, and will allow reducing costs. To demonstrate this, we need well-defined metrics and a large baseline of MAS applications.

Acknowledgments

This work has been funded by the Spanish Council for Science and Technology with grant TIN2005-08501-C03-01.

References

1. Barber, K.S., Martin, C.E.: Agent autonomy: Specification, measurement, and dynamic adjustment. In: Proceedings of the Autonomy Control Software Workshop (1999)
2. Bernon, C., Cossentino, M., Pavón, J.: An Overview of Current Trends in European AOSE Research. Informatica, An International Journal of Computing and Informatics 29(4), 379–390 (2005)
3. Boehm, B.W., DeMarco, T.: Software risk management. IEEE Software 14(3), 17–19 (1997)
4. Booch, G.: Handbook of Software Architecture,
   http://www.booch.com/architecture
5. Botía Blaya, J.A., Hernansaez, J.M., Gómez-Skarmeta, A.: Towards an approach for debugging multi-agent systems through the analysis of agent messages. Computer Systems: Science & Engineering 20(4) (2005)
6. Caire, G., et al.: Agent Oriented Analysis using MESSAGE/UML. In: Wooldridge, M.J., Weiß, G., Ciancarini, P. (eds.) AOSE 2001. LNCS, vol. 2222, pp. 119–135. Springer, Heidelberg (2002)
7. Carr, M., Kondra, S., Monarch, I., Ulrich, F., Walker, C.: Taxonomy-Based Risk Identification. Software Engineering Institute, Carnegie Mellon University. Technical Report CMU/SEI-93-TR-006 (1993)
8. Corchado, J.M., Laza, R.: Constructing Deliberative Agents with Case-based Reasoning Technology. International Journal of Intelligent Systems 18(12), 1227–1241 (2003)
9. Dijkstra, E.W.: The humble programmer. Communications of the ACM 15(10), 859–866 (1972)
10. Garijo, F.J., Bravo, S., Gonzalez, J., Bobadilla, E.: BOGAR_LN: An Agent Based Component Framework for Developing Multi-modal Services using Natural Language. In: Conejo, R., Urretavizcaya, M., Pérez-de-la-Cruz, J.-L. (eds.) CAEPIA/TTIA 2003. LNCS (LNAI), vol. 3040, pp. 207–220. Springer, Heidelberg (2004)
11. Garijo, F.J., et al.: Development of a Multi-Agent System for Cooperative Work with Network Negotiation Capabilities. In: Cairó, O., Cantú, F.J. (eds.) MICAI 2000. LNCS, vol. 1793, pp. 204–219. Springer, Heidelberg (2000)
12. Gómez-Sanz, J.J.: The Construction of Multi-agent Systems as an Engineering Discipline. In: O'Hare, G.M.P., Ricci, A., O'Grady, M.J., Dikenelli, O. (eds.) ESAW 2006. LNCS (LNAI), vol. 4457, pp. 25–37. Springer, Heidelberg (2007)

13. Gómez-Sanz, J., Pavón, J., Díaz Carrasco, A.: The PSI3 Agent Recommender System. In: Cueva Lovelle, J.M., Rodríguez, B.M.G., Gayo, J.E.L., Ruiz, M.d.P.P., Aguilar, L.J. (eds.) ICWE 2003. LNCS, vol. 2722, pp. 30–39. Springer, Heidelberg (2003)
14. Gómez-Sanz, J.J., Pavón, J., Garijo, F.: Intelligent Interface Agents Behavior Modeling. In: Cairó, O., Cantú, F.J. (eds.) MICAI 2000. LNCS, vol. 1793, pp. 598–609. Springer, Heidelberg (2000)
15. Gómez-Sanz, J.J., Pavón, J., Garijo, F.: Estimating Costs for Agent Oriented Software. In: Müller, J.P., Zambonelli, F. (eds.) AOSE 2005. LNCS, vol. 3950, pp. 218–230. Springer, Heidelberg (2006)
16. Iglesias, C.A., Garijo, M., Centeno-González, J., Velasco, J.R.: Analysis and Design of Multiagent Systems Using MAS-Common KADS. In: Rao, A., Singh, M.P., Wooldridge, M.J. (eds.) ATAL 1997. LNCS, vol. 1365, pp. 313–327. Springer, Heidelberg (1998)
17. Abran, A., Moore, J.W., Bourque, P., Dupuis, R., Tripp, L.L. (eds.): Guide to de Software Engineering Book of Knowledge. IEEE Computer Society, Los Alamitos (2004)
18. Jennings, N.: On agent-based software engineering. Artificial Intelligence 117(2), 277–296 (2000)
19. Jennings, N.R., Sycara, K., Wooldridge, M.: A Roadmap of Agent Research and Development. Int. Journal of Autonomous Agents and Multi-Agent Systems 1(1), 7–38 (1998)
20. Kephart, J.O., Chess, D.M.: The vision of autonomic computing. Computer 36(1), 41–50 (2003)
21. Luck, M., McBurney, P., Preist, C.: Agent Technology: Enabling Next Generation Computing (A Roadmap for Agent Based Computing). AgentLink (2003)
22. Luehrs, R., Pavón, J., Schneider-Fontán, M.: DEMOS Tools for Online Discussion and Decision Making. In: Cueva Lovelle, J.M., Rodríguez, B.M.G., Gayo, J.E.L., Ruiz, M.d.P.P., Aguilar, L.J. (eds.) ICWE 2003. LNCS, vol. 2722, pp. 525–528. Springer, Heidelberg (2003)
23. Naur, P., Randell, B. (eds.): Software Engineering: report on a conference sponsored by the nato science committee, Garmisch, Germany, NATO Science Committee (1968)
24. Pavón, J., Gómez-Sanz, J.J., Fuentes, R.: The INGENIAS Methodology and Tools. In: Henderson-Sellers, B., Giorgini, P. (eds.) Agent-Oriented Methodologies, pp. 236–276. Idea Group Publishing (2005)
25. Szyperski, C.: Component Software: Beyond Object-Oriented Programming, 2nd edn. Addison-Wesley, ACM Press (2002)
26. Software Engineering Standards Committee of the Software Engineering Technical Committee of the IEEE Computer Society. IEEE standard glossary of software enginering terminology. Institute of Electrical and Electronics Engineers, Inc. Standard IEEE Std. 610–612 (1990)
27. Weyns, D.: An Architecture-Centric Approach for Software Engineering with Situated Multiagent Systems. Ph.D. Dissertation. Katholieke Universiteit Leuven (2006)

A Characterization of Key Properties of Environment-Mediated Multiagent Systems

Hartmut Schmeck[1] and Christian Müller-Schloer[2]

[1] Institute AIFB, Karlsruhe Institute of Technology (KIT), Germany
[2] Institute of Systems Engineering, Leibniz University Hannover, Germany

Abstract. The increasing presence of application scenarios which are based on large collections of active components having to adapt continuously to changing environmental requirements has led to several research initiatives with the objective to create new concepts for the design and operation of environment-mediated multiagent systems. In particular, Autonomic Computing (AC) and Organic Computing (OC) have developed the vision of systems possessing life-like properties: They self-organize, adapt to their dynamically changing environments, and establish other so-called self-x properties, like self-healing, self-configuration, self-optimization etc. The impact of these initiatives will depend crucially on our ability to demonstrate the benefits of these systems with respect to some essential properties. Therefore, we need a clear understanding of some key notions like adaptivity, robustness, flexibility, or their degree of autonomy, allowing for self-x properties.

In this paper, a system classification of robust, adaptable, and adaptive systems is presented. Furthermore, a degree of autonomy is characterized to be able to quantify how autonomously a system is working. The degree of autonomy distinguishes and measures external control which is exhibited directly by the user (*no autonomy*) from internal control of a system which might be fully controlled by an observer/controller architecture that is part of the system (*full autonomy*). Finally, learning and of trustworthiness are briefly addressed, since these are further essential aspects of self-organizing, adaptive systems.

1   Introduction

Some of the major challenges for systems engineering arise from the trend of increasing complexity in the design, development, and maintenance of technical systems and from the necessity to adapt continuously to changing environmental requirements. Organic Computing (OC), like other initiatives such as IBM's Autonomic Computing [1] or Proactive Computing [2], postulates the necessity of a paradigm shift in the design of future technical applications, see e. g. [3]:

> "It is not the question whether self-organised and adaptive systems will arise but how they will be designed and controlled."

This emphasizes the inherent challenge to provide appropriate concepts and methods for dealing with intelligent, interacting systems, which might have to

D. Weyns, S.A. Brueckner, and Y. Demazeau (Eds.): EEMMAS 2007, LNAI 5049, pp. 17–38, 2008.

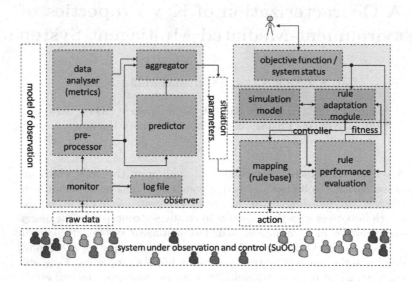

Fig. 1. Observer/controller architecture

cope with unanticipated events in their operating environment. In particular, we have to endow these systems with more degrees of freedom allowing them to self-organise in order to be able to *adapt* to potentially changing environmental conditions and external goals and constraints, and on the other hand we have to make sure that self-organization does not result in undesired behavior. Therefore, there is a need for concepts to achieve *controlled self-organization* as a new design paradigm. At first glance this seems to be a paradox, but it is necessary to cope in an acceptable way with the degrees of freedom required by the process of self-organization.

Within the German priority research program on OC [4] a generic architectural concept for the design and analysis of OC systems has been developed, the observer/controller architecture [5]. The (potentially) self-organizing *system under observation and control* (SuOC), which constitutes some productive system, will be endowed with a higher level of governance consisting of an *observer* and a *controller* (cf. Fig. 1). The observer monitors the underlying system by sampling the state and the properties of the different components and reports an aggregated quantified context (i. e. a description of the currently observed situation) to the controller. The controller evaluates this context with respect to a given objective function and takes appropriate control actions whenever it is necessary to influence the underlying system in order to meet the system goal. This loop of observing and controlling has to guarantee that the behavior of the SuOC stays within the external constraints. In particular, explicit control actions should not be necessary unless a deviation from the desired behavior has been detected or predicted, i. e. the SuOC would run autonomously as long as it behaves well and satisfies the requirements as specified by the developer or the user.

The feasibility of the control actions is evaluated continuously by comparing their predicted and observed impact. In this way, by on-line learning, every action gets an associated fitness value. The generic controller architecture provides an additional loop for off-line learning which consists of a simulation-based generation of new control actions having a minimal fitness level.

This generic observer/controller architecture bears similarities with concepts and techniques known from other scientific disciplines like control theory, mechanical engineering [6,7], or autonomic computing [1,8]. However, OC emphasizes the crucial difference from these disciplines that the resulting architecture is not a fully autonomous element. It is rather driven by external goals, and it reports its system status to the user (or to some higher level object). The user may intervene explicitly, e. g. by changing some system objectives or by initiating directly some control actions. Furthermore, the generic architecture allows for an adaptation of the control mechanism by utilizing on-line and off-line learning simultaneously.

An abstract view of the generic observer/controller loop is serving as our model for characterizing essential notions like robustness, adaptivity, or – ultimately – controlled self-organization in technical application systems. Our goal is to get significantly beyond the frequently followed attitude of using these terms in an almost magical sense based on some black box model. Despite of the long-term existence of these terms, in the context of technical applications based on advanced information processing systems we still lack a precise quantitative definition as a basis for a common understanding of these crucial concepts, which is a necessary prerequisite for a systematic comparison of different designs of self-organizing adaptive systems.

Based on a preliminary presentation at CEC 2007 [9], this paper elaborates on ideas towards this end that have been developed within the German priority research program on "Organic Computing" and it discusses some qualitative and quantitative characterizations of the essential properties of self-organizing technical systems. Section 2 introduces an abstract system model and provides an organic traffic light controller as an example of a self-organizing system. Characterizations of terms like robustness and adaptivity are given in Sect. 3, followed by a quantitative notion of autonomy and (controlled) self-organization. Aspects of learning and trustworthiness are briefly addressed in Sect. 5. Finally, Sect. 6 provides some concluding remarks.

2   System Description

Our characterization of terms uses a rather abstract description of a system which is based on the generic observer/controller architecture as depicted in Fig. 1. Let S be some productive system (the system under observation and control – SuOC), which processes some input and produces some output (cf. Fig. 2). The specific nature of the input and output is not essential for the purpose of this article, in a more detailed specification they would be specified as some parameter vectors.

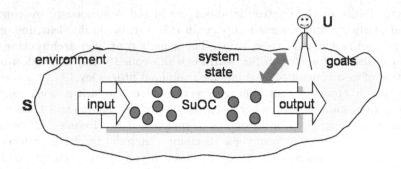

Fig. 2. System description

S is assumed to be a structured system, consisting of (many) elements and links, which interconnect these elements. We define the *system structure* to be an attributed graph, the nodes of which are the elements, and its edges correspond to the links between the elements. The *attributes* are associated to the system (*global attributes*) or to the edges and elements (*local attributes*) giving information like location, performance, storage capacity, communication bandwidth, reliability etc. A *re-organisation* of S adds or removes nodes and/or edges from the graph or modifies the attributes.

The behavior of the system may be influenced by its *environment*. This will subsume everything that is external to S, including input and output of S, and certain parameters (or attributes) which might have a disturbing effect on S.

At any given time t, the values of all the relevant attributes of the system constitute its *state* $z(t)$, i. e. if there are n attributes used to describe the state of S, $z(t)$ is a vector in some n-dimensional *state space* Z (also called *parameter space* of S).

These parameters include a description of the *evaluation criteria* (also called *objectives*) $\eta_1, \ldots, \eta_k$ which are provided by the (external) user U (or by some higher level entity). The evaluation criteria are assumed to map the system state into the set of real numbers. The evaluation of the system might involve rather complex operations, but this is irrelevant for the purpose of this paper. The criteria allow to define a hierarchy of subspaces of Z characterizing the performance of the system (cf. Fig. 3):

1. For simplicity, we assume that in an *ideal state* all the criteria evaluate to zero, i.e. their values are assumed to measure the deviation from an ideal state of the system. This set of ideal states is called *target space* TS. Typical examples of evaluation criteria could be (i) "The load of the worker nodes should be balanced.", (ii) "All the nodes with red colour should be in the upper half of the living space, the nodes with green colour should be in the lower half.", or (iii) "Move node x from A to B as fast as possible using not more than k units of fuel.". These examples show that the target space may be quite large (although, in some cases, it might be a unique single state z_Ω).

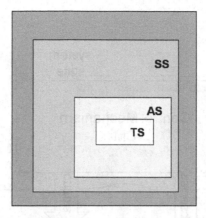

Fig. 3. State spaces of the SuOC

2. The system state $z(t)$ is called *acceptable* if an *acceptance criterion* or *threshold* θ on $\mathbb{R}^k$ is satisfied, i.e. $\theta(\eta_1(z(t)), \ldots, \eta_k(z(t)))$ is true. As a special case, θ might refer to a vector of threshold values, which should not be violated (i.e. surpassed) by the evaluation criteria. The set of all acceptable states is also called the *acceptance space AS*. Obviously, the target space is a subset of the acceptance space. A typical example of such a threshold would be some upper bound on the accepted level of energy consumption while the ultimate objective would be to achieve an optimal value.

3. If the system is in an inacceptable state (i.e. $z(t) \notin AS$), two cases are distinguished: If it is possible to modify the system state (by some control action), such that at some later time t' the state $z(t')$ is acceptable, the system state is in the *survival space SS*. For example, if a car has a flat tire, it can return into an acceptable state again by replacing the flat tire with a spare tire. This might lead to reduced performance, i.e. the new state might be acceptable, but not ideal. Otherwise, $z(t)$ is in the *"dead zone"*, i.e. the system cannot return into an acceptable state.

A crucial part of any system model is its dynamics, i.e. a specification of its state transitions. We assume that the potential state transitions are specified by some of the state attributes (e.g. a program or a transition table). Since we are explicitly interested in a distinction between internal and external control actions, we assume that there exist internal and/or external *control mechanisms CM*, which allow to control the behavior of the system by setting some attributes of the system and of its environment to specific values. Sometimes, it is assumed that it is not possible to control environmental parameters. But, as e.g. in traffic control, a speed limit could be viewed to be an environmental parameter which might be modified by some external control unit. As mentioned in Sect. 1, in the generic architecture of organic systems, CM will consist of an observer and a controller having a number of standard components as described in detail in

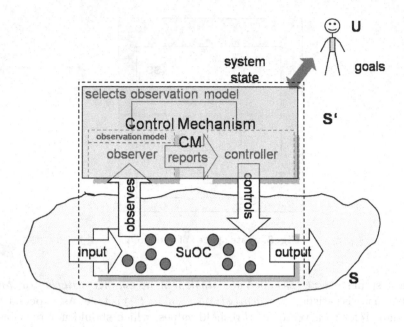

Fig. 4. System extended with control mechanism CM

[5]. The extended system model is sketched in Fig. 4; there, CM is external to S but internal to the extended system S'.

As a concrete example of such a system we refer to an organic traffic control system (OTC) as depicted in Fig. 5 (the example is taken from [10]). The system under observation and control is a traffic light controller which determines the length of the green periods for all the phases of a traffic light at some intersection. This could be a simple fixed-time controller or a more sophisticated traffic-adaptive controller which reacts to a number of different traffic parameters as indicated in Fig. 6. For OTC, the control mechanism consists of two levels:

- Layer 1 observes the current traffic situation (using appropriate sensors for detecting car frequencies, arrival rates etc.) and selects the most appropriate parameter settings for the traffic controller. This is done using a learning classifier system which is continuously evaluating the feasibility of its control actions by some kind of on-line learning.
- Layer 2 is triggered whenever there is no appropriate or insufficient response to a traffic situation: An evolutionary algorithm is used to generate more appropriate parameter settings which are evaluated off-line using a micro-scopic traffic simulator. Only those settings are transmitted to the lower level which show a sufficient performance. This is a crucial aspect of this application since it would not be acceptable to apply low quality control parameters in real traffic.

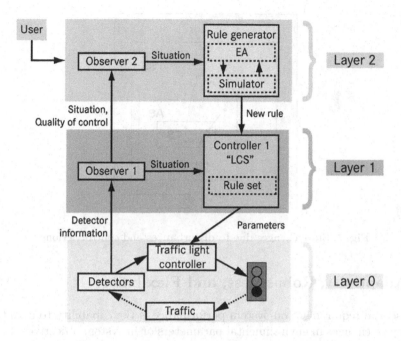

Fig. 5. Organic traffic control system (cf. [10])

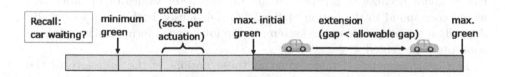

Fig. 6. Traffic-responsive traffic control (cf. [10])

For further details of the OTC architecture the reader is referred to [10]. The state vector of the OTC system consists of all the parameters that are relevant for its behavior: Traffic sensors, traffic light control parameters, elements of the rule base of the classifier system, the specification of the traffic simulator and the evolutionary algorithm. Obviously, this is a very long list of parameters. Therefore, the control mechanism has to select the most appropriate parameters by defining a *model of observation*, which is focusing the observer on the currently relevant attributes and selecting appropriate methods for analysis and prediction.

The following sections characterize crucial properties of self-organizing systems based on the system description outlined in this section.

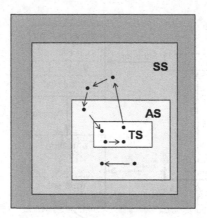

Fig. 7. State changes due to disturbances and control actions

3   Adaptivity, Robustness, and Flexibility

An essential requirement on system performance is the capability to adapt reasonably to changes in environmental parameters or in system objectives. In particular, a common objective is the capability to maintain a required behavior or functionality in spite of a certain range of parameter variations. The standard notion for this is *robustness*. Different from this, the requirement to modify the behavior because of certain changes of parameter values or of objectives would correspond to the notion of *flexibility*. Obviously, both notions crucially depend on the *adaptivity* of the system. In the following, a formalization of these concepts is presented.

The basic assumption underlying all these notions is the necessity of the system to react to changes of some parameter values. In our model, we are dealing with changes in the system state which might have very different origin, e. g. there might occur spontaneous changes of internal system parameters (e. g. due to component failures), or by environmental influences. Such a *disturbance* δ changes the state $z(t)$ into some state $\delta(z(t))$ (potentially with some time delay Δt and, consequently, the evaluation of the system changes from η $(= (\eta_1(z(t)), \dots, \eta_k(z(t))))$ to $\eta + d$ with $\eta_i(z(t)) + d_i = \eta_i(\delta(z(t)))$.

As shown in Fig. 7 the state changes due to disturbances can be differently severe with respect to the evaluation criteria. Some may leave the system within the target space whereas others might move it into the survival space such that it has to be "repaired" by some sequence of control actions. This leads to the following characterization of robustness:

Let D be a nonempty set of disturbances. A system S is called *strongly robust* with respect to D, iff all the disturbances $\delta \in D$ are mapping the target space and the acceptance space into themselves (i. e. they are mapping ideal states into ideal states and acceptable states into acceptable states).

Furthermore, a system S is called *weakly robust* with respect to D, iff all the disturbances $\delta \in D$ are mapping the acceptance space into itself (i. e. they might map ideal states into acceptable states, which would refer to a degradation in performance).

Obviously, strong robustness means that the system will continue to satisfy the evaluation criteria even under certain parameter changes, whereas weakly robust systems might show an acceptable deviation from an ideal behavior.

Example 1. An integrated circuit with automotive specification will function correctly from $-30 \,^\circ C$ to $+50 \,^\circ C$. Within this temperature range, there is no control action necessary, the system remains in an ideal state, and it is strongly robust with respect to changes in temperature that do not go beyond the specified range.

One could also define some quantitative notion of robustness by introducing a *degree of robustness*: The degree of robustness would grow with the size of D, and, if there exists some kind of distance measure on the state space, the degree of robustness would increase with the distances between the original and the disturbed state which do not lead to a significant deviation from ideal or acceptable states. In particular, a system S would be *more robust* than a system S', if it would be (strongly or weakly) robust with respect to more or stronger disturbances.

Using the distance measure on the state space, one could also characterize the robustness of S with respect to *smoothness*, i. e. small deviations in the parameter space should correspond to small(er) changes in the objective space.

By definition, if a system is in the survival space, there exists a sequence of control actions which move it back into the acceptance space. Therefore, we call a system *adaptable* with respect to a set of disturbances D, if the disturbances in D will not move the system out of the survival space. We could call it *perfectly adaptable* with respect to a set of disturbances D if for every state in the acceptance space and for every disturbance in D there is a sequence of control actions leading the system into an ideal state.

Now, while adaptability merely states that there is the potential to move a system back into the acceptance space or even into the target space, the much more interesting case would be the capability of a system to do so without any explicit external intervention. Consequently, a system S is called *adaptive* (with respect to some set of disturbances D), if – after some time interval Δt – it returns into an acceptable (or even ideal) state from any disturbed state without needing any external control.

This definition of adaptivity does not refer explicitly to any internal control actions by some (central or decentral) control mechanism. This is an essential point, since there are many examples of self-organising systems where the adaptation to environmental requirements is an emergent effect of interactions among the components of the system. The standard biological example for such an adaptive system is the capability of ant colonies to find the shortest paths around obstacles that are placed or moved spontaneously in their environment (cf. [11]). This capability is due to stigmergic interaction between the ants, placing pheromones on their paths and preferring directions with higher pheromone concentrations when they are moving in their environment. Hence, the difference between adaptable and adaptive systems is not just a matter of setting system borders appropriately (i. e. placing control mechanisms outside or inside the system) but it addresses also the crucial emergent effects of interactions in self-organizing systems (cf. [12]).

As is obvious from the definition, every (weakly or strongly) robust system is also adaptive (since, in a robust system, the time interval Δt equals zero).

While these definitions are referring to the complete sets of ideal or acceptable states, one could define analogous notions of robustness or adaptivity with respect to single states only. This would allow to define different degrees of robustness for individual states. In an inverse approach, one could also define the notion of critical states:

A system S is in a *critical state* with respect to a set of disturbances D, iff every disturbance in D will transform the current state of S into an inacceptable state.

Although we did not specify how an adaptive system manages to move into an acceptable state, we assume that in order to achieve adaptable and/or adaptive behavior, control inputs c are triggered (such as switching on a cooling device or lowering the clock frequency) whenever S enters a state outside of its acceptance space (but inside its survival space, cf. Fig. 7), or whenever such a leave from its acceptance space is predicted. These control inputs (which sometimes are also called *control actions*) have to come from an external source (the *user*) in the case of an adaptable system and will be triggered by the internal control mechanism CM in the case of an adaptive system.

Hence, adaptive systems increase their effective robustness with the help of the internal control mechanism, which modifies the values of some parameters of the system or of the environment and thus influences the system behavior or structure. However, this might involve a temporary deviation from the acceptance space and thus may lead to a (temporary) decrease in system quality.

The *quality* of an adaptive system may be measured in different ways, some of which are listed below:

1. The distance of S from an ideal state (which may be defined as the norm of $\eta(z(t))$ in $\mathbb{R}^k$, e. g. a maximum norm), or, alternatively, the distance from an acceptable state (both refer to distances in the objective space, not in the parameter space),

2. The time it takes to move S from the present state in survival space back into the acceptance space (this could refer to real time or to the number of control actions that have to be applied),

3. The time it takes to move S into an ideal state, or

4. The maximum deviation of the system state from an ideal state (or the sum of all such deviations) on the path from an initial state in the survival space into the acceptance space.

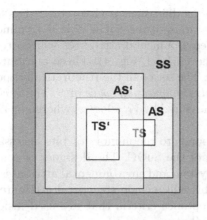

Fig. 8. Changes in state space structure due to changes in objectives

In general, we would like to distinguish two possible reasons for changes in the state of S:

1. The system state $z(t)$ changes due to a change of the system (e. g. a broken component) or a change of the environment (disturbance δ) without any changes in the evaluation criteria. If the system remains in the acceptance space, this corresponds to the common understanding of a *robust system*.
2. The state $z(t)$ changes due to modifications of the evaluation and acceptance criteria. This would modify the target space and the acceptance space (as indicated in Fig. 8). We call a system, which is able to cope with such changes in its behavioral specification, a *flexible system*.

After having defined these different types of adaptive behavior the next section focuses on a system classification with respect to different types of control mechanisms.

4   Degree of Autonomy and Controlled Self-organization

While in the previous section we have looked at whether the behavior of a system may be adjusted in response to changes in system or environmental attributes such that the acceptance criteria are eventually met, we now turn to the question to what extent this can be done by internal control actions only. That means we characterize essential properties of self-organizing systems.

In our extended system model (cf. Fig. 4) we assumed the existence of some control mechanism CM that could be used to influence the system appropriately, if it deviates from the desired behavior. This requires adequate possibilities for modifications of system parameters, either by using external control (by the user, who might modify parameters of the CM) or by internal control which would modify parameters of the SuOC only. In the following we assume that S is an adaptable system.

The range of possible modifications is characterized as follows:

An *(internal) configuration* of the SuOC S is determined by the values of a collection of system or environmental attributes which are open to be modified by control actions of the CM (cf. Fig. 4). These attributes will also be called *configuration attributes*. The set of all the (theoretically) possible configurations constitutes the *(internal) configuration space* of S. The *variability* of the internal configuration space is measured by $V_i = \log(n)$ where n is the number of internal configurations.

Obviously, V_i corresponds to the number of bits necessary to address all the different configurations of the SuOC. The designer of a system has to specify explicitly which of the system and environmental attributes will be configuration attributes. Typically, this will include structural attributes of S. Furthermore, any evaluation and acceptance criteria that are used inside of S will typically belong to this set of attributes.

The control mechanism CM is responsible for selecting specific configurations of S. Therefore, every control action influences the values of a subset of the configuration attributes. We denote the number of bits of a specific control action c by $\#c$.

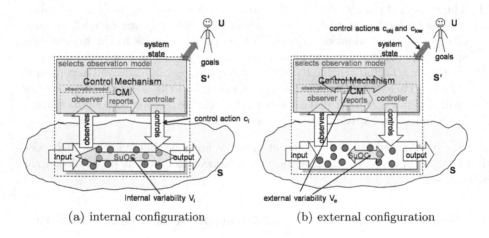

(a) internal configuration   (b) external configuration

Fig. 9. Configuration spaces and control options

As mentioned already, the system S is assumed to be adaptable. Therefore, the control mechanism CM has the task to direct the system back into the acceptance space whenever a violation of the acceptance threshold is detected or predicted. Hence, a successful control mechanism will result in an adaptive system S' which is the combination of S and CM as indicated in Fig. 9. On the next level, the user (or some higher level entity) should also be able to influence the system. Therefore, there should be an adequate collection of *external configuration attributes*, defining the *external configuration space* which has an *external variablility* V_e (cf. Fig. 9(b)). These will be attributes of the control mechanism

CM, including always the evaluation and acceptance criteria and possibly some further attributes of this and the lower level SuOC S, in order to allow for direct influence of the *user* on *internal* attributes of the system S. Corresponding to these internal and external configuration spaces we distinguish between internal and external control actions c_i and c_e, respectively.

An important design objective would be to reduce the variability of the configuration spaces going from the internal to the external level, i. e. in a multi-level design we should have an increasing degree of abstraction going from lower to higher levels. Nevertheless, it might be reasonable to provide direct higher-level control access to some configuration attributes of lower levels. Furthermore, in an adaptive system there should not be a necessity to specify anything more than evaluation and acceptance criteria by external control actions c_e. Therefore, we distinguish between external control inputs c_{obj}, specifying system objectives to be observed by the control mechanism CM, and control actions c_{low} directly related to attributes of the lower level SuOC. According to our definition of adaptive systems, there should not be a necessity for any control actions of type c_{low} as long as S remains within its survival space.

Using the definitions of internal and external variability, the *complexity reduction* from lower to upper level may be defined as $R = V_i - V_e$. R has a maximal value, if the external variability is zero, i. e. there is no externally visible variability which could be used for changing the configuration of the system. On the other hand, if the external configuration space includes attributes of the lower level system S, the external variability could even be larger than V_i. In such a case, the configuration task of the external user has even larger complexity than the configuration task of the control mechanism CM and, consequently, the complexity reduction R would be negative.

Now, these notions can be used to characterize the degree of autonomy of the extended system S'. Intuitively, the autonomy of a system should increase with a decrease in external interventions and vice versa. Therefore, the relationship between the variabilities V_i and V_e should be an intuitively reasonable indicator of the degree of autonomy. This leads to the following definition:

The *(static) degree of autonomy* α of system S' is defined as

$$\alpha = \frac{R}{V_i} = \frac{V_i - V_e}{V_i} \tag{1}$$

The value of α will be at most one (if V_e equals zero). In this case, there is no external variability, i. e. there is no possibility to modify any attributes of S' by external control actions. Therefore, such a system would be called *fully autonomous*. The only way to interact with such a system would be to influence the input values of S.

If the value of α is zero, the internal and the external variabilities are the same, which indicates that there is no reduction in complexity. If α drops below zero, we have a situation where the external configuration space contains more controllable attributes than the internal configuration space. In an extreme case, all the lower level attributes could be available externally, in addition to the configuration attributes referring to the control mechanism CM. In this case, the system S could be controlled completely by external control actions, which would be no autonomy at all. But, as is obvious from the definition, a low value of α is merely indicating a *potential* loss of autonomy, since it does not take into account, whether during any time interval any external control actions have been used actually. That means, even in a system with a rather low value of α the actual behavior might be more autonomous than indicated by α.

Referring to Fig. 7 and Fig. 9 again, CM influences (controls) S to keep it within its acceptance space by selecting a sequence of control actions $c_1, c_2, \ldots$ from its *behavioral repertoire* B. CM determines these control actions with respect to the evaluation and acceptance criteria as given initially or some time before by higher-level control. Ideally, it should be able to keep S within the acceptance space without additional intervention from a higher level. However, if the acceptance criterion is violated for too long, the higher level controller might intervene by sending further external control actions of type c_{obj} to modify the evaluation criteria or of type c_{low} to influence directly some of the configuration attributes of the SuOC.

Therefore, in order to characterize the actual degree of autonomy (or, the actual amount of external control) one should consider the number of bits that have been used in any control actions over some time period $[t_1, t_2]$. This leads to a more refined, time dependent quantitative notion of autonomy:

Let $v_e(t)$ and $v_i(t)$ be the number of bits of the external and internal control actions at time t, respectively.

(a) The *dynamic complexity reduction* r in S' over some time interval $[t_1, t_2]$ is defined to be

$$r_{t_1,t_2} = \int_{t_1}^{t_2} (v_i(t) - v_e(t))dt \tag{2}$$

(b) The *dynamic degree of autonomy* β in S' over some time interval $[t_1, t_2]$ is defined to be

$$\beta_{t_1,t_2} = \frac{\int_{t_1}^{t_2} (v_i(t) - v_e(t))dt}{\int_{t_1}^{t_2} v_i(t)dt} \tag{3}$$

This dynamic degree of autonomy measures the relative amount of external control that has been used during a specific time interval. Hence, a system could exhibit a fully autonomous behavior over some time period while being completely influenced by external control actions at a different time. This definitely allows for a much more accurate characterization of the autonomy of a system, based on the actual control flow. In particular, in the case of organic systems, we might have a fully autonomous behavior over some time period, but might use adequate control actions whenever the self-organized behavior of the system does not satisfy the external constraints.

After having characterized the (dynamic) degree of autonomy of a system, we may start to look at the so-called *self-x-properties*, as the degree of autonomy would correspond to the *degree of self*. One of the central notions is "self-organization", a term which has attracted growing attention by scientists from different diciplines. F. Heylighen has presented valuable surveys on the relevant literature (see e.g. [12]), and he provided concise specifications of a range of relevant terms (for a very recent publication see [13]).

Heylighen states: "Self-organization can be defined as the spontaneous emergence of global structure out of local interactions." And, in the FAQ list on self-organized systems [14], we find "The essence of self-organization is that system structure often appears without explicit pressure or involvement from outside the system.".

Following these characterizations, a self-organizing system is a multi-element system (consisting of m elements, $m > 1$), which needs no external control to restructure itself (i.e. it has a high degree of autonomy). Furthermore, a common assumption is that the internal control mechanism CM is distributed over the elements. In natural systems, such a distributed control mechanism might be difficult to localize which, sometimes, leads to almost magical connotations of self-organization.

Obviously, in a controllable technical system there must always be some control mechanism. It can be centralized (one CM), distributed over the m elements (m CMs) or distributed over a hierarchy of CMs (possibly more then m CMs). These architectural variants are depicted in Fig. 10). Following a recent discussion, the centralized variant could also be viewed to address only the aspect of adaptivity, and therefore correponds to top-down design, whereas the decentralized variant resembles self-organized systems, where the global behavior is rather developed bottom-up (as an emergent process). Finally, the multilevel design combines the two design approaches and corresponds to an intuitive idea of controlled self-organization.

We could define a *degree of self-organization* by counting the number of CMs ($= k$) in relation to the number of elements m of the system ($k : m$). An adaptive system with one centralized CM could then be denoted as ($1 : m$), an adaptive system with full distribution of CMs as ($m : m$). Definitely, an ($m : m$) system may be called self-organized. It is a matter of taste whether we want to call a system with lower degrees of self-organization still self-organized.

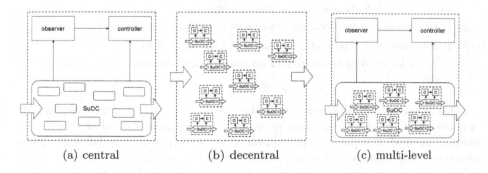

(a) central   (b) decentral   (c) multi-level

Fig. 10. Observer/controller realization

Let S be an adaptive system consisting of m elements ($m > 1$) with a large dynamic degree of autonomy (β) and fully or partially distributed k control mechanisms CM ($k \geq 1$) leading to a degree of self-organization of ($k : m$).

(a) S is called *strongly self-organized*, if $k = m$, i.e. the degree of self-organization is ($m : m$).

(b) S is called *self-organized*, if $k > 1$, i.e. it has a medium degree of self-organisation ($k : m$).

(c) S is called *weakly self-organized*, if $k = 1$, i.e. there is a central control mechanism and the degree of self-organization is ($1 : m$).

The weak definition would mean that any adaptive system is also called self-organized. The authors of this article tend to use the medium definition. Speaking about adaptive and self-organizing systems in an exact way requires to indicate (1) the degree of autonomy and (2) the degree of self-organization ($k : m$).

Here, a remark seems to be necessary: In the literature about self-organizing systems (see e.g. [15]) you sometimes find the additional requirement that a self-organizing system should be *structure-adaptive*. This is not explicitly stated in our definition, but it may be present in an implicit form: For example, if the system objectives refer to structural configuration attributes of S then, after some disturbance or after a change in the evaluation and acceptance criteria, an adaptive system will be able to re-organize its structure such that it is acceptable again.

A common way of characterizing changes in system structure would consider the resulting changes of the system's descriptional complexity or of the entropy of appropriate structural attributes of S (e.g. by computing the classical information theoretic entropy as defined by Shannon). This has been done in a systematic way in [16], it is beyond the scope of this paper.

Finally, we suggest the following characterization of controlled self-organization: A self-organized system S' allows for *controlled self-organization* iff

(i) it has a nonempty external configuration space, i.e. we have $V_e > 0$ (essentially we require that it has a small static degree of autonomy and allows for detailed information on its current state),

(ii) it has some external control actions of type c_{obj},

(iii) it has some external control actions of type c_{low}, and

(iv) it has a large dynamic degree of autonomy (i.e. external control actions are rare).

This characterization requires that the system is adaptive (which means that it is capable of returning autonomously into an acceptable state after certain disturbing events), but provides the option to the external user to redefine certain objectives (by using a control input c_{obj}) or to interfere directly with the operation of system S by using a control action of type c_{low}. The simplest example of the latter would be a control action to switch off the system.

5   Learning and Trustworthiness

A major motivation for the interest in environment-mediated multiagent systems is the expectation that they would be capable to overcome certain limitations caused by incomplete knowledge about the potential operation environment at design time.

In particular, the behavior of S' may be limited by

(a) a limited configuration space of S or
(b) a limited behavioral repertoire B of CM.

Limitation (a) may be caused by an inappropriate design, i. e. the necessity for including additional attributes of the system or of the environment into the configuration space has not been seen at design time. There might also be some system specific reasons that prohibit any external modifying access to certain structural attributes of the system. In these cases, it does not seem reasonable to expect a possibility to extend the configuration space at runtime of the system.

Limitation (b), however, might occur quite often in systems having a very large configuration space but only a limited behavioral repertoire. In particular, it might be a complex optimization problem to find the most suitable configuration for satisfying the system objectives, as e. g. in traffic light control, where you have to determine the most appropriate values for a number of control parameters of an adaptive controller system (cf. [10]). In this example, the quality of a particular parameter setting will be determined either off-line by a simulation or on-line by observing and analysing the system behavior. Whenever the control mechanism CM or the user detect that the currently available range of control actions is not sufficient to get acceptable behavior, it should be possible to extend the behavioral repertoire with new, more appropriate control actions. Definitely, it would be desirable to have a system that is capable of generating the necessary modifications of its behavioral repertoire in an autonomous way. This will be addressed in the following subsection.

5.1   Learning

In this subsection we briefly address the aspect of learning in adaptive and self-organizing systems.

In general, a system has the capability to learn, if it can improve autonomously its response to input values from some set X. That means, there are time values t_1 and $t_2 > t_1$ such that for any $t > 0$ the response to an input from the set X at time $t_2 + t$ has a higher quality than the response to the same input at time t_1. Consequently, the robustness and performance of a (self-)learning system should improve over time.

This learning capability requires some *learning mechanism LM* which may modify the behavior of the system S' by

(a) changing the values of some attributes of the system S or of its environment, or
(b) changing the behavioral repertoire B of the control mechanism CM.

An interesting mechanism for learning by modifying parameters of the environment is the stigmergic use of pheromones by ant colonies. This aggregation of individual experiences combined with some degree of evaporation leads to the amazing capability of constructing shortest path ant roads even in a dynamically changing topography. This has inspired a whole range of new design patterns for optimization algorithms (cf. [17]).

The design of the organic traffic control system may serve as an example for the second type of learning method (cf. [10] and Sect. 2): A classifier system for selecting parameter settings for a traffic light controller (in the real traffic system S) is using on-line learning by associating a fitness value to classifier rules based on the performance of their parameter settings in real traffic situations, combined with off-line learning which produces new classifier rules for inadequately handled traffic situations by using a genetic algorithm which generates new rules of some minimum quality level by evaluating their performance in a traffic simulator. In this way, the learning mechanism manages to improve the system performance on known traffic situations and it is also capable of generating adequate responses (i.e. control actions) to previously unknown traffic situations.

These are just two examples of a broad range of possible learning mechanisms, which could make use of learning by experience, trial-and-error, reinforcement learning, neural networks, or metaheuristics like genetic algorithms, ant colony optimisation, or simulated annealing, to name a few.

In highly complex systems, autonomous learning is the most attractive way of coping with the limitations of adaptivity as mentioned in the previous subsection.

5.2   Trustworthiness

Another important feature of systems that can adapt to their environmental requirements and that can cope with unanticipated situations in a self-organized way is their trustworthiness. That means, in spite of the flexibility and adaptiveness of the system, a user will ask, why or how she should build up trust in the behavior of such a system? Simultaneously, a designer or service provider should know what kind of methodology is appropriate to generate and comprehensibly demonstrate and maintain trust in a system or service (potentially operating in an insecure environment). Without adequate levels of trustworthiness we cannot expect sufficient acceptance of these systems!

Obviously, there are many facets characterizing trustworthiness. In particular, the following properties address essential aspects of trust:

- *Correctness*: Does the system actually do what it should do?
- *Security*: Does the system prevent any unauthorised access?
- *Safety*: Will there be any undesired effects by using the system or service?
- *Availability / Reliability*: What is the probability that a service is available when it is needed and what is the expected time duration of satisfactory service?
- *Robustness*: Will the service be provided even within an environment that is changing due to some disturbances?

- *Privacy*: Will the service use privacy information in an adequate way?
- *Performance*: Will the system show the expected response time or through-put?

Sometimes, trust is reduced to CIA:
- *Confidentiality*
- *Integrity*
- *Availability* to authorized users.

The final three properties all relate to security, they are quite often summa-rized as "Trusted Computing". But, trustworthiness extends far beyond these security-properties.

Some characterization has been given by S. Yau in his keynote talk at ATC 2006 [18] :

- Trust is a particular level of belief of an agent (the *trustor*) that some other agent (the *trustee*) will act or intend to act beneficially.
- Trust forms the basis for agents to make decisions on *what* to interact with, *when* to interact with, and *how* to interact with.

Consequently, trust management has to consider the (dynamic) relationship between trustor and trustee. The provision of *certificates* containing statements on the expected behavior of a system or service may be necessary for the es-tablishment of trust, but they do not suffice. In particular, trust is not a binary property, there will always be a certain, dynamically changing level of trust only. In our characterization of adaptable and adaptive systems we emphasized their capability to return to satisfying or even to ideal behavior after the occurence of failures. But, the level of trust will be reduced whenever a system shows unac-ceptable behavior, and it will be more difficult to regain trust after the system returned to its acceptance space again. Another mechanism besides certificates is to use *reputations* for sharing experiences on system usage and performance. In some way, these reputations have a similar impact as the pheromones in ant systems: They may be used as an additional source of accumulated information on the previous behavior of a system.

As emphasized in this paper, we are interested in robustness and adaptivity because of potential deviations in system behavior from an ideal state. Conse-quently, trust management is closely related to risk management. Self-organized, adaptive services will always bear the risk of unexpected behavior and even a well-engineered system may run into situations where it does not "behave well". Therefore, the more we know about the risks associated with using a system, the more we will be prepared to cope with failures. It is important to note that in-formation about the potential risks of a system provides the basis for the design of methods for preventing the occurrence of risky behavior and for building up trust. Hence, in order to fully appreciate the benefits of adaptive, self-organized behavior, it would be detrimental to ignore potential risks.

These few statements underline the necessity to develop a methodology for trust engineering for self-organizing environment-mediated systems which, among others, has to address the following:

- How do we build up initial trust?
- How can a trustor or trustee regain trust after failures?
- What can a producer do to create an initial level of trust for his product and to support a reasonable trust management?

Currently, we are still far away from satisfying answers to these questions, which might allow for coping with dynamic trust-relationships.

6   Conclusion

This contribution has given an overview on some recent characterization of important concepts and properties of self-organising and adaptive systems which are closely related to environment-mediated multiagent systems. Considering the increasing presence of interacting systems in our living environment, it is essential to design systems in a way which enables them to cope with unanticipated situations in a reasonable way and which – in particular – provides them with the capability to react appropriately to the frequently rather spontaneous and unexpected behavior of human users.

A common understanding of basic properties of these systems is a prerequisite for making reliable statements about their (expected) performance. Furthermore, as system designers and users, we have to know about the requirements for building up trustworthy relationships between services or systems and their users. We are beginning to be overloaded with undesired, unexpected, and sometimes even malicious information services. Therefore, we are in urgent need of systematic approaches to circumvent these problems and provide acceptable systems, which will respond as requested to environmental requirements.

The challenge for system design lies in building systems,

- which meet their target performance (stay within the target space)
- with little external control effort (high dynamic degree of autonomy)
- for a large set of environmental conditions and possible disturbances (large survival space).

It is essential for such a system to have a built-in control mechanism (constituting the *self*). A system will become more robust if the control mechanism is distributed, i. e. its degree of self-organization ($k : m$) is high since this avoids a single point of failure.

Adaptive and self-organising systems will not always outperform conventional systems but they may survive under a large diversity of environmental conditions. Self-organising systems may be especially robust due to their internal distributed architecture and their large structural variability.

The objective for system design should be to design controllable self-organising systems, i. e. systems, which allow for external control but have a high degree of autonomy as well. One major argument for the possibility of external control is the necessity to support the generation of trust into the dependability of a system.

Acknowledgement. This paper is based on intensive discussions and joint work with the members of our research groups at the Leibniz Universität Hannover and at the Karlsruhe Institute of Technology, we are deeply indebted to their valuable feedback and constructive suggestions. Furthermore, we gratefully acknowledge the support provided by the German Research Foundation (DFG) within the priority program on "Organic Computing".

References

1. Kephart, J.O., Chess, D.M.: The vision of autonomic computing. IEEE Computer 1, 41–50 (2003)
2. Tennenhouse, D.: Proactive computing. Communications of the ACM 43, 43–50 (2000)
3. Schmeck, H.: Organic Computing – A new vision for distributed embedded systems. In: Proceedings of the 8th IEEE International Symposium on Object-Oriented Real-Time Distributed Computing (ISORC 2005), pp. 201–203. IEEE Computer Society Press, Los Alamitos (2005)
4. DFG Priority Program 1183 Organic Computing (2005) (visited June 2007), http://www.organic-computing.de/SPP
5. Branke, J., Mnif, M., Müller-Schloer, C., Prothmann, H., Richter, U., Rochner, F., Schmeck, H.: Organic Computing – Addressing complexity by controlled self-organization. In: Margaria, T., Philippou, A., Steffen, B. (eds.) Proceedings of the 2nd International Symposium on Leveraging Applications of Formal Methods, Verification and Validation (ISoLA 2006), Paphos, Cyprus, pp. 200–206 (2006)
6. Oberschelp, O., Hestermeyer, T., Kleinjohann, B., Kleinjohann, L.: Design of self-optimizing agent-based controllers. In: Urban, C. (ed.) Proceedings of the 3rd International Workshop on Agent Based Simulation, Passau, Germany. SCS European Publishing House (2002)
7. Hestermeyer, T., Oberschelp, O., Giese, H.: Structured information processing for self-optimizing mechatronic systems. In: Araújo, H., Vieira, A., Braz, J., Encarnação, B., Carvalho, M. (eds.) Proceedings of the 1st International Conference on Informatics in Control, Automation and Robotics (ICINCO 2004), pp. 230–237. IEEE Computer Society Press, Los Alamitos (2004)
8. Sterritt, R.: Autonomic Computing. Innovations in systems and software engineering 1, 79–88 (2005)
9. Cakar, E., Mnif, M., Müller-Schloer, C., Richter, U., Schmeck, H.: Towards a Quantitative Notion of Self-organisation. In: Proceedings of the 2007 IEEE Congress on Evolutionary Computation, pp. 4222–4229 (2007)
10. Rochner, F., Prothmann, H., Branke, J., Müller-Schloer, C., Schmeck, H.: An organic architecture for traffic light controllers. In: Hochberger, C., Liskowsky, R. (eds.) Informatik 2006 – Informatik für Menschen. LNI, vol. P-93, pp. 120–127. Köllen Verlag (2006)
11. Dorigo, M., Maniezzo, V., Colorni, A.: Ant system: Optimization by a colony of cooperating agents. Technical Report 26 1. IEEE Transactions on Systems (1996)
12. Heylighen, F.: The science of self-organization and adaptivity. In: The Encyclopedia of Life Support Systems, pp. 253–280 (1999)
13. Heylighen, F.: Complexity and self-organization. In: Bates, M.J., Maack, M.N. (eds.) Encyclopedia of Library and Information Sciences. Taylor & Francis, Abington (2008)

14. Lucas, C.: Self-organizing systems (sos) faq. Frequently asked questions version 2.99 (2006) (visited June 2007), http://www.calresco.org/sos/sosfaq.htm
15. Mühl, G., Werner, M., Jaeger, M.A., Herrmann, K., Parzyjegla, H.: On the definitions of self-managing and self-organizing systems. In: Braun, T., Carle, G., Stiller, B. (eds.) Proceedings of the KiVS 2007 Workshop: Selbstorganisierende, Adaptive, Kontextsensitive verteilte Systeme (SAKS 2007), Bern, Switzerland, pp. 291–301. VDE Verlag (2007)
16. Müller-Schloer, C., Sick, B.: Emergence in Organic Computing systems: Discussion of a controversial concept. In: Yang, L.T., Jin, H., Ma, J., Ungerer, T. (eds.) ATC 2006. LNCS, vol. 4158, pp. 1–16. Springer, Heidelberg (2006)
17. Dorigo, M., Stützle, T.: Ant colony optimization. B&T, MIT Press (2004)
18. Yau, S.S.: Managing trust in distributed agent systems (keynote address). In: Proceedings of 3rd International Conference on Autonomic and Trusted Computing (ATC), pp. 17–25 (2006)

Toward Systemic MAS Development: Enforcing Decentralized Self–organization by Composition and Refinement of Archetype Dynamics

Jan Sudeikat[1,2] and Wolfgang Renz[1]

[1] Multimedia Systems Laboratory,
Department of Information and Electrical Engineering,
Faculty of Engineering and Computer Science,
Hamburg University of Applied Sciences,
Berliner Tor 7, 20099 Hamburg, Germany
Tel. +49-40-42875-8304
{sudeikat,wr}@informatik.haw-hamburg.de
[2] Distributed Systems and Information Systems,
Computer Science Department, University of Hamburg,
Vogt–Kölln–Str. 30, 22527 Hamburg, Germany
Tel. +49-40-42883-2091
4sudeika@informatik.uni-hamburg.de

Abstract. The utilization of self-organizing processes promises scalability, robustness and adaptivity in Multi-Agent Systems (MAS), solely based on decentralized coordination of individual actors. *Bionic* development approaches have been established, which reuse decentralized coordination mechanisms that are derived from natural self–organizing systems. In this paper, we address analysis activities in incremental MAS development, concerning with the derivation of system architectures that enable applications to meet system requirements. As the functional requirements to self–organizing MAS comprise recurring types of system wide dynamics, we propose a systemic approach to analysis and architectural design activities by the iterative refinement of macroscopic dynamics. Based on a catalog of dynamic models of currently applied environment–mediated design metaphors, we discuss how intended MAS dynamics can be modeled and refined to decentralized MAS designs. A systemic design procedure is proposed and exemplified in a case study that demands the combination of two established design metaphors to enable an projected level of MAS adaptivity.

1 Introduction

Agent technology is an established tool to the development of complicated distributed software systems, where applications are decomposed into sets of *autonomous* and *pro-active* agents that are embedded in an environment [1]. As the intended system functionality results from agent interplay, a major design

D. Weyns, S.A. Brueckner, and Y. Demazeau (Eds.): EEMMAS 2007, LNAI 5049, pp. 39–57, 2008.

challenge for these Multi–Agent Systems (MAS) is to break down the intended system functionalities into individual agent activities and interactions.

When MAS operate in highly dynamic environments, system *adaptivity* [2] is needed. Since MAS are composed of collections of autonomous actors the utilization of self–organizing processes, as observable in biological, physical and social systems, has been proposed [3]. These processes allow the decentralized establishment and maintenance of structures, i.e. MAS configurations and organization structures [4], solely based on local agent (inter–)actions and individual reasoning. The decentralized nature, i.e. the absence of dedicated controlling components, promises *robust* and *scalable* applications. However, the exploitation of decentralized coordinations of autonomous components in large scale distributed systems challenges traditional development techniques and methodologies [5].

Engineering efforts typically structure development procedures in *iterations*, composed of sequences of *activities* (so-called *workflows* or *disciplines*) that development teams are to complete successively. Development activities commonly comprise *requirements engineering, analysis, design, implementation* and *testing* (e.g. see [6]). Iterations typically start with requirements activities that purpose agreements between developers and stakeholders on the intended functionality of the system to be. The following system analysis (a.k.a. *architectural design*), results in an architecture that allows to meet the requirements and is refined during design activities to a level of detail that guides system implementation. Finally, resulting executables are tested, validating intended functionalities.

While these top–down development efforts facilitate cost– and time–oriented software development, their application to the construction of self–organizing MAS is complicated by the inherent nonlinearities of the macroscopic system behaviors that are introduced by self–organizing processes [7]. As these processes impair straightforward anticipations of system wide dynamics as well as the impact of changes of microscopic agent implementations on these dynamics, a trend toward the *recreation* of well–examined macroscopic dynamics can be observed [8,9,10,10]. Well studied natural self–organizing systems provide *design metaphors* and the implementation of similar behaving applications is facilitated by decentralized coordination mechanisms [9] that have been proposed as design pattern [11,12] for MAS development. As these provide means to the establishment of well understood dynamics, approaches to their selection and combination during application design, targeted to meet specific demands (requirements) of real world applications are still at early stages [13].

Based on the observation that development efforts to self–organizing MAS typically intend recurring types if macroscopic system behaviors [14,15], each inspired by natural design metaphors, we propose a *systemic* approach to MAS analysis efforts. As self–organizing processes originate from the presence of feedback loops [16,17], modeling notions from system dynamics research [18] are adopted that provide means to the description of causal relations between macroscopic system properties. We provide definitions of the causal structure and resulting dynamics of typically utilized design metaphors and show how these models can be refined from early requirements to detailed MAS designs. A systemic development procedure is demonstrated on the design of a simulation model that demands the combination of two environment–mediated design metaphors.

This paper is structured as follows. The next section summarizes current best practices to the construction of self–organizing MAS, focusing on the utilization of reusable decentralized coordination mechanisms. Afterwards, section 3 introduces a systemic modeling approach to these mechanisms. The modeling notion of causal loops – inspired by *system dynamics* research – is introduced, followed by a catalog of environment mediated template designs and an discussion how the consideration of the causal relations that are to be established enables a design perspective on self–organizing MAS (section 3.5). An exemplification is given in section 4 and finally, we conclude and give prospects for future work.

2 Engineering Self–organizing Multi–agent Systems

In [5], current best practices to the engineering of self–organizing MAS have been reviewed, ranging form formal tools [19] to development methodologies [20,21,22]. Decentralized, self–organizing processes are powerful tools to MAS adaptivity as they support macroscopic observable, nonlinear phenomena, e.g. *phase changes*. However, these phenomena hinder traditional *top–down* and *divide–and–conquer* design strategies [7,20,23] and are therefore usually not considered by general–purpose development methodologies [24]. Solely the *ADELFE* methodology provides an tailored extension of the *Rational Unified Process* [6] that addresses the development of adaptive MAS composed of *cooperative* agents [25]. ADELFE stresses the identification of cooperation failures (non-cooperative situations) and means for individuals to recover from these.

Currently, a trend toward *bionic* development approaches can be observed [8]. These approaches recreate well–known, field–tested template mechanisms. Recreations are supported by decentralized coordination mechanisms [3,9] and simulation based development procedures [20,21]. Figure 1 visualizes the support of these tools for the generic software engineering activities [6].

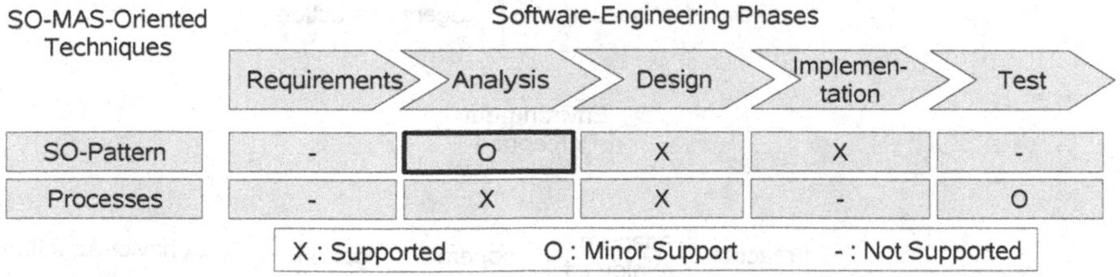

SO-MAS-Oriented Techniques	Software-Engineering Phases				
	Requirements	Analysis	Design	Implementation	Test
SO-Pattern	-	O	X	X	-
Processes	-	X	X	-	O

X : Supported   O : Minor Support   - : Not Supported

Fig. 1. The support for generic software engineering activities by pattern–oriented development approaches (extract from [5]). The bold cell is addressed in this paper.

Reusable coordination mechanisms (*SO–Pattern*) [9,12,11] require the, yet minor supported, selection of appropriate mechanisms during analysis activities and focus on design and implementation issues by guiding agent and environment models. Simulation–based development procedures (*Processes*) address the utilization of these mechanisms by iterative development activities, particularly system simulations and parameter adjustment [20]. Modeling the requirements for self–organizing solutions [14], the identification of appropriate mechanisms [13], their adjustment [8] and the testability of their correct utilization [15] are open research questions.

Figure 2 depicts a classification of applied coordination mechanisms from [5] that facilitate the establishment of decentralized feedback loops in agent populations. Feedbacks require that agents perceive the MAS state (*interdependency level*) and adjust their behavior (*behavior adaption level*) according to the gained insights. Interdependency-level mechanisms are distinguished between direct interactions of agents (right) and indirect interactions that are mediated by a (virtual) environment. Individual *behavior adaption* is controlled by the employed agent architectures, ranging from purely *reactive* mechanisms to, *adaptive, cooperative* and *generic* architectures (reviewed in [3]). Environment mediated mechanisms are attracting increasing attention [26] in MAS development and their classification is highlighted in figure 2 (a). According to [10], the propagation of information can rely on *diffusion* or on *serendipitous* perceptions from stochastic movement in shared data spaces.

Coordination mechanisms may depend on explicit data items (*marker–based*) or agents infer implicit information directly from the perceived environment

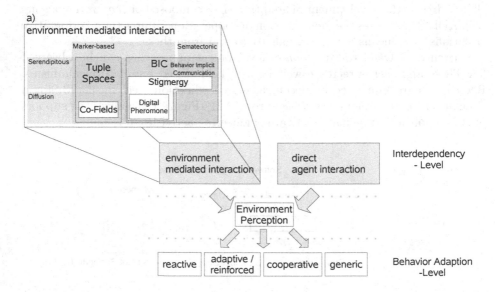

Fig. 2. A classification of decentralized coordination mechanisms (following [5]). Environment mediated mechanisms are highlighted (according to a taxonomy from [10]).

(*sematectonic*). *Behavior Implicit Communication* (BIC) [27] denotes agent coordination that is solely based on the observation and interpretation of neighboring agents activities. The required observations can be based on sematectonic
or marker–based perceptions. The prominent *stigmergy* mechanism [16] is an
application of BIC as it denotes the communication between individuals solely
via the modification of environment elements. Typically dedicated markers are
modified, e.g. *digital pheromones* are released which diffuse and evaporate [16].
The prominent *co-field* [28] approaches rely on virtual fields that are usually
computed within *tuple spaces* (see [10]).

Figure 3 relates the coordination mechanisms to the intended system behaviors and resulting MAS implementations. Self–organizing MAS developers
typically take inspiration from *self-regulatory design metaphors* (e.g. listed in
[10]) which exhibit a specific *behavior space*. Knowledge about the space of possible macroscopic system states, and transitions between them allows developers
to anticipate the system behavior and therefore select appropriate metaphors
to guide MAS design. Developers select metaphors and intend similar behavioral regimes to be exhibited by the implemented *MAS*. Metaphor designs are
realized by the utilization of *decentralized coordination mechanisms* [9,3] that
provide means to the establishment of feedback loops among agent populations.
Each mechanisms defines how agents (locally) perceive the MAS state (*interaction mode*), i.e. how information is communicated, and how individuals use the
perceived information to adjust their behavior (*behavior selection mode*) [5].

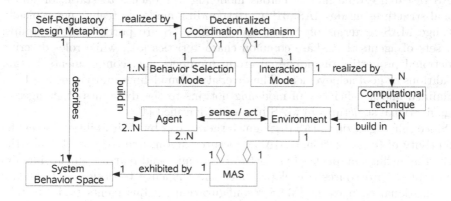

Fig. 3. The relation between design metaphors, distributed coordination mechanisms
and MAS implementations

MAS are composed of *agents* that perceive and modify an *environment*. Behavior selection modes directly guide agent implementations, while interaction
modes are to be implemented via specific *computational techniques* (e.g. described in [11]), which enable the propagation of information through the environment and define the sensory inputs of agents. Established computational

techniques for environment mediated MAS comprise *evaporation, aggregation* and *diffusion* [11]. E.g. *digital pheromone*–based coordination mechanism [29], a well–known exemplification of *stigmergy* [30], rely on a shared environment where communication is enabled by diffusion and evaporation. Diffusion ensures that pheromones are transported via the environment and evaporation degrades information that is not reinforced, therefore erasing old information.

MAS developers that aim to apply decentralized coordination mechanisms have to (1) select appropriate mechanisms, (2) map their constituent past (behavior selection and interaction modes) to the application domain at hand, (3) implement them in an agent architecture of their choice and finally (4) tune system / agent parameters to allow for the intended behavioral regimes (cf. [21]). While mechanisms have been examined in relation to the applied computational techniques to provide pattern languages [9,12,11], guidelines to their selection have yet caught minor attention [13]. In the following section, we discuss how intended macroscopic dynamics of future MAS implementations as well as nature–inspired design metaphors can be modeled. The proposed usage of systemic modeling notions facilitates the identification of appropriate design metaphors and coordination mechanisms.

3 Modeling the Dynamics of Decentralized Design Metaphors

MAS research established numerous modeling approaches to static, organizational structures inside MAS [31]. Corresponding modeling techniques typically arrange MAS in terms of *groups* and *roles*. MAS are partitioned in groups, i.e. sets of agents that share common characteristics [31], while roles describe functional properties of individual group members, e.g. commitments certain conditions or goal achievement. The diversity of modeling approaches has been examined and a deficiency of modeling notions to the dynamics of changes of organizational structures in MAS has been identified [4].

Since self–organizing MAS distinguish themselves by their ability to steer the adaptivity of (organizational) MAS structures at runtime (e.g. cf. [17,15]), the lack of modeling approaches to structural dynamics and rearrangements impairs development procedures. Developers face the challenge to design and validate organizational changes, i.e. MAS reconfigurations. Adjustments typically take place via group / coalition formations and run–time role adoptions. In [14,15], macroscopic models, inspired by modeling notions from *system dynamics* research [18], have been introduced and related to requirements engineering activities. In addition, it has been found that developers typically intend specific types of dynamics that recure in MAS from various applications domains [15].

In order to facilitate (iterative) design approaches to c omplex dynamics in MAS, we discuss how macroscopic models can be iteratively refined in order to allow derivation of the intended dynamics that map to the above discussed design metaphors. Since these metaphors are inherently linked to *decentralized coordination mechanisms* (e.g. [9]), prepares the metaphor identification the selection of coordination mechanisms that influence the design of individual agents and MAS environments. These refinement activities take place during analysis activities (cf. figure 7).

3.1 System Dynamics

Self–organizing processes rely on the presence of underlying *positive* and *negative* feedback loops [5,16,17]. Positive feedbacks are typically used to stimulate *coherent* and/or *cooperative* agent behaviors [32], while negative feedbacks are often applied to balance stimulations and remove obsolete stimuli. Combinations of feedback loops are observable in *physical, biological* and *social* systems and have been been examined and classified by interdisciplinary research communities.

These communities examine how the behavior of groups of interacting artifacts can be described and predicted. A family of *systems theories* (e.g. *cybernetics* [33]) have been revised that apply macroscopic modeling approaches to the analysis and simulation of complex systems. I.e. the relationships between system–wide observables are expressed by their rates of change. Available tools range from purely mathematical, numerical settings [34,35] to dedicated (equation–based) simulation packages.[1] Similar macroscopic modeling has been successfully applied to self–organizing MAS [36,37].

Among the system theoretic research communities, *systems dynamics* research focuses on the examination of the circular, possibly interlocking and/or time–delayed relationships among constituent entities ([38]). *Causal loop diagrams* (CLD) are used to model system entities and the causal relations between them. This notation is exemplified in the figures 5 and 6, where self-regulatory causal relationships in metaphoric MAS are described. *System observables* and respectively *system state variables* are connected via arrows that denote positive (+) and negative (−) contributions. *Positive* contributions (+) mark direct causal relations, where changes at origins produces changes at destinations in the same direction (increases causes increase). *Negative* (−) causal links describe inverted relations, i.e. the causation in the opposite direction. Circular relationships form feedback loops and are distinguished by their occurrences of positive and negative causal links.[2] *Reinforcing* loops (r) contain an even number of negative causal links while *balancing* (b) feedback loops contain an odd number of negative causal links.

While mainly focusing on business domains [18], interdisciplinary analysis efforts have lead to a number of common patterns of behavior – so–called *System Archetypes* [39] – that recur in various application domains and describe unique sets positive and negative causal loops. The identified archetypes provide generic causal loop structures, used as templates to classify structures and behavioral insights [40], by structuring causal relations between macroscopic system states and relating these structures to the exhibited *modes of dynamic behaviors* [18]. These templates can be applied either *diagnostically*, to predict system behaviors

---

[1] e.g.: http://ccl.northwestern.edu/netlogo/docs/systemdynamics.html
[2] http://www.public.asu.edu/~kirkwood/sysdyn/SDIntro/SDIntro.htm

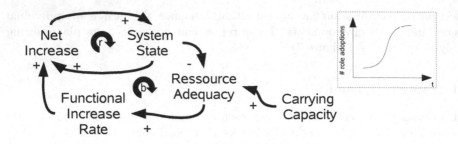

Fig. 4. CLD and canonical time series of logistic growth (according to [18])

from structural similarities, or *prospectively*, by anticipating structural changes as they introduce archetype structures [40]. To exemplify the utilized models, figure 4 shows a well–known *mode of dynamic behavior* [18], the *logistic growth*,[3] a.k.a *S-shaped growth*, that can be traced back to the occurrence of a reinforcing and a balancing causal loop (cf. [18]) steering the increase of a generic property limited by a carrying capacity. A catalog of actual archetypes and their relation to economic settings can be found in [39]. In the coming section, we show that typically applied design metaphors provide similar sets of recuring dynamics that can be understood in terms of sets of feedback loops.

3.2   A Catalog of Environment Mediated Coordination Mechanisms

While decentralized coordination mechanisms and bio–inspired design metaphors have been proposed as *design pattern* for self–organizing MAS [11,12], the causal link structures within them have not been considered yet. In the following, we examine these structures in common template designs, proposing a novel approach toward the dynamic MAS models. These complements to design pattern definitions are then used (section 3.5 and 4) for pattern selection and combination. Due to the targeted macroscopic description level, the here applied systemic modeling approach is applicable to general–purpose coordination mechanisms. Here, we exemplify this approach for situated, i.e. environment mediated coordination mechanisms. In [10], a comprehensive list of established design metaphors (named *mechanisms*) for environment mediated agent coordination have been summarized. In the following, we discuss their causal loop structures which steer self–organizing applications dynamics. Examination of constituent *reinforcing* and *balancing* feedbacks revealed a distinction between *single*–looped and *multi*–looped design metaphors.

3.3   Single–Looped Design Metaphors

The following MAS designs allow for system adaptivity by providing single causal loops that adjustments according to MAS external influences. Resulting

---

[3] see: http://mathworld.wolfram.com/LogisticEquation.html

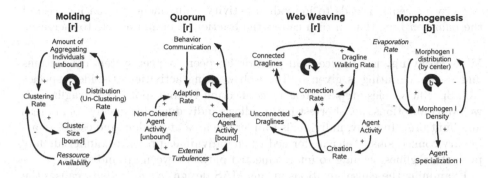

Fig. 5. Single Looped Design Metaphors: Prominent template designs that describe single looped dynamics

equilibrium states are established and maintained by either balancing or reinforcing feedback (cf. figure 5).

Molding and Aggregation. is a coordination scheme inspired by foraging in bacteria populations [41]. When resources are available, agents wander the environment to consume individually. If resources become scarce, individuals cluster. The resulting formation then moves as a whole. Individuals leave the cluster when an area is reached that allows individual foraging, i.e. resources are available. This behavior is particularly applicable to team coordinations (see [10]) allowing to aggregate group members.

   While coordination typically takes place via *pheromones* [16], the macroscopic model in figure 5 abstracts from the required implementation techniques of diffusion and evaporation and highlights the macroscopic observable dynamics. Molding is steered by a balancing loop that controlls the macroscopic observable numbers of *bound* (clustered) and *unbound* (not clustered) agents. Two rates control the binding (*clustering rate*) and release (*distribution rate*) of individuals. These are directly influenced by the availability of resources.

Quorum. describes the self–organized establishment of coherent agent activities, due to the ability of agents to sense the activities of population members, and adopt the sensed behaviors. In biological [10] as well as physical [35] systems, it has been observed that local agent activities can stimulate coherent activities of neighboring agents, leading to coherent agent states. Agent activities can be perceived either via communication of specific markers [10] or the observation of agent activities, due to *Behavior Implicit Communication* (BIC) [27]. Prominent examples are (ferro–)magnetic fields and laser phenomena [35].

   In these MAS (cf. figure 5), the numbers of bound (*coherent*) and unbound (*non–coherent*) agents are pertubated, i.e. driven out of sync, by *external* influences. Coherence of agent behaviors is (re–)established by a reinforcing feedback loop that originated from the *communication* and perception of agent activities.

Activity perception leads to individual activity adjustment, i.e. an increase of the *adaption rate*, that in turn causes the fraction of bound agents to increase.

Web Weaving. is a source of inspiration for peer–to–peer system connections and network routing is given by the web weaving activities of spiders species [10]. Specific species prepare areas by connecting ground spots with draglines. A web of connections, i.e. shortest paths, allows individuals to quickly roam areas and hunt prey. Initially, individuals wander the area at random and establish arbitrary connections. Webs are formed when individuals prefer to wander already present draglines, leading to interconnected paths between ground spots.

Examining the causal relations in this MAS design, *agent activity* causes the *creation* of *connected* and *unconnected* links (cf. figure 5). The *connection rate* of links depends on the rate of traversals of already present links (*walking rate*), which in turn is causally dependent on the amount of already present links, forming an reinforcing causal loop that increases link interconnections.

Morphogenesis. controls how cells in early development stages of organisms differentiate. It has been found that specific cells in an embryo emit diffusing morphogens [10]. Sensing gradients of these markers allow individual cells to measure their distance to emitting sources and therefore conclude their differentiation. Different morphogen types are typically combined to enforce adjustments due to sets of gradients.

The causal relations are dominated by balancing loops between the emitting distribution *center* and the morphogen density within the MAS (cf. figure 5). While several morphogens can be present in a MAS, figure 5 visualizes a single loop, originating from one morphogen type. An *evaporation rate* degrades (negatively contributes) to the morphogen density that triggers agent specialization.

The above presented mechanisms provide single causal feedback loops, therefore facilitating analysis, behavior anticipation and parameter adjustment. Due to the limited adaptivity of single steering forces enhanced mechanisms, i.e. combinations of causal feedbacks, are also utilized in MAS design.

3.4   Multi–looped Design Metaphors

The following design methaphors provide multiple, interplaying causal loops that steer MAS adjustments. These mechanisms take inspiration from biological systems where population members coordinate individual activities [10].

Brood Sorting. inside ant colonies inspired fully decentralized, collective sorting mechanisms [42,10]. Ants wander their nest randomly. When isolated or outnumbered items (egg, larvea, etc.) are encountered, they are picked up and transported till another item is encountered that satisfies a similarity criteria. Then the load is deposited nearby, leading to clusters of similar items [8].

The causal relations within this clustering scheme form two balancing and one reinforcing (b^2r) feedback loops (cf. figure 6). First, the numbers of bound

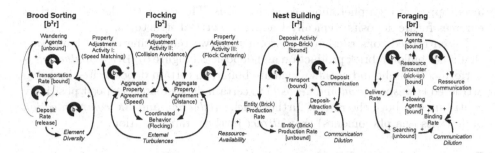

Fig. 6. Multi–looped design metaphors: Prominent template designs that describe system dynamics which result from combinations of causal loops

(*transporting*) and unbound (*wandering*) agents are balanced as agents successively adopt both behaviors. The *release* of items both decreases the *diversity* of elements and frees agents to adopt their initial wandering behavior. As the actual clustering is achieved by the negative contribution to item diversity, the remaining diversity contributes to the binding of (transporting) agents, forming a balancing causal loop. Since any deposit frees agents to search, a reinforcing causal loop is established.

Flocking, Schooling and Herding. behaviors in bird and fish swarms have inspired motion coordination mechanisms in MAS [10]. Formations of coordinated moving agents can be established by individual: *collision avoidance, speed matching* and *flock centering*. It is sufficient to form coordinated flocks of agents solely based on (1) the avoidance of direct collisions, (2) the adjustment of individual speed to the perceived speed of neighboring agents and (3) a constant movement toward the estimated center of clustered agents. The resulting formations move randomly as emergent macroscopic structures.

Concerning the exhibited causal relations, agents contribute to cluster formations by adopting common values for individual variables (*aggregate property agreement*), i.e. they agree upon similar *speed* and *distance* values (cf. figure 6). Agreements are constantly disturbed due to agent reactivity to *external turbulences*. These perturbations are balanced by two balancing loops (b^2) as the common agent distance is adjusted by collective movement toward the flocking center and the aggregate flock speed is adjusted by individual speed matching. Individual collision avoidance contributes positivley to the establishment of an aggregate distance, while it pertubates aggregate speed values as agents are forced to speed up and to slow down.

Nest Building. efforts in termite colonies have inspired approaches to the collective, decentralized construction, e.g. performed by robot swarms [10]. Termites produce building bricks from bodily waste that contain pheromones [16]. Individual transport of these bricks is guided by pheromone gradients, and bricks are dropped at high pheromone concentrations. Therefore, the deposit of bricks enforces future deposits, typically leading to vertical structures.

Decentralized construction is controlled by two reinforcing causal loops (r^2) that steer building brick production and deposit (cf. figure 6). Brick *production* is performed by unbound agents which are bound to certain deposit sites by being attracted (*transportation* and *deposit*) to certain deposit sites. Deposit positively contributes to both the rate of further brick *production* and the *communication* of deposits (via pheromones) that *attract* further transportation.

Foraging. behaviors, found in ant colonies, are prominent examples of swarming systems [26]. Agents stochastically wander an environment to forage resources. When clusters of resources are encountered individuals pick up a resource item and transport it to a home base (nest). During transportation, pheromones are released that diffuse and evaporate. Non–transporting agents sense pheromones and move toward the perceived gradient. As ants are attracted by resource trans-portation, the number of resource encounters increases leading to reliable estab-lishments of shortest path between resources and nest(s) [26]. Realizations of these dynamics typically utilize *stigmergy* mechanisms, i.e. the propagation of digital pheromones.

These causal relations control the numbers of unbound (*searching*) and bound agents that either *follow* a gradient, *pick–up* encountered resources or transport these (*homing*). As the bound actions take place in sequence (positive contri-butions), two causal loops (*br*) are established (cf. figure 6). Transported items are *delivered*, freeing agents to *search* and limiting the available resources by a balancing loop. As homing agents *communicate* their transportation, which contributes to the binding rate of unbound agents, these communications cause a reinforcing causal loop.

These combinations of causal feedback loops have been inspired by biological systems. While their *in vivo* resulting dynamics are well–known, the realization in software requires non-trivial parameter adjustments that are complicated by the (multiple) relations between system states. In the following, we discuss how the here modeled mechanisms can be selected and combined.

3.5   Using Dynamic Models in MAS Analysis

The previously examined design metaphors (cf. section 3.3) provide field–tested utilizations of single and multiple causal loops in MAS. As the dynamics of the embedded causal loops are well understood and their implementation is guided by pattern catalogues [9,12,11] as well as microscopic modeling approaches [43]. It is desirable to guide the reuse of this constructive knowledge. The utilization of these pattern requires developers to identify the decentralized coordination mechanisms that are suitable to satisfy application requirements. The selection of coordination mechanisms is typically approached by the examination of the macroscopic system properties that are to be established [13]. As these properties do not map uniquely to mechanisms (cf. [13]), we argue that non–ambiguous identifications also require comparisons of intended *dynamics*.

Different combinations of causal loops can lead to similar macroscopic states, e.g. equilibrium and fixed points. When self–organizing dynamics are utilized in MAS development, not only the established or maintained macroscopic properties but also the dynamics that steer establishment are of interest [14,15]. The time–dependent behavior of MAS adaptivity distinguishes different pattern a.k.a. design metaphors. To express metaphor dynamics, we propose the modeling of their inherent causal relations. The structure of the established causal loops is application independent (cf. section 3.3), while the macroscopic properties in these models are application dependent. Decentralized coordination mechanisms provide means to the establishment of these relations [12].

Building upon the elicitation and validation of requirements on self–organizing dynamics [14,15], we propose a procedure of *analysis* activities (cf. figure 7), which address the transition from *requirements* models to application *design* [6].

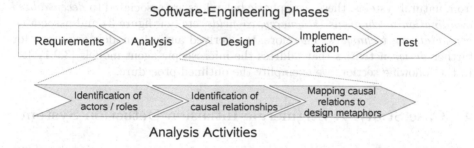

Fig. 7. Iterative causal link refinement activities. These activities guide the transfer from application requirements to the detailed agent design that applied decentralized coordination mechanisms.

These activities build upon descriptions of the macroscopic observable behavior. In [15], it has been shown how the intended macroscopic MAS adaptivity can be expressed in terms of CLDs and how the causal relations within these can be validated by macroscopic system simulations. The here proposed activities address application design by refining the *intended* dynamics to sets of metaphors that describe the required causal relations. These metaphors in turn provide input to subsequent design activities that derive agent models and utilize decentralized coordination mechanisms.

The derivation of application dependent models of MAS dynamics can be carried out in a three step iterative process. First, an initial *role model* needs to be derived from the system requirements. It denotes application dependent agent roles that are to be played by different agent types.

Secondly, definitions of causal links between these roles form a macroscopic model of the abstract MAS operation. The presence of causal loops indicates self–regulatory MAS behaviors. When developers decide to realize these behaviors via self–organization, i.e. decentralized agent coordination, applicable mechanisms can be identified by the refinement of the causal links within the intended feedback loops. As this refinement poses a considerable modeling effort, it is guided by the foreseen causal relations. Each of the identified causal links may exhibit dynamics, i.e. is subject to further causal loops and can therefore be refined incrementally.

After sets of causal loops have been identified, developers can reason about how to establish these. Intended loop structures are to be compared and mapped to established MAS designs, i.e. the previously cataloged design metaphors. This refinement may lead to combinations of mechanisms and the in principle possible mappings are not necessarily unique. Therefore, developers are guided in mechanisms selection and combination, but are also forced to decide qualitatively which mechanism, respectively mechanisms combinations, are appropriate for specific application scenarios. These decisions are not only to be made on the basis of the properties of the mechanisms at hand, but implementation and project dependent issues as well.

As the design metaphors describe intended dynamics by taking inspiration from natural systems, these metaphoric behaviors are associated to *decentralized coordination mechanisms* (*stigmergy, co–fields*, etc.; cf. figure 3) and associated *computational techniques*. Therefore, the derived analysis models are input for further *design* activities that address the microscopic agent models [3,9,11,12]. In the following section, we exemplify the outlined procedure.

4   Case Study: A Stigmergic Intrusion Detection System

A prominent example to self–organizing, nature inspired computational systems [44] are *intrusion detection systems* (IDS) (e.g. [45]). *Immune systems* have inspired agent–based IDS designs that exemplify the establishment of *self–healing* properties. IDSs maintain computational infrastructures by the identification and removal of *malicious* intruders. Detections are typically done by observing and interpreting agent actions [45]. In the following, we exemplify how a systemic view on MAS development and the iterative refinement of causal loop diagrams can be used to derive combinations of design metaphors to met application requirements [14]. The systemic analysis of an immune system inspired IDS is outlined in figure 8. An initial *role model* identifies (1) malicious *intruders*, (2) *searcher* agents that are equipped with specific algorithms to identify intruders and (3) *remover* agents that are capable to delete intruders. The foreseen interactions of these agent types describe macroscopic causal relations. Searcher agents execute a searching behavior and *detect* infected nodes. Upon detection, they *recruit* remover agents, i.e. trigger intruder removal. Remover agents get activated by infection communication and are responsible for *removals*. These relations are expected to establish a balancing causal loop (α) as the MAS behavior is to limit the amount of intruders. Developers are faced with the challenge to derive a MAS design that enforces this balancing loop in a totally decentralized manner. In order to identify design metaphors that enable self–organization of the intended causality (α), the participating causal links are refined (cf. figure 8; step 2). This refinement takes each of the relations between the elements of the initial role model (cf. figure 8; step 1) into consideration and reveals three

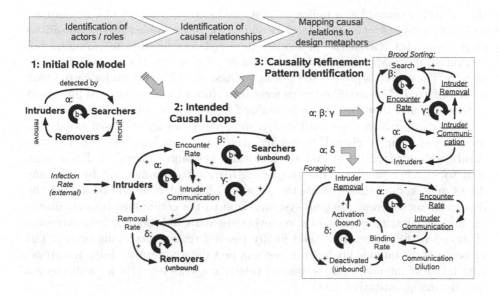

Fig. 8. Iterative refinement of the *Intrusion Detection System* case study. Based on an initial, immune system inspired role model (1), the intended causal loops are identified (2). Finally, the dynamics of these causal relations are refined by a mapping to the causal loops of design metaphors.

additional, auxiliary causal relations that steer agent type interactions. For each of the foreseen relations (*detected by*, *recruit* and *remove*), interaction rates can be introduced (*encounter rate*, *intruder communication* and *removal rate* respectively) that highlight the relations between agent roles.

In addition, the amount of intruders is related to an *external* infection rate, that controlls the entry of intruders to the system. Searcher and remover agents are refined to operate in two atomic states. They are either bound to the *communication* resp. *removal* of encountered intruders or are unbound, i.e. execute their default behaviors. Detection of intruders is based on an *encounter rate*. This rate denotes the binding of searchers to intruders, therefore balancing the amount of intruders (α) and bound searchers (β). Encounters trigger the communication of known malicious agents. These communications lead to the removal of intruders and searchers are freed to continue their searching behavior. Therefore, successful communication contribute to the amount of searching agents, forming a third causal loop (γ). Finally removing agents are supposed to perceive communications which binds them to agent removal. As successful removals free removing agents, a reinforcing loop (δ) is established.

The given refinement identifies two balancing and two reinforcing loops to be established in the MAS to be (b^2r^2). Comparing the intended causal structure with the given design metaphors reveals that the intended loop combination is not available as a generic structure and is therefore to be established by a combination of metaphors. Examination of the structural relationships between the identified causal loops indicates that the loops α, β and γ can be mapped to *brood sorting* (b^2r) and the loops α and δ can be resembled by the causalities of *foraging* (*br*). Given the previously modeled coordination mechanisms (cf. section 3), this mapping resembles the soonest the refined structure (cf. figure 8; step 2). The α loop is present in both mappings, since it is the major causal loop to be enforced. The auxiliary loops were introduced to refine the establishment of this loop and therefore are to be realized by single metaphors.

Taking inspiration from both design metaphors, an agent–based simulation model[4] has been developed. Searching agents perform *brood sorting*, i.e. randomly walk a virtual grid and stochastically encounter intruders. Encounters lead to searcher bindings that trigger stigmergic communication by releasing digital pheromones that indicate the presence of intruders in grid cells cause the dynamics known from *foraging* systems. Due to the communication via diffusing and evaporating pheromones, removers are attracted (bound) to occurrences of intruders, follow gradients and finally reach / remove malicious agents. The presence of the intended balancing loop can be validated by examining the cross–correlation of intruder and (activated) remover agents (see [15] for a discussion on this and quantitative data).

5   Conclusions

In this paper a macroscopic, systemic design approach to self–organizing MAS has been proposed, describing MAS run–time adaptivity. Self–organizing MAS development typically intends to establish nature–inspired pattern of system dynamics. Their construction requires the utilization of decentralized coordination mechanisms. Systemic modeling allows to express the dynamics of these design metaphors in terms of causal relations between macroscopic properties. A design procedure has been proposed and exemplified that relies on a given catalog of design metaphor dynamics. Starting from initial role models the intended causal relations between macroscopic properties can be iteratively refined and mapped to the causal relations that are exhibited inside design metaphors. After appropriate design metaphors have been identified, they guide the selection of suitable distributed coordination mechanisms, and knowledge of the intended feedback loops guide their utilization in MAS implementations.

Future work will examine further support of causal loop modeling for iterative development of self–organizing MAS. The here proposed notation has been adopted from *system dynamics* research [18,39] and will be revised to support refinement activities. Iterative development efforts require both the design of intended dynamics as well as the examination of causal relations in MAS implementations to validate MAS redesigns. Tool–support for static MAS analysis and macroscopic runtime simulation [46] will be revised, in order to support round–trip engineering. The modeling approach presented here addresses feedback loops on macroscopic scales and may be supplemented by explicitly modeling the information flows within microscopic agent implementations [43].

---

[4] Using the NetLogo simulation package: http://ccl.northwestern.edu/netlogo/

Enabling the mapping and mutual use of both micro- and macroscopic modeling levels promises full lifecycle support for self–organizing MAS design.

Acknowledgments

One of us (J.S.) would like to thank the *Distributed Systems and Information Systems* (VSIS) group at Hamburg University, particularly Winfried Lamersdorf, Lars Braubach and Alexander Pokahr for inspiring discussion and encouragement.

References

1. Jennings, N.R.: Building complex, distributed systems: the case for an agent-based approach. Comms. of the ACM 44(4), 35–41 (2001)
2. Zadeh, L.A.: On the definition of adaptivity. Proceedings of the IEEE 51, 469–470 (1963)
3. Serugendo, G.D.M., Gleizes, M.P., Karageorgos, A.: Self–organisation and emergence in mas: An overview. Informatica 30, 45–54 (2006)
4. Mao, X., Yu, E.: Organizational and social concepts in agent oriented software engineering. In: Odell, J.J., Giorgini, P., Müller, J.P. (eds.) AOSE 2004. LNCS, vol. 3382, pp. 1–15. Springer, Heidelberg (2005)
5. Sudeikat, J., Renz, W.: Building Complex Adaptive Systems: On Engineering Self–Organizing Multi–Agent Systems. In: Applications of Complex Adaptive Systems. IDEA (to appear, 2008)
6. Kruchten, P.: The Rational Unified Process: An Introduction. The Addison-Wesley Object Technology Series. Addison Wesley Professional, Reading (2003)
7. Edmonds, B., Bryson, J.J.: The insufficiency of formal design methods - the necessity of an experimental approach for the understanding and control of complex mas. In: AAMAS 2004: Proceedings of the Third International Joint Conference on Autonomous Agents and Multiagent Systems (2004)
8. Sudeikat, J., Renz, W.: On the redesign of self–organizing multi–agent systems. International Transactions on Systems Science and Applications 2, 81–89 (2006)
9. DeWolf, T., Holvoet, T.: A catalogue of decentralised coordination mechanisms for designing self-organising emergent applications. Technical Report Report CW 458, Department of Computer Science, K.U. Leuven (2006)
10. Mamei, M., Menezes, R., Tolksdorf, R., Zambonelli, F.: Case studies for self-organization in computer science. J. Syst. Archit. 52, 443–460 (2006)
11. Gardelli, L., Viroli, M., Omicini, A.: Design patterns for self-organizing multiagent systems. In: Proceedings of EEDAS 2007 (2007)
12. DeWolf, T., Holvoet, T.: Decentralised coordination mechanisms as design patterns for self-organising emergent applications. In: Proceedings of the Fourth International Workshop on Engineering Self-Organising Applications, pp. 40–61 (2006)
13. DeWolf, T., Holvoet, T.: A taxonomy for self-* properties in decentralised autonomic computing. In: Autonomic Computing: Concepts, Infrastructure, and Applications (2006)
14. Sudeikat, J., Renz, W.: Toward requirements engineering for self–organizing multi–agent systems. In: Proceedings of the First IEEE Internaltional Conference on Self–Adaptive and Self–Organizing Systems (SASO 2007), pp. 299–302 (2007)

15. Sudeikat, J., Renz, W.: On expressing and validating requirements for the adaptivity of self–organizing multi–agent systems. System and Information Sciences Notes 2, 14–19 (2007)
16. Parunak, H.V.D., Brueckner, S.: Engineering swarming systems. In: Methodologies and Software Engineering for Agent Systems, pp. 341–376. Kluwer, Dordrecht (2004)
17. Brueckner, S., Czap, H.: Organization, self-organization, autonomy and emergence: Status and challenges. International Transactions on Systems Science and Applications 2, 1–9 (2006)
18. Sterman, J.D.: Business Dynamics - Systems Thinking an Modeling for a Complex World. McGraw-Hill, New York (2000)
19. Rouff, C.A., Hinchey, M.G., Truszkowski, W.F., Rash, J.L.: Experiences applying formal approaches in the development of swarm-based space exploration systems. Int. J. Softw. Tools Technol. Transf. 8, 587–603 (2006)
20. Edmonds, B.: Using the experimental method to produce reliable self-organised systems. In: Brueckner, S.A., Di Marzo Serugendo, G., Karageorgos, A., Nagpal, R. (eds.) ESOA 2005. LNCS (LNAI), vol. 3464, pp. 84–99. Springer, Heidelberg (2005)
21. DeWolf, T., Holvoet, T.: Towards a methodolgy for engineering self-organising emergent systems. In: Proceedings of the International Conference on Self-Organization and Adaptation of Multi-agent and Grid Systems (2005)
22. Bernon, C., Gleizes, M.P., Peyruqueou, S., Picard, G.: Adelfe: A methodology for adaptive multi-agent systems engineering. In: Petta, P., Tolksdorf, R., Zambonelli, F. (eds.) ESAW 2002. LNCS (LNAI), vol. 2577, pp. 156–169. Springer, Heidelberg (2003)
23. Fromm, J.: On engineering and emergence. nlin.AO/0601002 (2006)
24. Henderson-Sellers, B., Giorgini, P. (eds.): Agent-oriented Methodologies. Idea Group Publishing (2005) ISBN: 1591405815
25. Picard, G., Gleizes, M.P.: An agent architecture to design self–organizing collectives: Principles and application. In: Alonso, E., et al. (eds.) Adaptive Agents and MAS. LNCS (LNAI), vol. 2636, pp. 141–158. Springer, Heidelberg (2003)
26. Bonabeau, E., Theraulaz, G.: Swarm smarts. Scientific American, pp. 72–79 (2000)
27. Omicini, A., Ricci, A., Viroli, M., Castelfranchi, C., Tummolini, L.: A conceptual framework for self-organising mas. In: WOA 2004: Dagli Oggetti agli Agenti. 5th AI*IA/TABOO Joint Workshop "From Objects to Agents:" Complex Systems and Rational Agents, November 30 - December 1, pp. 100–109 (2004)
28. Mamei, M., Zambonelli, F., Leonardi, L.: Co–fields: A physically inspired approach to motion coordination. IEEE Pervasive Computing 03, 52–61 (2004)
29. Parunak, H.V.D.: Go to the ant: Engineering principles from natural multi-agent systems. Annals of Operations Research 75(1) (1997)
30. Grasse, P.: La reconstruction du nid et les coordinations inter-individuelles chez bellicostitermes natalensis et cubitermes. sp. la theorie de la stigmergie: essai d'interpretation du comportement des termites constructeurs. Insectes Sociaux 6, 41–83 (1959)
31. Coutinho, L.R., Sichman, J.S., Boissier, O.: Modeling organization in mas: a comparison of models. In: Proc. of the 1st. Workshop on Software Engineering for Agent-Oriented Systems (SEAS 2005) (2005)
32. Parunak, H.V.D., Brueckner, S., Fleischer, M., Odell, J.: A design taxonomy of multi–agent interactions. In: Giorgini, P., Müller, J.P., Odell, J.J. (eds.) AOSE 2003. LNCS, vol. 2935, pp. 123–137. Springer, Heidelberg (2004)

33. Ashby, W.R.: An Introduction to cybernetics. Chapman and Hall, Boca Raton (1956)
34. Kaplan, D., Glass, L.: Understanding Nonlinear Dynamics. Springer, Heidelberg (1995)
35. Haken, H.: SYNERGETICS. Introduction and Advanced Topics. Springer, Heidelberg (2004)
36. Lerman, K., Galstyan, A.: A general methodology for mathematical analysis of multiagent systems. USC Inf. Sciences Tech.l Report ISI-TR-529 (2001)
37. Lerman, K., Galstyan, A.: Automatically modeling group behavior of simple agents. In: Agent Modeling Workshop, AAMAS 2004, New York (2004)
38. Forrester, J.W.: Industrial Dynamics. MIT Press, Cambridge (1961)
39. Braun, W.: The system archetypes. In: The Systems Modeling Workbook (2002)
40. Wolstenholme, E.F.: Towards the definition and use of a core set of archetypal structures in system dynamics. System Dynamics Review 19, 7–26 (2003)
41. Resnik, M.: Turtles, Termites, and Traffic Jams Explorations of Massively Parallel Microworlds. MIT Press, Cambridge (1997)
42. Deneubourg, J.L., Goss, S., Franks, N., Sendova-Franks, A., Detrain, C., Chrétien, L.: The dynamics of collective sorting robot-like ants and ant-like robots. In: Proceedings of the first international conference on simulation of adaptive behavior on From animals to animats, pp. 356–363. MIT Press, Cambridge (1990)
43. DeWolf, T., Holvoet, T.: Using uml 2 activity diagrams to design information flows and feedback-loops in self-organising emergent systems. In: Proceedings of the Second International Workshop on Engineering Emergence in Decentralised Autonomic Systems (EEDAS 2007) (2007)
44. Liu, J., Tsui, K.: Toward nature-inspired computing. Commun. ACM 49, 59–64 (2006)
45. Gardelli, L., Viroli, M., Omicini, A.: On the role of simulations in engineering self-organising mas: The case of an intrusion detection system in tucson. In: Brueckner, S.A., Di Marzo Serugendo, G., Hales, D., Zambonelli, F. (eds.) ESOA 2005. LNCS (LNAI), vol. 3910, pp. 153–166. Springer, Heidelberg (2006)
46. Sudeikat, J., Renz, W.: On simulations in mas development. In: Braun, T., Carle, G., Stiller, B. (eds.) KIVS 2007 Kommunikation in Verteilten Systemen – Industriebeiträge, Kurzbeiträge und Workshops, VDE–Verlag (2007)

Engineering Systems Which Generate Emergent Functionalities

Marie-Pierre Gleizes, Valérie Camps,
Jean-Pierre Georgé, and Davy Capera

Université Paul Sabatier, IRIT,
118 route de Narbonne, 31062 Toulouse Cedex 9, France
{gleizes,camps,george,capera}@irit.fr
http://www.irit.fr/SMAC

Abstract. Complexity of near future and even nowadays applications is exponentially increasing. In order to tackle the design of such complex systems, being able to engineer self-organising systems is a promising approach. This way, the whole system will autonomously changes its behaviour as its parts locally reorganise themselves, always providing an adapted function. This paper proposes to focus on engineering such systems generating emergent functionalities. We will first define two important concepts to take into account in such a context: Emergence and Self-Organisation. Building on these two concepts, we will highlight three main challenges researchers have to cope with: *(i)* how to control the system at the macro level by only focusing on the design of agents at the micro level, *(ii)* what kind of tools, models and guides are needed to develop such systems in order to help designers and *(iii)* how validation of such systems can be achieved? Each of these three challenges will be explained and positioned in regard to the main existing approaches. Our solutions combining emergence and self-organisation will be expounded for each challenge.

Keywords: Complex Systems, Engineering, Emergence, Multi-Agent System, Self-Organisation.

1 Context, Definitions and the Three Challenges

Complexity of near future and even nowadays applications is exponentially increasing. This is due to a combination of aspects such as the great number of components taking part in the applications, the fact that knowledge and control have to be distributed, the presence of non linear processes in the system, the fact that the system is more and more often open, its environment dynamic and the interactions unpredictable. In order to tackle the design of such complex systems, being able to engineer self-organising systems is a promising approach providing the needed robustness and adaptation in the light of the aforementioned difficulties.

D. Weyns, S.A. Brueckner, and Y. Demazeau (Eds.): EEMMAS 2007, LNAI 5049, pp. 58–75, 2008.

1.1 Understanding and Designing Complex Artificial Systems

The multidisciplinary community ONCE-CS (Open Network of Centres of Excellence in Complex Systems), clearly states the current interests in Complexity: "*the new Science of Complex System addresses the need to master the increasing complexity we see in natural and social systems. Examples include the human and new treatments for disease, managing the Internet, public administration, and business. This new science will revolutionise our world, causing irresistible changes*". In computer science, different kinds of techniques have been developed to tackle complexity such as those based on heuristics and metaheuristics [1], those based on learning such as genetic algorithm or neural network [2,3] and those based on self-organisation processes [4,5,6]. Since a Multi-Agent System (MAS) is defined as a macro-system composed of autonomous agents which pursue individual objectives and which interact in a common environment to solve a common task, it can be viewed as a paradigm to design complex applications.

To overcome difficulties coming from the openness and the dynamic of the environment, the system must be adaptive. Most natural systems have the ability to adapt themselves to a changing environment, such as the ability of the body to adapt its internal temperature when the temperature outside changes. It is well known that the process enabling these phenomena is self-organisation, defined by Bonabeau et al. as: "*a set of dynamical interactions whereby structures appear at the global level of a system from interactions among its lower-level components [...] The rules specifying the interactions are executed on the basis of purely local information, without reference to the global pattern*" [7].

1.2 Defining Self-organisation and Emergence for Artificial Systems

Self-organisation is a paradigm more and more used in MAS [8] and a definition with an artificial systems point of view has been provided by the European working group TFG SO (TFG SO[1] of Agentlink III) [9]:

Definition 1. *Self-organisation is the mechanism or the process enabling a system to change its organisation without explicit external command during its execution time.*

In general, the environment plays a fundamental role in the self-organisation process in constraining the system behaviour. It provides events which disturbs the system and leads the system to change its behaviour in self-organising. But some artificial systems can self-organise without interaction with the environment. In this case, when the system becomes stable it cannot evolve more.

The concept of self-organisation is often coupled with the concept of emergence [10]. And it seems that emergence is a suitable context to design complex systems that cannot be controlled by a human in a centralised way. We commonly agree with the fact that an emergent phenomenon must be observable.

---

[1] TFG SO: Technical Forum Group on Self-Organisation in MAS, see http://www.irit.fr/TFGSO.

From an observer point of view, we assume that if one can observe the content of the entities of a system and if one can observe at the system level a behaviour that cannot be reduced to the behaviour of the entities, the global behaviour can be qualified as emergent. In other words, we can say that a human cannot determine the global behaviour of the system only by looking at the agent behaviour. We can also qualify a phenomenon as emergent if we need different terms, vocabularies to explain the micro and the macro levels[2]. This leads to give the following operational definition of emergence in artificial systems, based on three points: what we want to be emergent (subject), at what condition it is emergent and how we can use it (method) [11,12].

1. *Subject.* The goal of a computational system is to realise an adequate function, judged by a relevant user. This "function" can be for instance a behaviour, a pattern, a property (which may evolve during time) that has to emerge.
2. *Condition.* This function is emergent if the coding of the system does not depend on the knowledge of this function. This coding has to contain the mechanisms facilitating the adaptation of the system during its coupling with the environment, so as to tend toward a coherent and relevant function.
3. *Method.* The mechanisms which allow the changes are specified by self-organisation rules, providing autonomous guidance to the components' behaviour without any explicit knowledge about the collective function nor how to reach it.

1.3   The Three Challenges for Engineering Systems Which Generate Emergent Functionalities

Designers of complex systems have been taking inspiration from natural systems in which complex structures or behaviours appear at the global level of a system from interactions among its lower-level components. The phenomenon observed at the macro-level emerges by self-organisation of the micro-level components making up the system. From an engineering point of view, the potential of this approach is important because it simplifies the design and diminishes the design delays. To develop a complex system, it is sufficient to design its components (called agents) which are less complex, to provide them with means to self-organise through local interactions and to enable them to interact with parts of the environment. But this is not so easy to do, as Parunak & Zambonelli [13] have claimed: "Such behaviour can also surface in undesirable ways". So, systems can reach undesirable states because the main difficulty lies in controlling global behaviour while designing at micro-level.

In our point of view, there are three main challenges to overcome to design self-organising applications. The first consists in answering the question: "how to control the emergence" or in others terms "how to control the system behaviour at the macro level by only focusing on the design of agents at the micro level?"

---

[2] This criteria has been highlighted in the working group TFG SO.

in order to avoid harmful global phenomena. The second challenge is to provide tools, models and guides to develop such systems. Because the goal of engineering self-organising systems is to deliver systems with a global behaviour which meets the requirements or realizes the desired function, the third challenge is about how to validate these systems. The aim of this paper is to briefly present these challenges in regard to the main existing approaches and to expound our ideas and solutions to address them.

In this paper, we first define the two important concepts to take into account in such a context: Emergence and Self-Organisation (Section 2). Then, the three challenges will be respectively explained in section 3,4 and 5, positioned in regard to the main existing approaches and finally our approach will be expounded. The paper ends by stating which research axes have to be pursued.

2 Challenge 1: An Emergence-Based Theory for the Designer of Complex Systems

Designing such MAS requires to find rules to make the system achieves the required collective behaviour, that is "functions that are useful to the system's stakeholders" [14], "the required macroscopic behaviour" [15], "a functionally adequate function" [11] ,... How does this produce a complex system with the right behaviour at the global level? The environment plays here its key role by constraining the system, and the system needs to be able to adapt to these constraints. There is an apparent antinomic situation in the idea of engineering applications with emergent functionalities. On one hand, emergent behaviour is a behaviour which occurs and in a certain manner cannot be under control. On the other hand, a software designer wants the system he is building to achieve a desired function. So, we can conclude saying that we want to *control the emergent behaviour* of the systems. The solution is then to better understand relations between micro and macro levels and to build a system able to self-adapt to environmental dynamics.

2.1 Some Mechanisms to Engineer Self-organising Applications

Currently, the objective of most researchers in self-organising MAS is to find relevant mechanisms to guide the agent behaviour at the micro level, helping the agents to self-organise and to obtain at the macro level, the behaviour of the system the designer expects. But the previous definition framework needs to be carefully instantiated with specific techniques enabling this self-organisation while allowing emergent functionalities to appear. Usual techniques are based on stigmergy, cooperation, gossip, natural selection, attraction and repulsion, potential fields, social relationships, trust...

One of the first kind of artificial systems related to self-organisation is based on the metaphor that only the better adapted individuals survive. In evolutionary computation and genetic algorithms [16,17], the system finds a solution in a huge state space in converging towards similar individuals which represent the solution. They are able to learn and adapt because the population evolves under the pressure of a specific function. Designer have to face two difficulties: on one hand, to give a well suited problem representation in terms of individuals and genes, and on the other hand to provide, in addition to mutation and cross-over operators, an efficient fitness function used by the individuals. This fundamental function is in general established from global knowledge about the solution the designer wants to achieve.

Neural networks [18,19] are usually composed of several layers: the entry, output and the hidden ones. Each layer has several neurons connected by weighted links. They are able to change the organisation between neurons of two consecutive layers during the learning phase by changing the weights. In general, it is difficult to find the right number of hidden levels and the number of neurons per level. The function used to update the weights of the links is dependent of the solution the system has to reach. Moreover, the learning corpus is not so easy to choose and requires a habit from the designer. The evolution of the system can be viewed as the self-organisation of the neurons, in particular in Kohonen maps [20].

Multi-agent systems are one of the most representatives among artificial systems dealing with *complexity* and *distribution* [21,22]. Self-organisation is a way to simplify the design of these systems in having a bottom up approach. Three kinds of inspirations are used to design these self-organising systems: the biologic and natural one [23], the social one [24], and the artificial one [25]. The mechanisms based on biologic approaches are closer to the work presented in this paper.

The stigmergy mechanism has been widely used and was first observed in societies of social insects by Grassé and can be summarised as "the work excites the workers" [26]. Agents leave information in the environment which can be perceived by the others. In general, this information evaporates after a given time. This mechanism allows task coordination and regulation within a group, using only indirect interactions and without central control. There is no method to develop this technique and the primary difficulty is to adjust the different parameters such as the speed of evaporation or the amount of information dropped. Because the solution must be represented in the environment, the final goal of the system guides the design phase. It is quite obvious that it cannot be applied if agents cannot act directly on an environment.

2.2 Adapt the System by Its Parts

In our approach, we consider that each part P_i of a system S achieves a partial function f_{P_i} of the global function f_S (cf. figure 1). f_S is the result of the combination of the partial functions f_{P_i}, noted by the operator "∘". The combination being determined by the current organisation of the parts, we can deduce $f_S = f_{P_1} \circ f_{P_2} \circ ... \circ f_{P_n}$. As generally $f_{P_1} \circ f_{P_2} \neq f_{P_2} \circ f_{P_1}$, by transforming the organisation, the combination of the partial functions is changed and therefore the global function f_S changes. So, enabling a MAS to self-organise consists in

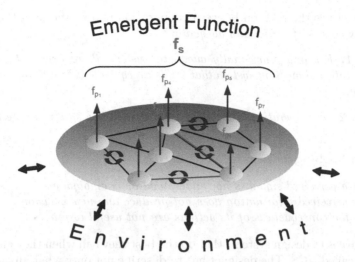

Fig. 1. Adaptation: changing the function of the system by changing its organisation

enabling the agent to change inside the organisation. The global function realized is the result of the organisation between agents in the system. This reorganisation technique can be extended with two other techniques, we are currently working on: *self-tuning* (parts can modify the parameters defining their behaviour) and *self-evolution* (parts can appear and disappear when needed). To ensure that the system will generate emergent behaviour, according to the definition of the emergence and to be able to *control* this emergence, it is necessary to provide to the agents a local criterion which enables them to self-organise. This requires both a theoretical and engineering framework.

The cooperation is the engine of the self-organisation and the heart of our bottom-up method. Cooperation is classically defined by the fact that two agents work together if they need to share resources or competences [27]. We add to this definition, the fact that an agent locally tries on one hand, to anticipate problems and on the other hand to detect cooperation failures called Non Cooperative Situations (*NCS*) and try to repair these NCS [28]. To anticipate NCS, the agent always chooses the actions which disturb the less other agents it knows. In others words, the agents, by trying to always have a cooperative attitude, act by reorganising their acquaintances and interactions with the others agents.

2.3 Controlling Emergence: The Theorem of Functional Adequacy

Cooperation was extensively studied in computer science by Axelrod [29] and Huberman [30] for instance. "*Everybody will agree that cooperation is in general advantageous for the group of cooperators as a whole, even though it may curb some individual's freedom*" [31]. In order to show how cooperation improves artificial complex systems design, we have developed the *AMAS* (Adaptive Multi-Agent System) [32,11] theory which is based upon the following theorem. This theorem describes the relation between cooperation in a system and the collective result which is *"functionally adequate[3] "*.

Theorem 1. *For any functionally adequate system, there exists at least one cooperative internal medium system that fulfils an equivalent function in the same environment.*

Definition 2. *A cooperative internal medium system is a system where no NCS exist.*

Definition 3. *An agent is in a (NCS) when:*

$(\neg c_{per})$ *a perceived signal is not understood or is ambiguous;*
$(\neg c_{dec})$ *perceived information does not produce any new decision;*
$(\neg c_{act})$ *the consequences of its actions are not useful to others.*

The objective is to design systems that do the best they can when they encounter difficulties called NCS. The designer has to describe not only what an agent has to do in order to achieve its goal but also which locally detected situations must be avoided and when they are detected how to suppress them (in the same manner that exceptions are treated in classical programs).

This theorem means that we only have to use (and hence understand) a subset of particular systems (those with cooperative internal mediums) in order to obtain a functionally adequate system in a given environment. We concentrate on a particular class of such systems, those with the following properties [32]:

- The system is cooperative and functionally adequate to the constraints of its environment. Its parts do not 'know' the global function the system has to achieve via adaptation (thus enabling emergent functionalities).
- The system does not have an explicitly defined goal, rather it acts using its perceptions of the environment as a feedback in order to adapt the global function to be adequate. The mechanism of adaptation is for each agent to try and maintain cooperation using their skills, representations of themselves, other agents and environment.
- Each part only evaluates whether the changes taking place are cooperative from its point of view – it does not know if these changes are dependent on its own past actions.

2.4   Architecture and Functioning of an *AMAS* Agent

A cooperative agent in the *AMAS* theory has the four following characteristics. First, an agent is autonomous. Secondly, an agent is unaware of the global function of the system; this global function emerges (from the agent level towards

---

[3] "Functional" refers to the "function" the system is producing, in a broad meaning, i.e. what the system is doing, what an observer would qualify as the behaviour of a system. And "adequate" simply means that the system is doing the "right" thing, judged by an observer or the environment. So "functional adequacy" can be seen as "having the appropriate behaviour for the task".

the multi-agent level). Thirdly, an agent can detect NCSs and acts to return in a cooperative state. And finally, a cooperative agent is not altruistic (it does not always seeks to help the other agents), but benevolent (it seeks to achieve its goal while being cooperative).

Cooperative agents are equipped with several modules representing a partition of their "physical", "cognitive" or "social" capacities. Each module represents a specific resource for the agent during its "perceive-decide-act" life cycle. The first four modules are quite classical in an agent model: *Interaction Module* (in fact composed of *Perception Module* and *Action Module*), *Skill Module*, *Representation Module* and *Aptitude Module*. The novelty comes from the *Cooperation Module* which contains local rules to solve NCS. All the cooperative attitudes of agents are implemented in this module: it must provide an action for a given state of skills, representations and perceptions, *if the agent is in a NCS*. Therefore, cooperative agents must possess rules to detect NCS. For each NCS detection rule, the Cooperation Module associates one or several actions to process to avoid or to solve the current NCS. During the perception phase of the agents' life cycle, the Perception Modules updates the values of the sensors. These data directly imply changes in the Skill and Representation Modules. Once the knowledge updated, the decision phase must result on an action choice. During this phase, the Aptitude Module computes from knowledge and proposes action(s) or not. In the same manner, the Cooperation Module detects if the agent is in a NCS or not. In the former case, the Cooperation Module proposes an action that subsumes the proposed action by the Aptitude Module. In the latter case, the only action[4] proposed by the Aptitude Module is chosen. Once an action is chosen during the action phase, the agent acts by activating its effectors or changing its knowledge.

According to the *AMAS* theory, agents have to be able to detect when they are in a NCS and how they can act to come back in a cooperative situation. Agents also always try to stay in a cooperative situation and so the whole system converges to a cooperative state within and with its environment. This leads – according to the theorem of functional adequacy (theorem 1) – to an adequate system.

Thus, this describes the typical decision process of a generic *AMAS* agent. But the NCS and the actions which could be applied to solve them are not generic: designers have to write their own specific NCS set and related actions for each kind of agent they wish the system to contain.

3   Challenge 2: A Method and Tools for the Designer of Complex Systems

The first and obvious problem software designers encounter when trying to engineer complex systems lies of course in their nature: complexity. How can we build something we do not even fully understand? Since the years 2000, agent

---

[4] There is only one action possible, otherwise an NCS is detected.

oriented methodology field is in full rise; numerous new methodologies devoted to particular problems appeared [33], but very few of them are devoted to design multi-agent systems generating emergent functionalities.

3.1 Existing Works for Engineering Self-organising Multi-agent Systems

Van Parunak and Bruckner propose a design guide for swarming systems engineering [14] consisting of ten design principles: the four first are derived from couples processes, the three next are derived from autocatalysis and the three last are derived from functional adjustment. Even if swarming systems have demonstrated their effectiveness as an alternative model of cognition and have been applied to number of applications, this approach is not very easy to apply because of the huge number of parameters to tune. The ten given principles are very general and no associated tool exists. No guide is given to indicate if the use of swarming systems is more relevant than conventional cognitive techniques for designing the current application or problem.

De Wolf [15] has defined a full life-cycle methodology based on the Unified Process customized to explicitly focus on engineering macroscopic behaviour of such kind of systems. This customization takes place in the following steps of the process:

- After the requirements analysis done, one checks if an autonomous behaviour is needed, if the available information is distributed, if the system is subject to high dynamics such as failures and frequent changes;
- In the design phase, general guidelines or principles, reference architectures, decentralised mechanisms allowing coordination between agents to achieved desirable macroscopic properties, have to be used to design self-organising emergent MAS. In that sense, De Wolf proposes an initial catalogue including the most widely used coordination mechanisms such as digital pheromones, gradient fields, market based coordination, and tag based coordination. Furthermore, he proposes "Information flow" as a design abstraction which enables designing a solution independently of the coordination mechanism.
- In the verification and testing phase, he combines agent-based simulations with scientific numerical algorithms for dynamical systems design. More detailed are given in the challenge 3 of this paper.

3.2 Engineering Adaptive Multi-agent Systems: ADELFE

ADELFE [5] is a methodology devoted to software engineering of adaptive multi-agent according to the AMAS approach. ADELFE enables the development of software with emergent functionality and consists of a notation based on UML (*Unified Modelling Language*) and AUML (*Agent-UML*) [34], a design process

---

[5] ADELFE is a French acronym for "Atelier de Développement de Logiciels à Fonctionnalité Émergente".

based on the RUP (*Rational Unified Process*), a platform made up of a graphical design tool called OpenTool and a library of components that can be used to make the application development easier.

The design process (see figure 2) covers all the phases of a classical software design (from the requirements to the deployment) in adding some specific steps to design adaptive systems. OMG's SPEM (*Software Process Engineering Metamodel*) has been used to express the ADELFE process and the SPEM vocabulary is used to expound the methodology: WorkDefinitions (WDi), Activities (Aj) and Steps (Sk).

ADELFE : Design Methodology

- Final requirements. The environment of the system is central in the AMAS theory; this is due to the fact that the adaptation process depends on the interactions between the system and its environment. This characteristic has led to the addition of one Activity (A6) and one Step (A7-S2) in the "Final Requirements" WD2. Designers must characterize the environment of the system by qualifying it as being accessible or not, deterministic or not, dynamic or static and discrete or continuous. These terms represent a help to later determine if the AMAS technology is required or not to build the studied system (A11). At this point, designers must also begin to think about the situations that can be "unexpected" or "harmful" for the system because these situations can lead to NCS at the agent level. Therefore, the determination of use cases has been modified to take this aspect into account (S2).
- Analysis. The use of AMAS theory is not a solution fitted to every application. For that reason, ADELFE provides an interactive tool (A11) to help a designer to decide if the use of the AMAS theory is required to implement his application. ADELFE does not assume that all the entities defined during the final requirements are agents. Therefore, this methodology focuses on the agents identification (A12) and some guidelines are then provided to help designers to identify agents [35]. A Step (S3) has also been added concerning the study of agents relationships.
- Design. Agents being identified and their relationships being studied, designers have now to study the way in which the agents are going to interact (A15) thanks to protocol diagrams. ADELFE also provides a model for designing cooperative agents (A16), following the agent architecture presented in section 2.5. The global function of a self-organising system is not coded; designers have only to code the local behaviour of the parts composing it. ADELFE provides some generic cooperation failures such as incomprehension, ambiguity, uselessness or conflict. Designers must fill up one table per NCS to give the name of each NCS, its generic type, the state in which the agent must be to detect it, the conditions of its detection and what actions the agent must perform to deal with it. A new Activity (A17) of fast prototyping based on finite state machine has been added to the process. It enables designers to verify the behaviour of the built agents. Now simulations tools is included into ADELFE to complete the life cycle of its development process [36,37].

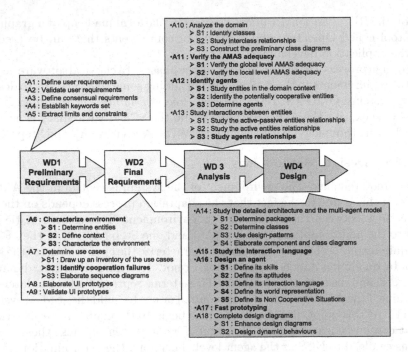

Fig. 2. ADELFE process

Tools Linked with ADELFE. Even if ADELFE is suited to develop applications based on the AMAS technology, it does not assume that the designer is specialized in this field. Therefore, some additional notations are provided as well as some tools to help or guide the designer throughout the process application [38]:

1. A tool enabling to know if the use of the AMAS technology is useful to implement the target system. Eleven questions are asked to designers using a graphical interface. This adequacy is studied at two levels: the global one (system) with 8 questions and the local one (components) with 3 questions. A designer uses a slider to answer a question and to give a rate among twenty possibilities ranging from "yes" to "no". His answers are then analysed by the support decision tool. The answers of ADELFE regarding the global level and the local one are then given in a graphical tool and an interpretation of the results can also be obtained.

2. An interactive tool which describes the process and helps the designer to apply it (it can be downloaded at http://www.irit.fr/ADELFE). The first functionality of the ADELFE interactive tool is to be a guide by describing the process; each activity or step of the process is depicted and exemplified by applying it to a timetabling problem (ETTO) [35]. The interactive tool also provides a means to support the adopted notations and draw the needed diagrams by integrating OpenTool which has been modified for ADELFE. It checks the project consistency by displaying what stages (activities or steps)

can be done depending on what has been already done or what documents have been produced yet.

3. OpenTool, a graphical modelling tool supporting the UML notation and embedded in the ADELFE toolkit. It enables applications modelling while assuring that the produced models are valid. As some lacks exist in the UML notation to deal with the specific modules composing a cooperative agent, nine stereotypes have been defined to show how an agent is formed and/or how its behaviour is expressed («cooperative agent» «characteristic» «skill», «aptitude», «representation», «interaction», «perception», «actions» and «cooperation»). On the other hand, to model interaction protocols between agents AUML interaction protocol model has been extended and included in OpenTool functionalities. OpenTool has also been modified to enabling expression of cooperation failures. In the fast prototyping stage (A-17), agents' behaviours are simulated using a functionality of OpenTool which requires a dynamic model (state-chart) for each simulated entity (object or agent). As agents' behaviours are modelled as AIP protocol diagrams and a method was proposed to transform a protocol diagram (a particular generic sequence diagram) into a state-chart that OpenTool is able to simulate.

4   Challenge 3 : A Validation Framework for the Designer of Complex Systems

It is quite obvious that the software validation phase, requested by industrials and end-users, is necessary before its commercialization. So, validation of self-organising applications is, even more, a mandatory step during development. In software engineering, there are often many validation activities but in this paper we focus on the global behaviour validation of the system which consists in verifying that the system complies to the desired function. Validation is not a new axis in computer science, but self-organising systems lead to new challenges not yet taken into account by classical methods. In large scale dynamic and adaptive systems such as self-organising systems, the methods, techniques and tools for validation are still in a research phase [39]. In general, formal methods [40] for validation, such as model checking, theorem proving... are adequate for checking/proving desired properties of the system when the code is showing the following properties: it is static and it runs in well-known environments. A static code is a code which does not evolve and there is no learning at this level. A well-known environment means that the system does not face unexpected events or unexpected scenarii.

4.1   Related Works in Multi-agent Systems

The question of validation becomes more and more crucial in self-organising MAS and some works attempts to deal with it. Tom De Wolf et all [41] use simulation-based scientific analysis for designing self-organising systems achieving the required system behaviour. They combine realistic agent-based simulation and existing scientific numerical analysis algorithms to design a system simulation. The main phase in the design process is to identify macroscopic properties desired at the system level, macroscopic variables for measuring the macroscopic properties and define microscopic variables for each macroscopic one. Then when an analysis algorithm is chosen, simulations are launched so as to analyse the global behaviour of the system in terms of desired properties linked to specific parameters. Parameters are adjusted iteratively until the systems exhibits a satisfactory behaviour. The difficulty in this approach is to define the different variables and express the link between the macro and micro levels.

Bruce Edmonds has shown in several papers [42,43] that formal methods are insufficient to show the reliability of self-organised systems. He proposes to use an experimental method to produce reliable self-organising systems and mixes in his approach engineering and adaptation. After the process of construction which constructs the multi-agent systems from the agents, the design process consists in adaptation cycles. A cycle begins with a test and comparison of the global behaviour of the system and the desired global behaviour. If it is not satisfying the system adapts to change its global behaviour. This cycle stops when the produced global behaviour fits the desired one. The validation is done by experiments and is considered by the authors as the sole mean at this time.

4.2   Validation of AMAS

In ADELFE, the reliability of the global behaviour of the system, ensured by the AMAS theory, is verified essentially at the design phase. In self-organising system, the desired function cannot always be well defined, for example: what is the global function of the Internet? What is the global function of a crowd? By consequence the automatic verification is not always possible and must be done by the designer. In ADELFE, this functional adequacy is checked at the end of the design but also during the design. Our aim is to give more tools to automate the verification-update cycle. We are very close to Edmonds's approach. The tests realized by simulation help to enhance the system and to improve the functional adequacy, i.e. to verify that the system fits the desired function.

As explained in [11], we can consider in agent-based software engineering that the object conceptual level and the agent conceptual level in the system design process overlap. The test phase of the code realized with the targeted programming language is done in parallel with the agent design phase (see figure 3). So, in ADELFE, what we call *Living Design* is defined by the link between design and test phases of the two processes. Namely, *Living Design* means "construct agents during run-time". Therefore, the designer is like a biologist who studies the behaviour of living creatures and who can modify its model according to his observations. For doing this, simulation is used in order to help the designer to develop the agents of the system by observing the system at the global level.

As we have say before, applying the AMAS theory consists in enumerating, according to the current problem to solve, all the NCS that can appear during the system functioning and then defining the actions the system must apply to return to a cooperative state. Currently, during the preliminary requirements phase, ADELFE provides tools to express NCS in the use case diagrams. During

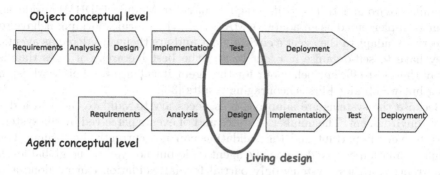

Fig. 3. Living Design

the design phase, it is possible to find if some deadlocks can take place within an interaction protocol, or if some protocols are useless or inconsistent. The protocol diagram notation has been extended to express these situations. Thus, the behaviour of several agents could be judged in accordance (or not) with the sequence diagrams described in the analysis phase. However, the core difficulty lies in identifying NCS and in helping the designer to find all these NCS. Simulation is used in ADELFE to help designers to find the correct behaviours of the agents during the design stage: by simulating a simplified system and observing it during execution, the behaviour of agents can be modified and improved. Currently, our work focuses only on situated multi-agent systems and not yet on communicative ones. The main reason for such a choice was that the observation of the behaviour in an environment is easier to be judged by an observer. Simulation enables to automatically identify these situations during execution of a prototype of a targeted MAS. A model of cooperative agents [37] is implemented under the *SeSAm* platform by using an architecture inspired from the subsumption architecture proposed by Brooks and reusing the notion of priority between the *(conditions, actions)* couple. This behaviour can be expressed with a set of behavioural rules which follow this pattern:

if **premise** then **consequent**

where **premise** is a logical predicate made up of elements coming from agent perceptions or characteristics, and **consequent** activates one of the possible actions this agent may perform. The difference between Brooks' architecture and ours is that our agents have representations. The cooperative agent model [37] automatically detects some NCS during the execution of a simulated MAS and shows where and when NCS appear. The designer has then to modify the agent behaviour.

In our more recent work [36], this goes a step further as during a simulation cycle, an agent has the ability to *self-design* its behaviour considering that *(i)* all the rules needed to design the decision process are given by a designer (that is the agent does not learn new rules during the process), *(ii)* the set of given rules is complete and correctly written and *(iii)* the system interacts with a dynamic environment. The Self-Design Behaviour Module (SDBM) inside an agent is implemented as an adaptive MAS. Behavioural rules forming it have to collectively adapt to the agent's environment and are then considered as agents. They have to self-organise in order to find the best hierarchy of rules that is to say the most efficient behaviour for the agent it belongs to. This work is on going but we obtained first encouraging results [36].

Because the systems are adaptive, it is necessary to validate them in a dynamic environment. The number of states and of events perceived by the system must be very important and the validation can not currently be formal. The formal validation can be done on the agent code but not yet at the global level, so currently on these systems only partial formal validation can be done and the global behaviour can be verified only by simulation. The role of the designer/observer is fundamental because he participates to the co-construction of the system. He plays the role of an environment which interacts with the system and causes the change of the system behaviour.

5   Conclusion

We have presented the three main challenges for engineering systems with emergent functionalities will be confronted with, as well as current investigated leads and work relating to the use of self-organisation and emergent phenomena.

1. System control related problems can be partially solved by providing the system with capability to self-adapt to the environment. Common decentralized mechanisms used to achieve such a control are inspired by existing natural systems (ants colony, collective movements) or social-related behaviours (co-operation, competition). This is the case for the AMAS theory which is based on an environmental constraints driven process and enables engineering systems whose parts self-organise according to local cooperative criteria.
2. In order to support those new ways to design complex systems, new tools and methodologies have to focus on local behaviours, environment characterization and emergent phenomena. Unfortunately, the few existing methodologies are yet in the research domain and/or incomplete (no deployment and maintenance phases). Moreover, system design analysis is still strongly focused on global ends analysis which cannot fit with some application requirements: for instance, in *Ambiant Intelligence* it is not possible to fully specify what the system has to do.
3. Given that emergence and self-organisation had not seriously been studied as hard science subject, classical formal methods are not suitable. Engineered complex systems verification and validation can only be achieved using simulation-based approaches. Nowadays, the most reliable way consists in iteratively improving the designed system using mathematical tools (statistical analysis, behavioural parameters optimisation) or semi-autonomous adaptive programming (*Living Design*).

Emergence and self-organisation have only recently been considered as serious alternatives in industrial software engineering. As anyone can notice by reading strategic agendas of some European platforms (ARTEMIS, eMobility, EPoSS), the main displayed concerns about these "new paradigms" are validation and verification aspects:

> " These system-design principles seem to be compatible with the good average-case performance. However, these often conflict with a design's predictability." (Artist2 Network of Excellence, 2006[6])

Nevertheless, in our opinion, industry does not really have a choice: as software becomes more complex, this approach is the only viable option currently known. True artificial complex systems will thus be built using emergence and self-organisation: Ambient Intelligence, Swarm Robotics, Autonomous Computing, e-Health-care, Computational Biology...

Another major effort has to be done towards methodologies supporting (enabling) pure local analysis without any need to specify what the system has to do or underspecified system. As a matter of fact, the core of the complex system engineering problem remains the lack of accepted theories (even non complete ones) of emergence and self-organisation. Without such a fundamental key, it will be difficult to legitimate and disseminate this approach, as well as to promote and explain any future successful "killer applications".

References

1. Dréo, J., Pétrowski, A., Siarry, P., Taillard, E.: Metaheuristics for Hard Optimization. Springer, Heidelberg (2006)
2. Mitchell, M.: An Introduction to Genetic Algorithms. MIT Press, Cambridge (1998)
3. Lawrence, J.: Introduction to Neural Networks. California Scientific, Nevada City (1993)
4. Di Marzo Serugendo, G., Karageorgos, A., Rana, O.F., Zambonelli, F. (eds.): Engineering Self-Organising Systems, Nature-Inspired Approaches to Software Engineering. In: Di Marzo Serugendo, G., Karageorgos, A., Rana, O.F., Zambonelli, F. (eds.) ESOA 2003. LNCS (LNAI), vol. 2977, Springer, Heidelberg (2004)
5. Brueckner, S., Di Marzo Serugendo, G., Karageorgos, A., Nagpal, R. (eds.): Engineering Self-Organising Systems, Methodologies and Applications. In: Brueckner, S.A., Di Marzo Serugendo, G., Karageorgos, A., Nagpal, R. (eds.) ESOA 2005. LNCS (LNAI), vol. 3464, Springer, Heidelberg (2005)
6. Brueckner, S., Di Marzo Serugendo, G., Hales, D., Zambonelli, F. (eds.): Engineering Self-Organising Systems. In: Brueckner, S.A., Di Marzo Serugendo, G., Hales, D., Zambonelli, F. (eds.) ESOA 2005. LNCS (LNAI), vol. 3910, Springer, Heidelberg (2006)
7. Bonabeau, E., Dorigo, M., Theraulaz, G.: Swarm Intelligence: From Natural to Artificial Systems. Oxford University Press, Oxford (1999)
8. Di Marzo Serugendo, G., Martin-Flair, J.-P., Jelasity, M., Zambonelli, F. (eds.): Proceedings of the First International Conference on Self-Adaptive and Self-Organizing Systems, SASO 2007, Boston, MA, USA, July 9-11, 2007. IEEE Computer Society Press, Los Alamitos (2007)

---

[6] http://www.artist-embedded.org/artist/-Research-.html

9. Di Marzo Serugendo, G., Gleizes, M.P., Karageorgos, A.: Self-Organization and Emergence in Muli-Agent Systems. The Knowledge Engineering Review 20(2), 165–189 (2005)
10. Wolf, T.D., Holvoet, T.: Emergence versus self-organisation: Different concepts but promising when combined. In: Brueckner, S.A., Di Marzo Serugendo, G., Karageorgos, A., Nagpal, R. (eds.) ESOA 2005. LNCS (LNAI), vol. 3464, pp. 1–15. Springer, Heidelberg (2005)
11. Capera, D., Georgé, J.P., Gleizes, M.P., Glize, P.: The AMAS Theory for Complex Problem Solving Based on Self-organizing Cooperative Agents. In: 1st International TAPOCS Workshop at IEEE 12th WETICE, pp. 383–388. IEEE, Los Alamitos (2003)
12. Georgé, J.P., Gleizes, M.P.: Experiments in Emergent Programming using Self-organizing Multi-Agent Systems. In: Pěchouček, M., Petta, P., Varga, L.Z. (eds.) CEEMAS 2005. LNCS (LNAI), vol. 3690, pp. 450–459. Springer, Heidelberg (2005)
13. Zambonelli, F., Parunak, H.: Signs of a revolution in computer science and software engineering. In: Petta, P., Tolksdorf, R., Zambonelli, F. (eds.) ESAW 2002. LNCS (LNAI), vol. 2577, pp. 13–28. Springer, Heidelberg (2003)
14. Parunak, H., Brueckner, S.: Engineering Swarming Systems. Kluwer, Dordrecht (2004)
15. De Wolf, T.: Analysing and engineering self-organising emergent applications. PhD thesis, Department of Computer Science, K.U.Leuven, Leuven, Belgium (2007)
16. Goldberg, D.: Genetic Algorithms in Search Optimization and Machine Learning. Addison-Wesley, Reading (1989)
17. Holland, J.: Adaptation in Natural and Artificial Systems. MIT Press, Cambridge (1992)
18. McCulloch, W.S., Pitts, W.: A logical calculus of the ideas immanent in nervous activity. Bulletin of Mathematical Biophysic 5, 115–133 (1943)
19. Rosenblatt, F.: The Perceptron: probabilistic model for information storage and organization in the brain. Psychological Review 65, 386–408 (1958)
20. Kohonen, T.: Self-Organising Maps, vol. 30. Springer, Heidelberg (2001)
21. Weiß, G.: Multiagent Systems, A modern Approach to Distributed Artificial Systems. MIT Press, Cambridge (1999)
22. Wooldridge, M.: An introduction to multi-agent systems. John Wiley & Sons, Chichester (2002)
23. Mano, J., Bourjot, C., Lopardo, G., Glize, P.: Bio-inspired Mechanisms for Artificial Self-organised Systems. Informatica 30(1), 55–62 (2006)
24. Hassas, S., Castelfranchi, C., Di Marzo Serugendo, G., Karageorgos A.: Self-Organising Mechanisms from Social and Business/Economics Approaches. Informatica 30(1) (2006)
25. Di Marzo Serugendo, G., Gleizes, M.P., Karageorgos, A. (eds.): Self-organisation in MAS - Tutorial at the 4th International Central and Eastern European Conference on Multi-Agent Systems (CEEMAS 2005), Budapest, Hungary, September 15 (2005)
26. Grassé, P.: La reconstruction du nid et les interactions inter-individuelles chez les bellicositermes natalenis et cubitermes sp. la théorie de la stigmergie: essai d'interprétation des termites constructeurs. Insectes Sociaux 6, 41–83 (1959)
27. Ferber, J.: Multi-Agent Systems: An Introduction to Distributed Artificial Intelligence. Addison-Wesley, Reading (1999)

28. Picard, G., Gleizes, M.P.: Cooperative Self-Organization to Design Robust and Adaptive Collectives. In: 2nd International Conference on Informatics in Control, Automation and Robotics (ICINCO 2005), Barcelona, Spain, September 14-17, vol. I, pp. 236–241. INSTICC Press (2005)
29. Axelrod, R.: The Evolution of Cooperation. Basic Books (1984)
30. Huberman, B.: The performance of cooperative processes. MIT Press / North-Holland (1991)
31. Heylighen, F.: Evolution, Selfishness and Cooperation; Selfish Memes and the Evolution of Cooperation. Journal of Ideas 2(4), 70–84 (1992)
32. Gleizes, M.P., Camps, V., Glize, P.: A Theory of Emergent Computation Based on Cooperative Self-Oganization for Adaptive Artificial Systems. In: 4th European Congress of Systems Science (1999)
33. Henderson-Sellers, B., Giorgini, P.: Agent-Oriented Methodologies. Idea Group Pub., NY (2005)
34. Odell, J., Parunak, H., Bauer, B.: Representing Agent Interaction Protocols in UML. Springer, Heidelberg (2001)
35. Bernon, C., Gleizes, M.P., Peyruqueou, S., Picard, G.: Adelfe: a methodology for adaptive multi-agent systems engineering. In: Petta, P., Tolksdorf, R., Zambonelli, F. (eds.) ESAW 2002. LNCS (LNAI), vol. 2577, pp. 156–169. Springer, Heidelberg (2003)
36. Lemouzy, S., Bernon, C., Gleizes, M.P.: Living design: Simulation for self-designing agents. In: Multi-Agent Systems and Simulation (MAS&S) Workshop at ESM 2007 (to be published)
37. Bernon, C., Gleizes, M.P., Picard, G.: Enhancing self-organising emergent systems design with simulation. In: O'Hare, G.M.P., Ricci, A., O'Grady, M.J., Dikenelli, O. (eds.) ESAW 2006. LNCS (LNAI), vol. 4457, pp. 284–299. Springer, Heidelberg (2007)
38. Bernon, C., Camps, V., Gleizes, M.P., Picard, G.: Tools for self-organizing applications engineering. In: Di Marzo Serugendo, G., Karageorgos, A., Rana, O.F., Zambonelli, F. (eds.) ESOA 2003. LNCS (LNAI), vol. 2977, pp. 283–298. Springer, Heidelberg (2004)
39. Slaby, J., Welch, L., Work, P.: Toward certification of adaptive distributed systems. In: Real-time and Embedded Systems Workshop (2006)
40. Clarke, E.M., Wing, J.M.: Formal methods: state of the art and future directions. ACM Comput. Surv. 28(4), 626–643 (1996)
41. Wolf, T.D., Holvoet, T., Samaey, G.: Development of self-organising emergent applications with simulation-based numerical analysis. In: Engineering Self-Organising Systems, pp. 138–152 (2005)
42. Edmonds, B., Bryson, J.: The insufficiency of formal design methods - the necessity of an experimental approach - for the understanding and control of complex mas. In: AAMAS, pp. 938–945 (2004)
43. Edmonds, B.: Engineering self-organising systems, methodologies and applications. In: Brueckner, S.A., Di Marzo Serugendo, G., Karageorgos, A., Nagpal, R. (eds.) ESOA 2005. LNCS (LNAI), vol. 3464, Springer, Heidelberg (2005)

Engineering Autonomic Electronic Institutions

Josep Lluís Arcos, Juan A. Rodríguez-Aguilar, and Bruno Rosell

IIIA, Artificial Intelligence Research Institute
CSIC, Spanish National Research Council
08193 Bellaterra, Spain
{arcos,pablo,jar,sierra}@iiia.csic.es

Abstract. There is a growing interest in the study and development of self-* systems motivated by the need for information systems capable of self-management in distributed, open, and dynamic scenarios. Unfortunately,there is a lack of frameworks that support the intricate task of developing self-* systems. We try to make headway along this direction by introducing a framework, EIDE-*, to support the engineering of a particular type of self-* systems, namely *autonomic electronic institutions*: regulated environments capable of adapting their norms to comply with institutional goals despite the varying behaviours of their participating agents.

1 Introduction

There is a growing interest in the study and development of self-* systems [12] (where the * sign indicates a variety of properties: self-organization, self-configuration, self-diagnosis, self-repair, etc) motivated by the need for information systems capable of self-management in distributed, open, and dynamic scenarios. A particular approximation to the construction of self-* systems is represented by the vision of autonomic computing [10], which constitutes an approximation to computing systems with a minimal human interference. Unfortuntately, there is a lack of frameworks that support the intricate task of developing systems with autonomic capabilities. As an exception we can consider the Living Systems framework [17]. Nonetheless, it is hard to conceive a general-purpose development framework for self-* systems. Therefore, our endeavour can be eased if we depart from a particular model of open system [9] that can eventually be endowed with self-management capabilities. A review of the literature indicates that electronic institutions (EIs) [5], regulated environments wherein the relevant interactions among participating agents take place, have proved to be valuable to develop open agent systems. Indeed, EIs do even count on a development environment (EIDE) to ease their engineering [1]. However, the challenges of building open systems as EIs are still considerable, not only because of the inherent complexity involved in having adequate interoperation of heterogeneous agents, but also because the need for adapting regulations to comply with institutional goals despite varying agents' behaviours. Particularly, when dealing with self-interested agents as noticed in [3].

D. Weyns, S.A. Brueckner, and Y. Demazeau (Eds.): EEMMAS 2007, LNAI 5049, pp. 76–87, 2008.

In this paper we try to make headway in the engineering of self-* systems by introducing a framework to support the development of a particular type of these systems, namely *autonomic electronic institutions*: EIs with self capabilities. The framework we introduce, EIDE-*, must be regarded as an extension of EIDE, the current development framework for EIs. Specifically, the new engineering requirements imposed by the autonomic capabilities brought about a new approach in the agent development tool (*aBUILDER*) and in the simulation tool (*SIMDEI*).

Furthermore, we illustrate the capabilities of the framework through the analysis of a power electricity market inspired on the actual operation of the Spanish electricity market. The main goal of an electricity market is to provide a set of rules for conciliating the demand of electricity and its generation. There are two issues that must be avoided: a lack of production that can leave customers without supply and an unwanted overproduction. Moreover, these goals have to be achieved while maintaining a reasonable electricity price. We show how EIDE-* can support self-configuration policies in such setting.

The paper is organized as follows: Section 2 introduces the formal concepts around autonomic electronic institutions. Section 3 describes the set of tools we provide for helping in the engineering of autonomic electronic institutions. Section 4 presents the electricity market problem and shows how all the concepts and tools are used to design a specific institution. Finally, conclusions and future work are presented in section 5.

2 Autonomic Electronic Institutions

Loosely speaking, EIs are computational realizations of traditional institutions (cf. North [14] pp. 3 ss.); that is, coordination artifacts that establish an environment where agents interact according to stated conventions, and in such a way that interactions within the (electronic) institution would *count as* interactions in the actual world.

According to the basic definition of an electronic institution (see [5]), an EI is composed of three components: a dialogical framework that establishes the social structure, the ontology, and a communication language to be used by participating agents; a performative structure defining the activities along with their relationships; and a set of norms defining the consequences of agents' actions.

MAS applications are usually concerned with some external environment. The environment is application-specific and refers to the part of the world that is relevant to the MAS application. For instance, in the electricity market example that will be presented in section 4, the power demand is modeled by an equation-based tool that simulates real electrical consumption patterns.

Environments are plugged into EIs as institutional services [2]. In our approach, agents cannot directly sense and act over the environment. Instead, and likewise all interactions of external agents in the realm of an EI, they are *mediated* by the institution wherein they interact. The link of an institution with an environment enriches the functionality of the EI components.

2.1   Self-organizing Capabilities

From this basic definition of an EI we have extended the model to support self-configuration [3]. The notion of Autonomic Electronic Institutions (AEIs) has been proposed as a model for providing self-configuration capabilities to EIs. AEIs incorporate three new main components: en explicit set of *institutional goals G*, an *information model I*, and a *normative transition function δ* that allows to transform interaction conventions.

The main objective of an AEI is to accomplish its goals. For this purpose, an AEI has to be able to both dynamically observe/analyze the performance of the institution and to adapt its interaction conventions. We assume that an institution can observe its environment, the institutional state of the agents participating in the institution, and its own state to assess whether its goals are accomplished or not. Thus, from the observation of environmental properties, institutional properties, and agents institutional properties, an AEI maintains the information model I required to determine the fulfillment of goals.

Formally, we define the goals of an AEI as a tuple $G = \langle V, C \rangle$ composed of : (i) a set of reference values $V = \langle v_1, \ldots, v_q \rangle$ where each v_j results from applying an evaluation function h_j upon the information model; $v = h(I), 1 \leq j \leq q$; and (ii) a finite set of constraints $C = \{c_1, \ldots, c_p\}$ where each c_i is defined as an expression $g_i(V) \lhd [m_i, M_i]$ where $m_i, M_i \in \mathbb{R}$, $\lhd$ stands for either $\in$ or $\notin$, and g_i is a function over the reference values. In this manner, each goal is a constraint upon the reference values where each pair m_i and M_i defines an interval associated to the constraint. Thus, the institution achieves its goals if all $g_i(V)$ values satisfy their corresponding constraints of being within (or not) their associated intervals.

Finally, the normative transition function δ defines the set of actions allowed for re-configuring the institution at runtime. The re-configuration is performed by changing the interaction conventions. Specifically, δ actions will have effects over the performative structure and the normative rules. For instance, the role flow policy among activities can be modified by δ.

Nowadays, we are not dealing with the re-configuration of the dialogical framework (i.e. the social structure, the domain ontology, and the communication language are invariant).

Because staff agents are those in charge of the institutional activities, only staff agents will be allowed to observe the fulfillment of the institutional goals and will be able to change the interaction conventions.

3   Development and Simulation Framework

In order to facilitate the engineering of AEIs we have developed a set of software tools that give support to all the design and execution phases. These tools are integrated in the Development Environment for Autonomic Electronic Institutions (EIDE-*). EIDE-* allows for engineering both the institutional rules and the participating agents. Figure 1 depicts the EIDE-* framework. The tools provided by the EIDE-* framework are: a graphical tool that supports the specification and

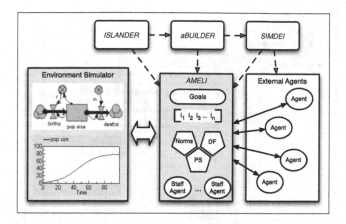

Fig. 1. The EIDE-∗ Framework

static verification of institutional rules (*ISLANDER*); an agent development tool (*aBUILDER*); a simulation tool to animate and analyse *ISLANDER* specifications (*SIMDEI*); and a software platform to run EIs (*AMELI*). All these tools have been enhanced to provide the new requirements of autonomic electronic institutions.

To design an AEI we have a tool, *ISLANDER* [6], that allows us to make a graphical specification of the AEI components and produces an XML file with the specification. That specification is used to enact instances of the institution, by agent designers to build agents that conform to the institutional conventions, and to design and run experiments with different agent populations.

The core of EIDE-∗ is *AMELI* [7], an institutional engine that provides a run-time middleware for the agents that participate in the enactment of a given institution. The middleware is deployed to *guarantee* the correct evolution of each scene, to *warrant* legal movements between scenes, and to *control* the obligations or commitments that participating agents acquire and fulfill. Furthermore, the middleware *handles* the information agents need within the institution. The *AMELI* generated middleware *mediates* between agents in order to facilitate agent communication within scenes. Broadly speaking, *AMELI* achieves those functions because on the one hand it generates the staff agents and the institutional *governors* that mediate all communications with external agents and, on the other hand, it handles all the institutional communication traffic by wrapping illocutions as messages that are handled by a standard agent-communication layer. *AMELI* has been extended so that staff agents can observe the fulfillment of the institutional goals and change the interaction conventions at run-time.

Additionally, *AMELI* provides a set of new monitoring facilities that allow a graphical depiction of all the events that occur during the enactment of an AEI. Fairness, trust and accountability are the main motivations for the development of a monitoring tool that registers all interactions in a given enactment of an electronic institution [13,18]. Giving accountability information to the

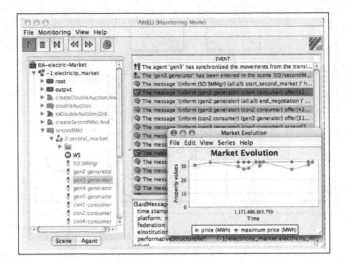

Fig. 2. Monitoring the Electricity Market

participants increases their trust in the institution. This is specially important for electronic institutions where people delegate their tasks to agents. Furthermore, the tool permits them to analyse their agent(s) behaviour within the institution in order to improve it.

Figure 2 shows some of the monitoring facilities activated for the electricity market. The left frame contains a list of the institution's scenes and transitions along with their executions. In the monitoring snapshot shown in the figure, the execution of the secondary market is monitored at state *W5*. The right frame depicts the events occurring during scene execution: agents' entrance (second event); the utterance of valid (third event) and wrong (fourth event) illocutions; transitions caused by timeouts; and agents' exit. Furthermore, the monitoring tool allows the tracking of the institution information model and the tracking of the institution goals achievement. For instance, figure 2 depicts the tracking of the energy cost parameter. The chart allows the tracking of the evolution of the energy cost along the time together with the maximum cost (calculated using the monitoring facilities of the tool).

External environments are plugged into *AMELI* by implementing a required Java interface, the so-called `EInstitutionService`, providing all methods for observing and acting with them. Thereafter, different interfaces to acces the service can be incorporated into *AMELI* as implementations of the `ServiceProfile` interface. These service profiles can be regarded as different views to an environment. The motivation to consider different profiles is that an AEI may require that external agents have different views to the environment depending on their roles. An example of a market forecast service for the electricity market is described in the next section.

EIDE-* provides a software tool, *aBUILDER*, for agent development based on *ISLANDER* specifications. Specifically, *aBUILDER* takes an *ISLANDER* specification and produces for each role that may be played in the institution an "agent skeleton". Those skeletons comply with all the conventions of the specified institution, in particular with its dialogical framework and the performative structure. The previous vesion of *aBUILDER* presented in [1] has been extended to support the graphical specification of agent skeletons. Hence, staff agents may be easily built —on top of the *aBUILDER* skeletons— by concentrating the programming efforts on the decision policies and having the skeleton take care of navigation and communication within the AEI. Additionally, external agents may be modeled as parametric skeletons and used in the simulation environment to validate the institution goals.

Validating the desired behavior of an AEI is a highly intricate and computationally expensive task, as illustrated by [8,11,21,22]. Such validation becomes even more complicated when we incorporate into the AEI an environment with a partially observable behavior. We have developed an extended version of *SIMDEI* (formerly introduced in [1]). *SIMDEI* allows to run discrete event simulations of *AMELI* along the lines of multi-agent simulations produced with the aid of libraries like Repast [16]. As to environment simulations, we must choose the modelling simulation tool (e.g. Simile [19], Simulink [20], EJS [4]) that best fits the domain features. Chosen a simulation tool, it is necessary to glue it with *AMELI* so that agents in an AEI can sense and act upon the simulated environment. This required *simulation bridge* (see the arrow connecting the simulation environment with *AMELI* in figure 1), is a software component whose main purpose is: (i) to synchronise both simulators; (ii) to forward environment variables' values to *SIMDEI*; and (iii) to translate actions within the simulated AEI into environment actions. At present, we do offer implementations of the simulation bridge to connect *SIMDEI* simulations to either Simulink [20] or EJS [4].

SIMDEI can exploit parametrised agent skeletons to generate agent populations by setting the number of agents to create from a given skelenton along with the means to set up values for their parameters. An agent's action can be parametrised in two ways: (i) by defining whether an action is carried out or not as a parameter; (ii) by defining (some of) the actual values of each action as parameters. Figure 3 illustrates how to generate a population of energy producers whose production capacity will be randomly generated by a normal distribution.

In summary, we have extended the original EIDE development framework providing a set of tools for engineering (specify and test) autonomic electronic institutions (EIDE-*). EIDE-* has been used for designing an testing the electricity market problem that is described below.

4   Electricity Market

We will illustrate the capabilities of the framework through the *Power Electricity Market* problem. The main goal of an electricity market is to provide a set of rules to conciliate the demand of electricity and its generation. There are two issues that must be avoided: a lack of production that can leave some customers

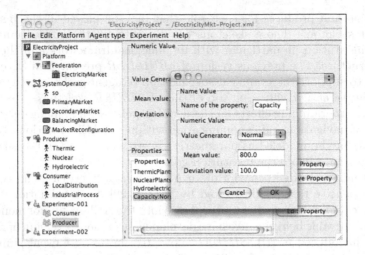

Fig. 3. Generating Agent Populations for the Electricity Market with SIMDEI

without electricity and an unwanted overproduction. Moreover, these goals have to be achieved while maintaining a reasonable electricity price.

We will model an electricity market as an electronic institution where the power demand is the environment where the institution is situated and the market is only able to partially observe the impact of their decisions in the environment.

4.1 Market Goals

As we mentioned above, the first goal of the electricity market AEI is to guarantee that the energy demand is always satisfied and that the overproduction is minimized. Because each producer is obliged to guarantee a safety power that is a 10% of its production, we are interested in minimizing the amount of safety power required.

The second goal of the electricity market AEI is to keep the power cost in a reasonable interval. For instance, the power cost in a working winter day oscillates from a minimum of 30 Euros/MWh to a maximum of 70 Euros/MWh.

Given these goals, we defined four reference values in the AEI: the power deficit percentage (PDP); the overproduction percentage (OPP); the power cost average (AvgC); and the power cost deviation (DevC).

Because we are interested in experimenting with different scenarios, the constraints associated to the reference values (the maximum and minimum ranges) will be parameters to be filled when enacting specific institutions.

4.2 Market Players

The players of the market are the producers, the consumers, and the system operator. Producers and consumers are external roles in the institution whereas the system operator is a staff role.

Producers: The producers use different technologies for electricity generation in order to satisfy the demand. The three main types of power stations modeled are: Thermic (coal-fired, gas fired and fuel-fired) stations, Nuclear stations, and Hydroelectric stations. Each type of power station has its own production features. For instance, nuclear and hydroelectric are cheap and come on stream rapidly. However, if nuclear plants are backed-off significantly, recovery time is slow. Thermic-based generation is relatively expensive and slow to come on stream.

Consumers: The consumers that participate in an electricity market are large industrial companies and local energy wholesalers that sell the energy to smaller or domestic consumers. The main goal of the consumers is to buy energy for half an hour periods according to the information provided by the demand model.

System Operator: The task of the system operator is to guarantee the voltage level and the dynamic security of the electricity network. Specifically, the system operator controls that the power deficit is never greater than a 10% of the total production, which is the obliged safety power that each power station must fulfill. Notice that, in our example, producers are autonomous about deciding their own production and the system operator is only responsible for the distribution of the demand.

4.3   Market Activities

The electricity market is organized in three different markets: the primary market, the secondary market, and the balancing market.

Primary Market: The primary market performs periodic auctions of transmission rights, in the form of tickets valid for the injection or extraction of energy over the next half an hour period. We have modeled the primary market with a double auction protocol. Every half an hour a new auction is launched.

Secondary Market: Once the auction has taken place, the goal of the secondary market is to provide an additional round for the trading of transmission tickets. The market allows the trading of a ticket until half an hour before the ticket time. This time is known as "gate closure".

Balancing Market: This market exists to permit the system operator to adapt the plans of production to the quality and security restrictions. Based on the analysis of the tickets held in the previous markets, the system operator is able to identify shortfalls or excesses of energy that will arise during the ticket window. The only actions available are: the dispatching of additional generation and the back-off of scheduled generation.

4.4   Simulation Environment

The power demand has been modeled following the electrical consumption in Spain every hour. The information has been taken from the "Red Eléctrica

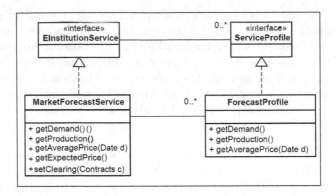

Fig. 4. Plugging a Forecast Service to the market

Española" [15] which controls the electrical power distribution in Spain. The power demand has been simulated using the EJS tool [4]. We have modeled four diffenent consumption patterns: working days, Saturday, Sunday, and holidays. Moreover, some perturbations can be introduced arbitrarily into the simulated patterns. We have developed the `MarketForecast` service that offers the forecast methods—namely expected demand (`getDemand`); expected energy production (`getProduction`); and expected MWh price (`getExpectedPrice`)—as well as a method to retrieve past market price on a particular date `getPrice(Date d)`. Furthermore, it provides a method for acting into forecast calculi: the method `setClearing(Contracts c)` sets the contract information corresponding to a market cleared by the system operator. THe `setClearing` method is employed by affecting the demand simulation and, consequently, the subsequent forecasts. The idea behind this method is to disturb the estimation of the next expected price by means of analyzing the production and consumption mismatches.

The `ForecastProfile` profile only allows external agents to obtain information about past market prices on particular dates, and the expected energy demand and production. The `ForecastProfile` has been further split so that only consumers can access the production forecast, whereas only producers can access the demand forecast. Figure 4 summarizes the `MarketForecast` service.

4.5   Self-configuration Policies

The system operator is the agent in charge of tracking the fulfillment of the institutional goals and the one responsible for re-configuring them when necessary.

The interest of the institution is the market autonomy, i.e. that producers and consumers would reach all the required agreements in the primary and secondary markets with the minimum mismatch between offer and demand. The intervention of the system operator in the balancing market has to be minimized and the task of the system operator is to dynamically adapt the institutional rules for enforcing this result.

After each execution round in the balancing market, the institutional goals are automatically updated by *AMELI*. First at all, the result of a balancing market round fires the updating of the reference values: the power deficit percentage (PDP); the overproduction percentage (OPP); the power cost average (AvgC); and the power cost deviation (DevC). Then, the fulfillment of the goals is updated by checking the constraints related to each goal, i.e. by contrasting position of the reference values into the desired intervals.

The most important goal of the institution is to minimize the amount of reserve power consumed (PDP). Because the guaranteed reserve power is only a 10% of the production, the priority of the system operator must be to avoid the usage of this reserve. The system operator uses the `MarketForecast` service for assessing whether a usage of the reserve power is the product of a punctual demand peak (the power demand usually has two maximum peaks per day) or reflects a problem between offer and demand. Only this second phenomenon is considered as an indicator to re-configure the institutional rules. We assume that producers and consumers follow a rational behavior. Producers are interested in offering all the energy they are able to produce when demand peaks arise because the price in those situations is usually high. On the counter part, consumers are aware that they have to pay an extra price when the global demand is high. Thus, the main reason of this market mismatch is the partial awareness that each consumer or producer has about the global market behavior. The scope for action of the system operator focuses the secondary and balancing markets. The system operator may change the role flow policies for enforcing the participation of producers in the secondary market and for re-configuring the protocol parameters in the secondary market providing more flexibility to the consumers.

The overproduction is preferable to the lack of production but also has to be minimized. Assuming again a rational behavior in producers and consumers, the system operator will change the role flow policies for inhibiting the participation of producers in the secondary market. Furthermore, the system operator may change the window of the demand forecast the producers are able to access, i.e re-configuring the `ForecastProfile` for helping the producers in the planning of their optimal production.

Finally, maintaining the energy cost in a reasonable interval should be a natural consequence of any balanced market. Because of the openness of participants this hypothesis cannot be assumed and the system operator has to prevent also unexpected low/high prices. The way a system operator may enforce reasonable prices is by modifying the normative rules of the institution by increasing/decreasing punishments.

5   Conclusions

In this paper we have tried to make headway in the engineering of self-* systems by introducing a framework, EIDE-*, to support the development of a particular type of these systems, namely *autonomic electronic institutions* (AEIs). We have introduced the formal concepts around autonomic electronic institutions and described the set of tools we provide for helping in the engineering of autonomic electronic institutions. Furthermore, we have illustrated the capabilities of the framework through the analysis of self-configuration policies in a power electricity market.

As future work, we plan to deal with the reasoning capabilities required by a participating agent in order to cope with institutional changes.

Acknowledgements

The authors would like to thank our anonymous reviewers for their very pertinent commens. This work was partially funded by projects AT (CONSOLIDER CSD2007-0022), IEA (TIN2006-15662-C02-01), OK (IST-4-027253-STP), EU-FEDER funds, and by the Generalitat de Catalunya under the grant 2005-SGR-00093. The authors would like to thank to the UDT-IA development team for their help in the deployment of the EIDE-* framework.

References

1. Arcos, J.L., Esteva, M., Noriega, P., Rodríguez-Aguilar, J.A., Sierra, C.: Engineering open environments with electronic institutions. Engineering Applications of Artificial Intelligence 18(1), 191–204 (2005)
2. Arcos, J.L., Noriega, P., Rodríguez-Aguilar, J.A., Sierra, C.: E4mas through electronic institutions. In: Weyns, D., Van Dyke Parunak, H., Michel, F. (eds.) E4MAS 2006. LNCS (LNAI), vol. 4389, pp. 184–202. Springer, Heidelberg (2007)
3. Bou, E., López-Sánchez, M., Rodríguez-Aguilar, J.A.: Towards self-configuration in autonomic electronic institutions. In: Noriega, P., Vázquez-Salceda, J., Boella, G., Boissier, O., Dignum, V., Fornara, N., Matson, E. (eds.) COIN 2006. LNCS (LNAI), vol. 4386. Springer, Heidelberg (2007)
4. Ejs, easy java simulations, http://www.um.es/fem/Ejs
5. Esteva, M.: Electronic Institutions: from specification to development. PhD Thesis Universitat Politècnica de Catalunya (UPC), 2003. Number 19 in IIIA Monograph Series. IIIA (2003)
6. Esteva, M., de la Cruz, D., Sierra, C.: ISLANDER: en electronic institutions editor. In: Castelfranchi, C., Johnson, W.L. (eds.) Proceedings of the First International Joint Conference on Autonomous Agents and Multiagent Systems, Bologna, Italy, July 15-19, vol. 3, pp. 1045–1052. ACM Press, New York (2002)
7. Esteva, M., Rosell, B., Rodríguez-Aguilar, J.A., Arcos, J.L.: AMELI: An agent-based middleware for electronic institutions. In: Jennings, N., et al. (eds.) AAMAS 2004, vol. I, pp. 236–243. ACM, New York (2004)
8. Esteva, M., Vasconcelos, W., Sierra, C., Rodríguez-Aguilar, J.A.: Norm consistency in electronic institutions. In: Bazzan, A.L.C., Labidi, S. (eds.) SBIA 2004. LNCS (LNAI), vol. 3171, pp. 494–505. Springer, Heidelberg (2004)
9. Jennings, N.R., Sycara, K., Wooldridge, M.: A roadmap of agent research and development. Autonomous Agents and Multi-agent Systems 1, 275–306 (1998)
10. Kephart, J.O., Chess, D.M.: The vision of autonomic computing. IEEE Computer 36(1), 41–50 (2003)

11. Khalil-Ibrahim, I., Kotsis, G., Kronsteiner, R.: Substitution rules for the verification of norm-compliance in electronic institutions. In: Proceedings of the 13th IEEE International Workshops on Enabling Technologies: Infrastructure for Collaborative Enterprises (WET ICE 2004), pp. 21–26. IEEE Computer Society Press, Los Alamitos (2004)
12. Luck, M., McBurney, P., Shehory, O., Willmott, S.: Agentlink Roadmap. Agenlink.org (2005)
13. Noriega, P.: Agent-Mediated Auctions: The Fishmarket Metaphor. Number 8 in IIIA Monograph Series (1997)
14. North, D.C.: Institutions, Institutional change and economic performance. Cambridge University press, Cambridge (1990)
15. Red Eléctrica Española, http://www.ree.es
16. Repast, http://repast.sourceforge.net
17. Rimassa, G., Greenwood, D., Kernland, M.E.: The Living Systems Technology Suite: an autonomous middleware for autonomic computing. In: Johnson, W.L., Castelfranchi, C. (eds.) Proceedings of the International Conference on Autonomic and Autonomous Systems (ICAS 2006), vol. 3, p. 33. ACM Press, New York (2006)
18. Rodríguez-Aguilar, J.A.: On the Design and Construction of Agent-mediated Electronic Institutions. Number 14 in IIIA Monograph Series (2003)
19. Simile, http://simulistics.com
20. Simulink, http://www.mathworks.com/products/simulink/
21. Vasconcelos, W.: Norm verification and analysis of electronic institutions. In: Leite, J., Omicini, A., Torroni, P., Yolum, P. (eds.) DALT 2004. LNCS (LNAI), vol. 3476, pp. 166–182. Springer, Heidelberg (2005)
22. Viganò, F.: A framework for model checking institutions. In: Edelkamp, S., Lomuscio, A. (eds.) MoChArt IV. LNCS (LNAI), vol. 4428. Springer, Heidelberg (2007)

Prediction Horizons in Agent Models

H. Van Dyke Parunak, Theodore C. Belding,
and Sven A. Brueckner

NewVectors. 3520 Green Court, Suite 250, Ann Arbor, MI 48105, USA
{van.parunak,ted.belding,sven.brueckner}@newvectors.net

Abstract. One motivation for many agent-based models is to predict the future. The nonlinearity of agent interactions in most non-trivial domains mean that the usefulness of such predictions will be limited beyond a certain point (the "prediction horizon"), due to unbounded divergence of their trajectories. The model's predictions are increasingly useful out to the prediction horizon, but become misleading beyond that point. We exhibit and characterize this behavior in a simple model, based on the polyagent modeling construct, which uses multiple ghost agents mediated through a shared environment to explore alternative futures concurrently for a domain entity. We also discuss how a single agent in such a model can estimate the prediction horizon based on locally available information, and use this estimate to modulate dynamically how far it seeks to look into the future.

Keywords: non-linear dynamics, complex adaptive systems, environment-mediated interactions, swarming multi-agent systems.

1 Introduction

"Det er svært at spå - især om fremtiden."[1] Nevertheless, prediction is important in any domain that requires planning, and has been the object of extensive study. Laplace believed that to an observer with enough information about the present and sufficient computing capability, no detail of the future could remain hidden [9], and many technologies have been developed in an effort to realize his vision.

Laplace's optimism foundered on the discovery of irreversible processes in thermodynamics, as well as sensitivity to initial conditions. Nonlinearities in the dynamics of most realistic systems drive the exponential divergence of trajectories originating close to one another, a phenomenon popularly denominated as "chaos." As a result, while we can predict a short distance into the future, our vision becomes blurred as we look further.

We cannot see as far as Laplace anticipated, but we can estimate how far we can see. A predictive tool that assists a planner in the short term will be a detriment if the planner relies on it beyond the prediction horizon, the point at which its predictions

---

[1] "Prediction is difficult, especially of the future." The most authoritative account of this variously attributed phrase traces it to the Danish parliament in the 1930's [1].

D. Weyns, S.A. Brueckner, and Y. Demazeau (Eds.): EEMMAS 2007, LNAI 5049, pp. 88–102, 2008.
© Springer-Verlag Berlin Heidelberg 2008

degrade. Predictive tools should incorporate mechanisms to monitor their own behavior, so that they can warn the user about their decreasing acuity with increased lookahead.

The polyagent modeling construct [12, 13] can fit a model of an agent to its observed behavior, and then extend this model into the future to provide predictions [14]. In experiments on military operations, this mechanism outperforms both experienced human soldiers and game-theoretic mechanisms, but it is not immune to the nonlinearities that defeated Laplace. This paper demonstrates the prediction horizon for polyagents in a simple experiment, and discusses how it may be detected. However, the polyagent mechanism is not the only one that is vulnerable to a prediction horizon. Any predictive mechanism is subject to this limitation, and the lessons we draw from a polyagent example apply to other predictive approaches as well.

Section 2 reviews the polyagent prediction mechanism and the dynamical concept of divergent trajectories. Section 3 describes the structure and behavior of a simple experiment demonstrating this phenomenon. Section 4 offers discussion and analysis. Section 5 concludes.

2 Polyagents and Divergent Trajectories

The two technical foundations of this paper are polyagent-based prediction and trajectory divergence in nonlinear systems.

The Polyagent Modeling Construct

The *polyagent* modeling construct associates each domain entity with multiple agents: a single persistent *avatar* (which may use complex reasoning) and a swarm of transient *ghosts* (which typically coordinate stigmergically [10]). The avatar manages the stream of ghosts, which explore alternative behaviors in order to advise the avatar. This concept has been applied to a number of applications, in manufacturing [3], robotic routing [17], and combat modeling [15], and is related to the delegate systems developed at Katholieke Universiteit Leuven [7, 19].

The polyagents use their ghost populations to jointly emulate their interactions with each other and with the (physical) environment their domain entities are embedded in. Each ghost is a simple probabilistic abstraction of the domain entities, exploring a possible trajectory around the current space-time location of that entity from its recent past to the near future. Ghosts of different polyagents may emulate the interactions of their entities (e.g., military engagements of fighting units) through successive manipulation of markers in a shared computational environment that also presents states (e.g., weather conditions) or constraints (e.g., buildings, roads, rivers) of the domain to the ghosts. Thus, our polyagent modeling construct relies heavily on the mediation of multi-agent interactions through a shared environment.

To use the polyagent for prediction, we borrow a model from nonlinear dynamics. Many systems can be described by a time-varying state vector, often analyzed as vector differential equations, $\frac{d\vec{x}}{dt} = f(\vec{x})$. When f is nonlinear, the system can be formally chaotic, making long-range prediction impossible. However, one can anticipate the system's near-term behavior, by fitting a convenient functional form for f to the system's trajectory in the recent past, and then extrapolating this fit (Figure 1, [8]). Iterating this process provides a limited look-ahead.

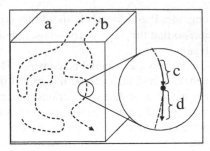

This approach requires systems described by mathematical equations that can be fit using regression methods such as least squares. It can be applied it to ghost agents whose behaviors are derived from digital pheromones that they sense in their environment. Each ghost has a

Fig. 1. Tracking a nonlinear dynamical system

personality vector of weights in [-1, 1] that describes how strongly it is attracted or repelled by each flavor of pheromone. To predict the future, the avatar generates ghosts with random personality vectors and inserts them into the recent past in a faster-than-real-time simulation of the domain. The ghosts follow their personalities in moving through the recent past to the present, at which point the avatar selects the fittest ghosts (based on their behavioral similarity to the observed entity) and breeds their personality vectors genetically. The fittest ghosts are then allowed to run into the future to predict likely futures of the entity (Figure 2). In realistic wargames, this mechanism predicts the future better than both experienced human staff and game-theoretic reasoners [16].

Trajectory Divergence in Nonlinear Dynamics

Nonlinear systems (which in principle account for virtually all realistic systems) exhibit sensitive dependence on initial conditions (known informally as "chaos" or the "butterfly effect") [23]. That is, if otherwise identical instances of the system are started with initial condi-tions that differ only min-utely, their state trajectories may ultimo-ately diverge arbitrarily far.

For example, consider the logistic equation,

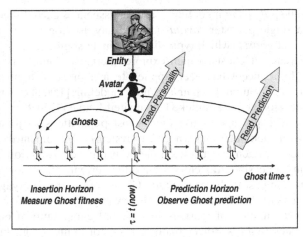

Fig. 2. Behavioral Evolution and Extrapolation

$$p_{t+1} = p_t + 3p_t(1 - p_t).$$

The 1000th iterate of this equation from $p_0 = 0.01$ is[2] 0.136739. However, if we add 10^{-13} to p_0, the result is 0.0423537, a difference of more than three times.

---

[2] Readers may obtain different results due to differences in the numerical processors, algorithms, or system libraries.

In physical systems, this divergence lies at the root of the failure of Laplace's program. Crutchfield et al. have argued that the only true randomness in the universe originates at the quantum level, and that pervasive evidence of randomness at the macro level is due to the action of chaos in effectively pumping quantum-level uncertainty to macroscopic levels [6].

Nonlinear systems *may* exhibit the butterfly effect. But is this effect a rarely-occurring academic curiosity, or a common problem? The question is empirical, but we can build intuitions from the behavior of a very simple system, the one-dimensional cellular automaton. Perhaps the simplest such system to exhibit nontrivial behavior is one in which each cell can have one of two states, and the state of a cell at time t depends on the state of itself and its two immediate neighbors at $t - 1$. The behavior of 256 such automata has been extensively studied [24]. Sixty show high-entropy evolution with the potential for the butterfly effect. Thus sensitive dependence characterizes a sizeable region of the behavioral space of a very simple system. Furthermore, as the size of the CA's rulespace increases (with more possible values per cell and a wider neighborhood), chaotic rules become more frequent, and ordered rules less frequent [25]. For systems whose complexity is comparable with the real world, chaotic behavior is likely to be ubiquitous.

Thus responsible use of any predictive mechanism requires that we recognize that the farther we look into the future, the less accurate our predictions will be. At some point, looking further into the future will stop being an advantage, and will lead to decreased performance. We call this point, the "prediction horizon." We must recognize the existence of this horizon and take steps to estimate it if we are to make responsible use of predictive tools.

Superficially, the challenges of the prediction horizon resemble those of overfitting in pattern recognition as was pointed out by reviewers of our research. In both cases a system is trained against one set of data and its output compared against another, and in both cases failure to attend to the issue reduces the accuracy of the output. But the two issues are fundamentally different (Table 1).

Table 1. Distinguishing the Prediction Horizon from Overfitting

	Overfitting	**Prediction Horizon**
Cause	Defective model (over-specializes to the data)	Divergence of correct model due to nonlinear dynamics
Detection	Information criteria (e.g., [1])	Local estimates of divergence
Correction	Detune the model (e.g., regularization [2])	Detect horizon and don't predict too far

- They have different *causes*. Overfitting yields a defective model that is overspecialized to the training data. The prediction horizon results from the inevitable divergence of a perfectly correct model due to nonlinear dynamics.
- Different mechanisms are used to detect them. Information criteria (e.g., the Akaike or Schwartz information criteria) can *detect* overfitting, by balancing the information content of a model against the degree of fit that it offers. Such criteria are inappropriate for dealing with the prediction horizon, which can arise even

when the information content of the model is at the appropriate level. Local estimates of divergence must be sought, some of which we discuss in this paper.

• The *correction* differs in the two cases. Overfitting is corrected by detuning the model (e.g., omitting some degrees of freedom by regularization). The correction for the prediction horizon is to detect it and not try to predict past it.

3   A Simple Experiment

We demonstrate the prediction horizon with a simple experiment involving pursuit and flight. Our experimental setup consists of two randomly distributed populations of avatars, c Cowards and r Rambos[3], situated in a toroidal arena k units on a side (a *kxk* square whose top and bottom are connected, as are its left and right sides). Cowards flee from Rambos, while Rambos approach Cowards. Each avatar deposits a digital pheromone in the environment, tracking its location. At each time step, each avatar samples the pheromone of avatars of the other side in its environment, and probabilistically decides whether it has engaged the adversary. The higher the pheromone concentration, the more likely an engagement is. If an engagement takes place, the Coward avatar dies with probability p (1.0 in our current experiments). Rambo avatars are immortal. When a Coward avatar dies, a new one is born at a random location, keeping the population constant.

Each avatar generates ghosts (one per time step) to guide its movement. The ghosts execute a random walk starting with their avatar, for a number of steps (the lookahead of the prediction). The ghosts determine the likelihood of an encounter by sampling the other side's pheromone. Rambo ghosts sense the Coward avatar pheromone, while Coward ghosts sense the Rambo ghost pheromone. When a Coward ghost and a Rambo ghost encounter each other, with probability p (again 1.0 in current experiments) they kill each other, and their avatars are notified of the location where the encounter took place. (Rambo ghosts, unlike Rambo avatars, are not immortal.)

Rambo ghosts live for 100 time steps (but only report their deaths within 10 steps of the avatar). The lifetime of Coward ghosts is the main independent variable in our experiment, and represents the distance into the future that the Coward looks ahead.

Periodically, each avatar takes a step. The interval between steps is the maximum of the Rambo and Coward ghost lifetimes. Each Rambo avatar wants to find Coward avatars, so it is attracted toward locations where its ghosts have died in encounters with Coward ghosts. It takes one step in the direction of the weighted sum of unit vectors from its current location to each of its ghosts that have died since it last moved. We call this weighted sum, the avatar's "guidance vector."

We weight the distances to dead ghosts to give more emphasis to nearby threat locations. The weighted sum is computed by scaling the distance r of dead ghosts from the avatar by

$$r' = Max\left(\frac{e^{-r} - e^{-10}}{1 - e^{-10}}, 0\right)$$

and summing the resulting vectors.

---

[3] We use this term as the semantic opposite to "Coward," to denote an agent that aggressively seeks to engage its adversaries.

Coward avatars want to avoid Rambo avatars. Each Coward avatar computes a weighted sum of unit vectors to its dead ghosts and takes a step in the opposite direction.

Preliminary probes show that the optimum lookahead for the configurations we explore is in the range [0, 25], so we run the system with settings of Coward lookahead ranging over [0,25] in steps of 1 and then over [25,100] in steps of 25. Rambo lookahead is fixed at 100 for all runs. Each run of the system has a fixed length of 500 avatar cycles.

We expect performance of Cowards first to increase as the lookahead increases, and then to decrease as it passes the prediction horizon. Success for a Coward means evading the Rambos, and thus experiencing fewer casualties. Since runs are of a fixed length, we use the total number of Coward avatar casualties as a performance figure. Thus our dependent variable can be interpreted in terms of the death rate of Cowards.

The mechanism leading to decreased performance beyond the prediction horizon in this case is confusion arising from detecting multiple adversaries. When the lookahead is too small, the Coward ghosts seldom reach any Rambo ghosts, and thus cannot give the Coward any information on the direction of danger, so it cannot avoid Rambos. When the lookahead is too long, the ghosts of both sides can reach all areas of the arena. Now a Coward learns of dead ghosts in every direction. Again, it cannot learn the direction of greatest danger. The predictive functionality enhances the Coward's performance most at an intermediate level of lookahead, the prediction horizon.

We are also interested in information that reflects the guidance available to a single avatar. For this purpose, we collect the number of dead ghosts on which each avatar bases each movement decision, the magnitude and angle of the sum of vectors to those ghosts (both scaled and unscaled), and the total distance covered by the avatar in its lifetime.

4 Analysis and Discussion

We consider evidence for the existence of a prediction horizon in our simple scenario, then explore its variation with configuration, and describe some ways that an agent can estimate it locally. Finally, we compare our work with related research. Unless otherwise noted, points in these plots are the mean over five separate runs.

As a general note referring to the initial discussion of the practicality of predicting non-linear complex systems, this model is very simplistic and should be considered an illustration of the proposed problem and the suggested approach to identifying and controlling

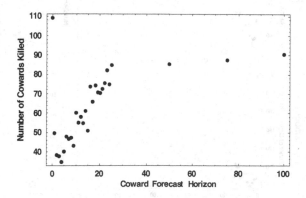

Fig. 3. Coward deaths as function of lookahead, 10x10 arena

prediction horizon effects. The "complexity" of the space of future states that we are trying to control is primarily due to the random walk of the ghosts that rapidly accumulates variance in estimating the future.

Evidence for the Prediction Horizon

For a run of 500 steps with ten Cowards and five Rambos on a 10x10 arena, Figure 3 plots the number of Coward deaths at prediction horizons ranging from 0 to 100. As expected, the number of deaths at first drops rapidly with increasing lookahead, from nearly 110 with 0 lookahead to about 35 with a lookahead of 4. Then it climbs rapidly and asymptotes around 90. Cowards can usefully predict and avoid threats for horizons on the order of 3-5, but then the future becomes increasingly murky.

Variation of the Prediction Horizon

The prediction horizon depends on the system's configuration. To illustrate this, Figure 4 plots the same statistic as Figure 3, but for different configurations, varying the overall arena size (in the columns) and the relative number of Cowards and Rambos (in the rows). The absolute numbers of Cowards killed varies with both parameters: smaller arenas and larger Rambo populations lead to higher casualties. Furthermore, all the curves have the same basic shape, with casualties at first decreasing rapidly with increasing lookahead, then increasing to an asymptote (incompletely achieved in the 20x20 arena).

The dip in the curve, indicating the region of useful predictions, varies considerably in width. The x-axis is the same in all four figures. On a larger arena, Cowards

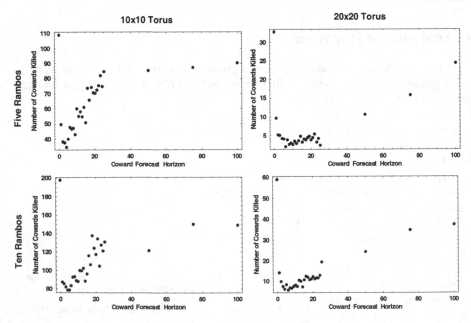

Fig. 4. Effects of Configuration Change

can make useful predictions out to a lookahead of 20 or 25 (upper-right), a point at which their predictions would seriously degrade on the smaller arena. The ratio of Rambos to Cowards also impacts the width of the useful region, most noticeably on the 20x20 arena, where fewer Rambos lead to a much broader minimum and much gentler approach to the asymptote.

This simple example shows that the prediction horizon is not constant for all agents or for a single agent at all times. It depends on the complexity of the agent's environment (illustrated in our example by the overall density of agents and the relative population of Cowards and Rambos). This complexity varies from agent to agent and from one moment to the next. For example, in real combat, agents are not reborn to keep the population constant, as they are in our system, so the density will vary over time. In addition, the density will vary spatially, leading agents in different portions of the arena to require different lookaheads. The dependence on density is a characteristic of our application, and other applications might depend on some other parameter, but the point remains. To use prediction effectively, agents must not only recognize the existence of the prediction horizon, but also learn how to estimate it dynamically.

Estimating the Prediction Horizon Locally

The prediction horizon is a global emergent feature of the system. We observe it by looking at the number of dead Coward avatars per fixed-length run (equivalently, the rate of Coward deaths). Making such information available to each agent compromises the locality of agent interaction that many applications require [11]. It would be much better if we can identify local indicators that an agent can use to adjust its lookahead dynamically, indicators that are available to each agent without directly consulting other agents or some system-level oracle.

We have studied three possible local indicators: the avatar's net speed over its lifetime, and two features (length and angle) of its guidance vector. All three are motivated by the intuition that an

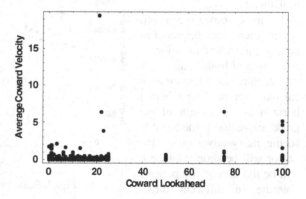

Fig. 5. Mean Coward avatar speed as function of lookahead

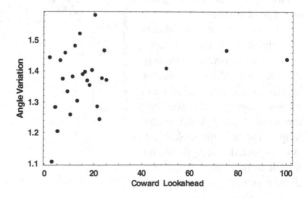

Fig. 6. Angle variation with lookahead

agent that is getting useful information from its predictive process should show this in its movement. Its guidance vector should tend to be longer and will tend to point in the same direction from one step to the next, and its overall speed should be greater than if the avatar were executing a random walk. These are only heuristics. An agent that is effectively evading numerous adversaries could exhibit as many sudden turns as one that is wandering randomly. But it is instructive to evaluate all three candidates.

Figure 5 shows the dependence of Coward avatar speed (total distance covered divided by lifetime) as a function of lookahead on the 20x20 arena. There is no clear correlation between speed and the prediction horizon. The most effective avatars in terms of survival cover no more territory overall than do those executing a random walk.

Given this result, we might not expect any correlation in angle changes. Computing angle changes is subtle, because at some steps an avatar may not have any dead ghosts, and in this case the angle of the ghost's vector is not defined. For each avatar, we compute the angle (in $[0, 2\pi]$) of its vector at each step, dropping those steps for which its angle is undefined. Then we compute the smallest difference in angle between each pair of succe-ssive vectors. We compute the mean value of angle differ-ence for each avatar, and then over all avatars with the same lookahead.

Figure 6 shows the result. Again, there does not seem to be any significant variation as a function of lookahead.

Our third candidate for a local indicator of the prediction horizon is the len-gth of the guidance vector. If the agent is seeing many adver-saries, the vector will be shorter (since it will be the sum of components pointing in different directions). So we expect a large vector to correspond to good agent performance.

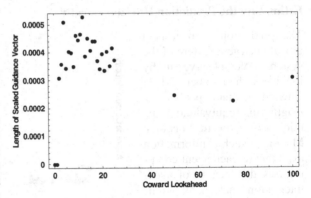

Fig. 7. Scaled vector length (20x20 arena)

The number of dead ghosts contributing to the guidance vector varies from step to step. So we normalize the vector length by the number of dead ghosts. Figure 7 shows how the scaled, normalized vector length varies with lookahead. As expected, scaled vector length is maxi-mal at the pre-diction horizon, and drops off on both sides.

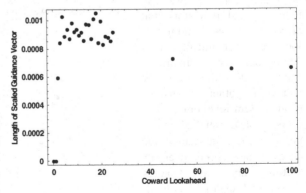

Fig. 8. Scaled vector length (10x10 arena, five Rambos)

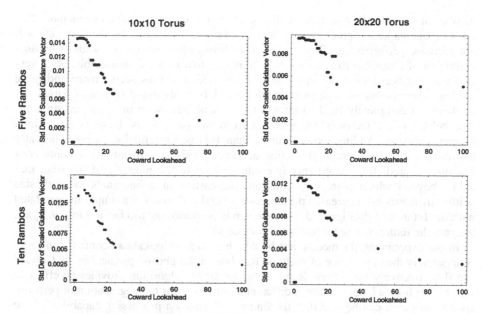

Fig. 9. Standard Deviation of Scaled Guidance Vector length (running medians of 5)

However, the length is not adequate to guide a Coward's decision. Figure 8 shows the same plot for the 10x10 arena. Even though the region of accurate prediction is much narrower for this case than for the 20x20 arena (Figure 4), the scaled vector length is too noisy to capture this difference.

But there is still hope. Figure 9 shows the standard deviation of the scaled guidance vector as a function of lookahead for the same configurations as Figure 4. This statistic clearly shows the broader width of the useful prediction region in the 20x20, five Rambo configuration. To use this information, the agent should keep a record of the length of its guidance vector, and adjust its forecast horizon to maximized the variance of this history. In the case of a polyagent, the avatar would not allow its ghosts to run past the point at which the variance of guidance vector length drops off.

The usefulness of the variance of normalized length depends on the decision scheme used by the agents in this experiment, whose structure has been kept simple to highlight the basic processes in operation. Brueckner *et al.* in [4] describe the more general principle. The entropy over the set of choices available to the agent at any time (the "option set entropy") is a local estimator of a system's global convergence. High entropy corresponds to low guidance for the agent, suggesting that it should not take further action. In this case, the length of the guidance vector directly reflects the guidance given to the agent, so it should be correlated with the option set entropy, consistent with their work. (It is not immediately clear why the variation in the guidance vector length is a more discriminating indicator than the length itself.)

Relation to Other Work

Our research bears comparison with several other bodies of work.

Crutchfield and Shalizi [21] have developed a theory of *ε-machines*, the minimal state machines that can accurately predict the future behavior of a system. The number of states in the ε-machine corresponds to the minimal amount of memory that must be maintained to predict the system's behavior. Increasing the memory size will not increase performance. Their theory also draws upon Kolmogorov and Chaitin's definition of a random time series of data as one that is not compressible. As a system's output becomes more and more complicated, and thus seems more and more random, the amount of state memory that must be maintained increases. However, predicting a completely random system requires no past state information, since future behavior is effectively uncorrelated from the past. Thus, there is an optimal memory horizon. Adding more memory than this is wasteful but is not inherently harmful to the ε-machine's prediction accuracy. This system admits a continuous measure of prediction uncertainty (the entropy) up to the memory of the state machine, beyond which point it is constant. Increasing an ε-machine's memory size neither increases nor decreases performance - outdated states are simply uncorrelated with the future and thus ignored. Our concern is with looking too far, not into the past, but into the future, where performance does degrade.

In our experiment, the mechanism by which increased lookahead confuses an agent is apparently the appearance of multiple Rambos in the ghosts' predictions. A Coward can flee effectively from a few Rambos, but its simple algorithm provides no effective way to flee from a large number at different azimuths. Thus the degradation of performance in this case can be traced to the limited information processing capability of the agents.[4] The effect of cognitive overload on agents, and the resulting pattern of increasing, then decreasing performance as the amount of information is increased, has been described in the context of a predator-prey experiment [22]. That system, unlike ours, is not predictive, and does not involve agent reasoning over multiple time steps.

The curves in Figure 3 and Figure 4 have the same general shape as the loss curve as-sociated with the Minority Game, a simple model of multi-agent competition for scarce resources [5]. In the classic form of this game, n agents (an odd number) repeatedly choose between two resources, each with capacity $\lfloor n/2 \rfloor$. Thus at every step, exactly one resource will be overloaded. The agents have available a history of which resource was not overloaded at each round in the past, and they base their decision on a suffix of length m of that history. The score for each round is the population of the under-subscribed resource. The loss function for the system is the variance of that population. For an agent population of a given size, as m (and thus the amount of information available to each agent increases, the loss decreases to a minimum (a performance maximum), followed by an asymptotic return to an intermediate level (Figure 10). This general shape is the same as that of the death rate in our game (Figure 4 and Figure 6).

The two systems differ in their superficial structure. The minority game is driven by competition for scarce resources, while our example is based on pursuit and evasion. But there are important similarities.

First, one could consider the space occupied by the agents in our game as a resource that is in contention. The desire of Cowards to avoid Rambos is analogous to the desire of agents in the Minority Game to avoid overloading the same resou-rce, though in our case the space being deconflicted is continuous rather than discrete.

---

[4] This explanation does not invalidate our motivation of the prediction horizon by the theory of nonlinear processes. The nonlinear interactions between Cowards and Rambos include the mechanisms of perception and analysis that they employ, and the horizon we observe is due to the emergent divergence of trajectories as these processes are iterated over successive steps of the game.

Second, the behavior of both systems varies as agents make decisions based on information that is increasingly remote in time. In our system, performance first improves, then declines, as we apply knowledge of the present to predictions that reach farther into the future. In the Minority Game, the same pattern of perfor-mance change appears as agents use information farther and farther into the past to inform a decision in the present.

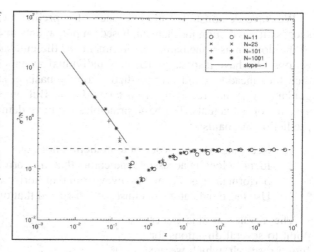

Fig. 10. Loss function in the minority game [20]

In the Minority Game, the asymptotic performance approached as m increases is what the agents would achieve if they made their selections randomly. The approach to the asymptote might be due[5], not to dilution of the information in the history from nonlinear effects, but to the limited processing capacity of the population of agents. If one increases the size of the agent population, the point of optimal performance moves higher, suggesting that there is information in longer suffixes that can be retrieved by a more complex mechanism (i.e., a larger population). However, the history is not identical with the history analyzed by fewer agents, since the agents themselves generate the history by their interactions, and it may be that the asymptote does in fact reflect dilution of the history's information content by nonlinear effects. To our knowledge, the relation of nonlinear divergence of trajectories to the dynamics of the Minority Game has not been studied. The similarity between Figure 10 and Figure 4 may be another instance of universality in multi-agent systems [18], in which similarly constrained patterns of interaction lead to similar outcomes in systems whose internal reasoning mechanisms are very different from one another. We intend to explore a deeper connection between the two systems in further research.

5 Conclusion

Prediction is an important task in planning, but must be applied with care. If one seeks to look too far into the future, one may be deceived, for the nonlinear dynamics of realistic problems impose a prediction horizon. Beyond this point, increased lookahead leads to a decrease, rather than an increase, in performance. Systems that look into the future must be aware of this horizon, and should take steps to monitor their approach to it so that they do not mislead their users with useless information.

---

[5] Proposed by Prof. Robert Savit of the University of Michigan.

We have demonstrated the existence of a prediction horizon in one particularly successful prediction mechanism, based on polyagents that use a computational model of the domain as a mediating environment for the emulation of complex entity interactions. We have also suggested how individual avatars in such a system can adjust their lookahead to avoid over-predicting, on the basis of local estimators of how much guidance they are receiving from their ghosts. But our results are not restricted to systems of polyagents. The basic principles we have demonstrated are critical for any prediction mechanism:

1. Recognize the existence of a prediction horizon.
2. Identify locally accessible indicators that are correlated with the degradation of performance as one moves away from that horizon.
3. Use these indicators to adjust the lookahead that one uses to inform decisions.

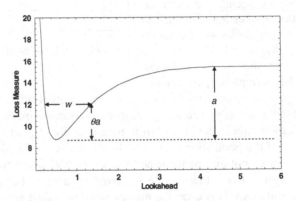

Fig. 11. Notional fit to predictive loss data

The results in this paper point to several directions for future research, which we are pursuing.

We have compared the area of effective prediction for different configurations somewhat qualitatively, by reference to visually apparent differences in the width of the region of low loss. We need a more quantitative measure of this region. A possible course is to fit an analytic form to the loss function. Figure 11 shows an instance of one promising family of functions, $y = 15 + 3/x - e^{-(x-3)}$. Then the width w of the dip at a specified fraction θ of the distance a between the bottom of the dip and the asymptote will serve as a consistent measure of the region of useful predictions.

More work is needed on local heuristics that an agent can use to avoid predicting beyond the prediction horizon. The criterion that we have identified, standard deviation of the length of the guidance vectors, is correlated only crudely with the useful prediction region (compare Figure 4 with Figure 9). Application of the option set entropy concept from [4] should permit derivation of more satisfactory local heuristics.

The shape of the performance curve as a function of lookahead is qualitatively similar to the performance curve for the Minority Game. This similarity may reflect a deeper relation between the dynamics of these superficially similar systems, which we plan to explore.

Acknowledgments. This research was conducted with the support of the office of Naval Research (Contract # N00014-06-1-0467). The results presented do not necessarily reflect the opinion of the sponsor.

References

1. Akaike, H.: A new look at the statistical model identification. IEEE Transactions on Automatic Control 19(6), 716–723 (1974)
2. Bishop, C.M.: Pattern Recognition and Machine Learning. Springer, New York (2006)
3. Brueckner, S.: Return from the Ant: Synthetic Ecosystems for Manufacturing Control. Dr.rer.nat. Thesis at Humboldt University Berlin, Department of Computer Science (2000), http://dochost.rz.hu-berlin.de/dissertationen/brueckner-sven-2000-06-21/PDF/Brueckner.pdf
4. Brueckner, S., Parunak, H.V.D.: Information-Driven Phase Changes in Multi-Agent Coordination. In: Proceedings of Autonomous Agents and Multi-Agent Systems (AAMAS 2003), Melbourne, Australia, pp. 950–951. ACM, New York (2003), http://www.newvectors.net/staff/parunakv/AAMAS03InfoPhaseChange.pdf
5. Challet, D., Marsili, M., Zhang, Y.-C.: Minority Games: Interacting Agents in Financial Markets. Oxford University Press, Oxford (2005)
6. Crutchfield, J.P., Farmer, J.D., Packard, N.H., Shaw, R.S.: Chaos. Scientific American 255, 46–57 (1986)
7. Holvoet, T., Valckenaers, P.: Exploiting the Environment for Coordinating Agent Intentions. In: Weyns, D., Van Dyke Parunak, H., Michel, F. (eds.) E4MAS 2006. LNCS (LNAI), vol. 4389. Springer, Heidelberg (2007)
8. Kantz, H., Schreiber, T.: Nonlinear Time Series Analysis. Cambridge University Press, Cambridge (1997)
9. Laplace, P.S.: Essai Philosophique sur les Probabilités (1820)
10. Parunak, H.V.D.: 'Go to the Ant': Engineering Principles from Natural Agent Systems. Annals of Operations Research 75, 69–101 (1997), http://www.newvectors.net/staff/parunakv/gotoant.pdf
11. Parunak, H.V.D.: Making Swarming Happen. In: Proceedings of Swarming and Network-Enabled C4ISR, Tysons Corner, VA, ASD C3I (2003), http://www.newvectors.net/staff/parunakv/MSH03.pdf
12. Parunak, H.V.D., Brueckner, S.: Concurrent Modeling of Alternative Worlds with Polyagents. In: Antunes, L., Takadama, K. (eds.) MABS 2006. LNCS (LNAI), vol. 4442. Springer, Heidelberg (2007), http://www.newvectors.net/staff/parunakv/MABS06Polyagents.pdf
13. Parunak, H.V.D., Brueckner, S.: Modeling Uncertain Domains with Polyagents. In: Proceedings of International Joint Conference on Autonomous Agents and Multi-Agent Systems (AAMAS 2006), Hakodate, Japan. ACM Press, New York (2006), http://www.newvectors.net/staff/parunakv/AAMAS06Polyagents.pdf
14. Parunak, H.V.D., Brueckner, S.: Polyagents Model Multiple Futures Concurrently. In: Proceedings of Social Agents: Results and Prospects (Agent 2006), Chicago, IL, Argonne National Laboratory (2006)
15. Parunak, H.V.D., Brueckner, S., Matthews, R., Sauter, J., Brophy, S.: Real-Time Evolutionary Agent Characterization and Prediction. In: Proceedings of International Joint Conference on Autonomous Agents and Multi-Agent Systems (AAMAS 2006), Hakodate, Japan. ACM Press, New York (submitted, 2006), http://www.newvectors.net/staff/parunakv/BEE.pdf
16. Parunak, H.V.D., Brueckner, S., Matthews, R., Sauter, J., Brophy, S.: Real-Time Evolutionary Agent Characterization and Prediction. In: Proceedings of Social Agents: Results and Prospects (Agent 2006), Chicago, IL, Argonne National Laboratory (2006)

17. Parunak, H.V.D., Brueckner, S., Sauter, J.: Digital Pheromones for Coordination of Unmanned Vehicles. In: Weyns, D., Van Dyke Parunak, H., Michel, F. (eds.) E4MAS 2004. LNCS (LNAI), vol. 3374, pp. 246–263. Springer, New York (2005), http://www.newvectors.net/staff/parunakv/E4MAS04_UAVCoordination.pdf
18. Parunak, H.V.D., Brueckner, S., Savit, R.: Universality in Multi-Agent Systems. In: Proceedings of Third International Joint Conference on Autonomous Agents and Multi-Agent Systems (AAMAS 2004), pp. 930–937. ACM, New York (2005), http://www.newvectors.net/staff/parunakv/AAMAS04Universality.pdf
19. Parunak, H.V.D., Brueckner, S., Weyns, D., Holvoet, T., Valckenaers, P.: E Pluribus Unum: Polyagent and Delegate MAS Architectures. In: Antunes, L., Paolucci, M., Norling, E. (eds.) MABS 2007. LNCS(LNAI), vol. 5003. Springer, Heidelberg (2008)
20. Savit, R., Manuca, R., Riolo, R.: Adaptive Competition, Market Efficiency, and Phase Transitions. Physical Review Letters 82(10), 2203–2206 (1999)
21. Shalizi, C.R., Crutchfield, J.P.: Computational Mechanics: Pattern and Prediction, Structure and Simplicity. Journal of Statistical Physics 104, 817–879 (2001), http://xxx.lanl.gov/ps/cond-mat/9907176
22. Takashina, T., Watanabe, S.: The Locality of Information Gathering in Multiagent Systems. In: Proceedings of Second International Conference on Multi-Agent Systems (ICMAS 1996), p. 461 (1996), http://homepage.mac.com/t_takashina/paper-dir/ICMAS96_takashina.pdf
23. Wikipedia. Butterfly Effect (2006), http://en.wikipedia.org/wiki/Sensitive_dependence_on_initial_conditions
24. Wolfram, S.: Universality and Complexity in Cellular Automata. Physica D 10, 1–35 (1984)
25. Wuensche, A.: Classifying Cellular Automata Automatically: Finding gliders, filtering, and relating space-time patterns, attractor basins, and the Z parameter. Complexity 4(3), 47–66 (1999)

Combining Interface Agents and Situated Agents for Deploying Adaptive Web Applications

Andrea Bonomi[1], Marcello Sarini[2], and Giuseppe Vizzari[1]

[1] Complex Systems and Artificial Intelligence research centre
University of Milan–Bicocca
Via Bicocca degli Arcimboldi 8, 20126 Milano, Italy
{andrea.bonomi,giuseppe.vizzari}@csai.disco.unimib.it
[2] Department of Psychology
University of Milan–Bicocca
Piazza dell'Ateneo Nuovo 1, 20126 Milan - Italy
sarini@disco.unimib.it

Abstract. A web site presents a graph–like spatial structure composed of pages connected by hyperlinks. This structure may represent an environment in which situated agents associated to visitors of the web site (user agents) are positioned and moved in order to monitor their navigation. This paper presents a heterogeneous multi-agent system supporting the collection of information related to user's behaviour in a web site by specific situated reactive user agents. The acquired information is then exploited by interface agents supporting advanced adaptive functionalities based on the history of user's movement in the web site environment. Interface agents also interact with user agents to acquire information on other visitors of the web site and to support a context aware form of interaction among web site visitors.

1 Introduction

Adaptive web research area [1] aims at considering the problem of how large web sites that encompass several heterogeneous topics can be adapted so to take into account the heterogeneous information needs of different visitors who have very different characteristics, goals, backgrounds and needs. In this vein, we aim at designing adaptive web applications considering a web site as a graph representing a spatial structure composed of pages connected by hyperlinks. Consequently, we propose to exploit the graph-like structure of a web site as a Multi–Agent System (MAS) *environment* [2] on which agents representing visitors of the web site (hereafter *user agents*) are positioned and moved according to their navigation.

In particular, the environment represents a virtual structure where it is possible to gather information related to users' navigation in the web space in a more structured way, simplifying subsequent phases of analysis and adaptation of site contents. Though this approach can be used to propose additional links providing shortcuts to the terminal web pages as a sort of suggestion to the web site visitor, our proposal provides more than just gather information on users'

D. Weyns, S.A. Brueckner, and Y. Demazeau (Eds.): EEMMAS 2007, LNAI 5049, pp. 103–114, 2008.

behaviours for sake of web pages adaptation or navigation support, but exploits the MAS environment to provide users a means for mutual perception and interaction. In fact, information related to users' positions on the environment representing the web site can also be used to supply them awareness information on other visitors who are currently browsing the same page or pages close to it within the site. Moreover, keeping track of this information allows to make possible a form of interaction among users that is based on their positions on the site. Essentially, more than just showing a user the other registered visitors that are "nearby" (i.e. viewing the same page or adjacent ones), the system could also allow them to communicate each other. This form of interaction, in addition to the web page adaptation function, requires the adoption of a supporting technology that goes beyond the request/response model.

The overall system architecture we designed requires thus proper *interface agents*, able to interact with user agents situated in the previously introduced environment in order to exploit the acquired information on users' behaviours. This second type of agent is totally different from user agents, both from a modelling point of view and with reference to the supporting technology. In fact, the web interface agent must be active as long as the related web page is being viewed by a visitor and it must be able to proactively modify the page to improve the user's browsing experience. The overall system architecture, summarized in Fig. 1, includes thus heterogeneous agents collaborating to achieve this goal.

The following section describes the general framework of this approach, the mapping between the web site structure and user agents' environment. Section 3 describes an application providing the exploitation of this information for the adaptation of web pages by proper interface agents. A brief comparison of this approach and related work can be found in Sect. 4, and finally concluding remarks and future developments will end the paper.

2   Site Structure and Reactive User Agents

A web site is made up of a set of HTML pages (generally including multimedia contents) connected by means of hyperlinks. It is possible to obtain a graph-like structure mapping pages to nodes and hyperlinks to edges interconnecting these nodes. This kind of spatial structure could be exploited as an *environment* on which user agents related to site visitors are placed and move according to the related users' activities. This structure can be either static or dynamic: for instance it could vary according to specific rules and information stored in a database (i.e. database driven web sites). However, this kind of structure (both for static and dynamic web sites) can generally be obtained by means of a crawler, then it could be maintained by having periodic updates.

Given this spatial structure, a multi-agent model allowing an explicit representation of this aspect of agents' environment is needed to represent and exploit this kind of information. Situated agents models represent a useful source of abstractions and mechanisms supporting the definition environments for MAS, towards a precise definition of concepts such as *locality* and *perception*. There are

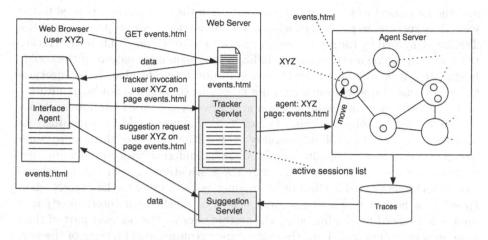

Fig. 1. A diagram showing the different components of system architecture and their interactions

not many models for situated agents, which provide an explicit representation of agent's environment. Some of them are mainly focused on providing mechanisms for coordinating situated agent's actions [3], others provide the interaction among agents through a modification of the shared environment (see, e.g., [4,5]). The Multilayered Multi Agent Situated Systems (MMASS) [6] model, that was adopted for the proposed system, supports an explicit representation of agents' environment through a set of interconnected layers whose structure is a graph of nodes (also referred to as sites in the model terminology; from now on we will use the term node to avoid confusion with web sites). The model was adopted due to the similarity among the defined spatial structure of the environment and the structure underlying a web site. Moreover, the model defines a set of allowed actions for agents' behavioural specification (including a primitive for agents' movement), that are useful to support the specification of situated agents mimicking the behaviour of web site visitors, for sake of monitoring and acquisition of user related data.

A platform for the specification and execution of simulations based on the MMASS model [7] was exploited to implement the part of the system devoted to the management of agents in their environments. The definition of spatial structure of the environment was supplied by a web crawler, while agents' movement is guided by external inputs generated by the requests issued by the related web site visitor. The general architecture of the system is shown in Fig. 1: the *Agent server* module is implemented through the MMASS platform, while the *Web server* is a Tomcat servlet container hosting SnipSnap[1], a Java-based weblog and wiki software. The highlighted *Tracker* module is a implemented through a Java Servlet, which is invoked by every page of the site but does not produce a visible effect on the related web page. The Tracker is responsible for triggering the creation

---

[1] http://snipsnap.org

and the movement of agents related to visitors in the environment related to the
web site structure. In particular, when a user makes his/her first page request the
Tracker is invoked by the interface agent associated to the page. Then the Tracker
tries to set a cookie on the client including the session information. If the cookie
is accepted, it is possible to use the session information to identify the user; on
the other hand, requests from clients not accepting cookies will not be monitored.

The management of agents creation and movement is not as simple as its intuitive description might indicate. In fact, the same user could be using different
browser pages or tabs to simultaneously view distinct pages of the site. In other
words, a user might be simultaneously following different trajectories in his/her
web site navigation. In order to manage these situations, a user can be related
to different agents, and his/her requests must be associated to the correct agent
(possibly a new one). Finally, agents related to finished (or interrupted) user
navigation should be eliminated by the system, storing the relevant part of their
state in a persistent way, until the related user requires again a page of the site.
In particular, remote users' requests may be divided into two main classes, according to their effects on the Tracker and Agent server. A request may bring
to the *creation of a new agent*: whenever a new user requires a web page, the
Tracker will invoke the Agent Server requiring the creation of an agent whose
starting position is the node related to the required page. On the other hand,
a request might *generate the movement of an agent*: when the viewer of a page
follows one of the provided links, the related web browser will generate a request
for a page that is adjacent to one of the related agents which must be moved to
the node related to the required page.

Consequently to the movements of user agents in the nodes of the graph
structure which mimic the navigation of the users within a web site, the system
is able to keep tracks of them into proper data structure called *traces*. A trace
keeps three kinds of information: the identifier of the user agent to which the
trace is related (that, in turn, can be related to an authenticated user that
actually generated the trace in one of its navigations in the web site), the starting
node related to the agent and destination node related to the browsing sequence
related to the trace. Additionally, this information is stored with other data
(e.g. a time stamp) in a database to allow for the provision of more advanced
functionalities and for the evaluation of the system.

3   The Web Interface Agent

The aim of the Interface Agent is to improve the browsing experience of a user
by adapting the page he/she is currently viewing to his/her preferences, needs
or habits. To do so, it must be active during the time–span in which the page is
visualized by the browser, and it must be able to dynamically alter its appearance. To do so, it must also be able to interact with the previously introduced
system to be informed about past user's behaviour. In other words the interface
agent is a client–side component, "living" in the web browser and interacting
with it in a proactive way.

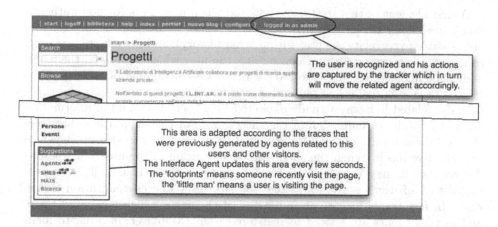

Fig. 2. A screenshot of a web page adapted according to gathered traces

After the analysis of the various candidate technologies for the design of the interface agent, we have chosen to adopt AJAX to this aim. With AJAX (shorthand for Asynchronous JavaScript and XML)[2] in fact it is possible to create an agent hosted in the web browser that remains alive and active during the visualization of a web page. AJAX makes it is possible to go beyond the classic web request/response model and develop proactive interface agents. Conversely, other approaches have different drawbacks: Java applets[3] lack of facilities to be integrated with the web browser, since they are confined in a sandbox and cannot manipulate the data of the page in which they are executed. Flash[4] instead, lacks of a proper full-featured Open Source IDE due also to its commercial nature. More details on the actual implementation of the interface agent can be found in [8].

3.1 Direct Guidance Adaptive Functionality

Every interface agent provides personalized suggestions about items that a given user could find interesting, according to the navigation history of the user and of other site visitors. These suggested links are selected from the previously introduced traces. As shown in Fig.1, in fact, interface agents can access the database of stored traces through the *Suggestion Servlet*. The strategy adopted to select the most relevant traces to be presented to a given user considers the occurrence of trace generation and the success rate of the traces that were proposed.

---

[2] Garrett, J.J.: AJAX: A new approach to web applications. Technical report, Adaptive Path Essay (2005). http://www.adaptivepath.com/publications/essays/archives/000385.php

[3] http://www.sun.com/applets/

[4] http://www.adobe.com/products/flash/

A first element of this strategy is adopted when new users (or non authenticated ones) enter the site. In this case the user has no previous history (or it is not possible to correlate the user with his/her history), and the adopted strategy considers all stored traces, not considering the user which generated them. An additional information that is stored with traces is the number of times that the related trace was really selected and shown to a user and the number of times that the related link was actually exploited by a user. This kind of information allows to obtain an indication of the success rate of the suggestions that were chosen by the agent, and can be exploited to select the traces to be shown in the adaptive block. When the agent has an indication of the user which issued the request, it may focus the selection activity to those traces that compose the history of user's activities in the web site, in a web customization framework. In fact traces include an indication of the agent which generated them, and in turn agents are related to registered users. Moreover, in order to focus on a specific user's history but do not waste the chance to exploit other users' experiences, just two of the three available slots for emergent links are devoted to traces that were generated by that user and one is selected according to the strategy adopted for anonymous or new users. Because the time spent on a page had a strong correlation with explicit interest [9], the adopted strategy uses this information to refine the proposed suggestions.

An example of page adaptation refers to the adoption of a recurrent trace leading from the index of the web site to a content page, that is not directly connected to the index but that is visited very frequently. This kind of "vertical"[5] adaptive hyperlink is frequently observed in the prototypal implementation of the system, which is installed in a web site presenting information about a research laboratory as well as information on courses held by members of the group[6]. Since the number of students of some of these courses is very high, they frequently generate traces connecting the index to the page related to those courses. These traces represent effective shortcuts allowing to bypass intermediate index pages related to education activities and university courses. However, suggested links can also connect pages deep in the site structure. For example, a page related to a project might not be explicitly connected to another page describing a particular modeling approach adopted in that project, but a user might browse the web site and effectively discover that page, causing the generation by the system of a correspondent trace connecting the project and the modeling approach. This trace might not be extremely relevant to all visitors of the web site, due to the fact that this navigation path will probably be not very frequent, but if the visitor is a registered user the trace could be stored and suggested anyway, since a number of slots in the adaptive area of the page is reserved to user–generated emerging links.

This strategy for the exploitation of the gathered and stored traces, based on users' behaviours and movement in the web site environment, represents a very

---

[5] Here vertical is intended as describing the typical navigation path starting from an index page and going deeper into the web site.

[6] http://www.lintar.disco.unimib.it

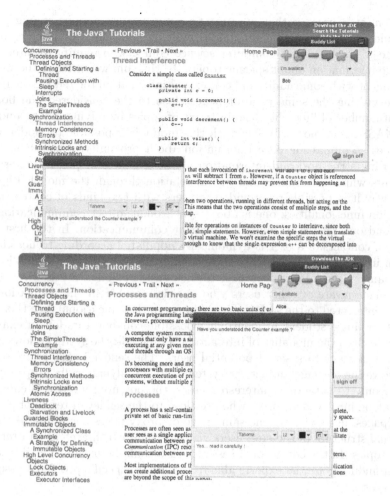

Fig. 3. An example of users interaction through the messanger component of the interface agent

simple way of exploiting this kind of information without requiring an off-line analysis of the logs generated by the web server.

3.2 Context-Aware User Interaction Functionality

In addition to more traditional functionalities usually provided in relation to web adapation, we provided also a functionality aiming at supporting interactions among users. In fact, we are aware about the current trends of web which is being always more considered not only as an information space, but also as a social space. Accordingly, we are focusing on a specific aspect of how the web could be considered as a social space, i.e. a *web in the small* vision. This vision is about considering not the support to sociality involving a large number of undifferentiated users, rather we aim at promoting interactions among people who could constitute small communities built dynamically around common interests, e.g., students of a computer science course who require to interact to exchange information about specific topics. To this aim we enriched the web interface agent with some additional contextual information related to other users who are visiting the same page or pages close to the considered one both in terms of number of links, but also in terms of topics by relying on the underlying MMASS agent model. In fact with this model it is possible to model different spaces encompassing both information about proximity of pages (in terms of hyperlink structure) and information about closeness of pages (in terms of arguments which are similar and put in relation through the modeled space). In this way it is possible to provide the users with two kinds of context-aware interaction functionalities: one is about synchronous direct communication and the second one relates to multicast indirect communication. In the first case, the list of contacts of a user is dynamically populated according to her current position in the space; in this case the system gather all the user agents located on the same page and on pages close to the considered one. In this way a single user is made aware of other users who are close to her in the navigation and could be interested to the same topics. Always in the educational case this could facilitate a single student in identifying possible collaborators for an exam. In the second case, the modality of interaction is different: the system allows a user to send a message to a set of potential users. The sender is not aware of who will receive the message, in fact the system is able to dynamically propagate the message only to potentially interested users: the potential interest is computed again taking into account users who are close to the sender in terms of position on the pages: users visiting the same page or proxy pages according to the hypertextual structure of the site; users visiting pages which are close in terms of related topics. In the educational case this also could be useful to facilitate students in finding potential experts able to answers to specific problems described in the message.

In order to test the above mentioned user interactions' functionalities, we designed a multi user Java Tutorial scenario. In this scenario, we integrated the pages related to Sun's Java Tutorial [7] with the MMASS system and an Ajax-based instant messenger. Three different MMASS layer has been defined: one layer represents the web 'physical' space, with the links between the pages, the other two layers represent the links between the pages by topics and by difficulty levels. Through the instant messaging interface, users are allowed to show the list of users who are viewing the same page of the tutorial or related pages and to communicate with them. The spaces are used both to diffuse the messages and to build the list of the neighbors.

In this scenario, we used ajax im[8] to build the messenger interface. ajax im is a browser-based instant messaging client written in JavaScript, employing AJAX to interact with the server. In particular, the client communicates with the server

---

[7] http://java.sun.com/docs/books/tutorial/
[8] http://www.unwieldy.net/ajaxim/

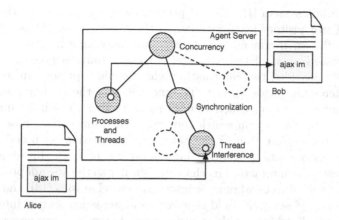

Fig. 4. The flow of information in the system in a case of user interaction

through JSON (JavaScript Object Notation) [9] messages. JSON is a lightweight data-interchange format, supported both by the client side JavaScript and the server-side Java (the language used by the Agent Server).

An example of users interaction is shown in Fig. 3. In this example, Alice, who is viewing the Java Tutorial "Thread Interference" page, needs some help on the topic. According to the current context, the Alice's interface shows the list of users who are proxy to her. In this case Bob, who is viewing a page related to "Processes and Threads", is considered to populate Alice's contact list. In fact, as shown in Fig. 4, Alice's and Bob's user agents are located in the 'physical' space just at a three links distance. Since the system is configured for building neighbors considering up to four links distant user agents, then Bob becomes part of the Alice's contact list. In this way, Alice can contact directly by using the IM interface to ask him some hints about the topic. The message is then delivered as a field by the MMASS Agent Server through the space to Bob, who is viewing the "Processes and Threads".

4   Related Work

There are several different approaches and relevant experiences in the area of web site adaptation, and some of them are also related to agent technologies. In particular, a relevant approach provides the adoption of information agents supporting users in their navigation [10]. These agents generally consider both the specific behaviour of the user and the actions of other visitors, and adopt multiple strategies for making recommendations (e.g. similarity, proximity, access frequency to specific documents). Instead in [11], Letizia is a user interface agent that assists a user browsing the Web by suggesting some links that are identified considering her past browsing behavior.

---

[9] http://www.json.org/, RDF 4627

The Footprints system [12] instead provides a site optimization through the metaphor of site visitors leaving traces in their navigation. These signals accumulate in the environment, generating awareness information on the most frequently visited areas of the web site. No user profile is needed, as visitors are essentially provided this information which could represent an indicator of the most interesting pages to visit. The metaphor of the structure of the web site as an environment on which visitors move in their search for information is very similar to the one on which the proposed framework is based, but we also propose the exploitation of the gathered information on users' paths for user specific customization. Another interesting recent work [13] represents an attempt to integrate interaction mechanisms similar to the one adopted by Footprints, often referred to as stigmergic interaction mechanisms [14], and cognitive agents. This line of research could represent an interesting way to integrate the proposed approach, which is able to generate and manage awareness contextual information, with higher level mechanisms and strategies of adaptation.

Other approaches provide instead the generation of index pages [15], that are pages containing links to other pages covering a specific topic. These pages, resulting from an analysis of access logs aimed at finding clusters grouping together pages related to a topic, are proposed to web masters in a computer-assisted site optimization scheme. A different approach provides the real-time generation of shortcut links [16], through a predictive model of web usage based on statistical techniques and the concept of expected saving of a shortcut, which considers both the probability that the generated link will be effectively used and the amount of effort saved (i.e. intermediate links to follow). In particular, this framework is very similar to the one proposed here with reference to the aims of the overall system, but it incorporates a complex algorithm for off-line analysis of logs, while the proposed approach provides a light and dynamic generation of most probable useful links and the storage of these proposals and high level information on site usage for a possible further off-line analysis.

A different approach to web site adaptation provides the adoption of a learning network to model the evolution of a distributed hypertext network, such as a web site [17]. Also in this case the adaptation provides a modification in the structure of a web site, and the concept of emergent link and the underlying mechanisms present a similarity with the learning rules adopted for that kind of learning network. However that approach also provides a deep modification in the architecture of the site and modifications in the web protocols, while this work aims at providing a solution that can be easily integrated with a traditional web architecture.

A final but significant note, regarding in general all adaptive web applications, must be mentioned: there is a tension between personalization and privacy. The former in fact, needs gathering information about the behaviors of web site visitors to provide the enhanced personalization functionalities, and this may contrast privacy concerns. However, some approaches tries to reconcile this tension [18], we aim at considering also these approaches to deal with this privacy issues in the future.

5 Conclusions and Future Developments

This paper introduced a heterogeneous multi-agent system, comprising an environment on which agents related to visitors move and possibly interact. This approach allows the gathering of a structured form of information on users' behaviours and activities in the web site. The concept of traces has been introduced in order to support an application exploiting information on users' browsing history for sake of web pages adaptation. The introduced framework and the application to web site adaptation have been designed and implemented, exploiting a platform supporting systems based on the MMASS model.

A campaign of tests aimed at evaluating the effectiveness of the adaptation approach, and also for sake of tuning the involved parameters (e.g. timings, number of presented possible emerging links) is currently under way. Some preliminary results [19] show that the suggested links are effectively used as shortcuts leading to interesting pages. A more comprehensive evaluation of the system will be based on user interviews in addition to quantitative data on the frequency of use of adaptive hyperlinks. The results of this evaluation might also lead to consider the modelling, design and implementation of more complex trace selection strategies, and thus a more complex behaviour for the interface agent.

A prototype supporting context-aware interaction among web site visitors through the introduced architecture was also implemented and it is currently being evaluated in a specific case study. In this framework, the environment related to the web site also supports the mutual perception of the agents situated in it and it also supports a form of interaction among them depending on their relative positions. The latter can be thus considered as a form of context–dependant interaction. A more thorough analysis of the possible applications of this approach can be found in [19].

Additional future works will be focused on the introduction and exploitation of higher level semantic information related to the site structure and contents, in order to design additional forms of adaptation also working on images and multimedia contents.

References

1. Perkowitz, M., Etzioni, O.: Adaptive Web Sites: an AI Challenge. In: Proceedings of the Fifteenth International Joint Conference on Artificial Intelligence (IJCAI 1997), pp. 16–23 (1997)
2. Weyns, D., Parunak, H.V.D., Michel, F., Holvoet, T., Ferber, J.: Environments for Multiagent Systems State-of-the-Art and Research Challenges. In: Weyns, D., Van Dyke Parunak, H., Michel, F. (eds.) E4MAS 2004. LNCS (LNAI), vol. 3374, pp. 1–47. Springer, Heidelberg (2005)
3. Weyns, D., Holvoet, T.: Model for Simultaneous Actions in Situated Multi-Agent Systems. In: Schillo, M., Klusch, M., Müller, J., Tianfield, H. (eds.) MATES 2003. LNCS (LNAI), vol. 2831, pp. 105–119. Springer, Heidelberg (2003)

4. Mamei, M., Zambonelli, F., Leonardi, L.: Co-Fields: Towards a Unifying Approach to the Engineering of Swarm Intelligent Systems. In: Petta, P., Tolksdorf, R., Zambonelli, F. (eds.) ESAW 2002. LNCS (LNAI), vol. 2577, pp. 68–81. Springer, Heidelberg (2003)
5. Hadeli, K., Valckenaers, P., Zamfirescu, C., Brussel, H.V., Germain, B.S., Hoelvoet, T., Steegmans, E.: Self-Organising in Multi-Agent Coordination and Control Using Stigmergy. In: Di Marzo Serugendo, G., Karageorgos, A., Rana, O.F., Zambonelli, F. (eds.) ESOA 2003. LNCS (LNAI), vol. 2977, pp. 105–123. Springer, Heidelberg (2004)
6. Bandini, S., Manzoni, S., Simone, C.: Dealing with Space in Multi–Agent Systems: a Model for Situated MAS. In: Proceedings of the first international joint conference on Autonomous agents and multiagent systems, pp. 1183–1190. ACM Press, New York (2002)
7. Bandini, S., Manzoni, S., Vizzari, G.: Towards a Platform for Multilayered Multi Agent Situated System Based Simulations: Focusing on Field Diffusion. Applied Artificial Intelligence 20(2-4), 327–351 (2006)
8. Bonomi, A., Sarini, M., Vizzari, G.: A heterogeneous multi-agent system for adaptive web applications. In: De Paoli, F., Di Stefano, A., Omicini, A., Santoro, C. (eds.) WOA 2006 – Grid, P2P and Self– Systems. CEUR Workshop Proceedings, vol. 204, pp. 66–75 (2006)
9. Claypool, M., Le, P., Waseda, M., Brown, D.: Implicit Interest Indicators. In: Intelligent User Interfaces, pp. 33–40 (2001)
10. Pazzani, M.J., Billsus, D.: Adaptive Web Site Agents. Autonomous Agents and Multi-Agent Systems 5(2), 205–218 (2002)
11. Lieberman, H.: Letizia: An agent that assists web browsing. In: Proceedings of the Fourteenth International Joint Conference on Artificial Intelligence, IJCAI 1995, pp. 924–929. Morgan Kaufmann, San Mateo (1995)
12. Wexelblat, A., Maes, P.: Footprints: History-Rich Tools for Information Foraging. In: Proceedings of the SIGCHI Conference on Human Factors in Computing Systems, pp. 270–277. ACM Press, New York (1999)
13. Ricci, A., Omicini, V.M., Gardelli, L., Oliva, E.: Cognitive Stigmergy: a Framework Based on Agents and Artifacts. In: Weyns, D., Van Dyke Parunak, H., Michel, F. (eds.) E4MAS 2006. LNCS (LNAI), vol. 4389, pp. 44–60. Springer, Heidelberg (2007)
14. Theraulaz, G., Bonabeau, E.: A Brief History of Stimergy. Artificial Life 5, 97–116 (1999)
15. Perkowitz, M., Etzioni, O.: Adaptive Web Sites. Communications of the ACM 43(8), 152–158 (2000)
16. Anderson, C.R., Domingos, P., Weld, D.S.: Adaptive Web Navigation for Wireless Devices. In: Proceedings of the Seventeenth International Joint Conference on Artificial Intelligence (IJCAI 2001), pp. 879–884 (2001)
17. Bollen, J., Heylighen, F.: Algorithms for the self-organisation of distributed, multi-user networks. possible application to the future world wide web. In: Trappl, R. (ed.) Proceedings of the 13th European Meeting on Cybernetics and Systems Research, Austrian Society for Cybernetic Studies, pp. 911–916 (1996)
18. Kobsa, A.: Privacy-Enhanced Web Personalization In The Adaptive Web. In: Brusilovsky, P., Kobsa, A., Nejdl, W. (eds.) Adaptive Web 2007. LNCS, vol. 4321, pp. 628–670. Springer, Heidelberg (2007)
19. Bandini, S., Sarini, M., Simone, C., Vizzari, G.: WWW in the Small: Towards Sustainable Adaptivity. World Wide Web Journal 10(4), 471–501 (2007)

Situating Cognitive Agents in GOLEM

Stefano Bromuri and Kostas Stathis

Department of Computer Science,
Royal Holloway, University of London,
Egham, Surrey, TW20 0EX, UK
{stefano,kostas}@cs.rhul.ac.uk

Abstract. We investigate the application of a logic-based framework representing an agent environment as a composite structure that evolves over time. Such a complex structure contains the interaction between two main classes of entities: *agents* and *objects*. Interactions between these entities are specified in term of *events* whose occurrence is governed by a set of *physical laws* specifying the possible evolutions of the agent environment, including how these evolutions are perceived by agents and affect objects and processes in the agent environment. We illustrate the work using GOLEM[1], a protype platform whose aim is to implement the framework to build situated cognitive agents in a distributed agent environment.

1 Introduction

It is widely acknowledged in the agent literature the need to model the agent environment in which agents are situated [1, 2, 3]. Early attempts to engineer MAS applications involved a MAS platform that implemented such an agent environment by enabling agents to interact with each other by sending and receiving messages [4, 5]. However, these early attempts in modeling the agent environment as a message transport system (or broker infrastructure) has been criticized to be inadequate for complex applications [6] requiring the treatment of an agent environment as a first class entity [7, 8].

1.1 Motivation

We are concerned with situating cognitive agents in an agent environment. Informally, by an "agent environment" we mean the virtualisation of an electronic or real environment inside an agent middleware, in such a way that agents deployed in the agent middleware can access virtual or real resources by means of standard interfaces and abstractions. As a running example, we consider the electronic environment of a virtual world called Packet-World [9]. This example has been proposed to evaluate the behaviour of Multi-Agent Systems (MAS) in which agents are explicitly situated in an environment. As shown in Fig. 1,

---

[1] GOLEM stands for **G**eneralised **O**nto-**L**ogical **E**nvironment for **M**ulti-agent systems.

D. Weyns, S.A. Brueckner, and Y. Demazeau (Eds.): EEMMAS 2007, LNAI 5049, pp. 115–134, 2008.
© Springer-Verlag Berlin Heidelberg 2008

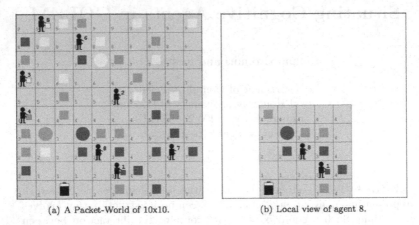

(a) A Packet-World of 10x10.   (b) Local view of agent 8.

Fig. 1. The Packet-World [9]

the basic setup of the Packet-World consists of a number of differently coloured packets inside a rectangular grid, whose destination is a circle with the same colour. Each agent living in the Packet-World has a battery that discharges as the agent moves in different locations in the grid. The battery can be recharged using a battery charger. This charger emits a gradient whose value is larger if the agent is far away from the charger and smaller if the agent is closer to the charger. To locate the battery charger an agent must follow the direction of decreasing gradient values. The agents have the goal to bring the packets to the collection points and can communicate with other agents to create collaborations or to ask information about the position of the collection points.

Shortcomings of Previous Work. In an attempt to situate cognitive agents built according to the KGP model of agency [10] we have developed in previous work the PROSOCS platform [11]. The main assumption behind PROSOCS is that an agent must have a logical mind [12] that is situated in the distributed environment of network via a body [11]. For the agent's mind PROSOCS supported a developer with the generic reasoning capabilities of KGP, which had to be programmed to allow an agent to act in the environment it was situated. For example, in the context of the Packet World, a rule of the form:

```
[ self(Picker),
  observed(see(packet(P, Colour, Position)), T),
  my_position(MyPosition),
  is_close(P, Position, MyPosition),
  destination_for(Colour, Dest)
] implies
[ assume_happens_after_once(do(Picker, pick(P)), T)].
```

would make a picker agent to perform a pick action, provided the agent has observed a packet that is close to its position and the agent knows the destination for packets of this colour. In the rest of this paper, we will refer to agents that are capable of processing this kind of rules as cognitive agents. To support this basic kind of cognition PROSOCS relied upon the CIFF proof-procedure (see [13] for details). CIFF enabled KGP agents to react and plan within the environment in which they were situated, including support for temporal reasoning. A summary of the reasoning capabilities of KGP agents and their computational characteristics, as implemented in PROSOCS, are described in [14].

PROSOCS also provided the middleware for agents to be deployed and communicate with each other by sending and receiving messages via their body. Two implementations of the middleware were developed: (a) one built on top of the JXTA peer-to-peer infrastructure and (b) another based on the TuCSON blackboard-based infrastructure. What characterised PROSOCS from other platforms of its time was that generic sensor and effector components were linked to an agent's body to enable the agent send and receive messages, including support with physical interactions between agents and objects. Experimentation with the platform [15] showed that although the development of a reusable middleware to enable communicative interaction was generally straightforward, providing general rules for the interaction between agents and objects for different applications was more a limitation than a strength. The issue here was that different applications imposed different requirements on how agents and objects need to be manipulated and coordinated. A more acceptable solution was to allow the developer to specify the low-level physical interaction for different applications, as if this developer designed the agent environment and programmed its middleware to serve the purpose of the application.

Contribution, Scope, and Significance. This paper develops a logic-based framework representing an agent environment as a composite structure that evolves over time. Such a complex structure contains the interaction between two main classes of entities: agents and objects. Interactions between these entities are specified in term of events whose occurrence is governed by a set of physical laws specifying the possible evolutions of the agent environment, including how these evolutions are perceived by agents and affect objects and other agents in the environment. The emphasis of the work is to specify the representation of the agent environment declaratively, in a logic-based way, so that the programming of the agent environment is easy to understand and change. To specify what is perceived in the agent environment we use of the notion of *affordances*, to enable cognitive agents to perceive the external states of objects and other agents in order to interact with them. Through affordances a designer specifies what is possible in the agent environment at a level that can be processed directly by cognitive agents. We show how to turn the overall representation from a specification to an implementation that we call GOLEM, which is a general and reusable platform across applications and whose features are examplified by the Packet World simulation in the context of this paper. The significance of the implemented system is that it can support complex applications through the deployment of cognitive agents situated in a distributed environment over a network.

1.2   Organisation

Section 2 introduces the general architecture of GOLEM, following the ideas presented in [16]. Section 3 shows how to represent interaction in a GOLEM agent environment on top of an extension of the *Event Calculus* based on objects [17], including any implementation issues. Section 4 places our research in the context of existing literature and compares it to related work. We summarise our effort in Section 5 where we also chart out directions for future work.

2   Description of Environment Affordances

We propose to investigate the design of the agent environment using the concept of *affordances*. This concept is normally taken to describe "all the action possibilities latent in the environment, objectively measurable, and independent of an agent's ability to recognise those possibilities" [18]. As with research in HCI [19], we rely upon *perceived affordances* where entities of an environment "suggest" to agents (whether artificial or human) how they should interact with them. In other words, we do not expect our agents to learn how to interact with an object by randomly taking actions [20] according to previous experience[21]. Instead, we propose an agent's environment to be designed in advance, assuming a particular ontology, very much like an interactive system, with the aim to treat cognitive agents like we treat users. This does not prevent an agent from learning how to use the object, because knowing the interface of the object, the agent could just try to explore the functionality by observing an action's effect on the agent environment.

We answer what the developer needs to design by relying on the conceptual framework described in [16]. This defines an agent environment as a *container* where *agents* interact with other agents and *objects* using *sensors* and *effectors*. We expand this preliminary work by providing a framework stating how to specify logically these entities and their interaction using *events*. Events describe what happens in the agent environment as a result of actions being executed by effectors. According to the happening of an event the agent environment notifies those sensors capable of perceiving the action of the event. For the purposes of this paper we distinguish between three types of acts embedded in an event: *speech acts* - to allow agents to communicate with other agents and users; *sensing acts* - to allow an agent to perceive the environment actively; and *physical acts* - to allow the agent to interact with other entities, in particular objects, but also agents as well. To simulate these acts we will rely upon different kinds of sensors and effectors the agent should possess to capture the interaction in the agent environment. Our primary concern is to provide a computable specification of the interaction rather than a formal definition; the latter is beyond the scope of this paper.

2.1   Objects

GOLEM uses a particular architecture for objects shown in Fig. 2. As part of this architecture the object is described in terms of the perceived affordances.

To present these perceived affordances we use the object-based notation used by C-logic [22], a formalism that allows the description of complex objects. A description of the form:

```
packet: p1[ colour ⇒ red,
            methods ⇒ {pick, drop, hit},
            position ⇒ square:sq1,
            receptors ⇒ { receptor:r1 },
            emitters ⇒ { emitter:em1 }
          ]
```

states that p1 is a complex term of class packet, with a functional attribute describing that the colour is red, a multi-valued attribute methods stating that the actions afforded by the object the term represents are pick, drop, and hit, a functional attribute asserting that the position of the packet is in square sq1, a multi-valued attribute receptors containing one receptor sensor r1, and a multi-valued attribute emitters containing one emmiter effector em1. Some of the attribute values are complex terms themselves, for example, sq1 is a complex term containing information such as the coordinates of the packet in the Packet-World grid. The C-logic syntax to represent the perceived affordances of an object as a complex term has a first-order logic translation, as we can see for a packet object below:

is_a(p1, packet).	method_of(p1, hit).	attribute(packet, colour, single).
colour(p1, red).	position(p1, sq1).	attribute(packet, method, multi).
method_of(p1, pick).	receptor_of(p1, r1).	attribute(packet, receptors, multi).
method_of(p1, drop).	emitter_of(p1, em1).	attribute(packet, emitters, multi).

In this way, we represent all the related information that is perceived of an object, including its relationship with other entities in the agent environment.

The idea behind having receptor sensors for an object is that they receive notifications from the agent environment as a results of actions executed on that object. In general, the receptor sensor of an object can only capture notifications of *physical acts* performed on the object by entities in the agent environment

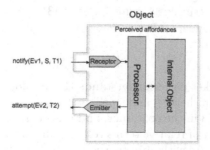

Fig. 2. A GOLEM object whose receptor S is receiving a notification of an event Ev1 at time T1 and whose emitter attempts to make event Ev2 happen at time T2

that are capable of executing these actions. To represent events that receptors can capture we use complex terms too. The term:

do:e1 [actor ⇒ agent:ag1 [effector ⇒ ef1], act ⇒ hit, object ⇒ packet:p1]

describes an event e1 where the effector ef1 of agent ag1 performs a physical act hit on packet p1. Such an event will be captured by the receptor of the object via notification sent to the object by the environment. Then the object's *processor* will call a *method* of the *internal object*. The general idea behind the internal object is that it wraps in it a resource of the external environment, thus hiding from the agents the complexity of interfacing with the external resource. In other words the object abstraction can be a virtual entity, as for objects in Packet World, or a virtualisation of an external resource of the external real environment. The method call will typically result in the output of the call transmitted as another event via the object's *emitter* effector. As before, emitted events are complex terms. To simulate a packet's reaction to the physical act represented by e1, the event description:

hearing:e2 [emitter ⇒ packet:p1 [effector ⇒ em1], sound ⇒ packet_hit]

showing the kind of event emitted by the object. Events may be emitted by the processor also upon conditions determined entirely upon the state of the internal object and not necessarily as a reaction to an external trigger. The details we omit as these events can be described similarly, the only part that changes is the type and content of the event.

2.2   Cognitive Agents

GOLEM agents are organised as an extension of the PROSOCS anthropomorphic architecture of an agent [11], shown in Fig. 3. In this architecture an agent has a *body* whose affordances can be perceived by other agents. A description of the form:

picker: ag1[understands ⇒ ontology:o1,
           sensors ⇒ {sight:s1, hearing:s2, smell:s3},
           effectors ⇒ {speak:ef1, arm:ef2, arm:ef3},
           position ⇒ square:sq3,
           activity ⇒ idle
        ]

states that ag1 is a packet picker understands the ontology o1 (of packet world), has sensors of class sight, hearing and smell, and effectors of class speak and arm, its position is square sq3 in the container, and it is currently idle. The position of the agent describes a set of relative terms relating the agent with other entities in the agent environment. As with objects, the effectors of an agent attempt to execute physical actions in the agent environment. Similarly, agent sensors respond to event notifications by the agent environment. These notifications enable an agent's sensors to *passively* observe the agent environment [10]. Alternatively, sensors actively observe the agent environment through sensing acts, giving rise to active observations [10]. Active observation is expressed as a sensing act that attempts to perceive certain properties of the agent environment. For example, the term below shows how agent **ag1** focuses on a specific part of the agent environment:

sensing:e3 [actor⇒ ag1[sensor⇒ s1], act ⇒ look, focus ⇒ p1[color⇒ X]]

by looking with sensor **s1** to find the colour of packet **p1**, denoted by the variable X. The outcome of such a request will result in an asynchronous call to the agent environment to return the variable substitution, as we will see later in section 3.2.

Apart from situating the agent in the agent environment, the body contains a *brain* to connect the various sensors attached to it. The brain also provides an interface to the *mind*, a cognitive component giving the agent the ability to reason logically and make decisions. This mind-brain separation allows different cognitive models of agency to be interfaced to the body, thus making the architecture more flexible. From an agent environment perspective, a user can use an agent's body to access the electronic environment, in which case the brain of the agent provides simply a convenient interface for the user to select actions using his own mind.

2.3   Containers

An agent environment in GOLEM is a first class entity referred to as a set of *containers*. As shown in Figure 4 the container has a *state* that acts as a directory of all the present agents and objects in it, including information about their topology and configuration. Interactions between the entities of an agent environment are governed by a set of *physical laws*. These laws specify the

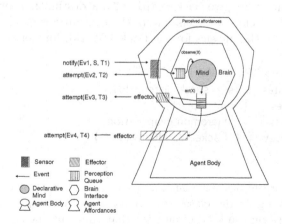

Fig. 3. The anthropomorphic agent architecture in GOLEM (adapted from [11])

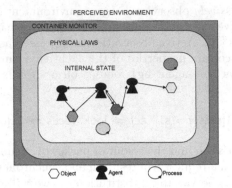

Fig. 4. A GOLEM Container

possible evolutions of the container, including how these evolutions are perceived by agents and affect objects and processes in the environment.

As with agents and objects, the container has its own perceived affordances that include the ways in which an agent can configure itself (or other basic, object, agent, and containers) to became part of the container's internal state. For example the description:

container:c1[address ⇒ "container://one@134.219.7.1:13000",
            laws ⇒ physics:pw1,
            type ⇒ open,
            entities ⇒ {agent:ag1, packet:p1, packet:p2, destination:d1, battery:b1}
            ]

describes a container whose address is container://one@134.219.7.1:13000, its laws are represented by another object pw1 of class physics, it is an open container in that any agent can enter it, and whose internal state contains five entities, one agent (ag1), two packets (p1, p2), a destination for packets (d1), and a battery (b1). Before an agent enters the container it can inspect the laws attribute containing the physics for the Packet-World, further specified as:

physics:pw1[name ⇒ "PacketWorld"
            mediates ⇒ {see, speak, listen, do},
            entities ⇒ {agent, object},
            processes ⇒ {pheromon_evaporation},
            ontology ⇒ {"PacketWorldOntology"}
            ]

By examining a physics term such as pw1 above, an agent can perceive the container by looking at the classes of events a container mediates, and other information regarding the kind of entities that the container contains, and the ontology specifying the features of these entities.

3   Interactions in a GOLEM Environment

The main task of our work has been to describe an agent environment in a form that is usable by the cognitive agents situated in it. So far we have discussed how a domain application can be described in terms of the perceived objects and agent bodies that are part of a container that acts as the agent environment. We have also shown how such a container can be represented as a complex term. In this section, we show how to describe the evolution of a container as an event calculus theory extended with a part that enables objects and agents to interact. We close the discussion with a summary of our implementation.

3.1   The Agent Environment and Its Evolution

To represent how phenomena change the state of a GOLEM container we use the object-based event calculus (OEC) described by Kesim and Sergot in [17]. The OEC extends the data model of the original event calculus with one that describes how instances of complex terms evolve over time. This framework allows the developer of a GOLEM application to specify the effects of actions to/from objects and agents as events. A subset of the clauses describing the OEC is given in Fig. 5.

Clauses C1-C2 provide the basic formulation of OEC deriving how the value of an attribute for a complex term holds at a specific time. Clause C3 describes how to represent derived attributes of objects treated as method calls computed by means of a solve_at/2 meta-interpreter as specified in [23]. C4-C5 support a monotonic inheritance of attributes names for a class limited to the subset relation. As C1-C2 describe what holds at a specific time, C6-C7 determine how to derive the instance of a class at a specific time. The effects of an event on a class is given by assignment assertions; the clause C8 states how any new instance of a class becomes a new instance of the super-classes. Finally, deletion of objects is catered for by clauses C9-C11. C9 deletes single valued attributes that have been updated, while C10-C11 delete objects and dangling references.

To describe how the affordances in the agent environment evolves as a result of events happening in it we need to define domain specific **initiates** and **terminates** clauses. For example, to describe an agent moving in the Packet-World grid, we write:

initiates(E, picker, A, position, Pos, T) ←
        do:E [actor ⇒ A, act ⇒ move:M [destination⇒ Pos]].

To complete with describing the effects of the event we also need to terminate the attribute holding the old position of the agent, in this case, this is handled by the general rule described in clause C9.

3.2   Representation of Interaction

Given the OEC to support the evolution of the agent environment's state we use on top of it a set of logic programs that work together with the event calculus,

(C1) holds_at(Id, Class, Attr, Val, T)←
        happens(E, Ti), Ti ≤ T,
        initiates(E, Id, Class, Attr, Val),
        not broken(Id, Class, Attr, Val, Ti, T).
(C2) broken(Id, Class, Attr, Val, Ti, Tn)←
        happens(E, Tj), Ti < Tj ≤Tn,
        terminates(E, Id, Class, Attr, Val).

(C3) holds_at(Id, Class, Attr, Val, T)←
        method(Class, Id, Attr, Val, Body),
        solve_at(Body, T).

(C4) attribute_of(Class, X, Type)←
        attribute(Class, X, Type).
(C5) attribute_of(Sub, X, Type)←
        is_a(Sub, Class),
        attribute_of(Class, X, Type).

(C6) instance_of(Id, Class, T)←
        happens(E, Ti), Ti ≤ T,
        assigns(E, Id, Class),
        not removed(Id, Class, Ti, T).
(C7) removed(Id, Class, Ti, Tn)←
        happens(E, Tj), Ti < Tj ≤ Tn,
        destroys(E, Id).

(C8) assigns(E, Id, Class)←
        is_a(Sub, Class),
        assigns(E, Id, Sub).

(C9) terminates(E, Id, Class, Attr, _)←
        attribute_of(Class, Attr, single),
        initiates(E, Id, Class, Attr, _).

(C10) terminates(E, Id, _, Attr, _)←
        destroys(E, Id).
(C11) terminates(E, Id, _, Attr, IdVal)←
        destroys(E, IdVal).

Fig. 5. A subset of the *Object-based Event Calculus* from [17]

to represent the interactions in a GOLEM environment. In what follows, we are presenting extracts of our formulation, to exemplify the approach.

Action Execution. As we discussed in section 2, the execution of actions in GOLEM are represented as attempts. Attempts are the same as what Ferber [24] calls influences, we prefer the use of attempt because it captures better our intention, namely the action that is about to occur as an event in the agent environment. Attempts are described by assertions of events at a specific time. We keep the description of events separately from attempts. Suppose for instance that an agent (ag1) is attempting to make a move to square sq3 at time 120. In GOLEM this will be represented by an attempt as shown below:

attempt(e14, 120).
do:e14 [actor ⇒ ag1, act ⇒ move:m1 [destination⇒ sq3]].

Such an attempt causes the event of moving to happen, provided the event described in the attempt is possible according to the physics of the agent environment. There are two ways we propose to define this:

(H1) happens(Event, T)←
        attempt(Event, T),
        possible(Event, T).

(H2) happens(Event, T)←
        attempt(Event, T),
        not impossible(Event, T).

Definition H1 suggests that we must describe for every agent environment when an event is possible at a specific time. Often, as the number of events that happen is large, H2 suggests that it would be easier if we described what events are impossible at a specific time. Depending on the application, the developer of an agent environment can choose between H1 or H2. In the Packet-World, for example, we have found easier to describe what is impossible rather than what is possible, and rely upon the use of negation-as-failure to handle what is possible by default. As an example of an impossible event description, consider how to define what is impossible when an agent attempts to move to a square in the grid that is occupied already:

impossible(E, T)←
        do:E [actor ⇒ A, act ⇒ move:M [destination⇒ Pos]],
        holds_at(Pos, square, status, occupied, T).

We need to define similarly additional impossible/2 constraints of this kind to deal with situations where an agent is trying to move outside the grid, for example. Impossibility constraints can also be used to handle more than one event attempted at the same time, thus making the approach quite expressive.

Using the definition H1, a developer has also the option to combine possible/impossible constraints if the following general rule is added:

possible(E,T)← not impossible(E,T).

This new definition makes H1 more general, since the developer is now in a position to specify both domain specific rules of both what is possible or what is impossible, case by case, thus allowing representations that are more expressive.

Passive Perceptions. When an event happens, it is notified instantaneously to all types of sensors that are capable of detecting it. Put another way, certain types of sensors will be filtering out specific kind of perceptions. This fact is reflected in the definition of event notification that takes into consideration the type of event that happens. For passive perceptions we need to check that the event does not contain a sensing action, so the notification is defined as:

notify(E, S, T) ←
    happens(E, T),
    not sensing(E),
    detectable(E,S,T)
    not interfered(E, S, T).

We assume that event types contain, as part of their description, the sensor types that can detect it. We use the notion of *detectable* as possibility for percepts. For the packet world we define it as:

detectable(E,S,T) ←
      E [is_detected_by ⇒ SensorClass],
    instance_of(S, SensorClass, T),
    holds_at(S, SensorClass, status, open, T).

The definition of notify/3 also checks that when an event is notified it is not interfered by an obstacle. Interference is a domain specific constraint that for some applications may remain undefined. To exemplify it in the Packet-World, we try simulate the fact that some events will not be possible to perceive because there is an entitiy (object or agent) that hides its occurrence. To do this we define the following rule:

interfered(E, S, T) ←
    E [coordinates ⇒ XYe],
    instance_of(S, sight, T),
    holds_at(A, picker, sensor_of, S, T),
    holds_at(A, picker, coordinates, XYa, T),
    holds_at(Entity, entity, coordinates, XYent, T),
    in_between(XYent, XYa, XYe).

In other words, a notification is interfered only when there is an entity between the position of the agent and the location in which the event happened.

Active Perceptions. Agents in GOLEM are enabled to actively perceive objects in the agent environment. Such perceptions assume that the agent has attempted to perform a sensing act with a specific focus query for the object. This is initiated by an attempt of an sensing act with a particular focus. We specify this as:

perceive(E, S, T) ←
    happens(E, T),
    sensing(E),
    detectable(E, S, T),
    E [sensor_of⇒ S, focus⇒ Focus],
    solve_at(Focus, T).

The call to solve_at is assumed to be an asynchronous call to the agent environment which returns the variable substitutions to the Focus, if any. It is important to note that the time T is not instantiated by the agent who is trying to perceive, but by the agent environment who receives the call.

3.3   Implementation Issues

We have implemented GOLEM according to the reference model of Fig. 6. In this figure actions coming from containers, agents, objects, or internal *Processes*, are collected by an *Attempts* module. Attempts of action are mediated by a *Physics* component ensuring that these actions are possible before they happen as events in the state. The physics module is in charge to mediate the three kind of events described in section 2. As a consequence, physics acts, speech acts and sensing acts are mediated before taking place in the agent environment, or, in other words, the agent environment allows to define laws of interaction for these three kind of events. The physics also describe how events cause changes

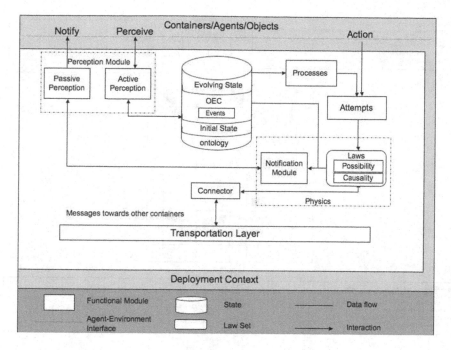

Fig. 6. The GOLEM Reference Model

to the perceivable state of the agent environment. Once an event has happened, it is directed by the notification module to the *Passive Perception* module that notifies the sensors of agents and objects.

Active perceptions of agents on objects are handled by the *Active Perception* module that accesses the state of the agent environment to support the requested perceptions. Containers are recursively deployed as objects, so that the agents in the agent environment can access a container from another container. The use of a *Connector* component allows the agent environment to forward/receive messages to/from other containers via the transportation layer.

We have implemented our framework according to the above reference model using tuProlog [25] and Java. Using this combination we use Java to implement Agents, Objects and the Container. The container has inside a Physics component that uses tuProlog to define the logic-based agent environment. To implement the specification we need to slightly change some of the rules specified earlier. For example, the rule H1 is rewritten so that attempts become agent environment calls that assert event descriptions in the state of the agent environment:

attempt(Event, T):- not impossible(Event, T), add(happens(Event, T)).

Agents, objects, containers, or internal processes will instantiate the Event at the time of the call, while the time T is instantiated by the agent environment. add/2 asserts separately the happening of the event from the event's description.

Other features of the tuProlog/Java combination include allowing a developer to support asynchronous communication and primitives to register Java objects

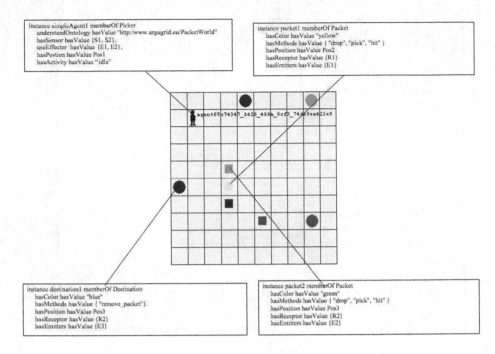

Fig. 7. A container node with Packet World inside

inside a Prolog context, using the Java Reflection API [26]. We use these facilities to define declaratively how to deploy agents, objects, agent sensors and services to create the GOLEM distributed environment. Defining the rules of the agent environment using a Prolog theory is particularly helpful when a developer needs to change the interaction inside a container. With the GOLEM's toolset, we allow a platform administrator to open a container, inspect it, and subsequently change the physical laws governing it. There are a number of issues that we have to take into consideration here, in particular, ensuring consistency of the physics and the atomicity of action execution. A detailed discussion of these issues, however, is beyond the scope of this paper.

To allow a container's affordances to be discovered within a distributed environment, we translate our complex terms describing a GOLEM container to WSMO [27] ontologies and concepts. This mapping is straightforward as there is a syntactic link between OEC and F-logic[28] upon which WSMO relies. For example, a picker agent description in GOLEM can be translated to a WSMO concept as follows:

```
concept Picker subConceptOf Agent
    UnderstandOntology ofType (1 1)_iri
    hasSensors ofType Sensor
    useEffectors ofType Effector
    hasPosition ofType Square
    hasActivity ofType (1 1)_string
```

The motivation behind the use of WSMO is to use it as a standard for allowing agents from other platforms to discover and use resources of GOLEM. A cognitive agent that looks at the affordances of an entity, knows immediately the messages to interact with the entity, as well as its observable properties. Fig. 7 shows an example of execution where GOLEM entities and their affordances are described in WSMO.

4 Related Work

There is a growing research and development effort on how to model situated multi-agent systems, see [6] for a discussion. Our work is inspired by the *influence-reaction* model by Ferber and Müller [2] and its extensions as formalised by the work of Weyns and Holvoet [29]. In our framework influences are represented as attempts of events and reactions as environment notifications. However, in this work we are not concerned with synchronisation issues as [2] and [29] but rather with how to specify interaction in computational logic, thus providing executable specifications of agent environments. Despite an apparent similarity of our container with the description of the agent environment in [8], at a closer look the two approaches rely upon different reference models.

Our representation of active perception relates naturally to the work of Weyns et al [30] who divide an agent's perception in three parts: *sensing, interpreting* and *filtering*. Our work is really about the first part, namely, the mapping of the external environment to a symbolic representation suitable for the agent using what we called *sensing* acts. As in Weyns et al, the agent can select a set of *foci* that enables an agent to direct its perception and perceive only specific types of information, simulating a kind of artificial sight for agents. The interpretation part of the perception mechanism of Weyns et al maps the representation of the agent environment in the actual percept of the agent. These percepts have the function to describe the sensed agent environment in the language understood by the agent. In our approach, we have tried to minimize interpretation and standardize it to be logical terms. We have left filtering outside the framework as this part concerns the way sensors work, which is beyond the scope of this work.

Vizzari in [31] models the concept of environment as a multi-layer multi-agent situated system (MMASS). The environment is composed by a set of graphs interconnected by interfaces, forming thus a multilayered structure with some interfaces among layers. Every layer, and thus every graph, may represent a specific aspect of agents' environment: for instance one of them may represent an abstraction of agents' physical environment, while other ones may be related to other conceptual topologies such as organization charts or dependency graphs. In GOLEM, instead of defining layers, we define rules. Different sets of rules can then describe different layers of the agent environment. What we have presented here is only a framework for the physical interaction where attempts for action result in events, which for Vizzari generate fields, signals capable to diffuse through the layers, according to the interfaces between these layers. In addition, signals in Vizzari's framework can be perceived by agents according to specific rules of perception based on functions such as *diffusion, composition* and *comparison*. For us diffusion is notification, composition is complex term creation, while comparison is our use of having different sensors capturing different types of events.

The coordination artifact theory [32] defines as an abstract model that takes inspiration from concrete objects supporting the interaction of physical entities. Agents perform their activities in the environment helped by coordination artifacts, generally passive entities that defines a usage interface, a set of operating instruction and a coordination behaviour specification. For an agent to understand how to interact with an artifact one has to understand the interfaces of that artifact. GOLEM follows the TuCSoN idea that the infrastructure must be programmable. While coordination artifacts for agent interaction take inspiration from actual concrete objects of the real world, our approach brings the metaphor of agent environment to the extreme by taking into account spatio-temporal features. These features are represented (possibly in an explicit way) and have an influence on perception, interaction and as a result on agent behaviour.

A more recent technology supporting the coordination artifact model is called CartAgO, proposed by Ricci et al in [33], which is in the process of being integrated with Jason [34]. This technology proposes a model of perception and actions that is similar to the one proposed by Weyns et al in [30]: Agents can have sensors that perceive well-defined kind of perceptions and filter them at runtime. The notion of *workspaces* contain artifacts and agents, used also to define the topology of the working environment. Through workspaces it is possible to model a notion of locality, in terms of the artifacts that an agent can use and observe.

There are many similarities of GOLEM with CArtAgO: they both use sensors and effectors for agents, as PROSOCS did [11], CArtAgO workspaces correspond to GOLEM containers, and as in CArtAgO we distinguish between speech acts, physical acts, and sensing acts. Moreover the Jason integration offers the possibility to defines user defined agent environments specifying pre-conditions, post-conditions and effects of the action in the environment, as well as offering a language to define BDI agents acting in the agent environment. However, there are many differences as well, the most important being that in GOLEM we keep the rules of the physical environment in the container, not in the artifacts, and we expect the implementation to enforce them in a distributed manner. Finally, instead of manuals keeping operating instructions for artifacts GOLEM uses affordances.

Affordances are also strongly related with the work reported by Platon et al. in [35], [36], and [37]. As in PROSOCS, this work puts forward the use of an *agent soft body* which has a state that is public and available to an observer. The act of observing such a state in the Platon et al. framework is based on the notion of *oversensing* [35] and *overhearing* [36]. In our work the oversensing/overhearing acts are modelled as active perception on the affordances of environment entities. Other differences with the Platon et al. work are that GOLEM affordances express more than a simple state, they express also the interaction interface of both agents and objects, rather than only agents.

5 Conclusions

We have presented a logic-based framework representing an agent environment as a composite structure that evolves over time. Such a complex structure contains *agents* and *objects* in *containers*, whose interaction is specified in term of *events*. Occurrence of events is governed by a set of *physical laws* specifying the possible evolutions of the environment, including how these evolutions are perceived by agents and affect objects and processes in the environment.

We have implemented the framework in GOLEM, a prototype platform exemplified here using the Packet-World. The benefits of our approach can be summarised as follows. By using a declarative approach we define the rules that constrain the interactions in an agent environment and then update them at run time, without the need to restart the application (an important issue if we want to incrementally introduce patches to an application environment). We do not need to translate the perceptions from the environment to the mind of the agent as the agent environment and mind of an agent use the same representation language, thus making the situating of cognitive agents easier. By introducing the idea of affordances and wrapping external resources in objects we hide the complexity of how an agent can interact with the external world; knowing the affordances of an object the agent has the interface of that object standardised by the use of ontologies. Finally, by keeping a history of events we can easily playback interactions and therefore debug an application through a log, in the case that the agent environment models a simulation that does not involve external resources, wrapped in the object abstraction.

We are currently studying the benefits of our approach in the ArguGRID project [38], where the mind of the agent is defined using argumentation [39]. Now interaction with objects is interaction of agents and/or users with semantic web-services defined in WSMO. As part of this work we are seeking to build upon the lemma generation mechanism discussed in [23] to improve the scalability of the GOLEM's approach.

Acknowledgments

This work was partially supported by the IST-FP6-035200 ArguGRID project. We would like to thank Danny Weyns and the anonymous reviewers for their comments in a previous version of this paper.

References

[1] Russell, S., Norvig, P.: Artificial Intelligence: A Modern Approach, 2nd edn. Pearson Education (2002)
[2] Ferber, J.: Multi-Agent Systems. Addison-Wesley, Harlow (1999)
[3] Kowalski, R.A.: Reconciling Logic and Objects. In: 6th Mexican Intl. Conference on Computer Science (ENC), IEEE Computer Society Press, Los Alamitos (2005)

[4] JADE: Java Agent DEvelopment framework Home Page:
http://jade.tilab.com

[5] Nwana, H.S., Ndumu, D.T., Lee, L.C., Collis, J.C.: ZEUS: A Toolkit for Building Distributed Multiagent Systems. Applied Artificial Intelligence 13(1-2), 129–185 (1999)

[6] Weyns, D., Parunak, H.V.D., Michel, F., Holvoet, T., Ferber, J.: Environments for Multiagent Systems State-of-the-Art and Research Challenges. In: Weyns, D., Van Dyke Parunak, H., Michel, F. (eds.) E4MAS 2004. LNCS (LNAI), vol. 3374, pp. 1–47. Springer, Heidelberg (2005)

[7] Odell, J., Parunak, H.V.D., Fleischer, M., Brueckner, S.: Modeling Agents and their Environment: The Physical Environment. Journal of Object Technology 2(2), 43–51 (2003)

[8] Weyns, D., Omicini, A., Odell, J.: Environment as a first class abstraction in multiagent systems. Autonomous Agents and Multi-Agent Systems 14(1), 5–30 (2007)

[9] Weyns, D., Helleboogh, A., Holvoet, T.: The Packet-World: a Test Bed for Investigating Situated Multi-Agent Systems. In: Software Agent-Based Applications, Platforms and Development Kits. Whitestein Series in Software Agent Technology (2005)

[10] Kakas, A.C., Mancarella, P., Sadri, F., Stathis, K., Toni, F.: The KGP model of Agency. In: Proceedings of the 16th European Conference of Artificial Intelligence, Valencia, pp. 33–37 (2004)

[11] Stathis, K., Kakas, A.C., Lu, W., Demetriou, N., Endriss, U., Bracciali, A.: PROSOCS: a platform for programming software agents in computational logic. In: Müller, J., Petta, P. (eds.) Proceedings of the 4th Intl. Symposium From Agent Theory to Agent Implementation (AT2AI-4), Vienna, April 13-16, pp. 523–528 (2004)

[12] Bracciali, A., Demetriou, N., Endriss, U., Kakas, A., Lu, W., Stathis, K.: Crafting the Mind of a PROSOCS Agent. Applied Artificial Intelligence 20(4-5), 105–131 (2006)

[13] Endriss, U., Mancarella, P., Sadri, F., Terreni, G., Toni, F.: Abductive Logic Programming with CIFF: System Description. In: Alferes, J.J., Leite, J.A. (eds.) JELIA 2004. LNCS (LNAI), vol. 3229, pp. 680–684. Springer, Heidelberg (2004)

[14] Bracciali, A., Demetriou, N., Endriss, U., Kakas, A.C., Lu, W., Mancarella, P., Sadri, F., Stathis, K., Terreni, G., Toni, F.: The KGP Model of Agency for Global Computing: Computational Model and Prototype Implementation. In: Priami, C., Quaglia, P. (eds.) GC 2004. LNCS, vol. 3267, pp. 340–367. Springer, Heidelberg (2005)

[15] Stathis, K., Toni, F.: Ambient Intelligence using KGP Agents. In: Markopoulos, P., Eggen, B., Aarts, E., Crowley, J.L. (eds.) EUSAI 2004. LNCS, vol. 3295, pp. 351–362. Springer, Heidelberg (2004)

[16] Stathis, K., Kafetzoglou, S., Papavasilliou, S., Bromuri, S.: Sensor Network Grids: Agent Environments combined with QoS in Wireless Sensor Networks. In: The 3rd Intl. Conference on Autonomic and Autonomous Systems (ICAS 2007) (June 2007)

[17] Kesim, F.N., Sergot, M.: A Logic Programming Framework for Modeling Temporal Objects. IEEE Transactions on Knowledge and Data Engineering 8(5), 724–741 (1996)

[18] Gibson, J.J.: The Ecological Approach to Visual Perception. Lawrence Erlbaum Associates, Mahwah (1979)

[19] Norman, D.A.: Affordance, Conventions, and Design. Interactions 6(3), 38–43 (1999)

[20] Child, C., Stathis, K.: Rule Value Reinforcement Learning for Cognitive Agents. In: Nakashima, H., Wellman, M.P., Weiss, G., Stone, P. (eds.) 5th Intl. Joint Conference on Autonomous Agents and Multiagent Systems (AAMAS 2006), pp. 792–794. ACM Press, New York (2006)

[21] Sequeira, P., Vala, M., Paiva, A.: What can I do with this? Finding possible interactions between characters and objects. In: Proceedings of the 6th Intl. Conference of Autonomous Agents and Multi-agent Systems (AAMAS 2007). IEEE Computer Society Press, Los Alamitos (2007)

[22] Chen, W., Warren, D.S.: C-logic of Complex Objects. In: PODS 1989: Proceedings of the eighth ACM SIGACT-SIGMOD-SIGART symposium on Principles of database systems, pp. 369–378. ACM Press, New York (1989)

[23] Kesim, N.: Temporal Objects in Deductive Databases. PhD thesis, Imperial College (1993)

[24] Ferber, J., Müller, J.P.: Influences and Reactions: a Model of Situated Multiagent Systems. In: ICMAS 1996 (Intl. Conference on Multi-Agent Systems), AAAI Press, Menlo Park (1996)

[25] tuProlog: http://www.alice.unibo.it:8080/tuProlog/

[26] Denti, E., Omicini, A., Ricci, A.: Multi-paradigm Java-Prolog integration in tu Prolog. Science of Computer Programming 57(2), 217–250 (2005)

[27] WSMO: Web Service Modelling Ontology, http://www.wsmo.org/

[28] Kifer, M., Lausen, G., Wu, J.: Logical Foundations of Object-Oriented and Frame-Based Languages. Journal of the Association for Computing Machinery (May 1995)

[29] Weyns, D., Holvoet, T.: A Formal Model for Situated Multi-agent Systems. Fundam. Inform. 63(2-3), 125–158 (2004)

[30] Weyns, D., Steegmans, E., Holvoet, T.: Towards Active Perception in Situated Multi-Agent Systems. Applied Artificial Intelligence 18(9-10), 867–883 (2004)

[31] Vizzari, G.: Dynamic Interaction Spaces and Situated Multiagent Systems: from a Multilayered Model to a Distributed Architecture. PhD thesis, University of the Studies of Milan Bicocca (2003-2004)

[32] Omicini, A., Ricci, A., Viroli, M., Castelfranchi, C., Tummolini, L.: Coordination Artifacts: Environment-based Coordination for Intelligent Agents. In: Autonomous Agents and Multi-agent Systems, Washington, DC, USA, pp. 286–293 (2004)

[33] Ricci, A., Viroli, M., Omicini, A.: CArtAgO: A Framework for Prototyping Artifact-based Environments in MAS. In: Weyns, D., Van Dyke Parunak, H., Michel, F. (eds.) E4MAS 2006. LNCS (LNAI), vol. 4389, pp. 67–86. Springer, Heidelberg (2007)

[34] Hübner, J.F., Bordini, R.H.: Jason, a java-based interpreter for an extended version of agentlink, http://jason.sourceforge.net/

[35] Platon, E., Sabouret, N., Honiden, S.: Oversensing with a softbody in the environment - another dimension of observation. In: Proceedings of Modelling Others from Observation 2005 (2005)

[36] Weyns, D., Van Dyke Parunak, H., Michel, F. (eds.): E4MAS 2005. LNCS (LNAI), vol. 3830. Springer, Heidelberg (2006)

[37] Platon, E., Sabouret, N., Honiden, S.: Tag interactions in multiagent systems: Environment support. In: Gleizes, M.P., Kaminka, G.A., Nowé, A., Ossowski, S., Tuyls, K., Verbeeck, K. (eds.) EUMAS, Koninklijke Vlaamse Academie van Belie voor Wetenschappen en Kunsten, pp. 270–281 (2005)

[38] ArguGRID: ARGUmentantion as a foundation for the semantic GRID, http://www.argugrid.eu/

[39] Morge, M., McGinnis, J., Bromuri, S., Toni, F., Mancarella, P., Stathis, K.: Towards a Modular Architecture of Argumentative Agents to Compose Services. In: Proc. of the 15th Journees Francophones sur les Systemes Multi-Agents (JFSMA), Carcasonne, France (November 2006)

Modeling Agent-Environment Interactions in Adaptive MAS

R. Zalila Mili* and Renee Steiner

University of Texas at Dallas
Department of Computer Science
Box 830688, Richardson, TX 75083-0688, USA
{rmili,rsteiner}@utdallas.edu

Abstract. In this paper, we discuss a way to model Agent-Environment interactions in adaptive multi-agent systems. We describe the interactions at various levels of abstraction starting with the highest. For each level, we specify the interactions from four viewpoints *functional, behavioral, data* and *structural*. This results into a set of models that capture the main properties of agent-environment interactions.

1 Introduction

This paper focuses on a specific category of MAS, the Agent-Environment System (AES) [1,2,3]. AESs are adaptive systems where the environment is *open* (i.e., inaccessible, non-deterministic, dynamic, and continuous) and can be modeled as a MAS. An AES can be viewed as a system composed of an agent-MAS, an environment-MAS , and interaction mechanisms between the two MASs. Hence it can be defined as $(agMAS, envMAS, Interaction(agMAS, envMAS)$. An example of an AES is an agent-based social simulation system where $agMAS$ consists of the population of social entities and their interactions, $envMAS$ consists of the environment entities and their interactions, and $Interaction(agMAS,-envAS)$ consists of the interaction mechanisms between the social and physical MASs (see Figure 1).

In this paper, we discuss an approach to model AES. We do not propose a methodology but rather discuss a software engineering modeling approach that can be incorporated in existing agent-oriented processes. For the sake of conciseness, we restrict our discussion to the specification of interactions between $agMAS$ and $envMAS$.

In Software Engineering, when dealing with a complex, multi-faceted problem, it is customary to describe the system from various levels of abstraction and different viewpoints. Abstraction allows an engineer to concentrate on those features that are the most important at a particular stage of the process while multiple viewpoints allow the engineer to address different concerns of the same problem.

---

* Correspondence author.

D. Weyns, S.A. Brueckner, and Y. Demazeau (Eds.): EEMMAS 2007, LNAI 5049, pp. 135–147, 2008.
© Springer-Verlag Berlin Heidelberg 2008

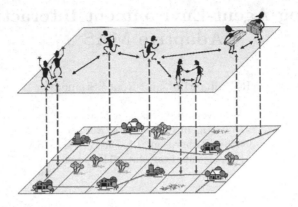

Fig. 1. Interactions in AES

In this paper, we propose to specify agent-environment interaction from four viewpoints. The *data* viewpoint describes the interaction in terms of its conceptual entities and associations; the *functional* viewpoint describes the interaction in term of its functionality; the *behavioral* viewpoint describes the interaction in terms of its reaction to events, and state changes; finally the *structural* viewpoint describes the interaction in terms of its design components. We start by discussing the problem at the highest level of abstraction, considering agents and environment as black boxes, then proceed through the next three levels of detail.

2   Agent-Environment Interactions in MAS

The environment only recently has been proposed as a "first-class entity" [4]. As such, the amount of engineering practices and methodologies focusing on this topic is limited.

There exist many Agent Oriented Software Engineering methodologies that have a foundation in object orientation, requirements engineering and knowledge engineering. However, most of them fail to address the needs of the environment. Falling into this category are Tropos [5], Prometheus [6], Zeus [7], MESSAGE [8], OPM/MAS [9], and MaSE [10]. These methodologies consider the environment as external to the MAS (i.e., actors on the MAS [10]) or consider it the operating system on which the MAS executes. This approach tends either to trivialize the environment's function or couples it too tightly with the agents.

Recently, Gaia has been extended to accept the environment as a primary abstraction for MAS [11]. To the best of our knowledge, this is the only AOSE methodology that does so. Gaia treats the environment in terms of *abstract computation resources* that the agent can sense, affect or consume. However, in the hope of keeping the environment general, Gaia recommends that the environment only holds components that are capable of performing simple tasks and operations such as a data lookup. Anything more complex should be *agentified*, i.e., complex tasks should be handled by a *proper* agent and not be considered a service of the environment. Regarding communication with the agent, the environment has sensors and effectors.

Another general methodology that considers the environment is SODA [12]. SODA focuses on societies and inter-agent issues. During the analysis phase, the resource model which represents the highest level of abstraction of the environment is defined. In the design phase the environment model is described by mapping resources onto an infrastructure. Recently, "zooming" has been applied to SODA which enables MAS to be viewed at different layers of abstraction. However, the layers start at a low abstraction and miss showing truly higher abstractions. Also, zooming would benefit from showing a clear distinction between agent and environment.

Another methodology used to describe environment functionality is presented using *artifacts*[13]. According to the authors, artifacts reside in the environment independent of agents and expose a set of operations. Agents are aware of these artifacts and invoke operations and perceive their effect as necessary. Artifacts generalize the research done for SODA regarding the coordination infrastructures [12]. Artifacts are responsible for providing the services that agents may need to achieve their goals.

One methodology that follows RUP and the traditional workflow is ADELFE [14]. This methodology covers the entire software process. The environment is addressed during the final requirements phase. The outcome of requirements describe the interaction, the context and the characteristics of the environment. During analysis, the modules of the environment are identified. However, during design, no explicit modeling of the environment occurs.

In [15,16], Ferber presents a agent-environment model based on the principles of influences and reaction. Once agents execute actions, they produce influences that are synchronously communicated to the environment. The environment interprets these influences, reacts to them, and changes its state. The new state is then synchronously communicated to the agents. In this manner, all agents have the same information about the environment at the same time.

In [16], Ferber proposes a formal approach to specify the influence reaction model for two categories of agents, i.e., *tropistic* and *hysteretic* when the environment is centralized.

In our work, Agent-Environment interactions follow the influence-reaction model. To illustrate our functional viewpoint, we build on Ferber's formal model and propose a model of interactions where agents are hysteretic and the environment decentralized.

Before going into the details of our approach, in the next section we discuss the properties of Agent-Environment Systems.

3   Agent Environment Systems

In our approach, we use the word *agent* to refer to a *structured abstract data type* that has the well known properties of autonomy, awareness, sociality/interactivity, pro-activeness and reactiveness.

In the remainder of this paper, and for the sake of clarity, we illustrate our discussion on AES through the example of a social simulation system, where social entities represent "humans", and the environment represents the world. In this case, it is clear that the agent concept is a natural abstraction of "humans". From the environment perspective, we might consider the case where the environment includes entities (i.e., components) that exhibit the properties discussed above. For example, a plant is an entity that is autonomous, aware of its surroundings, able to interact with other environment entities, proactive (its goal being to stay alive) and reactive. Hence, the agent abstraction can be used to model this type of environment entity.

From a Software Engineering perspective, when dealing with large *open* environments [17] it is necessary to split the environment into cells. Cells represent a division of continuous space. They are not necessarily contiguous and hence can form a network. The cell's main purpose is to divide the environment into easily manageable partitions.

Also, from a Software Engineering perspective, when dealing with adaptive environments, it is necessary to relieve the agents from the continuous burden of finding the environment's latest state. The principle of *separation of concerns* leads to the definition of *cell controllers* [1,2,18,19]. A cell controller is a design entity whose responsibility is to 1) manage and control its own portion of the environment (i.e., cell); 2) inform other controllers of any change that may affect their cell; and 3) inform its local agents of the latest state of the environment. Since these controllers serve as an *interface* between the environment and the agents, in a layered architecture, they will form the *middle layer* (see Figure 2).

From a requirements perspective, a cell controller is expected to 1) be autonomous; 2) be aware of the agent population and environment composition; 3) be able to interact with agents to provide them with a "picture" of their surroundings, interact with environment components to get information about their latest state, and communicate with other cell controllers to inform them of the propagation of the effect of external events [1]; 4) be proactive, its goal being for example to maintain a stable state for its cell; and 5) be reactive. Given these properties, it seems clear that the agent *abstraction* can also be used to model cell controllers.

To summarize our discussion, an AES might be viewed as a system that includes two types of agents, *conceptual agents* and *design agents*. Conceptual agents include agents which represent application specific entities such as social-agents and environment-agents. Design agents represent entities that are defined solely for engineering purposes such as controller-agents. It is clear that the level of proactivity (and therefore "intelligence") is higher in social-agents than it is in controller-agents and environment-agents. Due to size limitation, in the remainder of this paper, we restrict our discussion to social and controller agents.

Definitions. We define an *Agent-Environment System* (AES) as a system composed of a) a set of interacting social-agents, b) a distinct open environment in which these agents are situated, and c) a mechanism for social-agent/environment interactions [3,2].

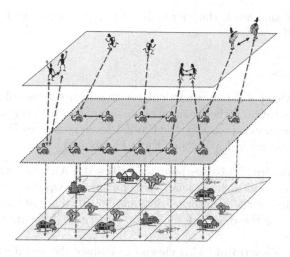

Fig. 2. AES layers

A *social-agent* is a software entity which 1) is driven by a set of tendencies in the form of individual objectives; 2) can 4) has a partial representation of this environment; 5) acts in an environment; 6) reacts to external events; 7) possesses skills and can offer services; 8) is mobile.

A *cell controller-agent* is a software entity which 1) is driven by a set of tendencies in the form of individual objectives; 2) can communicate with other environment entities; 3) possesses resources of its own; 4) has a partial representation of the agent population; 5) reacts to agents 6) reacts to external events; 7) possesses skills and can offer services.

4 Levels and Viewpoints for AES

In this Section, we introduce a means for expressing the AES at various levels of abstraction. We discuss representations for the data, functional, behavior, and structural viewpoints.

4.1 UWEA Levels

There exist few methodologies that allows the software engineer to view a MAS at finer grained levels of detail [8,12,20,21]. In this paper we follow Humphrey's approach [22] and propose four telescoping levels of abstractions:

- **Universe.** This level is the highest level and is appropriate when the viewer is an observer of the situation.
- **World.** This abstraction is appropriate when the viewer has a closer view of the situation.
- **Entity.** In this layer, the viewer is an entity in the situation. Protocols are available and for each entity more detail is known.

- **Atomic.** At this level, the viewer is within the entity and knows all the atomic details.

4.2 Viewpoints

The notion of a viewpoint puts a particular emphasis upon the role of a representation. A representation is the means that we use to capture certain properties of a design [23]. Design viewpoints for the UWEA levels consist of *Data*, *Functional*, *Behavioral*, and *Structural*. We define these viewpoints as such:

- **Data Viewpoint.** This viewpoint describes the AES in terms of the conceptual objects and their associations. The data viewpoint is concerned with the description of the conceptual data model, if we are at the early stage of development, or the description of data structures if we are at the detailed design phase.
- **Functional Viewpoint.** This viewpoint defines the architectural elements of the AES's in terms of their tasks and emphasizes the functionality the AES provides.
- **Behavioral Viewpoint.** This viewpoint describes the causal links between events and system responses during execution. The main concern of this view is with the dynamic relationships between components.
- **Structural Viewpoint.** This viewpoint defines the static aspects of the system by defining the components and how they relate.

Several notations can be used to represent the various viewpoints. We use entity relationship diagrams to represent the data viewpoint, functions to represent the functional viewpoint, statecharts to represent the behavioral viewpoint, and class diagrams to represent the structural viewpoint. This choice of notation is arbitrary and it can be complemented with other notations.

5 Agent-Environment Interaction Models

In this section we discuss the various models for AES interactions. Given that there has been much work regarding agent modeling, when discussing interactions, will give more weight to the environment.

5.1 Data Viewpoint Illustrations

For the Universal level, the only information available is that social agents influence the environment and the environment reacts to agents. At the World level, we are exposed to more detail. For example, we learn that the environment has a state and a structure, and is composed of cells. We also learn that each cell is managed by a controller agent. At this level, we determine that the interactions will happen between the social agents and the controller agents. At the Entity Level, more data is exposed (see Fig. 3). We can see that the controller agent has a synchronizer while cells form a hierarchy.

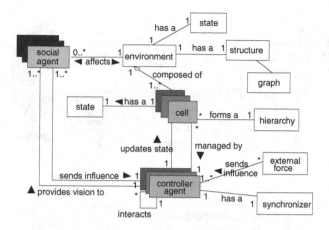

Fig. 3. E Level Data Model, Environment

5.2 Functional Viewpoint Illustrations

The levels of abstractions in this viewpoint correspond to the box structures in the Cleanroom methodology. A box structure is a description of functions that exhibit properties essential for effective system specification and design [24]. Hence, the UWEA levels can be mapped into four box structures: black box, grey box, white box and clear box. These structures exhibit identical external behavior, but increasing internal visibility.

At the Universal level, a social agent is a function that processes environment states, and produces influences. The environment is a function that processes social agent influences and external influences to produce a new state.

At the World level, the environment is composed of a set of cells. Each cell is managed by a controller agent represented by a function that takes as input the set of influences produced by the social agents within its boundaries, as well as external influences. It produces a new state that is passed onto the local social agents, and outputs information to be passed onto adjacent controllers.

At the Entity level (see Figs. 4- 8), we are able to see the main components that make up social agents and controller agents. A social agent consists of a *Perception*, a *Decision-Making* and an *Execution* component. A controller agent consists of two components, *Influence Combination* and *Decision Making*. A cell state is consumed by a social agent's *Perception* module. This produces a percept that is processed by the *Decision-Making* module resulting in an action. The execution of the action produces the social agent influences. External influences and local social agents influences are combined by the controller to determine the total influence on the cell. This is processed by the controller's *Decision Making* component to define the new cell state, and generate information to be passed onto adjacent controllers.

At the Atomic level, we realize that the decision making component of social agents and controller agents includes a memorization function. Hence, when a social agent perceives the cell's state, the new percept, the cell's previous state

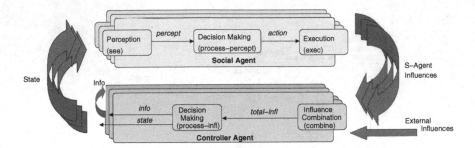

Fig. 4. E level Interactions

Σ : environment states

Σ_k: cell$_k$ states; $\Sigma = \cup \Sigma_k$

Γ_i: influences produced by social agent $_i$

Γ_{ext}: external influences

Γ: influence combinations

Λ: information sent to other controller agents

Π_i: set of percepts of social agent $_i$

Ω_i: set of actions of social agent $_i$

Fig. 5. E level Set Definitions

see_i : $\Sigma_k \to \Pi_i$

$deliberate_i$: $\Pi_i \to \Omega_i$

$exec_i$: $\Omega_i \to \Gamma_i$

S–Agent$_i$: $\Sigma_k \to \Gamma_i$

S–Agent$_i$: $(\sigma_k) = exec_i(deliberate_i(see_i(\sigma_k)))$

Fig. 6. E level Agent Functions

$combine_k$: $\Gamma_1 \times ... \Gamma_n \times \Gamma_{ext1} \times ... \Gamma_{extm} \to \Gamma$

$process\text{-}infl_k$: $\Gamma \to \Sigma_k \cup \Lambda$

$Controller_k$: $\Gamma_1 \times ... \Gamma_n \times \Gamma_{ext1} \times ... \Gamma_{extm} \to \Sigma_k \cup \Lambda$

$Controller_k$ $(\gamma_1, ..., \gamma_n, \gamma_{ext1}, ..., \gamma_{extm}) =$

$process\text{-}infl_k (combine_k (\gamma_1, ..., \gamma_n, \gamma_{ext1}, ..., \gamma_{extm}))$

Fig. 7. E level Cell Controller Functions

σ (t0): initial state of the environment (at time t0)

$$\sigma(t0) = \cup_{k=1}^{m} \sigma_k(t0)$$

$$\sigma(t+1) = \cup_{k=1}^{m} \sigma_k(t+1)$$

$$\sigma(t+1) = \text{process-inf}_k(\text{combine}_k(\text{S-Agent}(\sigma_k(t)), ..., \text{S-Agent}_h(\sigma_k(t)),$$
$$\gamma_{ext1}(t), ..., \gamma_{extm}(t))$$

Fig. 8. E level Interaction Specification

and the agent's previous state are used to determine the next action to perform. The same applies to the controller agent: after the influences are combined, the total influence and the cell's previous state are used to determine the cell's new state.

5.3 Behavioral Viewpoint Illustrations

At the Universal level, there is very little observable behavior. The social agents are either *idle* or *acting*, and the environment is either *idle* or *reacting*. At the World level, we see that the interactions occur between the social agents and the controller agents. The social agent can be either in state *idle*, *processing cell info* or *acting*. The controller agent can be in states *idle*, *processing influences* or *reacting*. When a social agent is created it will produce influences that will force the controller to move from state *idle* to state *processing influences*. Once the processing is complete, the controller transitions to state *reacting* that will produce event *new-cellstate-rdy*. Upon detection of this event, the social agent will transition from state *idle* to state *processing cell info*, then state *acting* that will produce new influences. And the cycle resumes.

At the E level (see Figure 9), we know more about the internal states of the social and controller agents. We also know that controller agents make use of

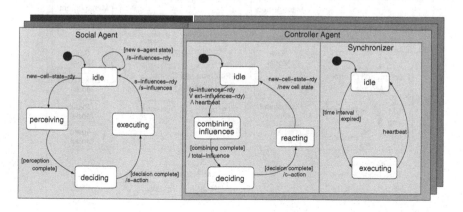

Fig. 9. E Level Behavioral Model

synchronizers. The synchronizer, if the time interval has expired, will execute a heartbeat. When the controller agent receives a heartbeat and influences, the controller *combines* all of the internal influences produced by the agents within its boundaries as well as the external influence received. The total influence is then passed to the *deciding* state which produces an action to be received by the *reacting* state. The event produced by *reacting* will cause the social agent to move from state *idle* to the *perceiving* state followed by the *deciding* state which determines the next course of action. *Executing* produces a new influence to be received by the cell.

5.4   Structural Viewpoint Illustrations

At the Universal level, we see, at a high level, the environment and the agent communication infrastructure. Agents communicate through an Agent to Agent Communication Service and the environment and agents communicate over the system's Message Transport Service.

At the World level, we can see that both social and controller agents have a means of interacting differently with different entities (Interaction Management component), a place to store information necessary for deliberating and communicating (Information Management component), a means of deliberating (the Planning and Control module), and a place to hold assigned tasks (the Task Management component).

At the Entity level (see Figure 10), we see deepest into the various components that make up the social and controller agents. For example, we see that detailed composition of the Planning and control Module as well as the Task Management component. We also see that the controller has a synchronizer as part of its Interaction Management component.

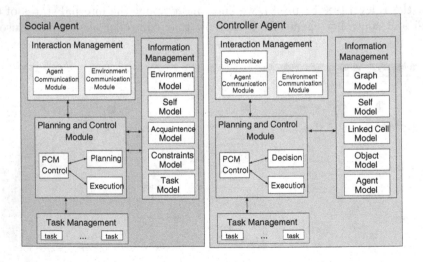

Fig. 10. E Level Structural Model

At the Atomic level, the Structural model is represented by UML class diagrams.

6 Conclusion

In this paper, we described a modeling approach for interactions in AES. These interactions were described at telescoping levels of abstraction with each level containing viewpoints for *functional, behavioral, data* and *structural* concerns. This approach results in a set of models that captures the main properties of agent-environment interactions. This concept was illustrated specifically for interactions between social-agents and controller-agents.

The presented approach was used to introduce students to the complex problem of modeling adaptive MAS. We discovered that students grasped the concepts more easily when we followed the levels of abstraction. Also, using standard software engineering notations as much as possible allowed our students to focus on the problem rather than on a notation. However, it should be noted that this approach is not intended to be complete and can be complemented with other viewpoints and notation as necessary. In addition, this approach can be included as part of existing AOSE methodologies.

Furthermore, while not discussed in this paper, we have defined additional models (e.g., communication model, social-agent organizational model, etc.) in order to specify other components of the AES. Given that the problem can be viewed from different perspectives, it seems natural to define several models. As with interactions, keeping these models separate and distinct allowed for a better understanding of the various aspects.

We conclude that, by describing the AES based on levels of abstraction, a clear understanding of the AES can occur and we believe that the consistency between diagrams at the same level can only increase that understanding. We also believe that one of the challenges with architecting environments for MAS is the fact that the environment typically is considered at different levels of abstraction from the agent. In order to architect a cohesive, unified MAS, the agent and environment should always be considered at the same level when describing MAS.

References

1. Mili, R.Z., Steiner, R., Oladimeji, E.: DIVAs: Illustrating an abstract architecture for agent-environment simulation systems. Multiagent and Grid Systems, Special Issue on Agent-oriented Software Development Methodologies 2(4) (2006)
2. Mili, R.Z., Oladimeji, E., Steiner, R.: Architecture of the DIVAs simulation system. In: Proceedings of Agent-Directed Simulation Symposium ADS 2006, Huntsville, Alabama (April 2006)
3. Steiner, R., Leask, G., Mili, R.Z.: An architecture for MAS simulation environments. In: Weyns, D., Van Dyke Parunak, H., Michel, F. (eds.) E4MAS 2005. LNCS (LNAI), vol. 3830, pp. 50–67. Springer, Heidelberg (2006)

4. Weyns, D., Parunak, H.V.D., Michel, F., Holvoet, T., Ferber, J.: Environments for multiagent systems: State-of-the-art and research challenges. In: Weyns, D., Van Dyke Parunak, H., Michel, F. (eds.) E4MAS 2004. LNCS (LNAI), vol. 3374, pp. 1–47. Springer, Heidelberg (2005)
5. Giunchiglia, F., Mylopoulos, J., Perini, A.: The tropos software development methodology: Processes, models and diagrams. Technical Report DIT-02-008, Informatica e Telecomunicazioni (2001)
6. Padgham, L., Winikoff, M.: Prometheus: A methodology for developing intelligent agents. In: Giunchiglia, F., Odell, J.J., Weiss, G. (eds.) AOSE 2002. LNCS, vol. 2585, pp. 174–185. Springer, Heidelberg (2003)
7. Nwana, H., Ndumu, D., Lee, L.: Zeus: An advanced tool-kit for engineering distributed multi-agent systems. In: Proceedings of PAAM 1998, London U.K., pp. 377–391 (1998)
8. Evans, R., Kearney, P., Caire, G., Garijo, F., Sanz, J.G., Pavon, J., Leal, F., Chainho, P., Massonet, P.: Message: Methodology for engineering systems of software agents. In: EURESCOM (2001)
9. Sturm, A., Dori, D., Shehory, O.: Single-model method for specifying multi-agent systems. In: Proceedings of the second international joint conference on autonomous agents and multi-agent systems, Melbourne, Australia (July 2003)
10. Deloach, S.A.: Analysis and design using mase and agenttool. In: Proc. of 12th Midwest Artificial Intelligence and Cognitive Science Conference, Ohio (2001)
11. Zambonelli, F., Jennings, N., Wooldridge, M.: Developing multiagent systems: the gaia methodology (2003)
12. Omicini, A.: Soda: Societies and infrastructures in the analysis and design of agent-based systems. In: Ciancarini, P., Wooldridge, M.J. (eds.) AOSE 2000. vol. 1957, pp. 185–193. Springer, Heidelberg (2001)
13. Omicini, A., Ricci, A., Viroli, R., Castelfranci, C., Tummolini, L.: Engineering mas environment with artifacts. In: Proceedings of 2nd Workshop on Environments for Multi-Agent Systems, Utrecht, Netherlands (July 2005)
14. Bernon, C., Gleizes, M., Peyruqueou, S., Picard, G.: ADELFE a methodology for adaptive multi-agent systems engineering. In: Petta, P., Tolksdorf, R., Zambonelli, F. (eds.) ESAW 2002. LNCS (LNAI), vol. 2577, pp. 156–169. Springer, Heidelberg (2003)
15. Ferber, J., Müller, J.P.: Influences and reaction: a model of situated multi-agent systems. In: Tokoro, M. (ed.) Proceedings of the 2nd International Conference on Multi-agent Systems (ICMAS 1996), December 10-13, pp. 72–79. AAAI Press, Menlo Park (1996)
16. Ferber, J.: Multi-Agent Systems: An Introduction to Distributed Artificial Intelligence. Addison-Wesley, Reading (1999)
17. Russell, S., Norvig, P.: Artificial Intelligence: A Modern Approach. Prentice-Hall, Englewood Cliffs (1995)
18. Mili, R., Leask, G., Shakya, U., Steiner, R., Oladimeji, E.: Architectural design of the DIVAs environment. In: Proceedings of 1st Workshop on Environments for Multiagent Systems, New York, USA, July 2004, pp. 57–66 (2004)
19. Steiner, R., Leask, G., Mili, R.Z.: An architecture for MAS simulation environments. In: Weyns, D., Van Dyke Parunak, H., Michel, F. (eds.) E4MAS 2005. LNCS (LNAI), vol. 3830, pp. 50–67. Springer, Heidelberg (2006)
20. Wooldridge, M., Jennings, N., Kinny, D.: The Gaia methodology for agent-oriented analysis and design. Autonomous Agents and Multi-Agent Systems 3(3), 285–312 (2000)

21. Rouff, C., Hinchey, M., Rash, J., Truszkowski, W., Gordon-Spears, D. (eds.): Agent Technology from a Formal Perspective. Springer, Heidelberg (2006)
22. Humphrey, W.S.: Managing the software process. The SEI Series in Software Engineering (1990)
23. Budgen, D.: Software Design. Addison-Wesley, Reading (2003)
24. Prowell, S., Trammell, C., Linger, R., Poore, J.: Cleanroom Software Engineering: Technology and Process. SEI Series in Software Engineering. Addison-Wesley, Reading (1998)

DECIDE: Applying Multi-agent Design and Decision Logic to a Baggage Handling System*

Kasper Hallenborg[1] and Yves Demazeau[2]

[1] Maersk Mc-Kinney Moller Institute,
University of Southern Denmark, DK-5230 Odense M, Denmark
hallenborg@mmmi.sdu.dk
[2] CNRS,LIG Laboratory,38000 Grenoble, France
Yves.Demazeau@imag.fr

Abstract. Behind the curtains at check-in desks in airports hide a very complex material handling systems, which manage to get your bag transported to the correct departure gate of your flight.

The conventional control software uses a strategy primarily based on a shortest path algorithm, not taking into account dynamical changes or utilization of less packed areas of the BHS.

We changed that perspective towards a decentralized multi-agent based solution by developing strongly collaborating agents. The agents replace the existing control software without modifying the layout of the BHS.

In this paper we describe the BHS problem and the agent-based design. We pay special attention to the impact of the local environments of the agents, and finally give examples of implemented decision strategies.

1 Introduction

Burdened by the fear of never seeing the suitcase again, you observe it disappearing in the back at check-in, even though is usually arrive out of nowhere at your destination. Looking into this "blackbox" one will experience a complex system unlike many others. Baggage-handling systems (BHS) of airports are shrouded in mystery due to both security reasons and the general size and complexity, which overshadows the entire air traffic industry.

In this paper we will present research experiences we have conducted by applying multi-agent technologies to a real BHS at a major airport hub in Asia. The intension was not to design a MAS-based system from scratch, but to evaluate an approach of exchanging the traditional control software with a multi-agent based solution, thus the solution described in the paper is truly mediated by the problems and constraints of the environment in which the BHS is situated.

1.1 DECIDE Project

The research case of the BHS is the primary case of a larger research project called DECIDE, which focus on promoting and proving the appropriateness of

---

* This research was supported by The Ministry of Science, Technology and Innovation in Denmark under the IT Cooridor Foundation.

D. Weyns, S.A. Brueckner, and Y. Demazeau (Eds.): EEMMAS 2007, LNAI 5049, pp. 148–165, 2008.

multi-agent based control in production and manufacturing systems. Other cases in the project have a focus on logistic control and scheduling of tasks in chemical processes. Major Danish manufactures are among the other partners of the consortium: Lego, Grundfos, Bang & Olufsen (B&O), and Odense Steel Shipyard.

1.2   Handling Baggage

To understand the baggage handling task of an airport, a short introduction is required. Handling baggage is usually not a problem in charter or minor airports, where almost all passengers are either departing or have reached their final destination, but sorting and routing baggage in airport hubs of modern airports with many connecting flight ought to be handled by an automatic BHS.

In principles the general task of a BHS is to bring baggage from one destination to another, A to B, but the number of bags, the unsorted inflow, the mechanics, and the number of different destinations complicates the task. Thus the BHS apparently shares several control characteristics with routing of packages in network traffic, but the density of alternative routes is much lower in the BHS than a typical telecommunication network. Also the important fact that lost packages cannot be resubmitted in the BHS introduces other foci in the control of the BHS. SWARM-based approaches like Schoonderwoerd's ant-based control [22] or Di Caro & Dorigo's AntNet are examples of intelligent agent-based approaches for routing in networks, but for the BHS we have to consider the settings and constraints of the environment to a much larger extend.

The BHS more or less covers an area similar to the basements of the terminals of an airport, and tunnels with pathways connect the terminals. The system is rather vulnerable around the tunnels, because typically there are no alternative routes and the tunnels only contain one or two FIFO-based lanes that could be several kilometers long. Thus the topology of the BHS could be regarded as connected clusters of smaller networks, but even within a terminal, the network of conveyors is far from being homogeneous, as special areas to some degree serve special purposes. A snapshot from a BHS is shown in figure 1.

A BHS is a huge mechanical system, usually composed of conveyor-like modules capable of transferring totes (plastic barrels) carrying one bag each. The BHS we have researched has more than 5000 of these modular components each with a length between 2-9 meters that run at speeds between 2-7 meters per. second. The BHS alone can easily be up to 20 km. in total length, may cover an area of up to 600.000 square meters, and should be capable of handling more than 100.000 pieces of baggage every day.

Besides the physical characteristics of the BHS, also a numbers of external factors from the environment influence the performance

- Arriving baggage from either flights or check-in are not sorted, but arrives mixed from different destinations[1].
- Identity and destination of bags are unknown until the bag is scanned at the input facilities, thus preplanning and traditional scheduling is not an option.

---

[1] Baggage for baggage-claim are usually separated and handled by other systems.

Fig. 1. Snapshot of a BHS with a moving tote containing a bag in the foreground

– Constant changes in flight schedules, due to both weather conditions and delayed flights.

Eliminating delayed bags are the top priority criteria for a BHS, because it can delay flights, and airports are charged to compensate the airline companies. Thus the BHS must comply with a specified maximum allowed transfer time on the BHS, which is our case is between 8-11 minutes. Besides that, the airport operates with the concept of *rush bags*. A bag becomes a rush bag, when it enters a certain timeframe (e.g. 20 min) before departure and then it cannot reach the plane using the standard procedures and moved by baggage wagons. Instead the bag will be discharged at a special location in the BHS and handled manually, and driven to the plane one by one. Naturally the number of rush bags should be minimized in order to keep handling expenses low.

Also if the bag enters the BHS very early (e.g. more than 3 hours before departure), a specific discharge point for this destination have not been allocated yet, and the BHS would not allow the bag to circulate on the system until that. Thus many BHSs have certain areas to temporally store early bags, called Early Baggage Storage (EBS). On a timeline the phase and concepts of moving bags on the BHS could be illustrated as in figure 2.

Fig. 2. The different states of a bag relative to departure time

Besides securing that bags reach their destination in time the capacity of the BHS should also be maximized, and the control system should try to distributed the load and utilize the entire system, if it should be capable of handling peak times.

Robustness and reliability is also of top priority, as breakdowns and dead lock situations inevitable will lead to delayed baggage, and in worst case stop the airport for several hours.

Given those criteria the traditional approach for controlling a BHS use a rather simplified policy of routing the totes along static shortest paths in the system. By the static shortest paths is meant the shortest path in an empty system, but during operation minor queues are unavoidable, which lengthen the static shortest routes. In the traditional control all totes are sent along the static shortest routes irrespective to the time of their departure in order the keep the control simple and reliable. A more optimal solution would be to group urgent baggage and clear the route by detouring bags with a distant departure time along less loaded areas. On top of the basic approach described above the control software are fine-tuned against a number of case-studies to avoid dead lock situations, but basically it limits the number of active totes in different areas of the system, which will be described later. The fine-tuning process is time-consuming and costly for the developers, a more general and less system specific solution is therefore one of the goals of an agent-based solution.

1.3   Worst Case Scenario

Apparently from the descriptions above there should be opportunities for improvement of the control logic in the BHS, and one might ask why it has not been tried before, but it has...

Still listed as one of the history's top ten worst software scandals are the BHS of Denver airport in Colorado, US. The Denver International Airport was scheduled to open in October 1993, but caused by a non-working BHS the opening of the airport was delayed in 16 months costing $1 million every day [25]. When it finally opened in 1995 it only worked on outbound flights in one of the three terminals, and a backup-system and labor-intensive system was used in the other terminals [13].

The original plan for the BHS developed and built by BAE was also extremely challenging, even compared to many BHS built today. Instead of moving totes by conveyors the BHS in Denver is based on more than 4,000 autonomous DCV[2] running at impressive speeds of up to 32 kph on the 30 km long rail system. It was a kind of agent-based with many computers coordinating the task, but the

---

[2] Destination coded vehicles.

first serious troubles was caused by the overloaded 10Mbit Ethernet. Also the optimistic plan of loading and unloading DCVs while running caused DCVs to collide, baggage to be damaged or thrown out of the DVCs. Even unloading a bag from one running DVC into another was part of the original plan, whereas many systems today still stops a tote or DCV before unloading, even at stationary discharging points.

2   Agent-Based Approach

Recent year's advancement in computer and graphics performance has made it possible to do realistic real-time simulations of very complex environments, including productions systems like the BHS. The ability to continuously interact with the simulation model during operation creates a perfect off-site test-suite for the control-software, which emulates the real BHS.

2.1   Emulation Model

Together with another consortium partner, Simcon, the BHS company FKI Logistex has created an emulation model of the researched BHS using the AutoMod simulation and modeling package [5]. AutoMod is a de-facto-standard for systems analysis of manufacturing and material handling systems. One of the strong advantages of using AutoMod is that you can communicate with the model over a standard socket connection, which is almost identical to the connection between the control server and the PLCs in the real hardware. Thus the control software cannot see the difference, if it is connected to the emulation model or the real hardware. The same protocol and telegrams are used, which simplifies the development process, and makes the emulation model reliable, whenever the basic communication has been tested correct. A snapshot of the emulation model is shown in figure 3. It shows the area with input facilities for terminal 3 of the airport.

2.2   Related Work

Multi-agent technologies have been applied to a number of both research and practical cases of production systems and material handling systems, such as the Production 2000+ project at DaimlerChrysler [7]. The Production P2000+ project has a strong focus on flexibility in a more traditional shop floor manufacturing environment, where high diversity in orders and production flow through operational stations is the main issue. The BHS could also be considered as a production system, because we have the input facilities (toploaders), which receive baggage from arriving planes or check-in. In production terms that would be the procurement of the production system [6]. There are a number of processing stations in the BHS as well, but primarily they fall into the category of diverters and mergers, which split or merge conveyor pathways respectively. There exists special processing stations in the system, such as manual handling stations, which are used e.g. for baggage, which have lost their tracking id. Also elements

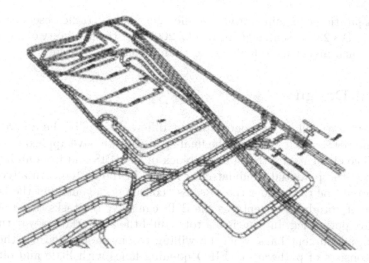

Fig. 3. Snapshot of the input area of the investigated BHS

as lifts or temporary storage elements are some specials versions elements that form the entire conveyor system of the BHS.

A number of research papers deal with agent-based manufacturing control or holonic manufacturing systems from a more general perspective, such as [20,16]. Primarily the research has focused on flexibility in scheduling and planning of resources in the productions environment. Approaches for planning are more or less formalized, such as the Generalized Partial Global Planning (GPGP) applied e.g. for scheduling and resource optimization in [9,10,11]. Other general strategies include the PACO planning, described in [17], and more deliberate agents using BDI-based agents for local optimizations [14]. But the BHS problem is highly constrained by the environment and less general in the required tasks to be handled than what could be described be general planning and routing.

With a focus on real-time decisions agent-based approaches have also been applied to material handling systems, such as [4], but compared to our case their approach is aiming for low-order systems (only tenth of orders to be produced are tested), and the approach taken is aiming for distributing jobs among machines. In contrast to our case the conducted research is based on designed scenarios that are being simulated, and not a real life applications, which must be converted into an agent-based system. There is a huge difference between designing a system to be agent-based or implementing agent-based control logic to an existing system. Flavor technology has applied their PIM and Paracell design model as an agent-based approach to the baggage-handling problem of a real BHS [15], but the case is quiet different from ours. First it contains check-in baggage which is addressed as a sorting problem, and the other problem addressed is batch processing of baggage to a particular departure, which is a classic scheduling problem. Whereas our system must handle mixed and unsorted baggage in the entire system, similar to a flexible manufacturing system with a high concurrent product variety.

Some inspiration can gained from real life agent-based traffic observation systems, such as [18,23] presented at EEMMAS 2007, but the flexibility of individual vehicles is much higher in traffic systems than a conveyor system.

3   Agent Design

In this section we will go into details about different tasks of the different elements of the BHS, which will form the final strategies we have applied to control the BHS. The elements are the building block of the BHS and from an intuitive point of view the potential candidates for agents in the system. An alternative approach would be to consider the totes as "consumer" agents and the BHS as a collection of "producer" agents, as the BHS can solve the tasks that the totes want to have performed. In principle a tote could then negotiate is way through the system, and urgent bags would be willing to pay more. Because the BHS generally consists of pathways of FIFO queuing lanes with little and often no possibilities of overtaking it is more appropriate to design the agents around the flow control of the BHS. The element agents should then coordinate their activities to optimize system performance and should therefore be considered as collaborative agents, rather than competitive agents.

3.1   Toploader

The input facilities of the BHS are called toploaders, as they drop bags into the totes from a conventional conveyor belt so they can be tracked at all times.

Basically the task of the toploader could be decomposed into id-scanning of the bag. Secondly it initiates the journey of the tote on the BHS. In order to start the routing of the tote, the endpoint (discharger) must be set for the tote, but several dischargers are often allocated to

Fig. 4. Toploader element; an empty tote is ready underneath the traditional conveyor belt, where the bags will arrive

the same flight destination. Therefore the toploader agents initiate a negotiation with the possible dischargers (a FIPA contract net) to find the best suited discharger, the evaluation of the proposals from the dischargers is not trivially chosen as the lowest offer, but weighted with the current route length to the dischargers, which is requested from a route agent - a mediator agent with a global focus on dynamic route lengths.

The toplader can take two different approaches for routing the tote.

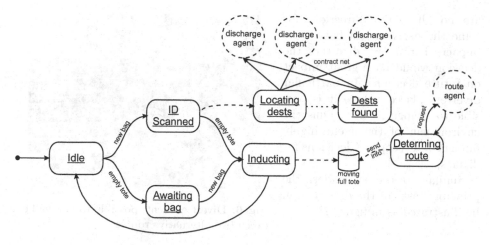

Fig. 5. The principal tasks of the toploader

Routing by Static Shortest Path. After the toploader has chosen the discharger it could instruct all diverters along the route to follow that path for the given tote, similar to the traditional control system, which send all totes along predefined static shortest routes.

Routing on the Way. Alternatively, the toploader could just send the tote to the next decision point along the shortest route. A more flexible approach, as the tote can be rerouted, if the route conditions have changed.

More formally the principal tasks of the toploader can be illustrated as the state diagram in figure 5, but it hides the advanced decision logic between the state changes and message interactions. Parts of that will be described in the next section.

It is important to note from the figure the destination and route information do not have to be fully determined, before the full tote can leave the toploader, and it can stay ready to induct the next tote.

3.2 Diverters

A diverter splits a conveyor lane into two, either a left or right turn and straight ahead.

In respect to the strategies described above the diverter would either just forward the tote in the direction determined by the toploader, or it would reconsider alternative routes by restarting the negotiation process.

A diverter should be concerned about the relevancy of reconsidering the route for a tote, because in many cases there is only one possible direction at a given diverter for a given tote. We want to generalize the control logic of the diverter agents instead of customizing it according to the placement of the diverter in the BHS layout. Thus initially it adjusts itself to the actual environment, such as possible destinations and route information. As mentioned for many diverters there are no alternative direction, for some the decision will have little impact. For a few diverters the decision would have great impact on future decisions. In particular diverters placed, where it is possible to change layers[3]. Thus the environment of the agent highly influence the scope of decisions for diverts.

Similar to the toploader, the principal tasks of the diverter can be illustrated as in figure 7.

Fig. 6. Divert element; possible to choose between two alternative routes

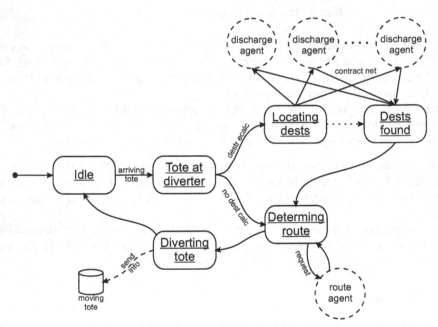

Fig. 7. The principal tasks of the diverter

3.3 Straight Elements

Most elements of a BHS are naturally straight or curved elements that connect the nodes of the routing graph. Straight or curved elements are not considered as agents in our current design, because mechanically they will always forward a tote to the next element if it free. In principle the speed of each element could be adjusted to give a more smooth flow and avoid queuing, but in the current setup it would generate an enormous communication overhead.

---

[3] The BHS is constructed as two layers of conveyor to save both space and cost.

3.4   Mergers

Mergers are the opposite of diverters, as they merge two lanes. Traditionally mergers are not controlled, as there are no alternatives to continuing on the single lane ahead, and the merger simply alters between taking one tote from either input lane, if both are occupied.

Obviously, more intelligent decisions could be considered than just switching between the input lanes. The ratio between merging totes from the input lanes should be determined by the aggregated data of the totes in either of the two lanes. E.g. if the number of urgent totes waiting to be merged are higher in one lane that lane should be given higher priority.

3.5   Dischargers

Dischargers are responsible for un-loading bags from the totes, when the tote reaches its destination. Dischargers also have to take care of the empty totes. Some BHSs have separate conveyor system for the empty totes, but many systems including the researched BHS use the same lanes for routing the empty totes back to the tote stackers at the toploaders.

The task is similar to routing full totes, but actually much more complex, due to several considerations that must be taken into account.

Fig. 8. Discharge element; unloads a tote by tilting it, so the bag falls onto a conventional conveyor belt

- The number of destinations (tote stackers) is larger than alternative dischargers for full totes (typically 2), whereas the number of tote stackers is equal to the number of toploaders, which is 12 in our case.
- The status of empty tote stackers. If a stacker runs empty, no totes will be available at the toploaders for new bags.
- The distance to the stackers. It is more appropriate to return the empty tote to a stacker nearby than sending it half way through the system.

Again also the principal tasks of the discharger can be illustrates as in figure 9.

3.6   Route Agent

As mentioned in section 3.1 the agents are assisted by a mediator agent, when they require information about the dynamic distances in the BHS. The static lengths of routes between nodes A and B are rather easy to measure, but also of

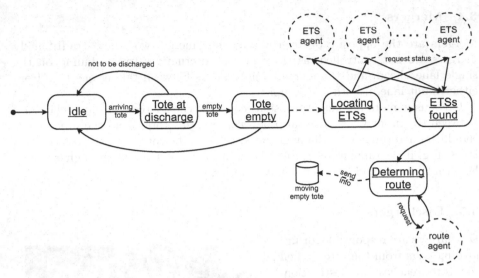

Fig. 9. The principal tasks of the discharger

less importance when the system starts to be loaded, as the distances (measured in seconds) increase when queues arise in the lanes and totes are delayed. Thus, the dynamic length of routes and distances is defined as the static length of routes add with the current delay of segments of the route.

The Route agent is an example of a mediator agent, which based on reported information from local agents can calculate the dynamic route length and distances between nodes, so they can be queried by other agents. In other words the route agent acts as a blackboard for the reactive node agents, so they do not have to maintain a world model by themselves.

In the initialization process the Route agent generates all possible routes in the system by building up a graph for the BHS with nodes corresponding to the element agents. During operation it constantly monitors traffic on edges of the graph by subscribing to such information of queues and the node agents and update the weights in the graph, so dynamic shortest paths can be calculated using classic Dijkstra for dynamic shortest path calculations [12].

4   Agent Strategies

In this section we present some of the implemented strategies for the agents evolved from the tasks and considerations mentioned in the previous section. The strategies includes basic local observations, which are used partly in some of the strategies. The strategies are highly influenced and mediated by the environment, as decisions are primarily based on observation of e.g. queues in the neighborhood of the agent.

All agents are implemented in the JADE™ agent platform [24], and all communication comply with the FIPA specifications [1]. One special agent, called the *AdapterAgent*, act as a gateway agent to the emulation model described in section 2.1, and communicate according to the telegram based protocol used for the real BHS system. To abstract message handling and queries among the agents we have defined and implemented an ontology for the BHS domain.

Three strategies will be described in the following subsections to give examples of the formulated problems above. The described examples do not complete the picture of the entire agent system, but present some of the decision formulas, which proved to be successful through simulation. We where aiming for heuristics that can solve the intended problem behind the strategies.

The mentioned queue statuses used throughout the strategies are local observations, where each element agent observes queue conditions of its input lanes. Only mergers have two input queues, other agents have only one. The dynamic queue conditions include measurements of average number of active totes lined up in the queue, the urgency of the totes, the delay if totes are moving slower than full element speed, etc.

4.1   Choosing a Tote Stacker for Empty Totes

Considering tote stackers in the return strategy of empty totes take into account the content state of stackers, the number of stackers, and the distance to each stacker. The full status of stackers are defined as ration between the full capacity and the current content. The status is converted into a priority for extra totes using a standard indeed fuzzy hedge [21]

$$s_i = \begin{cases} 2r_i^2 & 0 \le r_i < \frac{1}{2} \\ 1 - 2(1 - r_i)^2 & \frac{1}{2} \le r_i \le 1 \end{cases} \tag{1}$$

where r_i is the full-ratio for the i'th stacker, and s_i is its priority for requesting extra totes. The priority determined are used to scale the dynamic route length to each tote stacker, so an almost empty stacker will have a very low value, whereas a full stacker will be evaluated on its full route length.

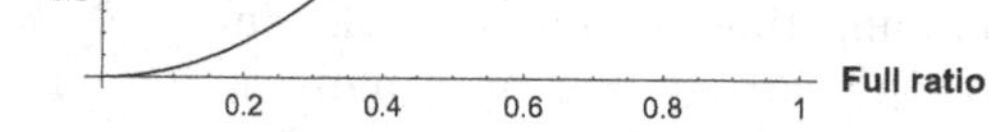

Fig. 10. Priority function for the tote stacker in routing strategy of empty totes

$$v_i = d_i \cdot s_i \tag{2}$$

where d_i is the dynamic distance to the stacker from the decision point.
Refer to section 3.6 for the definition of the dynamic length.

The strategy has clearly indicated that it can serve the task of filling up the tote stackers appropriately for the tested scenarios, but obviously it is also highly dependent on how good the forward routing algorithm is to distribute the load on the system, as it naturally complicates the job, if all totes are unloaded in the same area. As long as tote stackers are not running empty of totes, we can claim that the strategy is successful, and it is hard to say that one algorithm is better than another, but the load on the return lane is important at least for the segments shared with forward running totes. In the tested scenarios no problems with heavy loads on the return paths have been experienced.

4.2 Overtaking Totes within a Group of Diverters and Mergers

The overtaking strategy is an example of a collaborating strategy, which allows urgent bags to overtake non-urgent bags, by detouring non-urgent bags. A typical constellation of diverters and mergers in the discharging area can be seen in figure 11. The bottom lane is the fast forward transport line, the middle a slower lane with the dischargers and the upper lane is the return path. A diverter (in the bottom lane) has the option to detour non-urgent to the middle lane to give way for urgent baggage in the transport line. When the routes merge in the middle lane, higher priority is given to totes from the merging leg with most urgent totes.

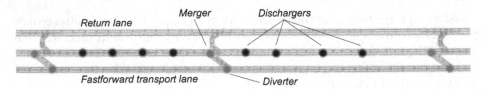

Fig. 11. Typical collection of diverters and mergers in the discharge area

The urgency is defined by a constructed function that serves the intension of giving high priority to urgent totes and negative priority to totes, which remaining time exceed a certain threshold value.

$$u_j = \begin{cases} \frac{1}{t_j^2} & t_j < U_T \\ \frac{1}{(U_{max}-U_T)^2}\left(-t_j^2 + 2U_T t_j - U_T^2\right) & t_j \geq U_T \end{cases} \tag{3}$$

where U_{max} is the maximum remaining time a tote can hold before departure, which usually is 180 min. U_T is the threshold value, which is set to 20 min, as no tote should be considered urgent, if it has more than 20 min left before the discharger closes. t_j is the remaining time for the j'th tote.

Again we convert this urgency factor to a scalar that can be multiplied to the dynamic route length of alternatives routes in order to

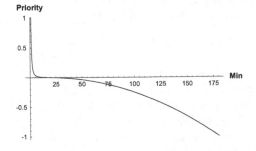

Fig. 12. Urgency function for totes

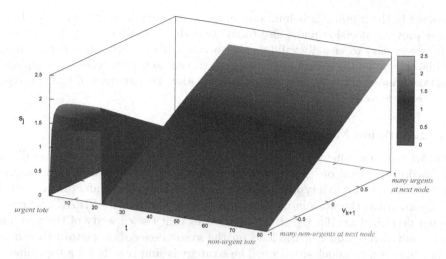

Fig. 13. The scalar factor given by urgency of current tote and next decision node of a route

stay with the simple principle that the decision of an agent is to chose the shortest route among alternatives. By shortening route lengths with a low scaling factor, it will be more likely that the agent will chose that route. Thus, for urgent totes the scalar should be low if the route is appropriate for urgent totes, and low for non-urgent totes if the route contains many non-urgent totes (a detour).

$$
s_j = \begin{cases} (1 - u_j)(1 + v_{k+1}) & u_j < 0 \quad \text{(non-urgent tote)} \\ (1 - u_j)(1 - v_{k+1}) & u_j \geq 0 \quad \text{(urgent tote)} \end{cases} \tag{4}
$$

where v_{k+1} is the aggregated urgency value for the next decision point along the route, which is requested from the divert agent. The aggregated urgency value of the next node is calculated as the average urgency of current totes between this agent and the next node.

Using this formula secures that urgent totes will group along the shortest route (as v_{k+1} is close to 1), whereas non-urgent are punished with a detour. If there are no queues on the routes the v_{k+1} is 0, and the scale factor has no effect. Figure 13 gives a visual explanation of the scalar-function, where it is rather easy to see that agents will have the requested switching decision principle based on if the tote is urgent or not, and that non-urgent totes groups with other non-urgent totes. Similar urgent totes ($t < 20$) will have lower scalars for routes with many urgent totes.

The mergers in the discharger lane, then simply give higher priority to input lanes with more urgent totes. The ratio between the aggregated urgency factors of the input lanes becomes the ratio for merging totes from the input lanes. Here it is important to note that the aggregated urgency value is the average urgency of totes queued at each input leg. An average value secures that the function is independent of the length of each input leg. In addition only a limited number of elements in the input legs behind the merger is observed, not the full lane back to the previous decision node, also to equalize the conditions of the input legs.

It is very easy to visually validate the success of the strategy in a live running simulator, and as the criteria for success is to enable urgent totes to group and overtake non-urgent totes, we can claim that also the intention of this strategy has been achieved.

4.3 Saturation Management

Saturation management is a strategy intended for avoiding queues at all by minimizing the load on the system in critical areas. Acceleration ramps and reaction times result in a typical characteristic of a flexible manufacturing system (FMS) known as the work in-progress against capacity curve (WIPAC), which is further described in [19]. By principle it states that the capacity of the systems goes dramatically down, if the load on the system exceeds a certain threshold value - almost a deadlock situation. The strategy is simply to block a toploader if the routes from the toploader are overloaded and let the system resolve. Queues close to the toploader are most critical, as the toploader have great impact on filling up those queues, whereas the parts of the route far from the toploader could be resolved before the new totes arrive. Instead of blocking the toploader completely, we can just slow down the release of new totes using the following fraction of full speed for the toploader.

$$v_t = \frac{\sum_i w_i q_i}{\sum_i w_i} = \frac{\sum_i \frac{\alpha}{d_i} q_i}{\sum_i \frac{\alpha}{d_i}} \tag{5}$$

where v_t is the velocity of the current toploader, when running at full speed, and w_i are weights of the queue statuses, q_i, along the routes. The weight is given by a fitted coefficient, α, and the distance from the toploader d_i. Queue statuses, q_i, are always a number between 0 and 1, where 1 indicates no queue. The effect of the saturation management strategy is clearly documented by the graph in figure 14, where it is compared to traditional centralized control approach.

One could argue that it is irrelevant to include all the nodes to the destination, as they are weighted less than nodes close to the toploader, but given the layout of a typical BHS the lanes near the toploader is shared for many routes, and then split closer to the destination. So the heavily scaled impact of the nodes close to the toploader is good for a quick response to overloaded lanes close to the toploader, and to even the load of all toploaders because the neighborhood varies. If the load is low around the toploaders, but distributed in the rest of the system around the dischargers, then the toploaders should still react by not as rapid.

The discussion of balancing local versus centralized observations was taken in section 3.6, but is the only decision point, where the decision actually is vital. Not choosing the optimal route at a node and perhaps be solved by choosing alternative routes later on the path, but here is it more or less a matter of releasing the tote into the system or not. Thus we allow it base its decision on a more global view of the status of the entire system.

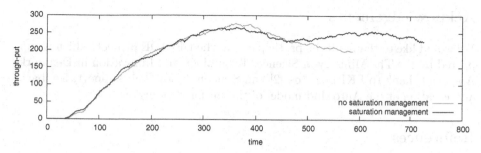

Fig. 14. Result of a test scenario with and without the saturation management strategy

5 Conclusion

Is this paper we have presented important research contributions from a baggage handling system (BHS) in a major airport hub in Asia. Agents were intended to substitute existing control logic, but not change the layout of the BHS, therefore design of the agent-based control software is highly influenced by the environment of the BHS, and the control logic of each individual agent constantly adapt to the current situation of the local neighborhood of the agent, by observing status of the environment like queues, urgent bags, etc. in spite of that we still believe, we have succeeded in keeping the decision logic of the agents rather general in order to improve reusability and understandability for the agent based control.

Special attention has been given to the task of the different type of agents, and examples of implemented decision logic have proven successful compared to the traditional approach.

Future Work

We continue our research on the BHS and will develop more new strategies for the local agents, and increase their mutual collaboration to maximize the utilization of the BHS during peak times. We will try to avoid the use of centralized mediator agents (the route agent) and rely on roles and profiles for the agents. Ideally a swarm of local agents would provide the most general setup, which easily can be ported to other manufacturing and material handling systems, which hopefully can lead to new abstract and general design methodologies for the topological domain of impact for agent collaborations.

Another important focus point of the future research will be to develop an application oriented agent platform, which is similar than the JADE framework that is the reason for serious performance problems. Environments and resources of material handling systems are more deterministic, than many other agent communities, thus interactions can be based on simpler and more efficient mechanisms.

Acknowledgements

We would like to thank all the participants in the DECIDE project, which is supported by the The Ministry of Science, Technology and Innovation in Denmark. A special thank to FKI Logistex [2] and Simcon [3] for their support, feedback, and creation of the AutoMod model of the major hub airport.

References

1. FIPA - The Foundation of Intelligent Physical Agents (2006),
   http://www.fipa.org/
2. FKI logistex (2006), http://www.fkilogistex.com/
3. Simcon (2006), http://www.simcon.dk/
4. Babiceanu, R.F., Chen, F.F.: Performance evaluation of agent-based material handling systems using simulation techniques. In: Proceedings of the 37th Winter Simulation Conference, Orlando, FL, USA, December 4-7, pp. 1022–1028 (2005)
5. Brooks Software. Automod - simulation and modeling software (2006),
   http://www.brookssoftware.com
6. Bussmann, S., Jennings, N.R., Wooldridge, M.: Multiagent Systems for Manufacturing Control. Springer, Heidelberg (2004)
7. Bussmann, S., Schild, K.: An agent-based approach to the control of flexible production systems. In: 8th IEEE Int. Conf. on Emerging Technologies and Factory Automation (ETFA 2001), Antibes Juan-les-pins, France, pp. 169–174 (2001)
8. Caro, G.D., Dorigo, M.: Antnet: A mobile angents approach to adaptive routing. Technical Report IRIDIA/97-12, Université Libre de Bruxelles, Belgium (1997)
9. Decker, K., Li, J.: Coordinated hospital patient scheduling. In: Proceedings of the Third International Conference on Multi-Agent Systems (ICMAS 1998), pp. 104–111 (1998)
10. Decker, K., Li, J.: Coordinating mutually exclusive resources using GPGP. Autonomous Agents and Multi-Agent Systems 3(2), 133–157 (2000)
11. Decker, K.S.: Environment Centered Analysis and Design og Coordination Mechanisms. PhD thesis, Department of Computer Science, University of Massachusetts (May 1995)
12. Dijkstra, E.W.: A note to two problems in connexion with graphs. Numerische Mathematik 1, 269–271 (1959)
13. Donaldson, A.: A case narrative of the project problems with the denver airport baggage handling system (dabhs). Technical Report TR 2002-01, Middlesex University, School of Computing Science, 1 (2002)
14. Flake, S., Geiger, C., Lehrenfeld, G., Mueller, W., Paelke, V.: Agent-based modeling for holonic manufacturing systems with fuzzy control. In: NAFIPS 1999, 18th International Conference of the North American Fuzzy Information Processing Society, New York, USA (1999)
15. I. Flavors Technology. Baggage handling systems,
    http://www.flavors.com/-Appnotes/Baggage.html
16. Giret, A., Botti, V.: Analysis and design of holonic manufacturing systems. In: 18th International Conference on Production Research (ICPR 2005) (2005)
17. Gufflet, Y., Demazeau, Y.: Applying the paco paradigm to a three-dimensional artistic creation. In: 5th International Workshop on Agent-Based Simulation, ABS 2004, Lisbon, Portugal, pp. 121–126 (2004)

18. Haesevoets, R., Eylen, B.V., Weyns, D., Helleboogh, A., Tom Holvoet, W.J.: Context-driven dynamic organizations applied in coordinated monitoring of traffic jams. In: Proceedings of Engineering Environment-Mediated MultiAgent Systems, Dresden, Germany, October 1-5, pp. 1022–1028 (2007)
19. Kragh, A.: K-Netvrksmodeller til Analyse af FMS Anlg. PhD thesis, Informatics and Mathematical Modelling, Technical University of Denmark (1990)
20. Maionea, G., Naso, D.: A soft computing approach for task contracting in multi-agent manufacturing control. Computers in Industry 52(3), 199–219 (1996)
21. Negnevitsky, M.: Artificial Intelligence – A Guide to Intelligent Systems, 2nd edn. Addison-Wesley, Reading (2005)
22. Schoonderwoerd, R., Holland, O., Bruten, J., Rothkrantz, L.: Ant-based load balancing in telecommunication networks. Adaptive Behaviour (5), 169–207 (1996)
23. Schumacher, M., Grangier, L., Jurca, R.: Modeling and design of an agent-based micro-simulation of the swiss highway network. In: Proceedings of Engineering Environment-Mediated MultiAgent Systems, Dresden, Germany, October 1-5, 2007, pp. 1022–1028 (2007)
24. Telecom Italia. Jade (java agent development framework) (2006), http://jade.tilab.com/
25. Wikipedia, T.F.E.: Denver international airport (2007), http://en.wikipedia.org/wiki/-Denver_International_Airport

Managing Agent Interactions with Context-Driven Dynamic Organizations

Robrecht Haesevoets, Bart Van Eylen, Danny Weyns,
Alexander Helleboogh, Tom Holvoet, and Wouter Joosen

DistriNet, Katholieke Universiteit Leuven
Celestijnenlaan 200 A, B-3001 Leuven, Belgium
{firstname.name}@cs.kuleuven.be

Abstract. Organizations are at the heart of multi-agent systems. To deal with the ongoing dynamics and changes in the system, organizations have to adapt. Typically, agents are responsible to deal with the complexity of organization dynamics. In this paper, we present an approach for context-driven dynamic organizations in which the agent environment takes the burden of managing organization dynamics. Driven by the context, the agent environment manages the evolution of organizations and actively advertises roles to the agents, supporting the necessary collaborations between agents needed in the current context. We introduce a conceptual model for context-driven dynamic organizations and present a software architecture that supports the model in a distributed setting. The proposed approach separates the management of dynamic evolution of organizations from the actual functionality provided by the agents playing roles in the organizations. Separating these concerns makes it easier to understand, design, and manage organizations in multi-agent systems.

We show how we have applied context-driven dynamic organizations in a concrete case of monitoring traffic jams. In this case, camera agents associated with traffic monitoring cameras collaborate in organizations. Depending on the context, camera agents play different roles, with responsibilities ranging from simple measurement to data aggregation. When a traffic jam covers the viewing range of multiple cameras, organizations are dynamically merged, assuring cameras detecting the same traffic jam can collaborate. Vice versa, when a traffic jam dissolves, the organization is dynamically split up. Test results indicate that context-based dynamic organizations is a promising approach to support decentralized traffic monitoring.

1 Introduction

Structuring and managing interactions among agents is a crucial part of the design of any multi-agent system. A typical way to manage these interactions is by means of organizations in which agents play roles [24,26,9]. Multi-agent systems are often applied to problems and domains which are very dynamic in nature. To deal with the ongoing dynamics and changes, organizations have to adapt. In many systems the interactions between agents in organizations are imposed or driven by the current context or environment of the system. Depending on the context, agents have to collaborate in organizations and play certain roles. Most of the existing work on organizations defines

D. Weyns, S.A. Brueckner, and Y. Demazeau (Eds.): EEMMAS 2007, LNAI 5049, pp. 166–186, 2008.

roles and organizations at the level of agents [11,13,14,30]. As such, agents have a dual role: on the one hand agents play roles providing the associated functionality in the organization, on the other hand agents are responsible to set up and manage organizations, and deal with the complexity of organization dynamics.

In this paper, we propose an approach called *context-driven dynamic organizations* that considers an organization as a first-class abstraction which is explicitly supported by the agent environment.[1] In particular, the agent environment takes the burden of managing organizations and their dynamics. Driven by the context, the agent environment manages the evolution of organizations and actively advertises roles to agents, supporting the necessary collaborations between agents needed in the current context.

The proposed approach separates the management of dynamic evolution of organizations from the actual functionality provided by the agents playing roles in the organizations. Separating these concerns makes it easier to understand, design, and manage organizations in multi-agent systems. We present a software architecture that supports our model for context-driven dynamic organizations in a distributed setting. In this architecture the agent environment consists of a group of distributed local agent environments. The local agent environment provides functionality to the agents for perception, action and interaction, and it manages organizations which it dynamically evolves according to the current context.

We apply context-driven dynamic organizations to a concrete case. The case covers the coordinated monitoring of traffic jams and clearly shows the need for context-driven dynamic organizations. In this case, camera agents associated with traffic monitoring cameras collaborate in organizations. Depending on the context, camera agents play different roles, with responsibilities ranging from simple measurement to data aggregation. When a traffic jam covers the viewing range of multiple cameras, organizations are dynamically merged, assuring cameras detecting the same traffic jam can collaborate. Vice versa, when a traffic jam dissolves, the organization is dynamically split up. Test results indicate that context-driven dynamic organizations is a promising approach to support decentralized traffic monitoring.

Overview of the Paper. Section 2 starts by introducing the concrete case on coordinated monitoring of traffic jams. In Sect. 3 we introduce the conceptual model for context-driven dynamic organizations and in Sect. 4 we present a software architecture that supports this model. Section 5 shows a prototype implementation for the traffic monitoring case, giving an initial validation of our model and applicability of our approach. Section 6 discusses related work, and in Sect. 7 we draw conclusions.

2   Case Study: Coordinated Monitoring of Traffic Jams

Intelligent transportation systems are a worldwide initiative to exploit information and communication technology in traffic monitoring and control, aiming to improve safety

---

[1] In line with [37], we consider the agent environment as an explicit building block in a multi-agent system that encapsulates its own clear-cut responsibilities, irrespective of the agents. Note that the agent environment should not be confused with the *environment* in which the system is deployed, i.e., the part of the external world with which the multi-agent system interact, and in which the effects of the system will be observed and evaluated [21].

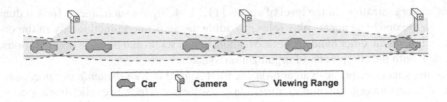

Fig. 1. An example of a highway with traffic cameras

and to reduce vehicle wear, transportation times and fuel consumption [20,12]. In this case, we focus on monitoring traffic jams on highways with a number of intelligent cameras. Traffic monitoring knows many applications, such as informing drivers about expected travel time delays, driving traffic control applications such as traffic light regulation, collecting data for long term structural decision making, etc.

The monitoring application we consider, consists of a set of intelligent cameras which are distributed evenly along the highway, as shown in Fig. 1. Each camera has a limited viewing range and cameras are placed to get an optimal coverage of the highway with a minimum in overlap. Each camera is able to measure three traffic variables within its viewing range: the current density ($k \approx$ number of vehicles per length unit), intensity ($q \approx$ sum of all speeds off all vehicles in the viewing range, devided by the total road length in the viewing range) and average speed (u). These three variables can be used to determine the current congestion level and decide whether there is a traffic jam or not in the viewing range of a camera [36]. Every camera is equipped with a data processing unit, capable of processing the monitored data, and a communication unit, to communicate with other cameras. The task of the cameras is to detect and monitor traffic jams on the highway. This case will follow an approach in which traffic jams are monitored in a decentralized way, avoiding the bottleneck of a centralized control center.

Because a camera has only a limited viewing range, no single camera will be able to monitor the complete highway or even a single traffic jam. Traffic jams can cover the viewing range of multiple cameras and can dynamically grow and dissolve. When growing or dissolving, traffic jams can enter and leave the viewing range of several cameras. To monitor a traffic jam, data observed by multiple cameras has to be aggregated. Because there is no central point of control, cameras will have to collaborate, and distribute the aggregated data to the necessary clients, such as traffic light controllers, driver assistance systems, etc.

By default each camera will simply monitor the traffic variables (density, intensity and average speed) of the traffic within its viewing range. When a traffic jam occurs, in the viewing range of a camera, the locally observed variables will pass a certain threshold. The camera will then have to collaborate with other cameras, detecting the same traffic jam. In the collaboration, the data each camera is monitoring is aggregated to get a complete image of the traffic jam. Cameras will enter or leave the collaboration, whenever the traffic jam enters or leaves their viewing range.

An example of such a collaboration is shown in figure 2. At t_0, there is no traffic jam and all cameras monitor the traffic variables. At t_1, an accident occurs in the viewing range of camera c_5 and a traffic jam arises. The traffic jam is only visible in the viewing range of camera c_5 and there is no collaboration necessary among the cameras. The

camera

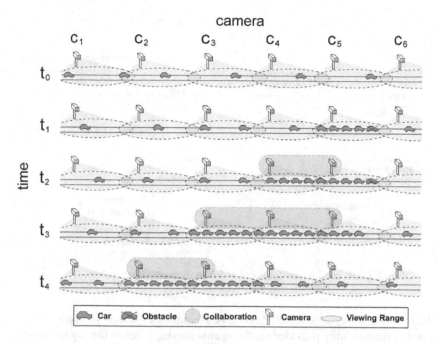

Fig. 2. An example of collaborations between traffic cameras

traffic jam, however, starts to grow and at t_2 it has entered the viewing range of camera c_4. Camera c_4 and c_5 start to collaborate because they are now both monitoring the same traffic jam. At t_3, the accident is solved but the traffic jam has further grown and entered the viewing range of camera c_3. Therefore, camera c_3 now participates in the collaboration between camera c_4 and c_5. At t_4, the traffic jam has entered the viewing range of camera c_2 but has dissolved in the viewing range of camera c_4 and c_5. Camera c_4 and c_5 have stopped collaborating while camera c_2 is collaborating with camera c_3. This example scenario illustrates how the collaboration between the cameras is driven by the context.

The dynamic nature of the traffic phenomena demands for dynamic collaborations between the cameras. Cameras will have to collaborate in organizations, which have to evolve dynamically according to the current traffic conditions, which make up the context of the highway. In the following sections, we will show how our conceptual model and architecture for context-driven dynamic organizations can be applied to the case of monitoring traffic jams and offer support for the complex collaborations required between the cameras.

3   Model for Context-Driven Dynamic Organizations

In this section, we present a conceptual model for context-driven dynamic organizations. The complete model is shown in Fig. 3. The model offers support for organizations and roles which dynamically evolve according to the current context. The idea

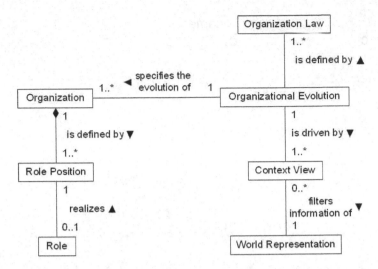

Fig. 3. Conceptual model for context-driven dynamic organizations

behind the model is to separate the context-driven dynamic evolution of organizations from the actual functionality provided by the agents playing roles in the organizations. This separation of concerns supports a system in which the agent environment provides support for organizations and manages organization dynamics, while the agents provide the actual functionality and behavior required in the organizations.

The main focus of the model is on how existing organizations dynamically evolve. How organizations are set up and what the relations are between roles is currently outside the scope of the model. Relations between roles, however, is a well researched topic, as we will cover in Sect. 6, and we consider it future work to add explicit support for this to our model.

Section 3.1 starts with explaining the conceptual model, and how the concepts allow to separate the dynamics of organizations from the actual functionality and behavior. After the introduction of each concept, it is mapped to the traffic monitoring case, introduced in Sect. 2. In Sect. 3.2 we illustrate how organizations can dynamically evolve, driven by the context, and finally in Sect. 3.3 we cover how the context itself is represented in the model.

3.1 Organizations, Role Positions and Roles

An organization (`Organization`) is defined by a set of related role positions (`Role Position`). A role position is very similar to a job opening in a company. It represents the specification of a coherent part of functionality required in an organization, but it can also include a part of the infrastructure needed to realize the required functionality. A role (`Role`) realizes the actual functionality specified by a role position. To collaborate with each other, agents can play one or multiple roles in one or more organizations. There is a potential conflict between the use of the terms role and role positions in our work and the use in other work. We will reflect on this issue in Sect. 6.

The abstraction of organization allows us to group collaborating agents as one entity, hiding the details of the individual agents. The abstraction of role position separates the dynamics of an organization, driven by the current context, from the actual functionality of the organization, provided by the agents playing the corresponding roles. It also allows agents to transparently swap roles within or between organizations, while leaving the decision to do so to the agents.

The difference between a role position and a role is clarified by the following analogy. A hospital has a role position for a surgeon. This role position represents the specification of the job as a surgeon, but also includes the necessary infrastructure, such as an office with a telephone and an internet connection, and an operating room, needed by the doctor playing the role of surgeon. It is clear that the role position of surgeon can exist without a doctor actually playing the role of surgeon, and that different doctors with the necessary qualifications and approval can decide whether or not to play the role of surgeon. The hospital management can decide whether or not to open a new role position for surgeon or to close an existing one, depending on the current demand of patients. The notion of role positions allows the hospital management to define and change the organizational structure, independent of the doctors providing the actual service of a surgeon.

Organizations, Role Positions and Roles in the Traffic Monitoring Case. In the traffic monitoring case, a software agent is deployed on every camera. The agent is capable of playing roles and will further be referred to as camera agent. An organization allows camera agents to collaborate, in order to detect and monitor traffic jams. When a camera agent enters the system, it is automatically added to a new organization. Within the organization, there are three kinds of role positions possible: data observer (Data Observer), data pusher (Data Pusher) and data aggregator (Data Aggregator). The data observer role is responsible for monitoring the three traffic variables (density, intensity and average speed) and deciding whether the congestion level is high enough to be considered a traffic jam. The data pusher role is responsible for pushing the observed data to the data aggregator role, which in turn is responsible for aggregating the data and distributing it to the necessary clients, such as traffic lights, driver assistance systems, etc.

3.2 Context-Driven Evolution of Organizations

The evolution of organizations and their role positions is context-driven. Organizational evolution (Organizational Evolution) uses one or more views on the current context (Context view) as input to evolve an organization and its role positions. Context consists of information such as existing role positions and their associated roles, information on external resources probed by sensors, or data related to physical entities. Organizations can evolve by splitting up or merging together, regrouping the agents to support the necessary collaborations between agents, needed in the current context. Role positions are evolved by opening new positions or closing existing ones.

Organizational evolution (Organizational Evolution) uses a set of laws (Organization Laws), which define the way organizations and role positions should evolve given the current context. Currently the model supports three kinds of

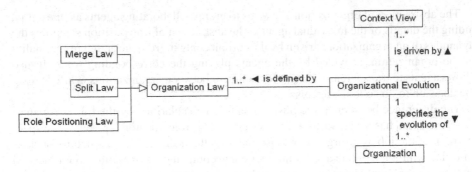

Fig. 4. Different kinds laws used by the organizational evolution

laws: split laws (Split Law), merge laws (Merge Law) and role positioning laws (Role Positioning Law).

Role positioning laws define whether existing role positions should be closed or whether new positions should be opened. Merge laws define whether two or more organizations should be merged into one organization, and split laws define whether an organization should be split up. Organizational evolution is the evolution of organizations according to these laws. Whenever something changes in the context, the laws are re-evaluated and organizations and role positions are updated accordingly.

The model assumes that laws are applied atomically and that laws can be executed in any order when multiple laws apply. Figure 5 shows a statechart representation of an example of a possible evolution of organizations and role positions. In the example, the current configuration of organizations and role positions, and the current context is represented as a state. Whenever something changes in the context or when laws are applied, a new state is reached. In the example the context in state S_0 is changed and a new state S_1 is reached. Because the context is changed, laws are re-evaluated and applied in an atomic and unordered manner. In the example law_B is first applied and a new state S_2 is reached, representing an updated configuration of organizations and role positions and an updated context. Next law_A is applied and a new state S_3 is reached, again with an updated configuration and context.

Context-Driven Evolution of Organizations in the Traffic Monitoring Case. When a camera agent enters the system, the agent is automatically added to a new organization. The further life of the organization is guided by the organizational evolution. Camera agents can not join or leave new organizations, but the existing organizations can be merged together or split up, regrouping the agents according to the current context. Role positions can be dynamically opened and closed.

Organizational evolution is defined by one merge law, one split law and one role positioning law per type of role position. The merge law states that organizations should

Fig. 5. Statechart representation of an example of organizational evolution

be merged when they are neighbouring organizations in space and when they are both monitoring a traffic jam. The split law states that camera agents in an organization with no traffic jam in their viewing range, should be split up in separate organizations, one per agent. The role positioning laws state that within an organization there is always a data observer role position available for every agent in the organization, which camera agents are supposed to play by default. The role positions for data pusher and data aggregator are only available when the organization is currently monitoring a traffic jam and data needs to be aggregated. If the organization is monitoring a traffic jam, the role position of data pusher will be available for every agent in the organization, but only one position will be available for the data aggregator role.

According to these laws, when there is no traffic jam, organizations will consist of single camera agents. The camera agents in these organizations will then play the default role of data observer, to detect whether a traffic jam arises. When a traffic jam is detected, the organization will grow along with the traffic jam in order to fully monitor it. Organizations grow by merging with neighbouring organizations, detecting the same traffic jam, as defined by the merge law. When the traffic jam dissolves or leaves the viewing range of a camera, the organization is split up again, as defined by the split law. This way, only camera agents with the traffic jam in the viewing range of their camera will be grouped in one organization.

Figure 6, shows a reprise of the example in Fig. 2, but now with the model applied to it. At t_0, there is no traffic jam and all camera agents are member of a separate organization. At t_1, an accident occurs in the viewing range of camera c_5 and a traffic jam originates. The traffic jam starts to grow and at t_2 it has entered the viewing range of camera c_4. The organizations of camera agents c_4 and c_5 are merged together because they are both monitoring the same traffic jam. At t_3, the accident is solved but the traffic jam has further grown into the viewing range of camera c_3. The organization of camera agent c_3 is therefore merged with the organization of camera agents c_4 and c_5. At t_4, the traffic jam has grown into the viewing range of camera c_2 but has left the viewing range of camera c_4 and c_5. The organization is split up, camera agents c_4 and c_5 are in separate organizations and the organizations of camera agents c_2 and c_3 are merged together. Whenever the organizations merge together or split up, new role positions are opened or existing role positions are closed, according to the role positioning laws.

3.3   World Representation and Context View

As mentioned before, context is an important concept in our model, it is used as input for the organizational evolution. World representation (`World Representation`) represents the current state or context of the world. World representation can contain information on the state of the real world, such as existing entities or input readings from sensors, as well as information on the state of the virtual world, such as existing organizations and role positions. However, world representation contains a lot of information which is often not relevant or needed and is therefore not accessed directly, but through a context view (`Context View`). A context view represents a specific view on the world representation, only focussing on relevant information. Organizational evolution can have one or more of these context views, e.g., each focussing on information of a specific organization.

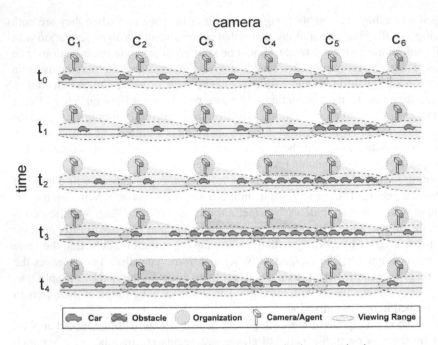

Fig. 6. An example of congestion monitoring organizations

World Representation and Context View in the Traffic Monitoring Case. In the traffic monitoring case the world consist of a highway with cars on it, a set of distributed cameras, their organizations and their roles. The organizational evolution will have a context view on each organization. The context view on an organization consists among other things of the open and implemented role positions, the current congestion level in the viewing range of individual cameras and information on neighbouring organizations it can be merged with.

4   Supporting Architecture

In this section, we present a high-level software architecture that supports the presented model for context-driven dynamic organizations. Figure 7 shows the collaborating components view of the software architecture that is deployed on each node or intelligent camera. The collaborating components view shows the agent system as a set of interacting components that use a set of shared data repositories to realize the required system functionalities. The main software components are `Local Agent Environment` and `Agent`. The local agent environment enables agents to coordinate their behavior [37]. It provides functionality to the agents for perception, action and interaction, but it also provides organizations, which it dynamically evolves according to the current context. The local agent environment is connected to the external world which contains the given hardware and software with which the software system interacts.

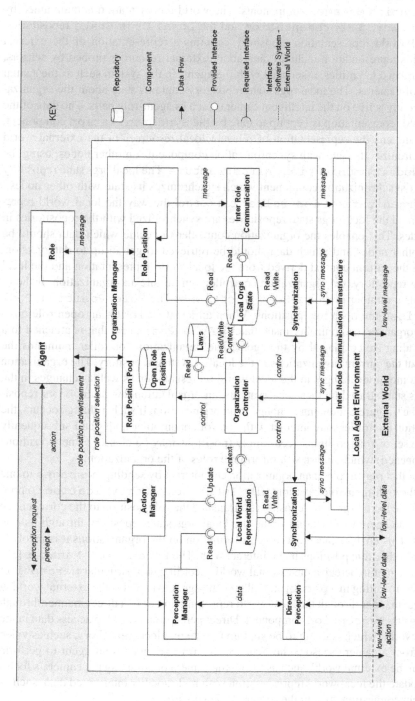

Fig. 7. Collaborating components view of the software architecture for context-driven dynamic organizations

The evolution of organizations, or organizational evolution, is managed by the Organization Manager components. The world representation is maintained by the Local World Representation and the Local Orgs State repositories. The local world representation repository contains a representation of the external world. This representation includes data about external resources probed by sensors, and data related to entities, associated with the agents in the system such as the spatial position of cameras. The local orgs state repository contains state about the organizations currently active on the intelligent camera, such as agent-role pairs. The data of the local world representation is kept up to date by the Synchronization component, which maintains the representation of relevant local resources in the external world and synchronizes its state with synchronization components on other nodes, using the Inter Node Communication Infrastructure. The local orgs state repository also has a synchronization component which synchronizes its state with other nodes.

The Organization Controller can control the way the local world representation and the local orgs state repositories are synchronized with the repositories in other nodes. This enables the organization controller to decide which data should be send to other nodes and which data should be retrieved to get an up to date version. Based on the current context derived from the local world representation and the local orgs state repository, the organization controller can initiate an organization. It therefore opens a number of Open Role Positions. The Role Position Pool advertises the open role positions. When an agent selects an open role position, the organization controller instantiates a Role Position that is attached to a corresponding Role played by the agent. The organization controller maintains the state about the current organizations in the local orgs state repository. The organization controller monitors changes in the local world representation as well as changes in the local orgs state. Based on these observations, an organization law in the Laws repository can be triggered, inducing a change in an organization. If such a change occurs, the organization controller may interact with controllers on other nodes and subsequently adapt the set of role positions accordingly (positions may be closed, or new positions may be opened) which in turn will inform the roles of the organization.

Agents that play a role in an organization can interact by sending messages to one another through their role positions. The Inter Role Communication component uses the local orgs state repository to translate the role position to the correct node address. The agent itself can also read the local orgs state repository through its role positions. This enables the agent to get information on the organizations it is involved in, such as other role positions it can interact with. The Perception Manager [38] enables an agent to perceive the external world according to a particular perception request, resulting in a percept. It allows the agent to perceive the external world in an indirect manner through the local world representation or in a direct manner through the Direct Perception component. Direct perception is used to access data in the external world, which is to big to be kept up to date in a local repository, such as video images from a camera sensor. The Action Manager enables an agent to perform actions in the external world, such as tilting the camera or adjusting the camera's focus, and to update the local world representation with high-level or interpreted data, such as the current congestion level in the camera's viewing range.

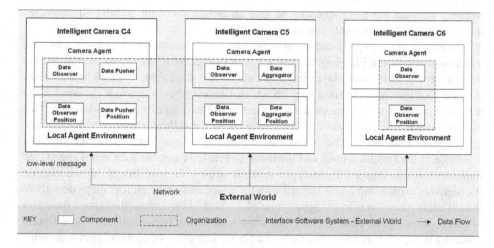

Fig. 8. Software architecture applied to the traffic monitoring application

Figure 8 shows an excerpt of the software architecture applied to the traffic monitoring application. The figure reflects the organization structure of cameras c_4, c_5, and c_6 at time t_2 in Fig. 6. In the depicted situation, the camera agents of c_4 and c_5 form an organization, monitoring a traffic jam. Since there is no traffic jam within the viewing range of c_6, the camera agent of c_6 makes up an organization on its own.

5   Prototype, Evaluation and Applicability

The goal of the prototype and evaluation is twofold. First, it is used as a validation for the model for context-driven dynamic organizations, introduced in Sect. 3, applied to the traffic monitoring case. Second, it is used to give an initial indication of the communication cost to support dynamic evolution of organizations and the applicability of our approach. This section will first explain the setup used for the validation and the assumptions the prototype is built on, before explaining the concrete experiments.

The prototype is built on a cellular automaton based traffic simulator [6]. It allows for the discrete simulation of individual vehicles, based on different selectable driver models. We extended the simulator with the notion of cameras, for measuring density, intensity and average speed. On top of the extended simulator, we built a prototype implementation of the architecture, presented in Sect. 4, explicitly supporting the abstractions provided by the model, introduced in Sect. 3. It is important to note that we have currently made abstraction from distribution issues.

5.1   Experiments

In our experiments we modelled a straight highway with a length of 4500 metres, one lane and one direction. Thirty cameras are equally distributed along the highway. First, we examined the dynamic evolution of organizations in four different scenarios.

Second, we used the same scenarios to give an indication of the number of messages needed for the dynamic evolution of organizations.

The results of the experiment are presented by a set of snapshots, an example of such a snapshot is given in Fig. 9(a), the key is given in Fig. 9(d). The top of the Fig. 9(a) is a space time plot. It shows the trajectory of each individual vehicle through time. Time t in the plot indicates the time step on which the snapshot was taken. Values on the time axis, smaller than t, happened at a time in the past relative to the snapshot. This way the space time plot shows the evolution of all the different vehicle trajectories in a fixed sized time frame. The color of each point in the graph represents the speed of a vehicle at the specified time and position. Green indicates the maximum speed, red indicates the lowest speed. Beneath the space time plot is a snapshot of the situation on the highway at time step t. It is aligned with the space axis and therefore maps directly to the different trajectories in the space time plot. At the bottom, another space time plot is given, showing the state of the congestion monitoring organizations. The different columns in the plot represent the thirty cameras. The color of each column represents the organizational situation of each camera. Green means that at that specific time the camera sees no congestion and sits all by itself in its organization playing the role of data observer. Blue means that the camera sees congestion but still sits alone in its organization, playing both the role of data pusher and data aggregator. Red means that the camera observes congestion and forms an organization with neighbouring cameras if they also have a red color. This way, adjacent red columns represent one organization.

Free Flow Traffic: In a first scenario we monitored free flow traffic, which constitutes of a continuous stream of vehicles traversing the highway. A snapshot of the situation is given in Fig. 9(a), which, as expected, shows that there is no congestion and all cameras are playing the role of data observer in their own organization.

Obstacle Blocking Highway: In a second scenario we simulated an obstacle in the middle of the highway to initiate a traffic jam. The evolution of this scenario is shown in Fig. 9(b), 9(c) and 10(a). In Fig. 9(b) we see in the space time plot at the top, that a traffic jam has emerged and is propagating backwards over the highway. The snapshot of the highway itself supports this finding. If we look at the bottom of the figure we see that the camera monitoring the congested part of the highway, is now also playing the role of data pusher and data aggregator, indicated by the blue color. Figure 9(c) and 10(a) show the further evolution of the traffic jam. Different adjacent columns have a red color indicating that these cameras are observing congestion and all form one organization. As expected, cameras detect the congestion and over time evolve into one large organization along the congested part of the highway.

Obstacle Removed: In a third scenario we removed the obstacle. The traffic jam slowly dissolved in the front, while propagating backwards. The organization formed in the previous scenario should adapt itself accordingly. Figure 10(b) and 10(c) show the outcome of this scenario. The traffic jam slowly dissolves at the front while propagating backwards. As expected, cameras in the front of the organization are split up in separate organizations, while the organizations of cameras in the back are merged in one large organization.

New Obstacle Introduced: Figure 10(d) shows the fourth and final scenario, in which after the initial obstacle was removed, a new obstacle is introduced at the same location. The initial traffic jam is still propagating backwards while a new traffic jam arises in the middle. This leads to two different organizations, which both evolve over time each following a traffic jam.

5.2 Communication Costs

Figure 11 shows the communication overhead throughout the four different scenarios. The counted messages are solely messages needed to dynamically evolve organizations. We make the following two observations. First, the larger an organization is the more overhead it takes to merge it, split it or change role positions in it. This can be seen in the second scenario in which a single organization grows larger and larger together with an increase in message overhead. When the organization splits up in smaller organizations in the third scenario, the number of needed messages also starts to drop. Second, the message overhead depends on the number of organizations. This can be observed in fourth scenario, in which the overhead starts to rise again because a second organization has formed.

5.3 Applicability

Although this is only an initial protoype and we made an abstraction of the distribution issues, it is clear that communication and synchronization are potential issues or bottle-necks, when applying our approach in a distributed setting. As an initial rule of thumb, we can say that context-driven dynamic organizations are applicable to problems where the phenomena or context (e.g., traffic jams) to which the organizations map are orders of magnitude slower than the speed at which the virtual organizations can evolve.

6 Related Work

We focus our discussion of related work on organizational concepts in multi-agent systems and on traffic monitoring techniques.

6.1 Organizations and Multi-agent Systems

We focus on two areas of related work with respect to multi-agent systems research: (1) representation of context information by means of an explicit environment model and (2) roles and organizations in multi-agent systems.

Research on environments in multi-agent systems devotes a lot of attention to representing context information of the external world in an explicit manner, i.e. by means of an explicit model of the environment. For example, to present relevant information of the physical world to agents, [7] introduces a *cognitive middle layer* in the environment that employs a shared ontology to present environmental information to the agents. MMASS [2] introduces a *multi-layered* model of the environment, with each layer an explicit representation of a particular spatial or conceptual structure of the real

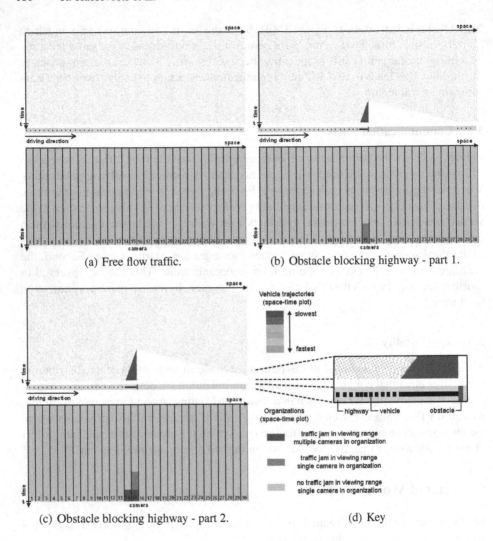

(a) Free flow traffic.

(b) Obstacle blocking highway - part 1.

(c) Obstacle blocking highway - part 2.

(d) Key

Fig. 9. Validation scenarios, part a

environment. ELMS [29] is an environment description language with explicit support for specifying perception and interaction of cognitive agents. The main difference between these approaches and our approach is that we employ the environment to support organizations. As such, the context information used in our approach exceeds a representation of the external world, and includes information about the organizational setting of the system.

Roles, organizations and groups are recognized to be valuable abstractions for building multi-agent systems [22,10,34,15]. For example, [27] analyzes role changes in dynamic environments, distinguishing between two categories of changes: dynamic activation of roles and dynamic classification of roles. In [8], the authors define relations between agents and roles, e.g., the way an agent *takes up* a role and *enacts* it. Possible

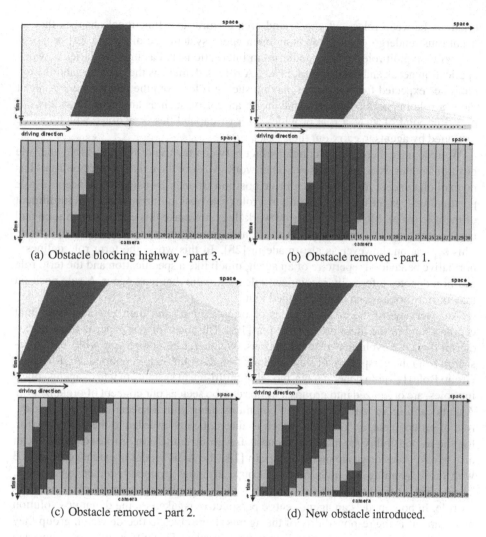

(a) Obstacle blocking highway - part 3.

(b) Obstacle removed - part 1.

(c) Obstacle removed - part 2.

(d) New obstacle introduced.

Fig. 10. Validation scenarios, part b

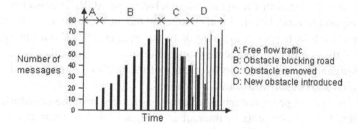

A: Free flow traffic
B: Obstacle blocking road
C: Obstacle removed
D: New obstacle introduced

Fig. 11. Message overhead throughout the four different scenarios

relations between roles and agents and architectural and functional changes that an agent must undergo when it enters an open agent system, are discussed. [5] proposes *XRoles* to exploit roles as intermediaries in interactions and as intermediaries between application needs and environment needs. A role is defined as the behavior and the capabilities expected from the agent playing such a role. From the environment point of view, a role imposes a defined behavior on an entity, such as an agent. From the application point of view, a role provides a set of capabilities or actions, which can be exploited by agents to carry out their tasks.

We recognize there is a potential conflict between the use of the terms role and role positions in our work and the use in other work. Most of the existing work on roles has no explicit concept for what we call role position. In fact, by using the concept of role position we separate the specification of a role (role position) from the actual fulfillment of the role (role). Most of the existing work does not make this explicit separation and uses the term role to denote a specification, assignment and a possible implicit position. This separation, however, is also made in [28]. In this work, the term role defines a normative behavioral repertoire of an agent, much like a specification and the term role position denotes a formally recognized role assigment that may occur. A role position may or may not have an agent assigned to it.

An overview of the different types of organizations and their characteristics that can be found in the literature, is given in [19]. The focus of our paper is the context-driven dynamic evolution of organizations. We therefore compare it with related research from the perspective of how organizational evolution is supported. AGR (Agent Group Role) [13] is a generic meta-model of multi-agent systems in which agents, playing roles, are organized into groups. Groups can be seen as our concept of organization. Agents can join or leave a group by communicating with a special agent playing the role of group manager. This role, which is automatically awarded to the group creator, has the responsibility for handling requests for group admission or role requests. It can also revoke roles or group membership. In [14] the AGR model is extended to AGRE with the E standing for environment. Groups are now grouped together into worlds. These worlds offer primitives for agents to join a particular group and to play a particular role. In both models an agent-centric perspective is taken on the dynamic evolution of groups. It is the responsibility of the agents themselves to decide which group they want to join or leave and which role they want to play. This differs from our approach in which the dynamic evolution of organizations is actively managed and driven by the agent environment instead of the agents themselves. The AGR(E) concepts also offer no explicit support to model evolutional changes at the inter-organization level. It is for example not clear how to model that two or more organizations should merge or split in function of the context of the agent system. Our model on the other hand allows to model inter-organizational evolution by means of the first-class concepts of organizational evolution and organization laws.

TuCSoN [31] offers programmable tuplespaces that encapsulate coordination rules between roles. It enables agents to interact at a higher level of abstraction, and in a way that is tailored to the their needs. In [30], TuCSoN is extended to support the description and enacting of organizational models. A TuCSoN node also serves as an organization node, hosting tuple centres as coordination artefacts/services available to agents. In order to access the tuple centres hosted by a node, an agent must join the organization and choose a role to play. As is the case with AGRE, this conforms to an agent-centric approach. Each node also has a special tuple centre that explicitly hosts the description of the organization, represented by that node. It contains, for example, dynamic information about the current set of roles and related relationships (agent-role and inter-role). These organizational settings can be dynamically inspected and changed by agents, by suitably reading and modifying the tuple contents. This allows agents, for example, to add or delete roles from the organization. However, it is only possible to make changes on the intra-organizational level this way. Reorganizations on the inter-organizational level are not supported.

In [11], reorganization issues in agent societies are discussed. It explores how and why organizations change, and how reorganization can be done dynamically, with minimal interference from the system designer (i.e., by the system itself). A classification is given of reorganization situations, based on the focus of the reorganization, the authority to modify the organization, and how reorganization decisions are taken. With respect to the latter, two possible approaches are identified. First, the decision making to change the organization could be the responsibility of one role in the organization. This corresponds to a master/slave relationship between agents acting at the different levels of autonomy and is called role-based control. Second, all or some roles are collectively responsible for a change decision. Changes are then achieved by collaboration or consensus among the agents. This is called shared control. This does not cover our model, in which it is the agent environment that has the authority and decision making power to change organizations.

6.2 Traffic Monitoring

Traffic monitoring is an extensively studied field of research. We discuss a number of representative approaches used for vehicle detection by means of image analysis and multi-sensor fusion.

A lot of research has been done on vision-based traffic surveillance. Many algorithms and processing techniques exist for vehicle detection and/or recognition from single or multiple frames obtained from a camera [3,17,23]. [32] describes an approach to identify vehicles in images of congested traffic. They rely on the strong shadows present under each vehicle to detect and localize vehicles. [25] proposes a tracking system, which processes traffic video streams, to track vehicles and to classify these vehicles into three classes, i.e. (1) sedans, (2) semi and (3) truck, SUV or van.

In the traffic monitoring research community, there is an increasing interest in combining footage from multiple (image) sensors to improve the analysis of a traffic situation. For example, [16] uses the imagery of three cameras, to track the trajectory of passing vehicles. [4] presents a color stereo vision system to extract 3D edges of an observed obstacle. [33] describes an approach, to detect traffic incidents, that relies on different types of sensors: i.e., image sensors and supersonic wave sensors. This allows more accurate detection of traffic incidents.

Support exists to underpin multi-sensor fusion. AROCCAM [35], is a software framework, to design and implement data fusion applications. It provides support for unsynchronized sensors and delayed observations. Other approaches for multi-sensor fusion are [18,1]. In contrast to our approach, these approaches provide no explicit support to enable sensors to play different roles, or to form organizations between sensors in a context-driven, dynamic manner.

7 Conclusion and Future Work

In this paper, we presented an approach for context-driven dynamic organizations. Contrary to most existing approaches, in which agents have the dual responsibility of playing roles, providing the associated functionality in the organization, and managing organization dynamics, in context-driven dynamic organizations the agent environment takes the burden of managing organization dynamics. Separating the management of dynamic evolution of organizations from the actual functionality, provided by the agents playing roles in the organizations, improves understandability, and enables better reuse, making the design and management of organizations in multi-agent systems easier.

The model is built around four key abstractions: organization, role position, role and context view. An organization is defined by a set of related role positions. A role position represents the specification of a coherent part of functionality required in an organization. A role realizes the actual functionalities specified in a role position. To collaborate with each other, agents can play one or multiple roles in one or more organizations. The dynamical aspects of the organizations are context-driven. The agent environment uses the context as input to manage the dynamic evolution of organizations. Organizations evolve by adapting available role positions, splitting up and merging together, regrouping the agents to support the necessary collaborations between agents needed in the current context.

We presented a high-level software architecture that supports the model for context-driven dynamic organizations and applied it to a traffic monitoring case. With an initial prototype we validated the model and implemented the presented architecture. We also gave an indication about the communication overhead for dynamically evolving organizations and the applicability of our approach. Test results indicate that context-based dynamic organizations is a promising approach to support decentralized traffic monitoring.

Future work consists of formalizing the model for context-driven dynamic organizations, investigating the feasibility of introducing explicit support for interaction protocols and relations between roles in the model, and expanding the software architecture to offer middleware support for the presented abstractions.

References

1. Abuhadrous, I., Nashashibi, F., Laurgeau, C.: Multi-Sensor Fusion (GPS, IMU, Odometers) for Precise Land Vehicle Localisation Using RTMAPS. In: 11th International Conference on Advanced Robotics (ICAR 2003) (2003)
2. Bandini, S., Manzoni, S., Vizzari, G.: A Spatially Dependent Communiction Model for Ubiquitous Systems. In: Weyns, D., Van Dyke Parunak, H., Michel, F. (eds.) E4MAS 2004. LNCS (LNAI), vol. 3374, Springer, Heidelberg (2005)

3. Bensrhair, A., Bertozzi, M., Broggi, A., Miché, P., Mousset, S., Toulminet, G.: A cooperative approach to vision-based vehicle detection. In: 4th International IEEE Conference on Intelligent Transportation Systems, ITSC 2001, Oakland, USA, August 2001, pp. 207–212 (2001)
4. Cabani, I., Toulminet, G., Bensrhair, A.: A color stereo vision system for extraction of 3d edges of obstacle. In: Proceedings of the 2006 IEEE Intelligent Transportation Systems Conference (ITSC 2006), pp. 307–312 (2006)
5. Cabri, G., Leonardi, L., Zambonelli, F.: Separation of concerns in agent applications by roles. In: Proceedings of 22nd International Conference on Distributed Computing Systems Workshops, 2002, pp. 430–435 (2002)
6. Cellular Automaton Traffic Simulators,
   http://rcswww.urz.tu-dresden.de/~helbing/RoadApplet/
7. Chang, P., Chen, K., Chien, Y., Kao, E., Soo, V.: From Reality to Mind: A Cognitive Middle Layer of Environment Concepts for Believable Agents. In: Weyns, D., Van Dyke Parunak, H., Michel, F. (eds.) E4MAS 2004. LNCS (LNAI), vol. 3374, Springer, Heidelberg (2005)
8. Dastani, M., Dignum, V., Dignum, F.: Role-assignment in open agent societies. In: Proceedings of the second international joint conference on Autonomous agents and multiagent systems, pp. 489–496 (2003)
9. Demazeau, Y.: Multi-Agent Systems Methodology. In: 2nd Franco-Mexican School on Cooperative and Distributed Systems, LAFMI 2003 (August 2006),
   http://lafmi.lania.mx/escuelas/esd03/ponencias/Demazeau.pdf
10. Demazeau, Y., Rocha Costa, A.C.: Populations and organizations in open multi-agent systems. In: Proceedings of the 1st National Symposium on Parallel and Distributed AI (1996)
11. Dignum, V., Dignum, F., Sonenberg, L.: Towards Dynamic Reorganization of Agent Societies. In: Proceedings of Workshop on Coordination in Emergent Agent Societies at ECAI (2004)
12. ERTICO: Intelligent Transportation Systems for Europe, http://www.ertico.com/
13. Ferber, J., Gutknecht, O.: A meta-model for the analysis and design of organizations in multi-agent systems. In: Proceedings of the 3rd International Conference on Multi Agent Systems, p. 128 (1998)
14. Ferber, J., Michel, F., Baez, J.: AGRE: Integrating environments with organizations. In: Weyns, D., Van Dyke Parunak, H., Michel, F. (eds.) E4MAS 2004. LNCS (LNAI), vol. 3374, Springer, Heidelberg (2005)
15. Gasser, L.: Organizations in multi-agent systems. In: 10th European Workshop on Modeling Autonomous Agents in a Multi-Agent World (MAAMAW 2001) (2001)
16. Goya, Y., Chateau, T., Malaterre, L., Trassoudaine, L.: Vehicle trajectories evaluation by static video sensors. In: Proceedings of the 2006 IEEE Intelligent Transportation Systems Conference (ITSC 2006), Toronto, Canada, September 2006, pp. 864–869 (2006)
17. Gupte, S., Masoud, O., Papanikolopoulos, N.P.: Detection and classification of vehicles. IEEE Trans. on Intelligent Transportation Systems 3, 37–47 (2002)
18. Hightower, J., Brumitt, B., Borriello, G.: The location stack: A layered model for location in ubiquitous computing. In: Proceedings of the 4th IEEE Workshop on Mobile Computing Systems & Applications (WMCSA 2002), Callicoon, NY, June 2002, pp. 22–28. IEEE Computer Society Press, Los Alamitos (2002)
19. Horling, B., Lesser, V.: A survey of multi-agent organizational paradigms. Knowl. Eng. Rev. 19(4), 281–316 (2004)
20. ITS America: Intelligent Transportation Society of America, http://www.itsa.org/
21. Jackson, M.: The Meaning of Requirements. Annals of Software Engineering, Special Issue on Software Requirements Engineering 3, 5–22 (1997)
22. Jennings, N.R.: On agent-based software engineering. Artificial Intelligence 177(2), 277–296 (2000)

23. Jung, Y.K., Lee, K.W., Ho, Y.S.: Content-based event retrieval using semantic scene interpretation for automated traffic surveillance. ITS 2(3), 151–163 (2001)
24. Kendall, E.: Role modeling for agent system analysis, design, and implementation. IEEE Concurrency 8(2), 34–41 (2000)
25. Morris, B., Trivedi, M.: Robust classification and tracking of vehicles in traffic video streams. In: Proceedings of the 2006 IEEE Intelligent Transportation Systems Conference (ITSC 2006), Toronto, Canada, September 2006, pp. 1078–1083 (2006)
26. Odell, J., Parunak, H.V.D., Fleischer, M.: The Role of Roles. Journal of Object Technology 2(1), 39–51 (2003)
27. Odell, J., Van Dyke Parunak, H., Brueckner, S., Sauter, J.A.: Changing roles: Dynamic role assignment. Journal of Object Technology 2(5), 77–86 (2003)
28. Odell, J.J., Parunak, H.V.D., Fleischer, M.: The Role of Roles in Designing Effective Agent Organizations. In: Software Engineering for Large-scale Multi-agent Systems: Research Issues and Practical Applications (2003)
29. Okuyama, F., Bordini, R.H., da Rocha Costa, A.C.: An Environment Description Language for Multiagent Simulation. In: Weyns, D., Van Dyke Parunak, H., Michel, F. (eds.) E4MAS 2004. LNCS (LNAI), vol. 3374, Springer, Heidelberg (2005)
30. Omicini, A., Ricci, A.: Reasoning about organisation: Shaping the infrastructure. AI* IA Notizie 16(2), 7–16 (2003)
31. Omicini, A., Zambonelli, F.: TuCSoN: a Coordination Model for Mobile Information Agents. In: Proc. of the 1st Workshop on Innovative Internet Information Systems (1998)
32. Sadeghi, M., Fathy, M.: A low-cost occlusion handling using a novel feature in congested traffic images. In: Proceedings of the 2006 IEEE Intelligent Transportation Systems Conference (ITSC 2006), Toronto, Canada, September 2006, pp. 522–527 (2006)
33. Sumiya, N., Familiar, K., Kamijo, S.: Incident detection system by sensor fusion network employing image sensors and supersonic wave sensors. In: Intelligent Transportation Systems Conference, 2006. ITSC 2006, pp. 1066–1071. IEEE, Los Alamitos (2006)
34. Tambe, M., Pynadath, D.V., Chauvat, N.: Building dynamic agent organizations in cyberspace. IEEE Internet Computing 4(2), 65–73 (2000)
35. Tessier, C., Cariou, C., Debain, C., Chausse, F., Chapuis, R., Rousset, C.: A real-time, multi-sensor architecture for fusion of delayed observations: Application to vehicle localisation. In: Proceedings of the 2006 IEEE Intelligent Transportation Systems Conference (ITSC 2006) (2006)
36. Traffic Congestion, http://en.wikipedia.org/wiki/Traffic_congestion
37. Weyns, D., Omicini, A., Odell, J.: Environment as a First-Class Abstraction in Multiagent Systems. Autonomous Agents and Multi-Agent Systems 14(1), 5–30 (2007)
38. Weyns, D., Steegmans, E., Holvoet, T.: Towards Active Perception in Situated Multi-Agent Systems. Applied Artificial Intelligence 18(9-10), 867–883 (2004)

Modeling and Design
of an Agent-Based Micro-simulation
of the Swiss Highway Network

Michael Schumacher[1], Laurent Grangier[2], and Radu Jurca[2]

[1] University of Applied Sciences Western Switzerland
Institute of Business Information Systems
CH-3960 Sierre
[2] Ecole Polytechnique Fédérale de Lausanne (EPFL)
Artificial Intelligence Laboratory
CH-1015 Lausanne, Switzerland

Abstract. Multiagent simulations can be elegantly modeled and designed by enhancing the role of the environment in which agents evolve, called the agent environment. In particular, the agent environment may have the role of a governing infrastructure that regulates with laws or norms the actions taken by the agents. The focus of modeling and design is thus shifted from a subjective view of agents towards a more objective view of the whole multiagent system. In this paper, we apply the idea of a governing environment to model and design a multi-agent system for a micro-simulation of the Swiss highway network. The goal of the simulation is to show how traffic jams and accordion phenomena may be handled with appropriate local regulations on speed limits. A natural modeling would give segments the capacity to regulate the speed based on observed local events. We developed the simulation platform from scratch in order to accommodate our design choices and a realistic complexity. This paper presents in details our modeling and design choices, and first experimental results.

1 Introduction

Agent-based micro-simulations are becoming a popular application area of multiagent systems (MAS), in areas such as social sciences, traffic management, biology, geography, or environmental sciences. Agent technology has opened a whole new methodology for studying real-world complex systems by simulating every individual through an autonomous agent. Individual behavior can thus be easily modeled, and the MAS captures the aggregated behavior of the collective. These agent-based *micro-simulations* help to better understand the emergence of specific reality; they can also be a mean to test virtually some settings that would be very costly to test in real experiment. Traffic management is a typical example. For instance, a micro-simulation may help to visualize the effect of constructing new roads on the overall traffic.

D. Weyns, S.A. Brueckner, and Y. Demazeau (Eds.): EEMMAS 2007, LNAI 5049, pp. 187–203, 2008.

Some MASs (and a fortiori agent-based micro simulations) may be elegantly modeled and designed by enhancing the role of the environment in which agents evolve. In particular, the environment may have the role of a governing infrastructure that regulates with laws or norms any action within the system. This has the strong advantage of a flexible modeling and design, where the focus is shifted from a subjective view of agents towards a more objective view of the whole MAS.

In this paper, we show first experiments on how we apply the governing environment to the modeling and design of a micro-simulation of the Swiss highway network. The goal of the simulation is to show how accordion phenomena and traffic jams may be handled with appropriate local regulations on the speed limit. For example, adaptive speed limitations my be implemented in order to maximize the throughput of the network.

A natural model gives segments the capacity to regulate the speed based on locally observed events. Therefore, regulating highway segments perfectly captures the design of a governing environment. Because of the complexity of the simulation and our choice in the above described modeling, we developed a simulation platform from scratch. This paper presents in details our modeling choices for the simulation platform. First experimental results of our implementation are also eluded. The adaptive distributed speed regulation will however be the subject of another paper, as it is still under development.

The paper is organized as follows. Section 2 introduces and explains the notion of governing environment. Section 3 explains our problematic of traffic simulation in Switzerland. After discussing our global modeling in Sect. 4 following the governing idea, we describe how we model the agent behaviors in Sect. 5. Section 6 presents our platform design. In Sect. 7, we discuss experiments. Section 8 concludes the paper.

2   The Governing Environment

Most research in MAS has focused on the internal capacities of agents, and not on the medium in which they evolve. This vision is however changing towards enhancing the function of the environment in MAS (see for instance [13,1]). Actually, such a vision was already implicit in the early days of software agent research. This is shown by a definition of an autonomous agent as *a system situated within and a part of an environment that senses that environment and acts on it, over time, in pursuit of its own agenda and so as to effect what it senses in the future* [3]. This description stresses the importance of the environment as the living medium, the condition for an agent to live, or the first entity an agent interacts with. Thus an agent is inextricably bound up with an environment. But it remains autonomous, so that the environment may not "force" the agent's integrity. It is in this environment that an agent (autonomously) senses and acts. The acting of the agent on the environment directly influences its future sensing, because the environment is changed by the agent actions.

Even if the notion of environment was stressed as a main component of MAS, most approaches have viewed it as something being modeled in the "minds" of the agents, thus using a minimal and implicit environment that is not a first-order abstraction, but rather the sum of all data structures within agents that represent an environment. This is a typical *subjective view* of the MAS inherited from distributed artificial intelligence, which contrasts with an *objective view* that deals with the system from an external point of view of the agents [10]. This objective point of view sees the environment as a central component for the modeling and design of MASs. Multiagent simulations belong to the type of systems that most explicitly model the environment.

The notion of environment in MASs has been an intensive topic of research. It is useful to differentiate its use in different contexts, as for instance discussed in [14]. In this paper, our notion of environment refers to the *agent environment* as explained in [14]. It is a design abstraction that offers services to agents, and that actually maps the *simulated environment* [5], i.e. the real environment that is simulated. Thus, through this paper, when we will simply refer to the environment, we will always refer to the *agent environment* as a design abstraction.

Whenever a MAS is to be implemented and deployed, an underlying *infrastructure* becomes essential [8]. It offers to the MAS basic services to be used by the agents. Example functionalities are agent communication, naming or life-cycle management. The abstractions provided by such infrastructures are essential for agent-oriented software engineering, as they should be as close as possible to the concepts used for analysis and design. Today's infrastructures primarily offer agent-related abstractions for the programming of agent architectures using for instance libraries for BDI agents [4], thus supporting subjective coordination. They only offer implicit support for objective coordination, as they establish the conditions necessary for running agent programs (e.g. life-cycle management) and for setting the basic interaction means (e.g. message-enabled middleware between agents).

An appealing way to exert the necessary level of control out of agents is the use of a *governing infrastructure* to structure and shape the space of actions within a MAS [8]. This governing perspective mainly allows managing agent interactions from an external point-of-view. This has the strong advantage that agents may be defined independently, and that some control is overtaken externally. In the area of virtual organizations, the Electronic Institutions (EI) approach [7] does this by defining so-called *governors* which are middle agents that mediate all (communicative) actions within a MAS [1]. This solution has, however, important disadvantages. Providing each agent with a governor puts a heavy computational burden on the infrastructure. But, more importantly, middle agents do not capture a natural modeling for the functionality they are expected to fulfill, i.e. mediation of communication. The governing or regulating responsibility should be transferred from specialized middle agents to the environment of a MAS, calling for the *environment as a governing infrastructure* [11]. This can be done with the idea of a *programmable coordination medium* [2], which essentially defines *reactions to events* happening in a shared dataspace. This schema has the strong advantage to allow the definition of laws that not only regulate agent

---

[1] All actions that the EI approach accounts for are communicative by nature.

interactions, but also any happening within an environment. Overall, we expect that viewing the environment as a governing infrastructure simplifies the design of MASs. We will show this in the area of agent-based micro-simulation applied to traffic management.

3   Micro-simulation of the Swiss Highway Network

We modeled, designed and implemented an agent-based micro-simulation that captures the ideas of governing environment. The application area is the simulation of the whole highway traffic in Switzerland of about 1700 km (see Fig. 1). We extended the platform also to the national roads, which are roads of national importance (e.g. the Gothard pass).

The highways are split into segments. This segmentation is given by the real data received from the Federal Office for Spatial Development[2]. Each segment has an arbitrary length, its own speed limit and can have multiple lanes (from one to a maximum of four). On a segment, cars can only drive in one predefined direction. This means that a standard highway part is composed of two segments: one for each direction.

The platform is bound to a geographical information system[3] that allows zooming from the global country view to the local view of each vehicle. We did not develop over an existing platform for agent-based simulation, because the complexity of the problem is much too big. Furthermore, it would be difficult to capture our modeling. We therefore built a new platform from scratch.

Our final goal is to study adaptive and decentralized speed limitation to have an optimal car throughput. Actually, there are some settings in which modern highways perform very poorly. First, the *accordion* is a transient mode in which cars accelerate to a given speed S, only to brake to almost a full stop immediately after reaching the speed S. Secondly, *traffic jams* usually occur in highway segments preceding a bottleneck (e.g. tunnels or accidents). Our goal of the simulation is to show that adaptive distributed speed limitations on the highway segments preceding (and including) the one where problems might appear will drastically decrease the negative effects previously discussed. Therefore we want to investigate whether speeding restrictions can increase the efficiency of highways, and to determine automatic speeding restrictions that optimize highway utilization. As a methodology we decided to develop an agent-based micro-simulation to investigate the above hypothesis and to determine optimal speeding policies. A distributed speed regulation needs to split highways into segments with constant length so that on each segment one speed limitation can be imposed. Constraints between the speed limit on neighboring segments have to ensure that the vehicles do not have to break too abruptly.

An adequate modeling of a micro-simulation allowing distributed decision making on segments can elegantly use the paradigm of a governing environment. Actually, the segment naturally build the environment of the MAS. Each

---

[2] http://www.are.admin.ch
[3] http://www.geotools.org

Fig. 1. Swiss national roads with limits of the cantons, as displayed in our simulation platform

segment has a set of rules that regulate the state of the highway segment (number of cars, average speed, etc) and can decide on the speed limitation for that segment. Neighboring segments can propagate events to one another. Each vehicle is modeled by one agent which takes decisions based on a local view: a driver wants to get to the destination as fast as possible and guides her action depending on the traffic in her immediate vicinity. We further assume that drivers respect the speed limits (within certain bounds).

This paper reports the modeling and design of our simulation platform, and *not* the distributed adaptive decision process for optimal speed regulation. Actually, we are currently working on this with the DPOP [9] algorithms for distributed constraint satisfaction. This will be reported in a future paper.

4   Modeling

We describe in this section the modeling of the MAS of the micro-simulation. According to the *governing environment* paradigm [11], laws are defined within the environment. The environment reacts to raised events according to the rules that we define. Unlike the agents, the environment has no behavior and does not act itself: it can just react to events which are intercepted.

Static Model. We identified two types of agents that are organized around highway segments that represent the environment (see Fig. 2). The Vehicle class[4] has three state attributes : its position (relative to its current segment), its speed and its lane position. Each vehicle has : a Plan which is an ordered collection of HighwaySegment telling it which way to take; a Behavior which describes its acceleration, deceleration and lane changing behavior. VehicleCreator is a dedicated agent which takes care of creating new agents in the system.

---

[4] We use the UML profile described in [12], where rounded rectangles are agents.

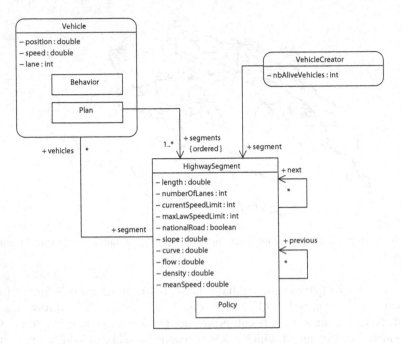

Fig. 2. Agent diagram of the system

The highway is divided in segments. Each Vehicle lives in a HighwaySegment which can be considered as a continuous space. Each one is connected to its next following segments and its previous preceding segments. Vehicles can only move from their current segment to one of the next segments. HighwaySegment has a few constant attributes (length, numberOfLanes, maxLawSpeedLimit, nationalRoad, slope, curve) and a few variable attributes (currentSpeedLimit, flow, density, meanSpeed). All these attributes are part of the environment and can be perceived by agents.

The choice for a continuous space is given by the better precision and the light implementation that follows, but one could consider a discrete space. Nagel [6] shows how to build a cellular automata simulation with discrete space. It should be easily transposed to our agent-based simulation.

Dynamic Description. The time of the simulation is discrete. We send a time step message to every agent at each step of the simulation, and they return an action depending on their perception and their internal behavior. The environment has a governor role and can react to some events.

The environment generates events. SpeedPolicyChangedEvent is generated by a segment each time the speed restriction is changed in a segment. The governing environment will tell the neighbor segments to reconsider their current speed limit. StepBeginEvent is an internal event which is generated by the environment itself to warn the segment that a time step has begun. StepEndEvent is the same type of event as StepBeginEvent, but it warns the segment against the end of a time step event. VehicleDestructedEvent is raised by the environment each time a vehicle finished its planning and should die. VehicleDensityChangedEvent is raised by a segment each time the density of the segment has changed. It tells the environment to reconsider its speed limit.

Agent actions generate events. VehicleCreatedEvent is launched by VehicleCreator each time it creates a new vehicle. VehicleChangedLaneEvent is posted by Vehicle every time it changes its lane position. VehicleChangedSegmentEvent is posted by Vehicle every time it leaves a segment and enters a new one.

5   Behavior Models

Vehicle behaviors are described by two different but connected models: i) the *car following model* describes how a car speeds up and brakes, and the ii) the *lane changing model* describes how a driver decides to change lane.

Car Following Model. Our model is inspired by the Intelligent-Driver Model (IDM) from Martin Treiber[5], which makes the vehicle accelerate to its speed objective (see Alg. 1). it does not have a constant acceleration. It decreases from the initial acceleration (a) to zero when approaching the speed objective (s_o). The deceleration value increases from b and is not limited in the theoretical model. Because of this, the vehicles can have unrealistic deceleration, but the system is collision free.

Algorithm 1. IDM car following model (acceleration computation)

Require: v, v_f, s, T, v_{limit}, a, b, s_{min}
1: $v_o \leftarrow humanizeSpeed(v_{limit})$
2: $\Delta_v \leftarrow v_f - v$
3: $s^* \leftarrow max\{s_{min}, s_{min} + vT + \frac{v\Delta_v}{2\sqrt{ab}}\}$
4: $a_c \leftarrow a\left[1 - \left(\frac{v}{v_o}\right)^4 + \left(\frac{s^*}{s}\right)^2\right]$
5: **return** $max\{-3b, min\{a_c, a\}\}$

In Alg. 1, T is a the safety time with the ahead vehicle, values can be from 0.8 to 2 seconds. Here we use a normal distribution ($\mu = 1.5$, $\sigma = 0.5$) for this value. a is the maximum acceleration (0.8 m/s^2 for cars, 1.5 m/s^2 for trucks). b is the minimum deceleration (-2.5 m/s^2 for cars and trucks).

This model has interesting advantages since it is not based on the fact that vehicles will always keep a safe distance with the vehicle ahead. On the other hand, deceleration can be high and this can lead to bizarre behaviors, like when cars drive at a high speed and suddenly brake down with a high deceleration because of a traffic slow-down or a slowest car.

Lane Changing Model. Each vehicle must at each iteration consider changing lane or not. This decision is based on two main criterions for the agent : *is it*

---
[5] http://www.traffic-simulation.de

safe to go on the other lane? (safety criterion) and *do I get a reward to go on the other lane?* (incentive criterion). In our model, the safety criterion just says that the car behind would be able to brake in order to avoid a collision. We also check that the car ahead is not to close and that if it brakes, we will have the time to avoid a collision. The incentive criterion is quite simple. Vehicles change lane every time they can increase their speed on the other lane. Furthermore we add a few biases to make vehicles go to the right lane whenever the highway is going to change from a N lanes to N-1 lanes. Informally, this gives algorithm 2.

Algorithm 2. Basic lane changing model (incentive criterion)

1: **if** lane will end soon and already on the correct lane **then**
2:    ← do not change lane
3: **end if**
4: **if** lane will end soon AND not on the correct lane **then**
5:    ← go to right lane with an increasing probability when approaching to the end of the lane
6: **end if**
7: **if** already changed lane in the last 10 seconds **then**
8:    ← do not change lane
9: **end if**
10: **if** distance to car ahead is more than 200 meters **then**
11:    ← do not change lane
12: **end if**
13: ← change lane if we can increase speed on the other lane

The two first conditions make the vehicle go to the right lane if its lane will end soon. The third condition (line 8) avoids an oscillation movement from a lane to another. Imagine five vehicles on the right lane, and no vehicles on the left lane. They all have an incentive to go the left lane, once they changed, there is no vehicles on the right lane, so they all have an incentive to change for the right, and so on. They will all change at each step to the other lane. Condition at line 10 tries to avoid cars going to the left lane when they have no other car in front of them.

Combining the Car Following and the Lane Changing Models. Alg. 3 presents how to execute the car following and the lane changing models together. It ensures that all agents will have the same information when taking the decisions. A problem can occur when two vehicles compete for the same lane and think it is safe. They both will have an incentive to change for the target lane and both think that it is safe. Figure 3 shows an example of this. To avoid it, we only change to the right at odd time steps and change to the left at even time steps.

Generation of Vehicles and Plans. For the *generation of vehicles*, we used the number of registered vehicles in the canton (swiss regions) where the segment is. We put a defined percentage of vehicles (N) on highways. We also generate

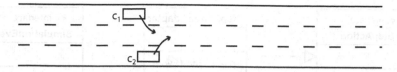

Fig. 3. Problem with +3 lanes highways

Algorithm 3. Vehicle state update loop

1: **for** all the vehicles **do**
2:   *state* ← current state of the environment
3:   decide to change lane or not according to *state*
4: **end for**
5: **for** all the vehicles **do**
6:   change lane if decided
7: **end for**
8: **for** all the vehicles **do**
9:   *newState* ← current state of the environment
10:   *acceleration* ← compute the new acceleration according to *newState*
11: **end for**
12: **for** all the vehicles **do**
13:   update the speed
14:   update the position
15: **end for**

---

trucks on the basis of country statistics. Concerning the starting place, vehicles are created uniformly in the canton. Therefore every canton generates a predefined flow of vehicles in respect to its registered car population. Because official data from the Swiss Federal Roads Authority[6] were not of sufficient granularity, we decided to create cars continuously. A realistic simulation should take into account different timing.

Each generated vehicle immediately has a deterministic assigned route plan, which can not change. This plan is however generated randomly. In future work, we will use demographic statistics and short-path algorithms to generate more realistic plans.

6   Platform Design

We describe in this section the design of our agent-based micro-simulation platform. After presenting the simulation engine interfaces, we discuss the simulation core.

6.1   Simulation Engine Interfaces

Figure 4 shows the class diagrams of the ch.epfl.lia.simengine package. This package intends to provide useful interfaces or classes in order to implement a simulation

---

[6] http://www.verkehrsdaten.ch/downloads/AVZ-StandorteStand012005.pdf

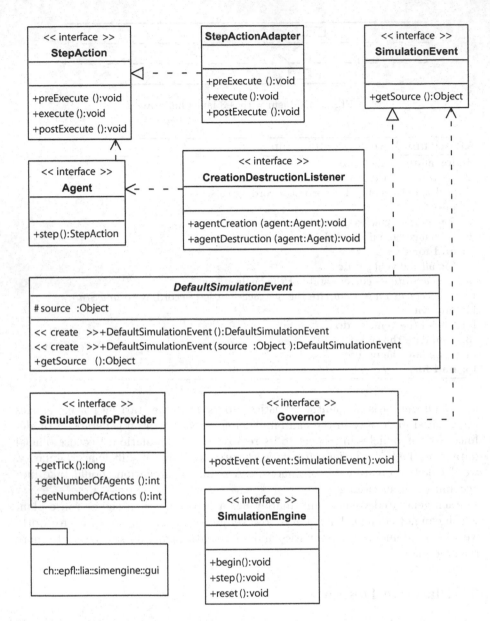

Fig. 4. Class diagram of the ch.epfl.lia.simengine package

core with a governing environment. Most of the types are abstract or even just interfaces:

StepAction represents an action made by an agent at one step of the simulation. A StepAction provides a way to execute a first piece of code (preExecute()), then execute a second piece of code (execute()) and finally execute a third

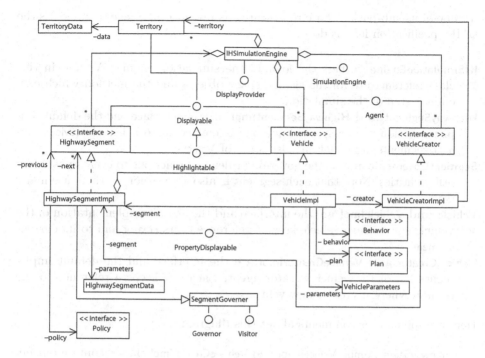

Fig. 5. Elided class diagram of the ch.epfl.lia.ih.sim

piece of code (postExecute). preExecute() will be called on every agent before the call to execute(), and execute on every agent before postExecute..

StepActionAdapter is just an empty StepAction provided for convenience.

Agent each agent should implement this interface. step() method is called at each step of the simulation and should return a StepAction instance.

Governor must be implemented by the governing environment classes, and provides a way to post events.

SimulationEngine must be implemented by the core class of the simulation engine.

SimulationInfoProvider is generally implemented by the same class as SimulationEngine. It helps other parts of the software to get a few basic informations about the simulation.

SimulationEvent represents a synchronous event of our event-based simulation engine.

DefaultSimulationEvent is a generic implementation of the SimulationEvent interface.

CreationDestructionListener should be implemented by classes which want to be warned about agent creations and destructions.

6.2   Simulation Core

Static Description. Figure 5 presents an elided and simplified class diagram of the simulation's core. Interfaces which are not part of the ch.epfl.lia.ih.sim package (or one of its sub-package) are represented as provided interface (a circle) as the UML specification lets us do it.

IHSimulationEngine gathers the logic of the simulation engine. We find in this class references to all the agents, space objects and the method which executes a step of the simulation.

HighwaySegment and HighwaySegmentImpl are the interface and the default implementation of our space. Each one is connected to a list of previous and next segments, and contains also a list of Vehicle.

SegmentGovernor contains the governing rules and reactions to events posted by other entities. Note that each segment is also a governor, so there are many governors.

Vehicle and VehicleImpl are the interface and the default implementation of the vehicle agent. Each vehicle keeps a reference to its creator and to its current segment.

VehicleCreator and VehicleCreatorImpl are the interface and the default implementation of the vehicle creator agent. Each one keeps a reference to the segment where it creates new vehicles.

Here are some other comments about this diagram :

- HighwaySegmentImpl, VehicleImpl and VehicleCreatorImpl classes contain our default implementation of the agent's logic.
- HighwaySegment, Vehicle and VehicleCreator interfaces define the method their implementation must follow. We designed it this way in order to let someone change completely the implementation without a huge change elsewhere in the software.
- HighwaySegmentImpl and VehicleImpl externalize a large part of their code. This is done in order to make a very clear separation between the logic of the agent and their intrinsic model or their constant parameters. For instance, VehicleImpl updates at each step of the simulation its speed according to the new acceleration which is computed by an instance of Behavior. This separation has a great advantage since it provides an easy way to change the behavior model or the plan computation of a vehicle. One can even have multiple instance of VehicleImpl with different types of behavior.

Dynamic Description. The core of the simulation is the class IHSimulationEngine. This class keeps references to every agent and space. At each step of the simulation, method step() is executed. Figure 6 shows a simplified activity diagram of this method.

Environment State. As we said in Sect. 5, we first need to execute some code on all agents and then execute another piece of code, and so on. This is easily done with StepAction facilities.

We also need to save the state of an agent. We can not simply perceive properties of the agent whenever we want. Even if the step method is theoretically

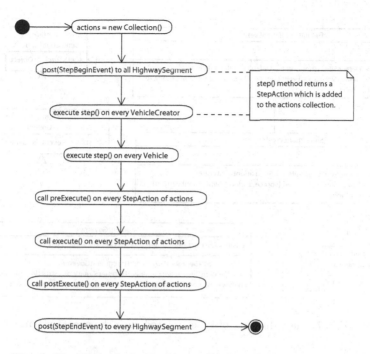

Fig. 6. The IHSimulationEngine.step() method activity diagram

executed simultaneously on every agent. In reality a few agents will change their state before others. Therefore agents need a way to correct state when taking decisions. To do this, we use VehicleState and LaneState which help to keep agent or environment state.

6.3   The Events

Static Description. Figure 7 presents the static description of the events system and Fig. 8 shows the attributes of every event.

We use here a visitor design pattern to make the implementation and extensibility easier. We could even imagine a way to generate automatically code of the SimulationEventVisited subclasses and the Visitor. It would be useful for a project with a huge amount of different events. The SimulationEventFactory is used here for performance reason.

Dynamic Behavior. Events are launched and treated synchronously (one would need to make a few design changes to make the system asynchronous). Events are launched each time it is needed. For instance, when a vehicle wants to move from one segment to the next one, it launches a VehicleChangedSegment by posting it to its current governor. Figure 9 shows how this event is posted and treated.

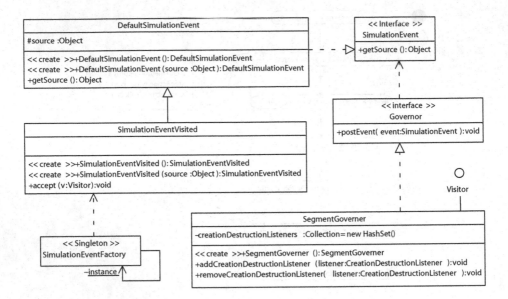

Fig. 7. Class diagram of types related with the event system

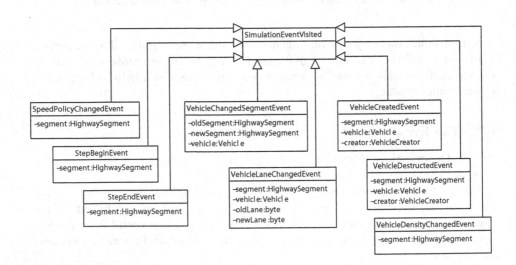

Fig. 8. Class diagram of all the events

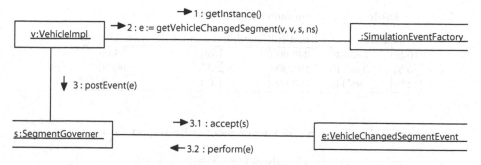

Fig. 9. An event launch example collaboration diagram

7   Experiments

Vehicle Generation. As said in Sect. 5, we can calibrate the simulation to generate a percentage of the registered vehicles. This is difficult since knowing how many vehicles can drive simultaneously on Swiss highways is not obvious.

Swiss highways are composed of 1'855 km of roads. Since these roads have two possible directions and can have multiple lanes, the total length of lanes is about 7'550 km. Supposing a high congestion of 40 vehicles/km everywhere (this means one car each 25 meters on every lane and every highway segment), this leads to an estimation of 302'000 vehicles. It means that $N = 6\%$ of the Swiss vehicles would be on the highways. It can seem very low but, we should not forget that all the cars are never used at the same time and that there is a lot of other roads than highways in Switzerland. And of course, in reality at some place there is much more vehicles than at others, 40 vehicles/km is just an overestimated value of what could be a maximal congestion level.

We have made tests with different values of N (the maximal percentage of alive vehicles at a precise time). Table 1 shows how many vehicles can be simultaneously alive and how much time it costs to simulate a certain time. The first remark is about the theoretical value which is not equal to the practical one. It comes from the way of generating vehicles. Each creator segment has a physical maximum flow of vehicles and depending of the local conditions (i.e. a traffic jam on this segment), it can be lower that what it should be to ensure the theoretical production of cars. Thus it is absolutely normal to have a lower value.

Tests of the Models. We ran the simulation with different values of N and looked at some randomly chosen place to see if the flow of vehicles we simulate is near reality or not. Vehicles were not always perceiving the current reality and were basing their decision on a partial future state. This was leading to many collisions, but since they are automatically cleared[7], the simulation was realistic. Table 2 shows the measures we found depending on the N value. The simulated time is the value given in table 1.

---

[7] The vehicle which causes the collision (the vehicle at the back) is deleted and everything continues as if nothing happened.

Table 1. Maximum number of vehicles with respect to N

N	Theoretical	Practical	Simulated time [h]	Real time [h][8]
10 %	492'230	249'000	1:30	24:00
5 %	246'115	192'000	2:35	60:00
2 %	98'445	95'000	1:00	8:00

Table 2. Mean flow measurements with respect to N

Place	Real flow	$N = 10\%$	$N = 5\%$
Muttenz	10700	4140	4551
Wuennewil	2342	3318	3533
Grandvaux	5662	3941	3798
Monte Ceneri	3243	3432	3732
Giessbachtunnel	983	2053	2103
Erstfeld	2192	2143	1366
Bardonnex	3656	1834	1783
Oftringen	5928	3304	3625

Values are very far from reality. However we remark that where there is a high mean flow value in reality, there is also a relative high mean flow in the simulation. This lets us think that even if our vehicle generation method is not realistic, it does not give arbitrary values.

8   Conclusion

We developed a micro-simulation of the Swiss highway network in order to show that the governing environment can be useful for the modeling and design of agent-based micro-simulations. In our simulation platform, the design has shown to be very flexible. Future work will consist in improving the vehicle behavior modeling and the performance of the platform, and in actually implementing the adaptive and distributed speed limit regulations in order to achieve an optimal car throughput. We shortly explain hereafter those points.

The model of a vehicle should become more realistic. Collisions should be avoided when two segments merge in one, including highway entries. We think this is very tricky to solve since road granularity information is not detailed enough to let us have finer grained models. The lane changing model should also be improved, especially at the end of lanes (when N ways merge to N-1 ways). Our model is not yet very good and produces unrealistic traffic jams.

Running a simulation with hundreds of thousands of agents is not costless. To simulate a real scenario with many vehicles in a reasonable time, we have to make deeper changes in the architecture. A way to do it is to distribute the computation on several computers. We estimate that our architecture should be easily

---

[8] Tests made on a 4 x 3 Ghz 64-bits processors computer with 4 Gb RAM.

transformable into a distributed one, for instance with segment distribution and asynchronous events.

However, the most important remains the realization and testing of an intelligent distributed speed restriction policy. We are currently working on this using a family of distributed constraint optimization algorithm [9].

References

1. Weyns, D., Van Dyke Parunak, H., Michel, F., Holvoet, T., Ferber, J.: Environments for Multiagent Systems, State-of-the-art and Research Challenges. In: Weyns, D., Van Dyke Parunak, H., Michel, F. (eds.) E4MAS 2004. LNCS (LNAI), vol. 3374, Springer, Heidelberg (2005)
2. Denti, E., Natali, A., Omicini, A.: Programmable Coordination Media. In: Garlan, D., Le Métayer, D. (eds.) COORDINATION 1997. LNCS, vol. 1282, pp. 274–288. Springer, Heidelberg (1997)
3. Franklin, S., Graesser, A.: Is it an Agent or just a Program? A Taxonomy for Autonomous Agents. In: Jennings, N.R., Wooldridge, M.J., Müller, J.P. (eds.) ATAL 1996. LNCS, vol. 1193, pp. 21–35. Springer, Heidelberg (1997)
4. Georgeff, M.P., Rao, A.S.: The Semantics of Intention Maintenance for Rational Agents. In: Proceedings of the International Joint Conference on Artificial Intelligence (IJCAI). LNCS (LNAI), vol. 1202, pp. 704–710. Springer, Heidelberg (1995)
5. Helleboogh, A., Vizzari, G., Uhrmacher, A., Michel, F.: Multi-agent modeling and simulation: Dynamism in the environment. Journal of Autonomous Agents and Multi-Agent Systems 14(1) (February 2007)
6. Nagel, K.: Multi-agent transportation simulation (draft) (2004), http://www.vsp.tu-berlin.de/archive/sim-archive/papers/book/book.pdf
7. Noriega, P., Sierra, C.: Electronic institutions: Future trends and challenges. In: Klusch, M., Ossowski, S., Shehory, O. (eds.) CIA 2002. LNCS (LNAI), vol. 2446, Springer, Heidelberg (2002)
8. Omicini, A., Ossowski, S., Ricci, A.: Coordination infrastructures in the engineering of multiagent systems. In: Bergenti, F., Gleizes, M.-P., Zambonelli, F. (eds.) Methodologies and Software Engineering for Agent Systems: The Agent-Oriented Software Engineering Handbook, ch. 14, pp. 273–296. Kluwer Academic Publishers, Dordrecht (2004)
9. Petcu, A., Faltings, B.: Dpop: A scalable method for multiagent constraint optimization. In: IJCAI 2005, Edinburgh, Scotland, August 2005, pp. 266–271 (2005)
10. Schumacher, M.: Objective Coordination in Multi-Agent System Engineering - Design and Implementation. LNCS (LNAI), vol. 2039. Springer, Heidelberg (2001)
11. Schumacher, M., Ossowski, S.: The governing environment. In: Weyns, D., Van Dyke Parunak, H., Michel, F. (eds.) E4MAS 2005. LNCS (LNAI), vol. 3830, pp. 88–104. Springer, Heidelberg (2006)
12. Giunchiglia, F., Odell, J.J., Weiss, G. (eds.): AOSE 2002. LNCS, vol. 2585. Springer, Heidelberg (2003)
13. Weyns, D., Schumacher, M., Ricci, A., Viroli, M., Holvoet, T.: Environments in multiagent systems. Knowledge Engineering Revue 20(2), 127–141 (2005)
14. Weyns, D., Helleboogh, A., Holvoet, T., Schumacher, M.: The environment in multiagent system: a middleware perspective. Multi-Agent and Grid Systems (to be published, 2008)

Environment Support to the Management of Context Awareness Information

Marco P. Locatelli and Giuseppe Vizzari

Department of Informatics, Systems and Communication
University of Milan–Bicocca
Viale Sarca 336, U14 Building, 20126 Milano, Italy
{locatelli,vizzari}@disco.unimib.it

Abstract. Collaborative Ubiquitous Environments (CUEs) are environments supporting collaboration among persons in a ubiquitous computing setting. This paper shows how results of the research in the Multi–Agent System (MAS) area, and in particular on MAS environments, can be used to model, design and engineer CUEs, with specific reference to the management of context–awareness information. The CUE reference scenario will be introduced, then the Multilayered Multi–Agent Situated System model will be briefly described and applied to represent and to manage several types of awareness information (both physical and logical contextual information). Finally, the paper introduces a prototypal framework based on DJess supporting the definition and management of MMASS based CUEs.

1 Introduction

The current trend of technological advancements allows foreseeing a radically new scenario for computer systems, a scenario in which persons will not be forced to sit down in front of a PC, representing the single spot of the environment in which both computational power and connectivity are concentrated. The environment is growingly endowed with sensors, information sources, hidden (or disappearing) computational devices that can exploit the pervasive presence of wired and wireless communication infrastructures [1]. One of the most current challenges for computer scientists and engineers is the design and realization of environments supporting human activities in this novel technological context, providing the possibility of a "natural" interaction and collaboration between the persons. We call such environments Collaborative Ubiquitous Environments (CUEs).

The full potential of this new technological setting is still not fully explored and exploited by current applications; according to [2] the new scenario provides possibilities and challenges that will necessarily lead to a revolutionary shift of paradigm in the way computer systems are modeled and engineered. To choose an approach to the definition of innovative computer systems trying to face the challenges posed by this new situation, we started considering one of the most relevant features of this scenario: the presence of devices that must interact in order to provide a rich and articulated support to human activities. This need to effectively establish suitable interactions in an opportunistic way lead us to consider Multi–Agent Systems [3] as a relevant source

D. Weyns, S.A. Brueckner, and Y. Demazeau (Eds.): EEMMAS 2007, LNAI 5049, pp. 204–222, 2008.

of abstractions, models and instruments to analyze the scenario and design systems effectively realizing CUEs. In fact, a device that is part of the overall system can be enhanced by the presence of an agent able to perceive the local context, detect relevant information sources, communicate its presence, and in general establish meaningful interactions. However, the single agent "reasoning" capabilities are not the most relevant element of this scenario. The abstractions and mechanisms supporting mutual agent perception and interaction are in fact extremely relevant, in the general setting of MAS research and even more in this specific application area. These abstractions and mechanisms are typical functions that can be ascribed to a MAS environment [4].

Even if agent definitions generally highlight the presence of an environment in which agents are situated, may perceive each other, act and interact, agent research has often been focused on specific aspects and features of agency, like the individual reasoning and decision making processes, the possibility to communicate by sending and receiving messages expressed into some shared language according to a given domain ontology. Recent research efforts have highlighted the general relevance of the environment as a *first class concept* that is on one hand a necessary element of a MAS, and on the other a source of abstractions and mechanisms to support the analysis, modelling and design of a MAS to solve a specific problem or face a specific requirement of the desired system.

The Multilayered Multi–Agent Situated System (MMASS) [5] is a formal and computational framework supporting the modeling of agents as well as the environment in which they are situated. One of the aims of this paper is to show how this model can be suitably adopted to design an infrastructure for the management and distribution of awareness information in CUEs. In particular, the following Sect. will introduce in a more extensive way the CUEs scenario and its specific requirements, while Sect. 3 will describe the MMASS model, and Sect. 4 will show how this model can be applied to effectively face these requirements, employing a sample CUE scenario related to a smart environment in a University. In this framework, this work differs from other existing proposals that employ agents and agent–based infrastructures simply as a middleware for the design and implementation of pervasive computing systems (see, e.g., [6,7]). Section 5 will thus present a prototypal platform realizing specific environmental mechanisms described by the MMASS model employing the DJess middleware [8]. The choice of this particular technological support is based on an analysis of different existing frameworks and middlewares that is extensively described in [9]. Section 5 will introduce the actual rules that were realized and tested in the realization of the sample CUE scenario, as well as specific support tools for the design of this kind of environment. Conclusions and future developments will end the paper.

2 Reference Scenario: Collaborative Ubiquitous Environments

The need of a support for collaboration in ubiquitous computing environments has emerged during the last years [10]; a Collaborative Ubiquitous Environment (CUE) is composed of objects (we also include electronic and computational devices in this term) that show a variety of computational capabilities: from sensors to wallboards, from actual documents to pieces of furniture, from desks to doors, and so on, up to traditional general purpose computers that can play the hidden role of servers or the visible role of terminals supporting individual work. The main characteristic of CUEs is that all the devices are explicitly intended to support collaborative work among persons instead of only the individual work of each one of them. To achive this aim CUEs require support both for *coordination* [11] to manage expected behaviours and *awareness* [12] to manage contextual information.

A way to connect ubiquitous computing and cooperation is through the notion of *context*, since ubiquitous computing and context-aware computing share the same goal: to make the environment "alive" and its context an important part of what determines the application's behaviour. More specifically, we like the idea to view context not as a representational problem but *as an interactional problem*, as proposed in [14]. In fact, this view is more coherent with what we consider the main advantage of ubiquitous computing (once adequately developed): to bring back the notion of context as currently mediated and constrained by the desktop metaphor to its natural connotation, that of physical context, with all its affordances, possibly augmented by computing capabilities to become more significant.

Additional motivations to the need of managing both *coordination* and *awareness* dimensions are presented in [13]. Our goal, however, is to maintain a strong separation between the computational abstractions and mechanisms devoted to them, in terms of their behavior, their language and the design approach; in particular, we actually have different interaction-space models and there is thus no reason to mix them.

From the *context awareness* point of view, it is important to represent information about both physical and logical aspects related to actors; in fact, people freely move in the physical space carrying and approaching objects that altogether provide different forms of computational connectivity, as well as meet other people and establish with them various forms of cooperation. Moreover, considering the logical dimension, which is the dimension where information and coordination resources are managed to support these forms of cooperation, we can recognize a similar kind of dynamism: actors own, make available, approach and coordinate their access to these resources in a flexible way according to their needs, interests, duties or simply because they realize that an opportunity is offered to them or that the current state of affairs requires their coordinated intervention.

The physical spatial representation is made possible by the use of suitable localization technologies but it is not limited by them in the sense that the representation does not necessarily reflect the technological localization (e.g., small localization areas identified by the technology could be aggregated in one localization area in the modeled space); of course, the logical dimension by its nature is not related to physical aspects, so the concept of granularity is not related to a physical property. However, we can model different kinds of relationships among actors and sometimes these can represent the "same" information but at a different level of abstraction, so granularity is a valid concept also for the logical dimension.

Beyond the representation of the space, both physical and logical, context awareness is built on the information dynamically diffused in the spaces in accord to the view of context as an interactional problem; the *modulated propagation of information* is a key requirement of CUEs and allows dynamic interaction and perception among actors in terms of perception by proximity, dynamic configuration of the environment, acquisition of contextualized information and so on.

The characteristics of CUEs depicted above as generic requirements can be found immediately in the typical situations managed by CUEs such as the ones described in Sect. 4, on one hand to analyze in a deeper way and exemplify the introduced reference scenario. Moreover, the MMASS model will be adopted to represent the notions and mechanisms regulating these CUEs. To this end, the following Sect. will briefly introduce the MMASS model.

3 Multilayered Multi-agent Situated System

The Multilayered Multi-Agent Situated Systems (MMASS) is a model supporting the definition of systems made up of a set of autonomous entities acting and interacting in a structured environment. It has been successfully applied to different contexts, from the simulation of complex systems (e.g. crowds [15]), to the support of human interactions in the Computer Supported Cooperative Work area [16]. This Sect. does not represent an extensive formal description of the model (that can be found in [5]), but it will briefly introduce its main concepts, specifically focusing on the environmental structure. In fact the latter deeply influences agents behaviour, as the environment is the source of their perceptions and a constraint limiting their actions (e.g. their movement), but it also provides them a medium to interact with other entities.

MMASS Environment – Agents in MMASS are necessarily situated in a *site*, that is, a node of the graph related to a single layer of the environment (i.e. a single Multi-Agent Situated System). The overall agent environment is generally composed of several interacting layers, each one representing a different aspect such as, for instance, a physical spatial abstraction (i.e. a discretization of a physical space), or the relationships among specific organizational roles related to the environment. We will now consider a single MASS to introduce its structure, as well as the abstractions and mechanisms supporting the definition of agents, their behaviours and interactions.

A MASS, from a structural point of view, is an *undirected graph*. An edge connecting two sites indicates possibility of agents to move from one of those sites to the other (and vice versa), to perceive the presence of signals (i.e. *fields*, which will be introduced later on) and agents in the adjacent site. Adjacency between sites enables thus agents' movements and local perception, but it also supports the diffusion of fields, according to specific rules managing their distribution in the environment (i.e. *diffusion function*). Originally edges were not weighted; however, in this specifica case of application, since it is possible to adopt one MMASS layer to represent the social relationships among individuals, it can be useful to support the definition of graph including weighted arcs: in social relationship representations a weight will be employed to indicate the strength of a given relationship between two roles. An additional difference between the adopted version of the model and the original definition is the possibility more than one agent to be situated in a given site. In fact, since there can be several coordinated spatial representations of the environment, for instance related to different levels of granularity, it could be necessary to relax the non-interpenetration principle that limited to one the maximum number of agents present in a site. Considering, for example, the representation of a physical environment based on the mapping of one room to a single MMASS site, it is necessary to allow different agents related to different electronic devices currently positioned in the room to be situated in that site.

Environment Mediated Agent Interaction – The main mechanism for environment mediated interaction defined by the MMASS model in the CUE context provides the possibility for agents to emit *fields*, that are signals diffused through the environment that can be perceived by other agents according to specific rules. This indirect interaction mechanism is also related to stigmergic approaches to agent communication, but fields are not just associated to an intensity value that persists through time in a given position, but it rather conveys more complex kind of information also through the spatial dimension of the environment. For every field type a *diffusion function* must be specified in order to define how related signals decay (or are amplified) during their diffusion in the environment, from the source of emission to destination sites. Additional functions must given to specify how fields of the same kind can be *composed* (for instance in order to obtain the intensity of a given field type at a given site) or *compared*. Fields are neutral, from a semantic point of view, even if they can have related information in addition to their intensity: in fact, they are only signals, with an indication on how they diffuse in the environment, how they can be compared and composed. The interpretation of these signals and the reaction to their perception is part of agents' behavioural specification.

Agent Perception and Action – Agents of different types may be able to perceive the same signal in a totally different way; moreover they may have completely different reactions to the perception of the same signal, according to their behavioural specification. With reference to perception, an agent may perceive a field with a non–null intensity active in the site it is situated on according to two parameters characterizing its type and related to the specific field type: the *sensitivity threshold*, indicating the minimum field intensity that an agent of that type is able to perceive and the *receptiveness coefficient*, representing an amplification factor modulating (amplifying or attenuating) field value before the comparison with the sensitivity threshold. Employing these parameters it is possible to model dynamism in the perceptive capabilities of agents of a given type, since these parameters are determined according to agent's state. In this way, for instance, the same agent that was unable to perceive a specific field value could become more sensitive (increase its own receptiveness coefficient) as a consequence of a change in its state. This allows to model physical aspects of perception, but also conceptual ones such as agent interests. Field emission is one of the possible actions available for the specification of agent behaviour. Other actions are related to the possibility to move (*transport* operation) and change the state upon the perception of a specific event in their local context (*trigger* operation) or according to a coordinated change of state among adjacent agents (*reaction* operation).

Representing and Integrating Different Aspects of the CUE – The overall agent environment, as previously mentioned, can be composed of several interacting layers. In order to allow this interaction (i.e. intra-MASS interaction) the model introduces the notion of *interface*. An interface of a given MASS specifies fields imported from and exported into each MASS, and more precisely it is defined as

$$Interface(MASS_i, export : E; import : I)$$

where E and I are respectively the set of fields exported into and imported from $MASS_i$. Imported fields (that must be correspondingly exported by another MASS), can be used in specifying agent actions exactly as fields that are internal to the agent MASS. The value of an external field in *any* site of the local *Space* of a MASS is the value specified at its emission.

The Model and the Other Parts of the CUE – In order to coordinate different aspects of the MMASS environment, layers must also be open to the influences and signals generated by sensors and devices spread in the actual environment. Additionally, the effects of the computation carried out in the MMASS environment, and more precisely the actions of agents situated in it, must have an effect on the world, not only through the MMASS environment, but also by communicating with the devices that are hosting them. To this aim, it is necessary to introduce both a new input primitive that can be included in the behavioural specification of a given agent type and the possibility to invoke an external input operation when expressing conditions triggering agents' actions, in order to represent both *intentional* and *reactive* behaviours. Both the operations must support the interaction of the MMASS agent with the coordination world (through the Manager agent as described in Sect. 4). The new primitive is defined as $request(s, o)$, as the specific intentional request operation for an external object o. The $input(e)$ function can instead be used as a conditional element for the activation of a primitive, specifying that an external object e can be used to express further conditional elements. To support the possibility of an agent to provide awareness information to the coordination world an output primitive must be provided by the model: the $output(s, o)$ primitive specifies that the agent triggers the Manager agent by sending an o message. The information specified by o is determined on the basis of the information locally accessible to the current agent, and precisely it state s and the elements of its local context.

4   MMASS and CUEs

As introduced in Section 2, CUEs treat both coordination and awareness facets. Of course they are tightly coupled to provide support to collaboration; thus, the entities of the two "worlds" must have a way to interact. Moreover, the awareness side of a CUE can encompass several different aspects, such as the physical position of an actor (it could be a person as well as a device endowed with an agent managing awareness information) in a given representation of the CUE as well as logical position, such as the role in an organization or project. Fig. 1 depicts the reference model for MMASS–based awareness management in a CUE. In particular, beyond k MMASS layers (the topological spaces related to the various aspects of represented awareness information) there are some additional elements:

- *Awareness agent* ($A_{i,j}$): this kind of agent is situated on the awareness graph j and it is associated to actor i of the CUE; its behaviour is described in accord to the MMASS model thus this agent reasons on fields, by perceiving and emitting them.

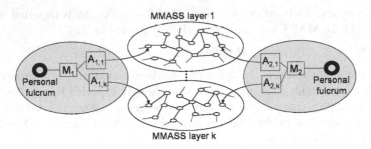

Fig. 1. Reference model for MMASS–based awareness management in a CUE

- *Manager agent* (M_i): the agent that bridges the awareness and coordination worlds for actor i; it translates information expressed in term of fields (exported by the A_i agents) into *awareOf* statements (the kind of information that the agents of the coordination world can understand) and, in the other direction, imports fields in the proper $A_{i,j}$ agent when requests of propagation come from the agents of the coordination world.
- *Personal fulcrum*: the space of interaction of the agents of the coordination world.

In this paper we do not provide details on the coordination component of a CUE (see [17,18] to have more information on this topic) because it is not strictly related to topological spaces and their representation, instead it is focused on information and behaviour exchange. However, to let the reader better understand the following sections and the Section 5 here we put in evidence that the coordination part of the model is implemented by adopting DJess [8] because it is a middleware that easily allows the sharing of facts (to represent statements) and rules (to describe behaviours). In the following we will show how to model a scenario that exploit the characteristics of CUE depicted in Section 2 by applying the MMASS model.

4.1 Lesson Setup Scenario

This scenario describes how the perception of entities in the neighborhood can be realized by the propagation of a *presence field*. Each agent situated on the topological space (can) emits a presence field in order to let the other ones to be aware of its presence. The presence field is characterized by the *emitter id* and by a *diffusion function* that decreases the field intensity (to obtain a small neighborhood a quickly decreasing function must be defined). When the agent moves around the space, it emits the presence field again and the neighborhood changes consequently; in fact, the presence field emitted before disappears and the new one defines the new neighborhood.

In an university department people can perceive the presence of the other ones thanks to the propagation of the presence field, moreover, agents that represent either tecnological (such as a desk) or logical (such as a lesson) artifacts can perceive the presence of persons, and eventually emit their own. Although it is not presented in this scenario, it is important to put in evidence that the presence field could be propagated both on physical and logical topological spaces, so the neighborhood could not necessary be driven by the physical proximity.

Scenario. In the smart department, classrooms are equipped with a minimal set of devices providing: people identification or localization, projection on a large surface, audio-video recording, and interaction with electronic documents. In addition, personal devices seamlessly operate into an organization-wide cooperative infrastructure.

Mrs. Jameson is a teacher of the Institute, and she is allowed to use its modern facilities. She can seamlessly work in her office or in a classroom: when she is sitting at her desk, she can use her habitual PC applications, and she is aided by the cooperative infrastructure when interacting with other devices (such as her PDA or mobile phone) and to access documents in a content management system. She can schedule lessons and prepare them by selecting the material to be used in the classroom (e.g., slides, videos), and the readings and exercises to be assigned. When Mrs. Jameson enters the classroom where one of her lessons is scheduled currently, the environment automatically sets up according to the situation: teaching materials are retrieved from the content management system and presented to the teacher on the interactive surface of her desk, the projecting equipment switches on to display the presentation, and the audio/video equipment starts recording and streaming to remote students.

Whenever Mrs. Jameson creates a new lesson, it can be considered to be located in the same site where she is. When she leaves her office, she moves in the institute and is localized by the system. Her lessons follow Mrs. Jameson in the topological space (thanks to the propagation of her presence field): the presence field is perceived to be weaker, the lessons check the source of the field (i.e., where the teacher is), and move to the same site. Then, the new position is confronted with lessons' location: if the place where a lesson is scheduled is reached, and the time is right, then the lesson activates the setup.

All the devices in the classroom, according to the services they are able to provide, react on the presence of the lesson and execute the proper behaviors. Such operation represents the setup of the system for the lesson that is beginning: once devices have set up, they are ready to provide the desired services, and feedback regarding the acquired status is published in the fulcrum.

When all the required services are available the lesson officially begins, its status changes accordingly, a webcam starts recording and streaming the lesson, the material for the teacher is retrieved from the CMS and displayed on the desk (ready to be shown on a larger screen to the audience), and a sign can automatically light outside, above the door to warn people passing by to be quiet.

4.2   Modeling the Environment

An environment for agents is designed to let them move and interact in the university department; in fact, they inhabit a topological space that represents the topology of the department as depicted in Fig. 2. The weights of the arcs of the topological space are defined both for the presence and lesson-setup fields (Fig. 3).

For the *presence* field, the weight of the arcs between a room (e.g. U701) and its entrance area (e.g. U701E) is 2 because the presence field has to be perceived only in

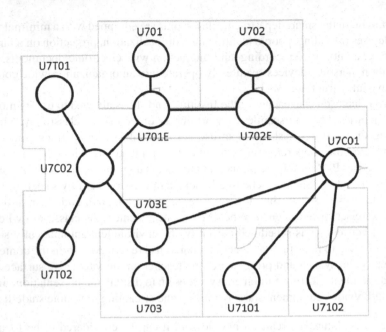

Fig. 2. The topological space that models the department. U7101 and U7102 are teachers' offices, U701-03 are classrooms, U701-03E are the corresponding entrances, U7T01 and U7T02 are areas with tables where students can stay, and U7C01 and U7C01 are the corridor areas.

the room when the agent is there; in fact, the default (emission) intensity of the presence field is 3 and its diffusion function is subtraction.

Instead, the *lesson-setup* field has to be perceived in all the department, so also students around the department are able to perceive this information. Its diffusion function is subtraction with 1 as minimum and its default intensity is 3: this allows to have a field that decreases its intensity in the first two sites it traverses and then diffuse with a constant intensity. In this manner the agents located in the first two sites perceive the field with a higher intensity and react accordingly.

4.3   Defined Agents

In this scenario we defined different types of agents: teacher, student, lesson, and desk. A teacher agent is instantiated for Mrs. Jameson; for each lesson she defined a lesson agent is instantiated. Of course, a student agent is instantiated for each student of the university.

Teacher and lesson are agents able to change their location in the environment in accord to the current location of the person they are related to. In particular, the Teacher agent is actually moved by the system according to localization information gathered by the smart department infrastructure; similarly, also student agents are moved to mimic the actual position of localized students. Lesson is instead an autonomous agent, that is programmed to follow the teacher of the lesson it represents (the actual implementation of this behavioural element is presented in Sect. 5.3) until they are both in the lesson classroom. Finally, desk does not move at all.

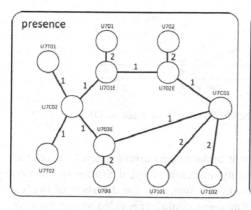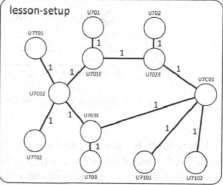

Fig. 3. Arcs' weights for the presence and lesson-setup fields

Lesson is an agent that perceives the presence field of its teacher, i.e. the teacher that created the lesson. Students agents perceive le lesson-setup fields, but only of the the lesson they are interested in, i.e. the lesson of the courses they are attending. All the other lessons are ignored to avoid information overload.

Finally, an agent is instantiated for each device that is deployed in the environment: for example, for each desk in the classrooms a desk agent is instantiated and it perceives the lesson-setup field and it is in charge of display the proper information to the teacher. In particular, they perceive only the lesson that is situated in the same classroom thanks to the topology of the space and the weights assigned to arcs for the lesson-setup field.

5   A DJess MMASS-Based Collaborative Ubiquitous Architectures

In this Sect. we describe a first effort in the realization of a prototypal framework supporting the definition of MMASS–based CUEs and provide real rules written to achieve the right behavior of the framework as defined for the model. Before describing the adopted approach, some considerations must be done on the specific features of the scenario and on the suitability of existing middlewares and frameworks to support the development of CUEs.

5.1   General Considerations

First of all, it must be noted that a CUE is surely (and not surprisingly) a distributed system. However, a single layer of environmental representation, such as those introduced in the previous Sect., can be suitably hosted by a single computational node of the network: the latter can act as an awareness server for the specific aspect of the CUE represented in the hosted layer. Devices scattered in the actual environment that are part of the CUE are assumed to be able to communicate with these nodes[1], in order to signal their presence and perceive the signals coming from the CUE.

---

[1] This is a basic assumption of the Ubiquitous Computing scenario, which is rapidly becoming a reasonable one at least in several urban contexts and built environments.

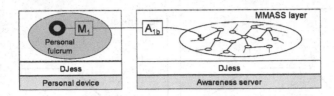

Fig. 4. A deployment diagram for the CUE architecture based on DJess

Every layer is thus responsible to maintain updated the current state of the related aspect of the overall environment (e.g. reflecting the actual physical position of a device on the discrete representation of the environment, managing the diffusion of fields). Information related to the current position of an agent could be provided by some *sensor installed on the device* hosting it (e.g. a GPS receiver, in case of physical position), by an *infrastructure of sensors* installed in the environment (e.g. a wireless network or a RFID infrastructure [19]), or by a *user* (e.g. its current availability to interact or carry out a task, in case of a conceptual position). In other words, according to the specific aspect of the environment represented in a given layer, the information on agent position could be provided by the agent, obtained by an infrastructure or even inferred. However, nodes managing environmental layers are currently assumed to be well known by every device that is part of the CUE (their addresses could be set during the configuration of the adopted middleware).

This kind of network structure had an influence on the preliminary selection of the frameworks and middlewares to consider and evaluate. The TOTA middleware [20], for instance, offers a rich and sophisticated support to the design and engineering of Pervasive Computing applications exploiting the abstractions of agents and MAS environment. However, one of TOTA's most distinguishing features is the possibility to diffuse and keep updated context–awareness information in a dynamic environment, and in particular it offers the possibility to maintain the structure of Co-Fields over a changing network. In this case, however, the structure of the network is not very relevant in determining the context of a given node, and instead the reference scenario requires the capability to integrate several spatial representations, related to different aspects of the CUE.

The relevance of environment related abstractions and mechanisms highlighted in the previous Sect. (i.e. spatial structure in which agents are situated, fields and related functionalities and services) in the representation of contextual information led us to focus on those MAS approaches actually providing some specific support to environmental aspects. The adoption of a middleware providing a communication infrastructure supporting direct agent interaction (e.g. JADE [21]) would require the design and implementation of additional structures and interaction mechanisms or the realization of an agent (or a set of agents) specifically devoted to the management of environment related abstractions and mechanisms to enable context-aware forms of agent interaction.

A relevant approach to the design and engineering of Environments for MASs is represented by *artifacts* [22]: artifacts are a conceptual, formal and computational framework supporting the realization of function–oriented elements of a MAS. In particular, a single layer of environmental representation could be suitably modeled and managed

```
;; Site template
(deftemplate Site "A site"
    (slot id))                      ;; identifier of the site (used to define arcs)
;; Arc between two sites template
(deftemplate Arc "An arc between two sites"
    (slot siteA) (slot siteB)       ;; the connected sites
    (slot id))                      ;; the identifier of the arcs
;; Weight of an arc, defined for a particular field type
(deftemplate Weight "The weight of an arc for a particular field type"
    (slot arc)                      ;; identifier of the arc
    (slot fieldType) (slot value))  ;; field type and weight
```

Fig. 5. Fact templates representing the configuration of the related MMASS layer

by means of an artifact, encapsulating the internal spatial structure of the layer as well as the various related mechanisms (e.g. field diffusion), realized in the form of reaction rules considering the TuCSoN [23] approach to artifact implementation. This approach can provide a suitable support to the design and implementation of an MMASS–based CUE, but since there is an ongoing activity aimed at realizing coordination aspects of a CUE adopting DJess, the latter was adopted for a prototypal implementation of a framework for MMASS–based CUEs. Most important, DJess allows to easily and naturally define an A-agent as a reactive agent and describe its reactive behavior in term of rules, and to distribute the execution of agents and topological spaces in a transparent way for the system designer and of course for the agents too.

5.2 DJess and MMASS: Environment Management

DJess [8] is a communication middleware whose main aim is to support the remote and transparent interaction of computational nodes hosting instances of the Jess[2] rule based inference system [24].

DJess is essentially an extension of Jess that adds a communication layer underneath its inferential capabilities. In particular, it is possible to define a web of inferential systems transparently sharing facts and rules across a network. For this specific application only the first functionality was exploited, in particular to support the possibility of A-agents to communicate with the related M-agents by means of the adoption of the *input* and *output* primitives introduced in Sect. 3. This is necessary to support the interaction between the awareness and the collaboration aspects of the CUE. However, it must be noted that the rule–sharing function was used in the modules that manage the coordination aspects of the CUE, that are effectively implemented in DJess. The overall deployment diagram of this architecture is shown in Fig. 4.

DJess was thus considered as a support for the modeling and implementation of MMASS–based environmental representations of CUEs. In particular, it is possible to define fact templates for basic configuration and state of a specific MMASS layer. Figures 5 and 6 show how the `deftemplate` command can be used to define a specific structure for a given fact type. In this case, templates are respectively defined for facts representing the building blocks of a MMASS layer (i.e. sites and weighted arcs connecting them) and other information related to the configuration and current state of the

---

[2] http://www.jessrules.com/

```
;; Field type template
(deftemplate FieldType "A field Type"
    (slot id)                          ;; identifier of the type
    ;; name of the diffusion function
    (slot diffuseFunction (default "diffuse-subtract"))
    ;; name of the composition function for fields of the same instance
    (slot composeInstanceFunction (default "compose-max"))
    ;; name of the composition function for fields of different instances
    (slot composeFunction (default "compose-avg"))
    ;; name of the comparation function
    (slot compareFunction (default "compare-great-then-or-equal"))
    ;; default arc weight for this field type (used in layer compilation)
    (slot defaultArcWeight (default 1))
    ;; default emission intensity
    (slot defaultEmitIntensity (default 1)))
;; Field instance template
(deftemplate Field "A field instance"
    (slot site)                        ;; id of the site on which this field is
    (slot instanceId (default "null")) ;; id of the field instance
    (slot fieldType (default "null"))  ;; id of the field type
    (slot spec (default "null"))       ;; specialization
    (slot intensity (default 1))       ;; intensity of the field
    (slot info (default "null"))       ;; additional information content
    ;; local source site for the field (used during diffusion)
    ;; defaults to 'nil' for newly emitted fields
    (slot sourceSite (default "null"))
    ;; level (or time step) in which this field was diffused,
    ;; defaults to 0 for emitted fields
    (slot level (default 0))
    ;; collection state of this field, can be "TRUE" or "FALSE"
    (slot collected (default "FALSE"))
    ;; this slot is true if the represented field is the result of a
    ;; composition, can be only "TRUE" or "FALSE"
    (slot isComposition (default "FALSE")))
```

Fig. 6. Fact templates representing field types and instances

layer (e.g. the specification of a field type and the format for a specific field instance). Other templates are used to represent information about the current state of the environment, such as the position of an agent, the presence of fields in sites (`Field`), and so on.

It is now possible to specify rules granting the layer the possibility to react to the stimuli represented by agent actions, such as a field emission. The basic idea is that the emission of a field (i.e. the assertion of a `Field` fact associated to a given site), triggers rules analyzing the surrounding of the emission site and evaluating the possibility to propagate the field value, modulated according to the diffusion function (the field is propagated when it is not voided by the diffusion function and the destination site was not already visited by the diffusion process). By modifying the working memory, adding new field value, this rule is able to recursively trigger further activations on different sites, stopping only when the emitted field has been propagated to all sites that are reached according to the spatial structure of the layer and to the diffusion function of the related field type.

More precisely, Fig. 7 shows the support structures and rules that were defined to manage field diffusion. This operation is actually triggered by the presence of a new `Field` fact that causes the firing of the `start-diffusion` rule, that asserts a `Diffuse` fact that is used to manage and monitor the diffusion. In particular, the `level` slot indicates the distance (in terms of number or arcs, not considering their weight) from the

```
;; Directives for diffusion start
(deftemplate Diffuse "A level diffusion directive"
    (slot instanceId)          ;; id of the field instance to be diffused
    ;; type of the field to be diffused (can be the original type or "*")
    (slot fieldType)
    ;; level to be diffused
    (slot level))
(defrule start-diffusion
    (declare (salience 1))
    (Field (isComposition "FALSE") (collected "FALSE") (instanceId ?id)
        (fieldType ?type) (site ?site) (sourceSite "null") (level 0))
=>
    (assert (Diffuse (instanceId ?id) (fieldType ?type) (level 0))))
;; Diffuse a field to one site of the current level
(defrule diffuse-level-not-present (declare (salience 3))
    (Diffuse (instanceId ?instId) (fieldType ?type) (level ?level))
    ;; ensure the field can be diffused (see template definition for details)
    (Field (collected "FALSE") (sourceSite ?source) (level ?level)
        (site ?site) (instanceId ?instId) (fieldType ?type) (spec ?spec)
        (intensity ?int) (info ?info))
    ;; get the diffusion function name
    (FieldType (id ?type) (diffuseFunction ?diffuse))
    ;; get an adjacent site (different from the local source site)
    (Arc (siteA ?site) (siteB ?dest&~?source) (id ?arcId))
    ;; verify that this same field does not exists on the adjacent site
    (not (Field (site ?dest) (fieldType ?type) (instanceId ?instId)
        (level ?l&:(<= ?l ?level))))
    ;; get the arc weight for the specified field type
    (Weight (arc ?arcId) (fieldType ?type) (value ?weight))
=>
    (bind ?newInt (apply ?diffuse ?int ?weight FALSE))
    (if (neq ?newInt nil) then
        (assert (Field (sourceSite ?site) (level (+ ?level 1))
                (site ?dest) (instanceId ?instId) (fieldType ?type) (spec ?spec)
                (intensity ?newInt) (info ?info)))))
;; this rule is identical to the diffuse-level-not-present except for
;; an 'exists' instead of a 'not' and a TRUE instead of a FALSE
(defrule diffuse-level-present (declare (salience 3))
    (Diffuse (instanceId ?instId) (fieldType ?type) (level ?level))
    ;; ensure the field can be diffused (see template definition for details)
    (Field (collected "FALSE") (sourceSite ?source) (level ?level)
        (site ?site) (instanceId ?instId) (fieldType ?type) (spec ?spec)
        (intensity ?int) (info ?info))
    ;; get the diffusion function name
    (FieldType (id ?type) (diffuseFunction ?diffuse))
    ;; get an adjacent site (different from the local source site)
    (Arc (siteA ?site) (siteB ?dest&~?source) (id ?arcId))
    ;; verify that this same field exists on the adjacent site
    (exists (Field (site ?dest) (fieldType ?type) (instanceId ?instId)
        (level ?l&:(<= ?l ?level))))
    ;; get the arc weight for the specified field type
    (Weight (arc ?arcId) (fieldType ?type) (value ?weight))
=>
    (bind ?newInt (apply ?diffuse ?int ?weight TRUE))
    (if (neq ?newInt nil) then
        (assert (Field (sourceSite ?site) (level (+ ?level 1))
                (site ?dest) (instanceId ?instId) (fieldType ?type) (spec ?spec)
                (intensity ?newInt) (info ?info)))))
(defrule increment-level (declare (salience 1))
    ?diffuse <- (Diffuse (instanceId ?id) (fieldType ?type) (level ?level))
    (exists (Field (instanceId ?id) (fieldType ?type) (level =(+ ?level 1))))
=>
    (modify ?diffuse (level (+ ?level 1))))
;; rule used to keep the facts base clean, retracts the diffusion directive if
;; no new field was asserted in the previous level
(defrule end-diffusion (declare (salience 1))
    ?diffuse <- (Diffuse (instanceId ?id) (fieldType ?type) (level ?level))
    (not (Field (instanceId ?id) (fieldType ?type) (level =(+ ?level 1))))
=>
    (retract ?diffuse))
```

Fig. 7. Jess rules supporting field diffusion

source site currently covered by the operation. Rules `diffuse-level-not-present` and `diffuse-level-present` actually propagate the modulated value of the field to sites having `level` distance from the source of emission. In fact a diffused field can actually reach a given site with different paths in the layer, and the framework must be able to manage this possibility[3]. The last rule, finally, detects the end of the diffusion operation, when the previously described rules do not cause the assertion of new `Field` facts for a given level.

5.3   DJess and MMASS: Agents

DJess can thus be adopted to represent facts about an MMASS environment and to manage its internal mechanisms, such as field diffusion. In addition, it can be suitably adopted to represent and manage abstractions related to agents. The behavioural specification of an MMASS agent is made up of a set of primitives, specifying an action to be carried out at certain conditions. These primitives can be easily mapped to Jess rules, whose left hand side specify conditions on the local context perceived by an agent, and whose right hand side cause modifications of the agent internal state (for *trigger* and *react* operations) and modifications in the environment (for *emit* and *transport*).

Note that *rules are preprocessed* when they are loaded; during this operation the match on a `Field` fact is replaced by `LAYER::Field` so for example:

`(Field (fieldType presence) (spec ?teacherId) (intensity ?int))`

is changed in:

`(LAYER::Field (fieldType presence) (spec ?teacherId)`
`    (intensity ?int))`.

In this manner the `Field` facts are matched on the LAYER's working memory instead of the agent's working memory.

We will now present two sample elements of an agent behavioural specification, to exemplify the adopted approach in the smart department scenario introduced in Sect. 4. In particular, Fig. 8 shows some sample rules respectively related to the Lesson and Student agents.

The first rule of the Lesson agent allows him to effectively exploit the perception of the teacher and to follow its movement in the spatial layer by means of a transport operation. The teacher is a human, an external entity moving in the environment according to his/her free will. However, we suppose that a localization infrastructure is present and that the system can be able to trace his/her position in the physical environment, mapping it to the MMASS spatial layer by means of a teacher agent. Whenever the teacher moves, for instance from his/her room to the corridor and then to one of the classrooms, the teacher agent moves accordingly and it emits a `presence` field, whose specialization is the teacher identifier. This field will thus be centered on the site associated to the current teacher position. For instance, when the teacher exits his/her room (U7-101 in Fig. 2) and enters the corridor the teacher agent moves too and the presence field, previously centered in the site associated to the room, is deleted from the layer and emitted from the site

---

[3] The decision on how to manage this case (e.g. consider only the shortest path and discard other diffusion paths, or combine the intensities) is actually delegated to the diffusion function definition; note that this function can distinguish the case fields reaching a site from the shortest path or deeper ones by means of the last parameter.

```
;; Lesson agent behavioural specification
[...]
;; ALL THE FOLLOWING FACTS ARE ASSERTED IN THE AGENT'S WORKING MEMORY
;; the ID of the lesson
(assert (LessonId operatingsystems))
;; the room of the lesson
(assert (LessonRoom U701))
;; the ID of the teacher to follow
(assert (Teacher Jameson))


;; rule to follow the teacher
(defrule follow-teacher
    (State following)
    (Teacher ?teacherId)
    (Field (fieldType presence) (spec ?teacherId) (intensity ?int))
    (test (< ?int 3))
=>
    (bind ?site (max-adj-site presence ?teacherId))
    (transport ?site))

;; rule to emit the lesson-setup field
(defrule emit-lesson-setup
    (State following)
    (LessonRoom ?site)
    (CurrentSite ?site) ;; matches if the current position is the lesson's room
    (LessonId ?lessonId) ;; to be used in the emit
=>
    ;; change state
    (trigger lesson-setup)
    (emit lesson-setup ?lessonId))
[...]

;; Student agent behavioural specification
[...]
;; THE FOLLOWING FACT IS ASSERTED IN THE AGENT'S WORKING MEMORY
;; the IDs of the lessons to which the student is interested in
(assert (InterestedIn (operatingsystems math1)))


;; rule to show a message when a lesson is about to start (using lesson-setup)
(defrule lesson-setup-notify
 (Field (fieldType lesson-setup) (spec ?lessonId) (intensity ?int))
 ;; the perceived lesson must be of interest
 (InterestedIn ?lessonsIds)
 (test (member$ ?lessonId ?lessonsIds)) ;; true if the lessonId is in the list
 ;; the intensity must be equal to 1
 (test (= ?int 1))
=>
 (printout t The lesson (id = ?lessonId ) is starting. crlf))
[...]
```

Fig. 8. A part of the behavioural specification for Lesson and Student agent

associated to the corridor (U7C01 in Fig. 2). Under this assumption, the Lesson agent can follow the teacher agent (and thus the teacher) in the MMASS spatial layer by perceiving this specific type of field (comparing the field specialization to the fact `Teacher` available to the lesson agent) in its site and adjacent ones and moving towards the one having the highest level of intensity (selected invoking the `max-adj-site` function). It must be noted that `transport` is a library function provided to agent designers by the framework. Similarly, the second rule causes the emission of a `lesson-setup` field whenever the Lesson agent reaches the room assigned for the related lesson (indicated by the fact `LessonRoom` also available to the lesson agent).

The only rule indicated for Student agents realizes the other side of this pattern of indirect interaction with the Lesson agent, that is, the perception of the `lesson-setup` field related to the lessons to which the student is interested in (this relation is checked by looking for the perceived lesson in the fact `InterestedIn`). Since also students are not automatic devices, the only action that can be carried out is the notification to the human student carrying the device in which the Student agent is deployed. Similar rules are present in the behavioural specification of device agents, that will instead actually start the classroom setup.

6   Conclusions and Future Developments

This paper has described a Multi–Agent approach to the modelling and design of CUEs, that are environments that support collaboration among persons in a context of ubiquitous computing. In particular, the paper has shown how results of the research in the topic of MAS environment has provided both modeling abstractions and concrete computational supports for the analysis, design and engineering of CUEs. In particular, the MMASS model was applied to represent and to manage several types of awareness information (both physical and logical contextual information), which is an essential part of a CUE. Moreover, an approach based on DJess to the design and engineering of CUEs was introduced. Support tools for the definition and design of this kind of environment were also realized (Fig. 9).

Future works are on one hand aimed at identifying a concrete situation for an evaluation of a CUE integrated with existing applications already adopted by users of the environment (e.g. the CMS of the smart department scenario), aimed at further evaluating the adequacy of the approach as well as testing the introduced prototype, in order to identify problems and necessary additional features.

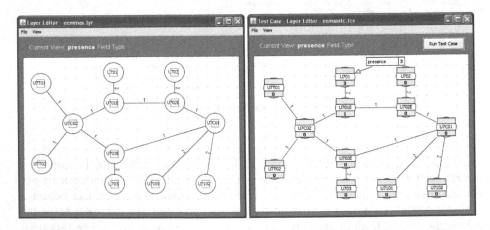

Fig. 9. A tool supporting the design of an MMASS spatial layer (on the left) and the testing of field diffusion in it (on the right)

References

1. Satyanarayanan, M.: Pervasive Computing: Vision and Challenges. IEEE Personal Communications 8, 10–17 (2001)
2. Zambonelli, F., Parunak, H.V.D.: Signs of a revolution in computer science and software engineering. In: Petta, P., Tolksdorf, R., Zambonelli, F. (eds.) ESAW 2002. LNCS (LNAI), vol. 2577, pp. 13–28. Springer, Heidelberg (2003)
3. Ferber, J.: Multi–Agent Systems. Addison Wesley, Reading (1999)
4. Weyns, D., Omicini, A., Odell, J.: Environment as a first class abstraction in multiagent systems. Autonomous Agents Multi-Agent Systems 14, 5–30 (2007)
5. Bandini, S., Manzoni, S., Simone, C.: Heterogeneous agents situated in heterogeneous spaces. Applied Artificial Intelligence 16, 831–852 (2002)
6. Lech, T.C., Wienhofen, L.W.M.: AmbieAgents: a scalable infrastructure for mobile and context-aware information services. In: 4th International Joint Conference on Autonomous Agents and Multiagent Systems (AAMAS 2005), Utrecht, The Netherlands, July 25-29, pp. 625–631. ACM Press, New York (2005)
7. Rodríguez, M.D., Favela, J., Martínez, E.A., Muñoz, M.A.: Location-aware access to hospital information and services. IEEE Transactions on Information Technology in Biomedicine 8, 448–455 (2004)
8. Cabitza, F., Sarini, M., Dal Seno, B.: DJess - a context-sharing middleware to deploy distributed inference systems in pervasive computing domains. In: Proceedings of International Conference on Pervasive Services, 2005. ICPS 2005, pp. 229–238. IEEE, Los Alamitos (2005)
9. Locatelli, M.P., Vizzari, G.: Awareness in Collaborative Ubiquitous Environments: the Multilayered Multi-Agent System Approach. ACM Transactions on Autonomous and Adaptive Systems 2 (2007)
10. Campbell, R.H.: Beyond global communications: the active world. In: PerCom, p. 211 (2005)
11. Beaudouin-Lafon, M.: Computer Supported Co-operative Work. Trends in Software, vol. 7. John Wiley and Sons, Chichester (1999)
12. Schmidt, K.: The problem with 'awareness': Introductory remarks on 'awareness in CSCW'. Computer Supported Cooperative Work 11, 285–298 (2002)
13. Cabitza, F., Locatelli, M.P., Simone, C.: Cooperation and ubiquitous computing: an architecture towards their integration. In: COOP 2006, IOS Press, Amsterdam (2006)
14. Dourish, P.: What we talk about when we talk about context. Personal and Ubiquitous Computing 8, 19–30 (2004)
15. Bandini, S., Manzoni, S., Vizzari, G.: Situated Cellular Agents: a model to simulate crowding dynamics. IEICE Transactions on Information and Systems: Special Issues on Cellular Automata E87-D, 669–676 (2004)
16. Simone, C., Bandini, S.: Integrating awareness in cooperative applications through the reaction-diffusion metaphor. Computer Supported Cooperative Work 11, 495–530 (2002)
17. Cabitza, F., Locatelli, M.P., Sarini, M., Simone, C.: CASMAS: Supporting collaboration in pervasive environments. In: Fourth Annual IEEE International Conference on Pervasive Computing and Communications, 2006. PerCom 2006, pp. 286–295. IEEE, Los Alamitos (2006)
18. Locatelli, M.P., Simone, C.: Supporting care networks through an ubiquitous collaborative environment. In: Nugent, C., Augusto, J. (eds.) Smart Homes and Beyond. Assistive Technology Research, vol. 19, IOS Press, Amsterdam (2006)
19. Mamei, M., Zambonelli, F.: Augmenting the physical environment through embedded wireless technologies. In: Weyns, D., Van Dyke Parunak, H., Michel, F. (eds.) E4MAS 2005. LNCS (LNAI), vol. 3830, pp. 235–250. Springer, Heidelberg (2006)

20. Mamei, M., Zambonelli, F.: Programming pervasive and mobile computing applications with the TOTA middleware. In: Proceedings of the Second IEEE International Conference on Pervasive Computing and Communications (PerCom 2004), Orlando, FL, USA, March 14-17, pp. 263–276. IEEE Computer Society, Los Alamitos (2004)

21. Bellifemine, F., Bergenti, F., Caire, G., Poggi, A.: Jade - a java agent development framework. In: Bordini, R.H., Dastani, M., Dix, J., Fallah-Seghrouchni, A.E. (eds.) Multi-Agent Programming. Multiagent Systems, Artificial Societies, and Simulated Organizations, vol. 15, pp. 125–147. Springer, Heidelberg (2005)

22. Omicini, A., Ricci, A., Viroli, M., Castelfranchi, C., Tummolini, L.: Coordination artifacts: environment-based coordination for intelligent agents. In: Jennings, N.R., Sierra, C., Sonenberg, L., Tambe, M. (eds.) 3rd international Joint Conference on Autonomous Agents and Multiagent Systems (AAMAS 2004), pp. 286–293. ACM Press, New York (2005)

23. Omicini, A., Zambonelli, F.: Coordination for Internet application development. Autonomous Agents and Multi-Agent Systems 2, 251–269 (1999); Special Issue: Coordination Mechanisms for Web Agents

24. Fiedman-Hill, E.: Jess in Action – Rule Based Systems in Java. Manning (2003)

Engineering Contextual Information for Pervasive Multiagent Systems

Gabriella Castelli, Marco Mamei, and Franco Zambonelli

Dipartimento di Scienze e Metodi dell'Ingegneria – Università di Modena e Reggio Emilia
Via Amendola 2 – 42100 Reggio Emilia – ITALY
{name.surname}@unimore.it

Abstract. Multiagent systems for mobile and pervasive computing should extensively exploit contextual information both to adapt to user needs and to enable autonomic behavior. This raises the problem of how to represent, organize, aggregate, and make available such data so as to have it become meaningful and usable knowledge, facilitating the design and development of agents, and enabling them to acquire high-degrees of context awareness at limited efforts. In this paper, we identify the key software engineering challenges introduced by the need of accessing and exploiting huge amount of heterogeneous contextual information. Following, we survey the relevant proposals in the area of context-aware pervasive computing, data mining and granular computing discussing their potentials and limitations. On these bases, we propose the W4 model for contextual data and show how it can represent an effective model to enable flexible general-purpose management of contextual knowledge, to facilitate agents in achieving high degrees of context-awareness and, overall, to facilitate the design and development of complex multiagent systems.

Keywords: Context-awareness, Autonomic services, W4 Model, Knowledge engineering.

1 Introduction

Pervasive and mobile computing scenarios consider the possibility of providing users with ubiquitous and on-the-move access to digital services, and of supporting users interactions with their surrounding environments [18, 24, 10]. For this possibility to become practical and satisfying, agents should be able to understand situations occurring in the surrounding physical context, autonomously adapt their behavior to the context from which they are requested, and proceed with their execution in an autonomic (i.e., self-organizing, self-adapting, and self-healing) way [24]. The enforcement of these features requires both the technology to capture contextual data and the capability of agents to exploit it.

The technology to acquire contextual information is becoming increasingly available, and it will soon become widespread via the increasing deployment of RFID tags, sensor networks, localization systems, users' and organizations' profiles. This fact, together with the increasing success of participatory Web 2.0 tools, will soon make available to agents overwhelming amounts of information about facts and events

D. Weyns, S.A. Brueckner, and Y. Demazeau (Eds.): EEMMAS 2007, LNAI 5049, pp. 223–239, 2008.

occurring in the physical and social world. This opens up the possibility of exploiting all such information for the provisioning of pervasive context-aware services for "browsing the world", i.e., for facilitating users in gathering information about the world, interacting with it, and understanding it. Those services require accessing to great amount of distributed and continuously updating data, however due to the amount of data and the inherent distribution the challenge is not getting the freshest data or all data available everywhere but getting a good approximation is real time. Accordingly, the real challenge for future pervasive applications is the investigation of principles, algorithms, and tools, via which this growing amount of distributed information can be represented, organized, aggregated, and made more meaningful, so as to facilitate the exploitation by agents [5].

In the past few years, a number of different research communities, from pervasive computing, to data mining and granular computing, have recognized the above problems, and have proposed solutions aimed at engineering large amounts of contextual data and at turning them into usable knowledge [DeyA00, 11, 13, 34]. Thus, a first contribution of this paper is to survey such diverse proposals in different areas and critically analyze their potentials and limitations. The result of our analysis is that, despite the potentials of specific approaches for specific problems, none of them can qualify as a fully-fledged general-purpose solution for the challenges raised by pervasive autonomic multiagent systems. Following, the second contribution of this paper is to present a novel data model to represent context information, and discuss its potential to act as a general-purpose model to handle several kinds of context information. The model, which we call "W4", is based on the consideration that most information about the world (i.e., about facts occurring in the world) can be simply represented in terms of four "W"s – Who, What, Where, When. Despite its simplicity, such a representation enables for very expressive and flexible data usages. In particular, W4 data can be easily queried and accessed by agents, tolerate the effective execution of semantic data organization and data aggregation, and can be effectively used to represent both primitive data and high-level knowledge related to a situation.

2   Agents and Context-Awareness

Our everyday environments (houses, offices, and cities) are increasingly populated by a variety of communication-enabled computing devices, forming the basis of a truly pervasive network and generating increasing amounts of information about the physical world and its processes. Embedded and wireless sensors collect and make available information about physical phenomena, RFID tags can be attached to objects to describe them and to track their usage. We, as humans, typically carry on a mobile phone and/or a PDA, possibly a GPS device and some additional wearable sensors, and can generate a lot of information about ourselves and about our own activities and movements. Similar considerations increasingly apply to cars and home furniture. In addition, the success of participatory Web tools (aka Web 2.0 technologies) and of geographic Web tools (e.g., Google Earth and alike), is increasingly making available nearly-up-to-date information about various facts and events occurring in the physical and social worlds. The above trend paves the way for the design and development of a wide variety of innovative, autonomic and context-aware, pervasive multiagent systems. However, it also raises peculiar challenges in engineering such agents, mostly due to the issue of engineering all available data and turning it into usable knowledge.

2.1 Context-Awareness vs. Situation-Awareness

Agents have to be inherently context-aware. In fact, collecting information about situations around and acting accordingly is the very core of their activities [24]. The need for context-awareness also arises when one wants to enforce autonomic behavior in agents, i.e., their capability of self-organizing their activities, self-reconfigure and self-heal on need. Given the intrinsic dynamics and decentralization of pervasive scenarios, where components and devices belonging to different stakeholders can come and go at any time and where the structure of the network is inherently dynamic and unreliable, autonomic behavior is necessary to ensure agents' continuity without forcing costly and hard to be managed human intervention. However, for such autonomic features to be enabled, agents require the capability of understanding what's happening around and react accordingly.

Given that, as stated at the beginning of this section, a number of technologies exists that contribute producing large amounts of contextual information, one may think that achieving context-awareness is simply a non issue. Whatever the data source producing some raw item of contextual information (i.e., "data atom"), all of them contribute populating a large cloud of data atoms and at making it available to agents (see Fig. 1-left). An agent in need of understanding what's happening around can access (i.e., internalize) the needed data atoms and analyze them.

Unfortunately, such description is far too simplistic and does not emphasize a number of complexities inherent in it. First, the process of data internalization can lead to high communication and computational costs for a multiagent system, in that it may require accessing large amounts of data atoms possibly distributed across different devices and analyze which data may serve its current purposes. Second, the process of analyzing retrieved contextual data atoms and turning them into useful knowledge may be non-trivial. In other words, getting access to context information does not automatically imply the capability of reaching "situation-awareness", i.e., the capability of recognizing a situation. That is, acquiring contextual information does not imply the capability of understanding situations, especially in the presence of an overwhelming amount of unrelated contextual data atoms. Such problem is even exacerbated by the increasing heterogeneity of devices and tools that contribute producing contextual information, and by the consequent need of handling heterogeneity in data representation and semantics.

In our view there must be an evolution from a model of simple context-awareness, in which agents access isolated pieces of contextual data and are directly in charge of digesting them, towards a model of situation-awareness, in which agents access properly structured and organized information, reflecting comprehensive knowledge that is related to a "situation" of interest and which can be exploited in a standardized fashion [5]. With reference to Fig. 1-right, we envision that the access by agents to contextual information does no longer occur directly, but rather via a "knowledge network" layer. Such layer should encapsulate mechanisms and tools to analyze and (self-)organize contextual information into sorts of structured collections of related data items, i.e. knowledge networks. Such knowledge networks, by pre-digesting contextual information and by providing compact and expressive information to agents, may support them in reaching, with reduced efforts, a comprehensive understanding of "situations" around and, consequently, a higher-degree of adaptability and autonomicity.

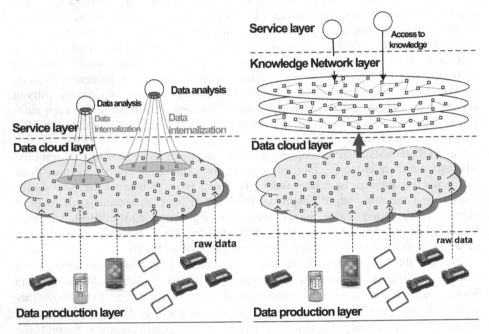

Fig. 1. (**left**) Pervasive devices and sensors make available to agents a sort of "data cloud layer", fed with large amounts of heterogeneous data atoms. To serve their purposes, a multi-agent system needs to retrieve contextual information (i.e., internalize data atoms from the cloud), analyze it to properly understand situations, and finally exploit such knowledge as needed for their own goals. (**right**) By exploiting a knowledge network layer, agents are no longer forced to access the raw data cloud layer. Knowledge organization and analysis is externalized in the middleware, and agents are given access to pre-digested information.

From the software engineering viewpoint, an approach based on knowledge networks has the advantage of providing a clear separation of concerns between data analysis and data exploitation. While data analysis and organization is delegated to the knowledge network layer, agents are left with the only duty of exploiting such data to reach specific functionalities. As always in software engineering, this separation of concerns can notably reduce the complexity of developing and maintaining agents. A possible criticism of the approach is that it does not eradicate the problem of analyzing large amounts of information, but simply passes it to a different component that either exists at application or at knowledge network level. However, in a distributed setting, knowledge networks can take care of knowledge management duties that would have been otherwise replicated inside each agent, with an overall saving in computation and communication efforts.

2.2 Engineering Challenges

For agents to effectively achieve situation-awareness, and for our general idea of knowledge networks to become a practical tool, several engineering challenges have to be faced.

Data Model. Our idea of knowledge networks requires the identification of a simple, general-purpose, and uniform model to represent contextual information. The model should enable representing very diverse facts about the context, typically generated by a variety of heterogeneous sources and at different levels of granularity. Also, the model should enable ease of manipulation of the data atoms, both by the algorithms and that will be embedded in knowledge networks and by agents. Furthermore, the model should enable to deal with incomplete information and information of limited accuracy.

Access to Data. The very goal of knowledge networks is to provide knowledge to agents and to digest data from any possible contextual data source. First, it is necessary to identify suitable methods (i.e., APIs) by which agents can be given access to the knowledge network layer and the information within. Such methods should enable flexible querying of the knowledge network layer, yet should limit the amount of information required by agents to fruitfully access it. Also, given the intrinsic distributed and decentralized nature of contextual information, access to knowledge networks by multiagent systems should abstract from the actual distribution and allocation of data and knowledge. Second, a similar general API should be provided for enabling data sources (which may include agents themselves) to inject new data in the knowledge network layer.

General Approaches for Data Aggregation and Networking. Our idea of knowledge networks is to have it as a "live" layer, which is in charge of continuously and autonomously analyzing information to aggregate data atoms, relate existing knowledge atoms with each other, and extract meaningful knowledge from the available data. Thus, it will be necessary to identify algorithmic approaches for performing such analysis without explicit human intervention. Also, it is necessary for such algorithmic approaches to be as general as possible, so as to be flexibly adaptable to a variety of application needs without having to re-think from scratch the knowledge network architecture for any new application needs.

Application-specific Views. Strictly related to the above, we have clear in mind that the idea of a single knowledge network capable of capturing of the possible needs of all possible agents, is illusionary. In a given pervasive environment, a variety of agents by different stakeholders may exist and new ones can be deployed at any moment, each with its own goals. Such agents may, of course, have very diverse needs for what concerns to accessing contextual knowledge, and may require organization/aggregation along different dimensions and based on different algorithms. For instance, some agents may be more interested in organizing/analyzing knowledge along the spatial dimension (e.g., for detecting spatial patterns of activities in an environment), some along the temporal dimension (e.g., for detecting temporal patterns of activities by users), some along some mixed spatio-temporal dimension or along any other application-specific dimension. Thus, agents may require the dynamic instantiation within the knowledge networks of application-specific algorithms for knowledge analysis. Accordingly, a general approach to knowledge networks should account for this possibility and enable the dynamic instantiation of any new knowledge analysis algorithm.

3   Critical Survey of Relevant Related Works

In the last years the role of the environment has being rapidly considered as a fundamental one in modeling and engineering multi-agent systems. The environment abstraction suits to some extent our idea of knowledge network. For this perspective, the knowledge network can be perceived as an information environment where agents live.

[3] provides an explicit representation of the spatial structure of the environment. They define a Multilayered Multi–Agent Situated System (MMASS) that describes the spatial structure of the environment as a multilayered network of sites. Agents diffuse fields throughout the environment, and since fields values can decrease during propagation, agents perceive them depending from where their position in space. The work in [32] interprets the environment as a locus to be explicitly designed and developed to provide agents with services. They introduce the notion of artifact for MAS, i.e. entities residing in the environment independently of the existence of agents. The artifact exposes a set of operations, which an agent aware of the artifact can invoke. [9] proposes a cognitive middle layer, starting from the idea that agents must be able to understand the environment and capture its dynamic nature. It is realized as a three-layered architecture. The bottom layer is the physical environment. The middle layer is the concept model, it is merged into the environment and shared among all agents providing a common conceptual basis. And finally the topmost layer is the subjective mind, which resides in an agent. [28] considers the problem of distributed mobile application where the interactions between agents is complicated by the dynamics of the environment. They propose a distributed interaction protocol based upon roles called ObjectPlaces.

All these approaches provides interesting models that could be applied to our knowledge network idea. However, even if the knowledge network base infrastructure could be based on environment-based modes, the fact that we are dealing explicitly with context acquisition and processing requires dedicated models and algorithms. In the rest of this section, we survey and analyze several approaches that, in different areas, are somewhat contributing pieces towards the realization of our knowledge network vision. Yet, none of the approaches we have analyzed properly addresses all the identified challenges.

3.1   Context-Awareness

In the past few years, a lot of research work has focused on identifying proper models for context-aware information, mainly with the goals of engineering usable context representation from low-level sensor data.

Early work in this area, as from Schmidt et al. [30] and Dey et al. [14], concentrates on the issue of acquiring context data from sensors and of the processing such data to make it available to processes/agents in the form of abstract components. Such approaches thus partially address the data model challenge, in that they recognize the need for a data model able to abstract raw contextual data at higher level. However, they generally miss in identifying a uniform model and a common semantics to describe the data. This forces developers to build new query languages and new components in dependence of the kind of information at hand.

A different thread of researchers focuses on the issue of providing rich data models for contextual information and of facilitating querying by agents. [29] proposes a context model in which each contextual data atom is represented by a set of environments variables – each one dealing with a different aspect of the context – that can be accessed in a flexible way. Similarly, [18] models contextual data by making possible to enrich it with several meta-information such as temporal aspects, information imperfection, etc. Such approaches well address the data model challenge, in that they aim at developing a general and flexible data model. However, working with data atoms made up of a long list of elements/variables does not go toward simplicity and generality, which we instead feel should both be goals. More recently, other proposals have adopted a similar endeavor but have considered the issue of adopting specific ontologies to model context-information and enable – other than efficient querying – also efficient context-reasoning [12, 27, 22]. Although such approaches tend to be application-specific, they attribute the importance of linking independent atoms of contextual information (with ontological relations) and of reasoning not only on individual data items but also on their relations, an idea which is fully shared by our knowledge network vision.

An increasing number of research work get inspiration from tuple space data models [1] and proposes representing contextual information in the form of tuples, storing them across a set of distributed tuple spaces holding local contextual information, and accessing them via associative (i.e., pattern-matching based) query operations on tuple spaces. Egospaces [20] adopts this perspective, without committing to a specific pre-defined structure for context tuple, which can make it difficult for agents to uniformly deal with tuples representing different aspects of the context represented in different formats. However, Egospaces proposes a so called "egocentric" notion of context, in which different agents can perceive a different context-dependent representation of the contextual information, depending on their current location. We consider such a feature very important in that it allows to tailor information to specific users' needs and viewpoints. The Context Fabric model [19] improved the Egospaces idea in that it relies on well-structured context tuples each describing a single piece of context data in terms of entities (people, place, thing), attributes (e.g., the name). Moreover, even if it does not propose solutions for enforcing application-specific views, it considers the possibility of identifying relationships between context tuples. Recent proposals focusing on sensor networks, suggest exploiting a tuple-based approach to flexibly access sensorial information [26]. The idea is to have agents inject code into the sensors for aggregating/elaborating data within the network, and eventually enabling agents to directly access aggregated data according to their own specific needs.

In general we consider tuple-based approaches very suitable for organizing and accessing contextual information, but we also think that there is need of more structuring and flexibility than those exhibited by the existing approaches.

Some recent proposals focus on providing models for contextual data that adopt a uniform well-defined structure, capturing those specific aspects which are of interest by agents, a characteristic which we consider very promising. The approach proposed in the Nexus platform [23] proposes representing different contextual data uniformly accounting for fields such as spatial references and temporal references, for enabling general spatial and temporal queries over a context database. Similarly, the proposal described in [33] suggests adopting a seven-field data structure to describe the context. The suggested fields include subject, predicate, object, time, area, certainty, freshness, which overall provide quite a complete characterization of contextual information. Finally, the system described in [7] proposes describing contextual information contained in RFID tags in terms of identity, purpose of tag, location of tag, time of information production. Although the system is a special-purpose one, having been applied to RFID tags only, we consider it interesting in that is consider a simple enough yet quite informative structured data model, able to represent in a uniform way different data coming from different sources. Indeed, our proposal accounts for a very similar structuring for contextual information, and enriches it with a well defined API, and with the possibility of linking data atoms and of providing application-specific views.

3.2 Data Mining and Pattern Discovery

As stated in Sect. 2.1, the potentially overwhelming amount of data that can be generated by pervasive sensing infrastructures does not constitute knowledge per se, in that agents have may have to face complex analysis tasks to get a meaning out of it. Such analysis task, which we think should be delegated to a knowledge network layer, is in the end a sort of data mining process [16].

Data mining concerns analyzing large amounts of typically unrelated data to infer hidden linkages, correlations, rules, constraints, (i.e., broadly speaking, patterns) in such data [15, 4], to present such inferences to user for subsequent interpretation, i.e., to have the user give a meaning to data by analyzing the identified patterns. In general, all the mechanisms proposed in this field can be naturally be employed within the knowledge network layer to extract knowledge from raw data collected by sensing devices.

In the wide data mining research area, a variety of algorithms and approaches have been proposed, most of which rely on a general two step process: identifying relevant sets of related data item within the global dataset and, following, inferring patterns from this sets. This two-steps process can be of inspiration for knowledge networks, and in particular with regard to the need of identifying flexible and general algorithmic approaches for continuously and autonomously aggregate and analyze data atoms. In fact, it may lead to a modular algorithmic approach, in which the two issues of relating data atoms and of extracting higher-level knowledge form such relations can be clearly separated.

Data mining activities may, in general, identify thousands of patterns from data sets, all of them of general interest. With this regard, several researches involve the specialization of association mining fundamentals to address the problems of specific application domains, e.g. spatial or temporal association rules, to limit the number of mined association to the most relevant ones [2, 31]. Of course, for applying the lessons of data mining to agents and knowledge networks, a similar application-specific approach must be taken.

Recently many researchers applied data mining techniques to wireless sensor networks. Sensor network offers new challenges to classical data mining. The large amount of sensed data has to be modeled has a stream, there may be a large number of nodes in the network, calling for decentralized approaches and should account for data losses, and finally the power consumption issue must be considered. Some approaches[6, 25] focuses on mining sensed data for prediction purpose. [6] proposes a framework for data mining upon sensor network for supervised learning (prediction, classification, etc.) according to a specified level of precision and quality. The framework is based on a two step process: the first step performs aggregation of sensors in clusters, in the second one, each cluster sends the aggregate to a data mining server that performs the analysis. Similarly, [25] proposes a framework for prediction based on the flow of local predictors through the network. At the root, predictors are combined via a voting mechanism. Other approaches [17, 21] focuses on the general problem of identification of pattern by using neural networks algorithm in a distributed setting. In particular, these approaches: (i) uphold the need for data mining for analyzing the vast amount of data in pervasive computing application, (ii) show that decentralized approaches are effective and operable in distributed network with several nodes.

As an additional note, typical data mining approaches are human-centered and query-based, i.e., assuming humans are the end users of data mining activities. In pervasive computing, instead, we require automatic methodologies for discovering relations between contextual data and for making these available to computational agents. Moreover, conventional data mining assumes the independence between the attributes and the independence between the values of these attributes, but in context-awareness diverse attributes and their corresponding values are often related. Some researches has been done in areas where correlation between attributes exist [16], however they result in human-centered and visual data mining methodologies that are not suitable for pervasive multiagent systems.

3.3 Data Aggregation Granular Computing

Granular computing is an emerging inter-disciplinary research area that considers the general issue of processing "information granules", i.e., collections of data atoms, and extract knowledge from them. The idea is to organize information granules together based on their similarity, functional properties, spatial/temporal adjacency, or identified regularities in data, and eventually provide higher knowledge-level views, at different scales, of the phenomena underlying information granules. Although the strict relations between data mining and granular computing are evident, the latter adopts a more theoretical and inter-disciplinary viewpoint, and specifically focuses on the idea that, at different level of observation and analysis, the same data can provide different knowledge [34].

The ideas and principles of granular computing have been investigated in many research fields from computer science to psychology: computational intelligence, artificial intelligence, the theory of hierarchy, divide and conqueror, the theory of small groups, etc. Such a wide range of researches demonstrates the potential of granular computing approach. Indeed, the underlying assumption of granular computing is that the basic principles and methodologies are independent from specific problem domains. Granular computing naturally fits also our perspective on context-awareness and situation-awareness, and specifically our idea of knowledge networks. First, the goal of extracting knowledge from information granules directly maps into the idea of introducing a layer above the cloud of contextual data to access higher-level information. Second, the idea of relating information granules based on different characteristics and rules directly maps into our idea of knowledge networks. Finally, the idea of granular computing of providing multi-level views for serving different purposes directly maps into our goal of providing application-specific views of knowledge networks.

To the best of our knowledge, there are no studies directly related to applying granular computing ideas to support context-awareness by pervasive multiagent systems. Nevertheless, there are studies related to applying granular computing techniques to model spatial and temporal data at different levels of granularity, an issue which is of specific relevance to pervasive multiagent systems (which are inherently situated in space and time). Camossi et. al. [8] proposes a spatiotemporal data model relying on an extended ODMG model, which provides a uniform management of both moving entities and temporal maps. The model allows for the multi-level management of such data, and also deals with temporal indeterminacy and spatial inaccuracy. Granular GeoGraph [13] provides a conceptual spatial data model with two granularity dimensions: a purely spatial one and a semantic one. Spatial granularity refers the possible variations of the geometry of an object with respect to different scales, semantic granularities refers to the possible variations of set of domain objects with respect to the levels of detail requested by different users/applications.

Although the above researches help us providing some inspiration with spatial and temporal data, context-awareness and situation-awareness especially, involves more contextual factors and more rich set of relations to be taken into account, something which we indeed try to account in our proposal.

4   The W4 Approach

The result of the previous survey is that, despite diverse approaches address specific engineering challenges, none of them propose fully-fledged solutions for the need of modern autonomic pervasive multiagent systems.

Our proposal for a novel, simple yet effective, data model for expressing contextual knowledge about the world starts from the consideration that any elementary data atoms as well as any higher-level piece of contextual knowledge, in the end, represents a "fact" which has occurred. Accordingly, our proposal simply account that any of such facts – and therefore any data/knowledge atom – can be expressed by means of a simple yet expressive 4-fields tuples (Who, What, Where, When): "someone or something (Who) does/did some activity (What) in a certain place (Where) at a specific time (When)".

W4 knowledge atoms may be created by proper software agents associated to data sources or sensor. Their four-fields structure is flexible and general enough to uniformly deal with information coming from sources as diverse as embedded devices, cameras, users, or Web 2.0 sites, and can account for adaptation to context and incomplete information (i.e., some of the four fields being unspecified). W4 knowledge atoms, as tuples in tuple spaces, can be stored in suitable shared data spaces, whatever distributed and implemented. Users and agents, from everywhere, can retrieve knowledge atoms via a simple API, based on "à la Linda" [1] pattern-matching query mechanisms. Such API supports context-aware queries and incomplete information, to enable agents to interact with the world and to enforce autonomic and context-aware functionalities. In addition, the simple W4 structure support general distributed algorithms for data aggregation and manipulation, and facilitates the building of semantic knowledge networks and of multiple, application-specific views.

4.1 Data Representation

The four-fields (Who, What, Where, When) of the W4 data model each describes a different aspect of a contextual fact.

The Who field associates a subject to a fact, and may represent a human person (e.g., a username) or an unanimated part of the context acting as a data source (e.g., the ID of an RFID tag). The Who field is represented by a type-value pair, in the form of a string, with an associated namespace that defines the "type" of the entity that is represented. For example, valid entries for this field are: "person:Gabriella", "tag:tag#567".

The What field describes the activity performed by the subject. This information can either come directly from the data source (e.g., a sensor is reading a temperature value), or be inferred from other context parameters (e.g., an accelerometer on a PDA can reveal that the user is running), or it can be explicitly supplied by the user. This field is represented as a string containing a predicate:complement statement. For example, valid entries for the What field are: "read:book", "work:pervasive computing group", "read:temperature=23".

The Where field associates a location to the fact. In our model the location may be a physical point represented by its coordinates (longitude, latitude), a geographic region (we currently adopt the PostGIS language to describe such regions), or it can also be a logical place. In addition, context-dependent spatial expressions like "here" or "within:300m" can be used for context-aware querying, as described in the following of this section.

The When field associates a time or a time range to a fact. This may be an exact time/time range (e.g., "2006/07/19:09.00am - 2006/07/19:10.00am"), or a concise description (e.g., 9:28am). For example 9:28am = 2006/07/19:9:28am ± 5min. Also in this case, context-dependent expressions can be defined (e.g., "now", "today", "yesterday", "before") and can be used for context-dependent querying.

In summary, in our current implementation, the content of each W-field is a string of formatted text containing either some keywords like "yesterday", "within", etc., or some general unformatted words "read", "work", "temperature", etc.

While the 4 Ws structure the information contained in a knowledge atom meaningfully, the content of each field is still difficult to be analyzed and, in general, to an agent something like "What = read:book" has the same meaning of "What = djhxf:wyktx". In our experiments and applications, this problem is trivially solved by using a predefined small ontology hardcoded into the agent and enabling the agent to recognize specific words. This of course, while vey simple to implement, presents all sorts of problems with regard to openness and scalability of the knowledge network. In any case, this kind of problem (i.e., the need to use shared ontologies) is not peculiar of our approach, and it troubles all open systems. Accordingly, in our future work, we plan to describe the content of each W-field by making use of well-defined ontologies supporting interoperability between agents also in open and large scenarios.

4.2 Data Access and Multiagent system Engineering

As already stated, it is fundamental to define a simple API for agents to access to contextual knowledge and enabling data sources and agents to inject new data in the knowledge network layer. Since knowledge atoms are stored in the form of W4 tuples in a shared data space (or in multiple data spaces), we took inspiration from tuplespace approaches to define the following API:

```
void inject(KnowledgeAtom a);
KnowledgeAtom[] read(KnowledgeAtom a);
```

The inject operation is equivalent to a tuple space "in" operation: an agent accesses the shared data space to store a W4 tuple there.

The read operation is used to retrieve tuples from the data space via querying. A query is represented in its turn as a W4 tuple with some unspecified or only partly specified values (i.e., a template tuple). Upon invocation, the read operation triggers a pattern matching procedure between the template and the W4 tuples that already populate the data space. A vector of all matching tuples – i.e., those for which all the defined fields match those provided in the template – is returned as the result of the query. In any case, pattern matching operations work differently from the traditional tuple space model. In fact, our proposal relies on the W4 structure to enforce more expressive pattern matching operations, which may exploit differentiated mechanisms for the various W4 fields. Current mechanisms work as follows:

Who and What. Pattern-matching operations in these fields are based on stringbased regular expressions. For example, "user:*" will match any user.

Where. Pattern matching in this field involves spatial operations inspired by PostGIS operations. Basically, the template defines a bounding box (e.g., "circle, center(lonY,latX), radius:500m") and everything within the bounding box matches the template. All tuples with a Where field within the circle will match this field of the template. Contextual places such as "within:300m" can be specified in the template and are translated into actual spatial regions – based on the current location from where the query is performed – before going through the pattern matching.

When. In this case, the template defines a time interval. Everything that happened within that interval matches the template. Concise time descriptions as well as contextual ones (e.g., "now" or "before") are converted into actual time intervals before pattern matching.

Two simple examples follow to illustrate the querying process. Let us assume Gabriella is walking in the campus and wants to know if some colleagues are near. She will ask (via a read operation):

```
Who: user:*
What: works:pervasive computing group
Where: circle,center(lonY,latX),radius:500m
When: now
```

Then, she will get in return the tuples representing all the colleagues of her group currently around (at least, of all those colleagues having decided to expose themselves via a W4 tuple). Similarly, Gabriella can ask if some of her colleagues have gone to work in the morning:

```
Who: user:*
What: works:pervasive computing group
Where: office
When: 2006/07/19:09am- 2006/07/19:10am
```

We emphasize that the returned answers have not to be "complete" W4 tuples. The pattern matching mechanism also allows for matches between incomplete information. Thus, unlike in traditional tuple space approaches, applications are based on components entering complete and incomplete context information and getting in response refined (but possibly still incomplete) information.

In summary, the proposed data access model reflects standard tuple-space operations, but can rely on a predefined structure in the tuples to support more meaningful and semantic kind of pattern matching.

4.3 Data Generation

In the W4 model, we rely on the reasonable assumption that software drivers (or, more in general, software agents) are associated with data sources and are in charge of creating W4 tuples and inserting them in some sorts of shared data spaces. In the end, any data source must be somehow associated with some software to gather and store data items, W4 agents have the additional goal of collecting all the necessary information to produce a W4 tuple which is as accurate and complete as possible. This occurs by sensing and inferring information from all the devices and sources available (e.g., RFID tags, GPS devices, Web agents), and by combining them in a W4 tuple. Three simple examples may clarify this concept.

Let us assume Gabriella is walking in the campus park. Agents running on her GPS-equipped PDA, can periodically create the following tuple:

```
Who: user:Gabriella
What: walk:4km/h
Where: lonY, latX
When: 2006/10/17:10.59am
```

Where the Who is entered implicitly by the user at the login, What and Where can be derived by the GPS (e.g., the speed of Gabriella as measured by the GPS can be used to deduce that she is walking), When can be provided both by the PDA or by the GPS. Viewing this from a different, more fine-grained perspective, we can imagine that one agent controlling the user profile can create a raw W4 tuple in which only the who and where are specified; another agent controlling the GPS agent create a tuple in which only where and what (i.e., the speed) are specified. Accordingly, the merging of these two raw W4 atoms into the complete one represented below can be considered as an action of the knowledge networking that produces a more complete and expressive information.

Now, let us assume that Gabriella's PDA is connected with a RFID tag reader. A specific RFID agent controls the reader and handles the event of "tag recognition" whenever a tag enters in the reading range. In this case, either the tag contains its own Who and What description in its limited memory, or the tag ID can be resolved in a database (mapping tag IDs into the associated Who-What descriptions) that the agent may access to fill in the W4 fields. Otherwise, the Who reduces to the tag ID (which enables to access to the database later) and the What is left empty. As in the previous example, the Where and When can be read from the GPS of the user. The resulting tuple is as follows:

> Who: tag:#456
> What: -
> Where: lonY, latX
> When: 2006/10/17:10.59am

The agent running in the knowledge network can use both the data coming from the GPS and the tag to provide a better localization of Gabriella. For example a good policy is that the RFID based location may be more accurate than the GPS one. So the resulting tuple describing Gabriella is the result of the merging between the previous ones:

> Who: user:Gabriella
> What: walk:4km/h
> Where: tag#456
> When: 2006/10/17:10.59am

This last example shows again a task of knowledge networking, in that it includes and action for relating individual atoms to increase their informative values.

5   Conclusion and Open Issues

The W4 Model is our proposal for expressing contextual knowledge about the world. It tackles the majority of challenges in Sect. 2.2. However we are still working on it to extend the aggregation mechanism and to test them in distributed environments. Its simple four-fielded structure can uniformly represents data coming from diverse sources, it can represent simple data atoms as well as aggregated atoms. The examples in Sect. 4 shows the expressiveness of the data model in diverse situations. The developed API to access the knowledge network layer and to inject new data is simple yet flexible in that it is based upon the classical tuple spaces mechanism, the query interface is based on expressive pattern matching upon the four fields. Respect to first works in the field of Context-awareness such as [30] and [14], the W4 Model can uniformly deal with multiple context information in a coherent way, without leading to a long list of all the characteristics of the context as [29] and [18]. Differently from the tuple based approaches ([20] , [19]) the W4 representation strongly structures the context representation, so that the context representation can be easily browsed. The W4 Model represents the context similarly to [23], [33] and [7], but our approach is general purpose and able to represent a large number of context information.

About the knowledge network, our idea is to exploit the four fielded structure to identify some preferential dimensions between atoms, and create new atoms represented the inferred knowledge. In this, the proposed approach is similar to the classical data mining process, in which in a first step is devoted to identify all data sets, and then patterns and rules are inferred from sets.

Although powerful some problems and limitations affects the current W4 Model. The first criticism of the W4 approach is that it does not eradicate the problem of analyzing large amount of data, but simply passes it to a different abstraction level. It should be considered that knowledge network can take care of knowledge management duties that would have been otherwise replicated inside each agent.

A serious limitation of our model is the lacks of meta data about the context, such as the freshness of the data, the source of the data, etc. that are traditionally available to the agents. We plan to tackle this requirements in the future works.

Another problem deals with the storage of historical information. Although historical data are useful to do inferences, for learning procedures and in general for querying, it is not possible to store all W4 atoms, some mechanism to aggregate or delete old data must be developed. Moreover it must considered that the knowledge network leads to a multiplication of new atoms coming from the inferences process.

In our future work we will try to tackle all these challenges to finally develop flexible and autonomic knowledge networks.

Acknowledgements

Work supported by the project CASCADAS (IST-027807) funded by the FET Program of the European Commission.

References

1. Ahuja, S., Carriero, N., Gelernter, D.: Linda and Friends. IEEE Computer 19(8), 26–34 (1986)
2. Al-Naymat, G., Chawla, S., Gudmundsson, J.: Dimensionality reduction for long duration and complex spatio-temporal queries. In: Proceedings of the 2007 ACM symposium on Applied computing, pp. 393–397. ACM Press, Seoul (2007)
3. Bandini, S., Manzoni, S., Simone, C.: Dealing with space in multi–agent systems: a model for situated MAS. In: Proceedings of the First international Joint Conference on Autonomous Agents and Multiagent Systems: Part 3, pp. 1183–1190. ACM Press, New York (2002)

4. Bartolini, I., Bertino, E., Catania, B., Ciaccia, P., Golfarelli, M., Patella, M., Rizzi, S.: PAt-terns for Next-generation DAtabase systems: preliminary results of the PANDA project. In: Rubettino, C. (ed.) Symposium on Advanced Database Systems, pp. 293–300 (2003)

5. Baumgarten, M., Bicocchi, N., Mulvenna, M., Zambonelli, F.: Self-organizing Knowledge Networks for Smart World Infrastructures. In: International Conference on Self-organization in Agents. Erfurt (2006)

6. Bontempi, G., Le Borgne, Y.: An adaptive modular approach to the mining of sensor net-work data. In: Proceedings of 1st International Workshop on Data Mining in Sensor Net-works as part of the SIAM International Conference on Data Mining, pp. 3–9. SIAM Press, Newport Beach (2005)

7. Bravo, J., Hervas, R., Chavira, G., Nava, S.: Modeling Contexts by RFID-Sensor Fusion. In: Conference on Pervasive Computing and Communications Workshops, pp. 30–34. IEEE Computer Society Press, Pisa (2006)

8. Camossi, E., Bertolotto, M., Bertino, E.: A flexible Approach to Spatio-temporal Multi-granularity in an Object Data Model. International Journal of Geographical Information Science 20(5), 511–534 (2006)

9. Chang, P.H.-M., Chen, K.-T., Chien, Y.-H., Kao, E., Soo, V.-W.: From Reality to Mind: A Cognitive Middle Layer of Environment Concepts for Believable Agents. In: Weyns, D., Van Dyke Parunak, H., Michel, F. (eds.) E4MAS 2004. LNCS (LNAI), vol. 3374, pp. 57–73. Springer, Heidelberg (2005)

10. Castelli, G., Rosi, A., Mamei, M., Zambonelli, F.: A Simple Model and Infrastructure for Context-Aware Browsing of the World. In: Proceedings of the Fifth IEEE International Conference on Pervasive Computing and Communications, IEEE Computer Society Press, New York (2007)

11. Ceglar, A., Roddick, J.F.: Association Mining. ACM Computing Surveys 38(2) (2006)

12. Chen, H., Perich, F., Finin, T., Joshi, A.: SOUPA: StandardOntology for Uiquitous and Pervasive Applications. In: Proceedings of 1st Annual International Conference on Mobile and Ubiquitous Systems (MobiQuitous 2004), Networking and Services, IEEE Computer Society Press, Boston (2004)

13. De Fent, I., Gubiani, D., Montanari, A.: Granular GeoGraph: a Multi-Granular Conceptual Model for Spatial Data. In: Aracne, (ed.) Proceedings of the Thirteenth Italian Symposium on Advanced Database, Bressanone (2005)

14. Dey, A.K., Abowd, G.D., Salber, D.: A Conceptual Framework and a Toolkit for Support-ing the Rapid Prototyping of Context-aware Applications. Human-Computer Interac-tion 16(2-4), 97–166 (2001)

15. Fayyad, U.M., Piatetsky-Shapiro, G., Smith, P.: Advantages in knowledge discovery and data mining. In: Data Mining to knowledge Discovery: An Overview. AAAI/MIT Press (1996)

16. Galloway, J., Simoff, S.J.: Network Data Mining: Methods and Techniques for Discover-ing Deep Linkage between Attributes. In: Proceedings of the 3rd Asia-Pacific conference on Conceptual modelling, Australian Computer Society Inc., Hobart (2006)

17. Ganesan, D., Estrin, D., Heidemann, J.: DIMENSIONS: Why do we need a new Data Handling architecture for Sensor Networks? ACM SIGCOMM Computer Communication Review 33(1), 143–148 (2003)

18. Henricksen, K., Indulska, J., Rakotonirainy, A.: Developing Context-aware Pervasive Computing Applications: Models and Approach. Journal of Pervasive and Mobile Com-puting 2(1), 37–64 (2006)

19. Hong, J.: The Context Fabric: An Infrastructure for Context-Aware Computing. In: Con-ference on Computer Human Interaction, Minneapolis (2002)

20. Julien, C., Roman, G.: EgoSpaces: Facilitating Rapid Development of Context-aware Mobile Applications. IEEE Transactions on Software Engineering 32(5), 281–298 (2006)
21. Kulakov, A., Davcev, D.: Data mining in wireless sensor networks based on artificial neural-networks algorithms. In: Proceedings of 1st International Workshop on Data Mining in Sensor Networks as part of the SIAM International Conference on Data Mining, pp. 10–16. SIAM Press, Newport Beach (2005)
22. Lee, D., Meier, R.: Primary Context Model and Ontology: A Combined Approach for Pervasive Transportation Agents. In: Proceedings of the 5th IEEE Conference on Pervasive Computing and Communications Workshops. IEEE Computer Society Press, White Plains (2007)
23. Lehmann, O., Bauer, M., Becker, C., Nicklas, D.: From home to world - supporting context-aware applications through world models. In: Proceedings of the Second IEEE International Conference on Pervasive Computing and Communications, p. 297. IEEE Computer Society Press, Orlando (2004)
24. Manzalini, A., Zambonelli, F.: Towards Autonomic and Situation-Aware Communication Agents: the CASCADAS Vision. In: Proceedings of the IEEE Workshop on Distributed Intelligent Systems: Collective Intelligence and Its Applications, pp. 383–388. IEEE Computer Society Press, Prague (2006)
25. McConnell, S.M., Skillicorn, D.B.: A Distributed Approach for Prediction in Sensor Networks. In: Proceedings of 1st International Workshop on Data Mining in Sensor Networks as part of the SIAM International Conference on Data Mining, pp. 28–37. SIAM Press, Newport Beach (2005)
26. Newton, R., Welsh, M.: Region Streams: Functional Macroprogramming for Sensor Networks. In: Proceedings of the 1st international workshop on Data management for sensor networks, pp. 78–87. ACM Press, Toronto (2004)
27. Roussaki, I., Strimpakou, M., Pils, C., Kalatzis, N., Anagnostou, M.: Hybrid context modeling: A location-based schemeusing Ontologies. In: Proceedings of the 4th annual IEEE international conference on Pervasive Computing and Communications Workshops. IEEE Computer Society Press, Pisa (2006)
28. Schelfthout, K., Weyns, D., Holvoet, T.: Middleware for Protocol-Based Coordination in Mobile Applications. IEEE Distributed Systems Online 7 (2006)
29. Schilit, B., Adams, N., Want, R.: Context-Aware Computing Applications. In: Proceedings of the Workshop on Mobile Computing Systems and Applications, pp. 85–90. IEEE Computer Society Press, Santa Cruz (1994)
30. Schmidt, A., Aidoo, K.A., Takaluoma, A., Tuomela, U., Van Laerhoven, K., Van de Velde, W.: Advanced Interaction in Context. In: Proceedings of the 1st international symposium on Handheld and Ubiquitous Computing, pp. 187–201. Springer, London (1999)
31. Verhein, F., Chawla, S.: Mining spatio-temporal association rules, sources, sinks, stationary regions and thoroughfares in object mobility databases. In: Proceeding of the 11th International Conference on Database Systems for Advanced Applications, Springer, Singapore (2006)
32. Viroli, M., Omicini, A., Ricci, A.: Engineering MAS environment with artifacts. In: 2nd International Workshop Environments for Multi-Agent Systems, Utrecht (2005)
33. Xu, C., Cheung, S.C.: Inconsistency Detection and Resolution for Context-aware Middleware Support. In: Proceedings of the 10th European software engineering conference held jointly with 13th ACM SIGSOFT international symposium on Foundations of software engineering. ACM Press, Lisbon (2005)
34. Yao, Y.Y.: Three perspectives of granular computing. Journal of Nanchang Institute of Technology 25(2), 16–21 (2006)

Engineering Business Ecosystems Using Environment-Mediated Interactions*

César A. Marín, Iain Stalker, and Nikolay Mehandjiev

Manchester Business School
The University of Manchester
Booth Street West, Manchester M15 6PB, UK
Cesar.Marin@postgrad.manchester.ac.uk,
Iain.Stalker@manchester.ac.uk,
Nikolay.Mehandjiev@manchester.ac.uk

Abstract. The increasingly complex and dynamic nature of contemporary markets demands that a business engages in an ongoing dialogue with all aspects of its environment, including other cooperative and competitive businesses. Whilst the concept of a *business ecosystem* captures the essence of such a domain, the lack of a convincing software architecture for its support has resulted in solutions which only partially leverages the potential of the forementioned concept. In this paper, we present an architecture for a business ecosystem supporting application based on Dynamic Agent-based Ecosystem Model (DAEM:) a novel and promising approach to support business ecosystems and their adaptation capabilities where the environment plays an identifiable mediating role.

1 Introduction

The increasingly complex and dynamic nature of contemporary markets means that to achieve a sustainable growth and improve competitiveness, many businesses participate in agile partnerships of collaborating organisations having complementary expertise. Typically, such partnerships form opportunistically and require that a business engages in an ongoing dialogue with other members of its environment.

The term *business ecosystem* denotes a strategic planning concept, introduced by Moore [1], that captures the essence of such a domain. Moore defined a *business ecosystem* to be a collection of companies which co-evolve developing capabilities in response to new, wide-ranging innovations; companies both cooperate and compete, as appropriate, as they contend for survival and dominance. A business ecosystem is obtained when a set of (initially randomly) interacting companies develops into a more structured community; and typically supports competition at a higher level, i.e., competition among business ecosystems.

* C.A.M. thanks the support provided by Consejo Nacional de Ciencia y Tecnología (CONACyT) through sponsorship No. 197297/218103; this work was supported in part by the European Commission under the research project SMEs Undertaking Design of Dynamic Ecosystem Networks (SUDDEN) through contract No. 035169.

D. Weyns, S.A. Brueckner, and Y. Demazeau (Eds.): EEMMAS 2007, LNAI 5049, pp. 240–258, 2008.

Natural ecosystems—where species compete for same resources and interact to create complex networks, such as food webs—do indeed offer a clarifying metaphor. A natural ecosystem is an example of a so-called complex adaptive system (CAS.) It comprises sets of individuals exhibiting emergent behaviours which are not apprehended by any one individual. Such systems continuously adapt to changes in their extremely dynamic environment, as defined by Holland [2]. Yet, whilst Holland has likened a business environment (cf. financial market) to a CAS, he has not provided any convincing means to explore the metaphor of a business ecosystem. Needless to say about any indication on how to develop one.

In this paper we present an architecture for a business ecosystem supporting application based on Dynamic Agent-based Ecosystem Model (DAEM) [3]. The latter comprises a synthesis of ideas from natural ecosystems and multi-agent systems (MASs) providing an approach to leverage the strategic concept of a business ecosystem along with its adaptation capabilities. In our architecture we assume the existence of an MAS layer supporting business transactions. We then add an extra layer where DAEM is played out. The novelty of our architecture over other approaches is that it makes use of a mediating environment to support all aspects of a business ecosystem according to [1] namely, encouragement to innovate, resource competition, creation of alliances, detection of innovations and changes, and the capability to react to those changes. Our motivation is to help businesses to survive in their dynamically changing environment. Thus, we focus on the uninterrupted and opportunistic discovery of potential long-lasting partnerships such as those in a supply chain.

We begin by briefly explaining DAEM and how adaptation emerges from local interaction occurring on a mediating environment. Then in Sect. 3 we present our architecture which allows us to connect the ecosystem aspects of DAEM to intra- and inter-organisational business interactions and supporting adaptation. Afterwards, we contrast some aspects of our architecture against others and discuss how it is related to other environment mediation views found in literature. Finally, we close the paper in Sect. 5 with a summary and future work.

This work lies in part within the EC-funded project SUDDEN (see [4].) Its aim is to empower SME suppliers to collaboratively design and coordinate supply networks in automotive ecosystems.

2 An Overview of the Dynamic Agent-Based Ecosystem Model (DAEM)

In [3] we presented DAEM as a synthesis of ideas from natural ecosystems and MASs. Its purpose is to provide an approach to leverage the strategic concept of a business ecosystem. Thus, we focus on the uninterrupted search and opportunistic discovery of potential long-lasting partnerships, such as those in a supply chain. We subscribe to the view that local, dynamic interactions are fundamental to the creation of ecosystems [5] and to the development of adaptive behaviours [6]. In addition, we abstract from the details of a particular trade or transaction between two organisations and assume the presence of only three elements in a business interaction, namely: services being offered; services being evaluated; and feedback of service evaluations. *That is, the actual exchange of money for services is not considered here.*

Typically, an organisation functions as both a supplier of one service and a customer (cf. consumer) of another. An organisation offers its services to potential customers and receives service offers from potential suppliers. As a customer, service offers are evaluated to determine who is more convenient to buy from, and therefore, to tag him as a preferred supplier. Service evaluations are sent back to the potential suppliers, so that they know how good their services are perceived. These evaluations are relativised (i.e. they have values within the range $[0, 1]$) according to the best service offer recently evaluated. Any customer sending a relative evaluation of 1 is telling the supplier that his service offer is considered the best one so far. Thus, the supplier knows he is the preferred one for that specific customer.

Likewise, suppliers determine who are their preferred customers according to received evaluations. Because these evaluations are relativised, the closer the evaluation is to 1 the better that customer is preferred over others. Therefore, any organisation knowing it is the preferred supplier of its preferred customer will seek to increase the interaction frequency with its counterpart; and vice versa. Preferred supplier and preferred customer will together become partners and constitute a link in a supply chain.

Relative evaluations give an idea of how good a service offer is perceived compared to the best one a customer has recently found. This information is useful to determine how much improvement the supplier needs to better the top supplier. This mechanism encourages competition so essential for a business ecosystem to function [1].

Because we are interested in the capacity of an organisation as a whole to respond effectively to changes in a business ecosystem, it is convenient to have a single agent to represent an entire organisation. Typically, organisations are in an uninterrupted process of potential partnership discovery. Thus, agents interact with certain frequency, i.e. service offers are re-sent in order to detect whether there has been any preference change.

Figure 1 depicts an agent interaction example in the automotive industry. For instance, say agent i represents a car manufacturer who is about to start a new car design. Among other parts, it needs a new instrument panel design (IPD.) Agents j and h represent each an instrument panel designing company. Say agent j sends his service offer $(ipdp, adv)_j$ to agent i where $ipdp$ represents the service description, i.e. IPD proposal, and adv is the service added value, i.e. a quotation along with manufacturing time, warranty, etc. Then agent i analyses the offer according to his own standards and grants an absolute evaluation of 400. Because this is the best offer i has received, he sends back a relative evaluation of 1.0 meaning that agent j knows his offer is the best one recently received (see Fig. 1(a).) Service offers are compared against other recent offers as a mechanism to implement the "forgetting" MAS engineering principle [7,3].

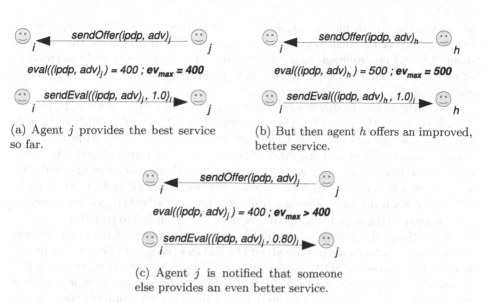

(a) Agent j provides the best service so far.

(b) But then agent h offers an improved, better service.

(c) Agent j is notified that someone else provides an even better service.

Fig. 1. Changes are detected through service evaluations

Now let us say that a similar situation occurs with agent h. He sends his service offer (with a different added value, though) to agent i. After analysing it, the latter concedes 500 as the absolute evaluation, i.e. higher that agent j's offer evaluation. Thus, agent i sends a relative evaluation of 1.0 to agent h. Thus now, agent h knows he is i's preferred supplier to do the IPD (see Fig. 1(b).)

Nevertheless, when agent i receives again a service offer from agent j, the former analyses again j's same offer and grants an absolute evaluation of 400 again. However, because now the highest absolute evaluation is 500 (agent j's,) agent i sends back a relative evaluation of $400/500 = 0.8$. At this point, agent j will know that a better supplier has appeared and that he has been replaced as the preferred supplier (see Fig. 1(c).) Notice that agent j re-sent his service offer even though he already knew he was the preferred supplier. In DAEM, agents interact with certain frequency in order to detect preference changes.

In summary, if an agent improves his service, offers a new service or stops offering one, it will be noticed in service evaluations and preferences will change: replacing a supplier for a better one or giving preference to one customer over another. This is how local adaptations (cf. innovations) are detected, which in turn encourages competition as required by a business ecosystem [1].

2.1   DAEM and Environment-Mediated Interactions

An environment is a fundamental element of both businesses and natural ecosystems, and is not omitted in DAEM. For our purposes, *an environment is defined as a virtually observable surface where inhabitants (i.e. agents) wander across and encounter others in order to interact.* It supports capabilities such as a sense of positioning and displacement, and surrounding awareness. These capabilities permit an agent to orient himself and follow notional gradients on the environment [7,8]. An environment as a surface allows spatial diversity and the creation of niches [8] around *keystone species* [9,5], complying with the view of business ecosystems [1].

The environment mediates agent interactions in a number of ways. In particular, it supports the use of "senses", namely proximity sensing, sight, and smell. The first one permits an agent to identify who are in his near vicinity and the services being offered and required. Moreover, the environment restricts agent communication, so that only agents close to each other are able to interact. The sight sense lets an agent to "see" beyond his near vicinity and identify others within a certain distance. This is mainly for deciding whether to come closer or not for interacting depending on the services the agent is interested in.

In addition, all agents leave a trail of evaporative marks on the environment. These marks contain information about the services the agent offers and requires, but not information about the agent himself. Thus, when agents move (i.e. walk) across the environment they can be tracked down by means of "smelling" the mark trail. The smell sense lets an agent to detect a notional gradient on the environment and guide his exploratory behaviour towards where it seems to be something of his interest. These senses permit agents to forage for services required and provided by those who have given the best evaluation and have offered the best service, accordingly.

It is important to remark that there is no mapping between *walking* in the DAEM environment and performing an action in the real world or acquiring new valuable knowledge. The DAEM environment is a place for agents to "sense" gradients, so that they easily explore interest gradients and track down the source to find a potential customers and suppliers. Equally, the DAEM environment allows DAEM agents to readily create these interest gradients around them by means of leaving trails. This sense of attraction and service foraging resembles food foraging in natural ecosystems and encourages the creation of niches around keystone species [9,5]. Therefore, complying with the original view of business ecosystems [1].

In particular, the idea of leaving and perceiving evaporative mark trails is inspired by the concept of *stigmergy* (cf. [7]); we use mark trails as an indirect communication medium to guide the agent exploratory behaviour and find other agents. Other approaches are inspired by the same concept and used for the same purpose, but applied differently. For instance, *digital pheromones* are used for guiding agent movements through a space, either in a virtual environment [10] or in the physical world [11]: pheromones left on the environment diffuse and disseminate producing different levels of pheromone concentration, thus creating gradient fields. The latter permits an agent to perform a hill climbing search guiding the agent displacements either away or towards the pheromone source, i.e. another agent.

In that approach, agents read the pheromone concentration on the spot. Thus, to determine the gradient field direction agents have to read at least

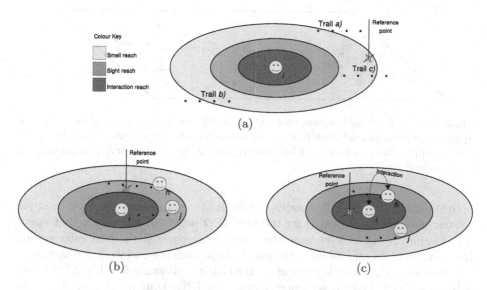

Fig. 2. An example of agent senses

two pheromones on two different spots. That is, they have to navigate through the environment first in order to decide what direction they want/have to take. Once a direction is determined, the agent have to actually follow the trail, either uphill or down hill, even though the pheromone source has already changed direction. In contrast, in our approach agents have a smell sense and perceive evaporative marks in a wider area. This permits agents to detect partial trails, hence a gradient, and immediately determine its direction whilst being on the same spot. Our approach permits agents to react promptly to a sudden direction change of the agent being tracked down.

There is yet another example inspired by stigmergy called *cognitive stigmergy* [12]: an approach to consider *annotations* as an alternative to pheromones for stigmergy coordination and cognitive agents rather than ant-like agents. Annotations keep information about mediating artifacts; they contain symbolic values representing an information piece along with a semantic, and denoting an ontology; they are created by agents and other mediating artifacts to provide feedback on other artifacts, e.g. session information, number of agents utilising the artifact, number of times an artifact is used, etc. Although this approach is motivated by stigmergy as well, its usage and purpose is completely different from ours.

Another difference between the approaches mentioned above and ours is that in those approached the agent is responsible for leaving the pheromone trail or the annotations on the environment. This allows the possibility for an agent to decide not to leave them. Thus, creating confussion among other agents and possibly an undesired system behaviour. Whereas in our approach, leaving mark trails is an environment property; they are managed by the environment through all their existence avoiding confusion among agents.

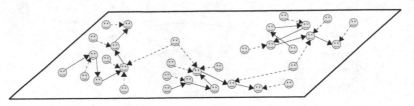

Fig. 3. Agents forming business ecosystems on the environment. Arrows exemplify supplier-to-customer relationship: solid arrows correspond to preferred interactions, i.e. links in supply chains, whereas dashed lines represent competitors trying to participate in the main links.

To illustrate how to utilise agent senses, let us resume our previous example of a car manufacturer looking for the best IPD provider. Let us say that agent i is foraging for agent h because the latter has provided the best offer so far. However, agent h is not found at the place where both agents interacted last time. Nonetheless, agent i smells three mark trails at the distance (see Fig. 2(a):) trail a) happens to belong to someone offering an IPD; trail b) was left by some requiring a car insurance; and trail c) also belong to someone offering an IPD as well. Thus, agent i moves towards the closest trail, i.e. trail c). Then it happens that the sources of both trail a) and trail c) appear at sight reach, thus mapping them to agent h and agent j, correspondingly. At this point, agent i identifies agent h —the agent originally being looked for— and decides to move closer to him rather than to agent j, thus changing its current route (see Fig. 2(b).) Finally, both agents i and h has moved close to each other to have an interaction (see Fig. 2(c).) Notice that agent j may decide on his own to move closer to agent i to interact anyway.

In general, when any agent p is the preferred supplier for agent q and at the same time q has given the highest evaluation p has received, they will forage for each other. If no other agent with a better service comes across, p and q will eventually reduce the distance between them on the environment, creating and strengthening in this way a link in a supply chain. Thus, a supply chain is a collection of links going from the supplier offering the basic service (cf. a basic resource) up to the final customer acquiring a transformed product or composite service.

Additionally, participating in more than one different supply chain by offering and/or requiring more than one service, agents become nodes in supply webs. Due to supply chain links formed by individual preferences on suppliers and customers, and on initial environment positions, two non-exclusive situations might arise: (1) competitors will be attracted closer to the links in their attempt to be part of the chain; besides, (2) one or more separate, similar, competing supply chains might emerge along with its competitors swarming around the links (see Fig. 3) resembling competition between business ecosystems [1].

Consequently, when an agent improves his service it will trigger changes to local preferences at the individual level: better suppliers will usually be preferred over others. Yet, at system level supply chains remain and survive to changes occurring at the individual level.

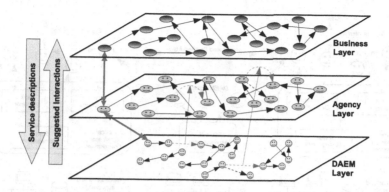

Fig. 4. DAEM architecture from a conceptual point of view; it is composed of three layers namely, business layer, agency layer, and the DAEM layer

3 DAEM Architecture

We are interested in the capacity of organisations to respond effectively to changes in a business ecosystem, thereby encouraging the survival of an organisation as whole, i.e. viewed as a single entity. Thus, as we have mentioned above, in DAEM we envisage a single agent representing an entire organisation and possessing (all) descriptions of the services provided and required by itself. This emphasises organisation interactions because it orients the agents towards service discovery and possible attendant interaction changes. However, we assume that a company might be already supported by a composite agent or a complete MAS with possibly high-level reasoning mechanisms to facilitate other different important goals. Thus, we have decided to project this MAS as a single agent onto a separate new conceptual layer where we have envisaged DAEM. This projection is inspired by the aggregation property of CAS where a collection of interacting individuals can be seen as a single organism when treated as a whole [2].

Conceptually, as we mentioned above the consider three major layers (see Fig. 4:) (1) a business layer where service descriptions and business rules exist; (2) an existing supporting agency layer where actual transactions are carried out, and (3) a DAEM layer where business ecosystem interactions are played out for opportunistic discovery of long-lasting partnership.

The business layer is where business rules exist and where (all) *actual* interactions between organisation systems and users occur. Each organisation specifies its services here and propagates service descriptions to the other layers for carrying out transactions (agency layer) and partnership discovery (DAEM layer.) Moreover, interactions in this layer consist of service fulfilment, e.g. shipping seats to the car assembly factory.

The agency layer is where software agents and associated MASs undertake various, disparate tasks within an organisation. An MAS interacts with another MAS (from another company) in order to engage transactions. When a

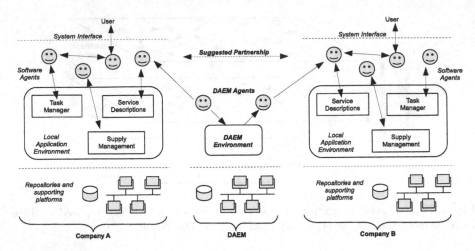

Fig. 5. DAEM architecture: a collection of many business interacting systems assisted by the DAEM layer to find potential partnerships

transaction needs more attention, e.g. a specific authorisation, it is sent to the business layer for further consideration.

The DAEM layer is where each MAS from the agency layer is projected into as a single agent. It is in this layer where the ecosystem interactions are played out (see Sect. 2:) both potential partnerships are discovered and preference changes are detected. Then, promising alliances are recommended to the upper layers for their actual arrangement.

Each organisation along with the its corresponding MAS and DAEM agent constitutes a system in the business ecosystem. Thus from the conceptual point of view, the DAEM architecture represents a collection of interacting systems portraying an open, collective system forming the business ecosystem. Then, the DAEM layer functions as a first point of contact between any two companies when looking for potential alliances. Figure 5 presents the DAEM architecture in more detail: it shows any two typical agent-based systems of different companies assisted by a unique DAEM layer for partnership discovery.

Users represent the business layer. A user interacts with the company's system for giving instructions or solving conflicts the underlying agents have not been able to sort out. An example will be given in Sect. 3.1.

Software agents represent the agency layer counterpart. In this context, agents engage transactions with peers from other companies. Moreover, they manage supplies and the services their company provides among other important activities specific to the company itself.

The local environment application is the generic environment where the software agents exist and perform their activities. The level of interaction mediation [13] as well as the deployment context may vary from company to company. We assume the existence of three main internal components namely, a service descriptor, a transaction manager, and a task manager. *The service descriptor* is used to keep track of all the details of the services the company provides or requires in order to then establish corresponding transactions. Changes in service provision are registered here as well as service evaluation standards. This component helps to send service information to the DAEM agents. *The transaction manager* is utilised for assisting in carrying out the transactions themselves, i.e. the actual exchange of money for services. Finally, the *task manager* is a generic component aiding agents in other important activities they are responsible for.

We now introduce the *DAEM layer* and its internal components. They are slightly based on the environment reference model presented by [13]. This layer is represented as a separate unique system with its own agents, environment, and corresponding deployment context. Typically, a keystone enterprise would be responsible for the development of such a system in order to coordinate its own business ecosystem members [14]. The DAEM layer internal representation basically contains two main entities: the DAEM environment and DAEM agents. The former represents the space where DAEM agents inhabit; it provides the mechanisms and dynamics to enhance DAEM agents with senses namely, proximity, sight, and smell. These are used to guide the DAEM agent exploratory behaviour on the virtual surface in order to find potential partnerships and detect preference changes in the business ecosystem. Each DAEM agent represents an MAS from the agency layer. DAEM agent interactions are mediated by the DAEM environment in such a way that they have to be close to one another on the virtual surface in order to interact. Figure 6 shows the internal structure of the DAEM layer.

The virtual surface manager deals with the maintenance of the virtual surface, i.e. it keeps a record of the current environment state. It is composed of four internal components, three entity registries (agent, mark, and service) and the map. *The agent registry* holds references of all DAEM agents existing on the environment. This means that they have to register to this component when entering the business ecosystem. *The service registry* keeps descriptions of all services offered by all DAEM agents. Service descriptions are registered upon entering the business ecosystem and whenever a new service is offered or one is no longer offered. The service registry assists on the creation of marks by providing the service descriptions only. *The mark registry* maintains all the actual marks on the environment. As can be appreciated in Fig. 6, the DAEM agents do not interact with the mark registry because the former do not decide whether to leave a mark on the environment: mark dropping is an environment property, thus it is managed by the environment itself. Finally, *the map* is the virtual surface itself: it is a toroidal grid containing all possible positions or cells. Cells contain pointers to an agent reference or a mark, in the corresponding registry, to indicate an occupied position. DAEM agents interact with this component when they want to move on the environment.

Dynamics is the component in charge of updating the virtual surface: it handles the rules for its operation. It controls agent displacements according to the direction the agent wants to move to. In addition, it manipulates directly the mark registry for managing the creation, evaporation and the eventual deletion of marks.

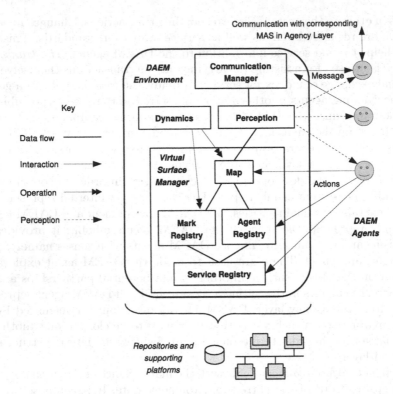

Fig. 6. DAEM layer internal structure: the DAEM environment is a separate entity from the DAEM agents; it mediates DAEM agent interactions

Perception periodically sends each to DAEM agent a set of information regarding his surroundings in the environment. This information is sent to all DAEM agents regardless of whether they have performed any action or not. This component queries the map to obtain the current position of all entities on the surface. Then it calculates what each agent senses in terms of proximity, sight, and smell. Afterwards, two lists are created containing agent identifiers and associated service descriptions. One list relates to the proximity sense and the other one to the sight sense. There is a third list created as well containing copies of marks "smelled" in the surrounding area. Let us recall that marks only contain service descriptions and no agent identifier.

The communication manager is the one that actually mediates DAEM agent interactions. When a DAEM agent sends a message to another one it passes first through this component. Then, it queries the perception component to see that the recipient of the message is within the proximity space of the message sender. If such is the case, then the message is delivered. Otherwise, the message is simply discarded. Notice that this component does not mediate inter-layer communication, i.e. communication between a DAEM agent and his corresponding MAS in the agency layer.

The mediating nature of the DAEM environment complies with the interaction mediation supporting level according to [13]. Moreover, the DAEM environment is a virtual surface mediating agent communication in such a way that DAEM agents have to be close to one another on such the surface in order to interact. Encouraging in this way local and dynamic interactions so fundamental for creating ecosystems [5] and developing adaptive behaviours [6]. These elements are fundamental for maintaining a business ecosystem because they allow agents to react timely to innovations and changes in preferences occurring in the environment.

Service-oriented architectures (SOAs) are commonly used for supporting business interaction due to their flexibility and modularity regarding economic transactions [14] (e.g. [15]), and their capacity to inter-operate regardless of the underlying implementation. Typically, an SOA consist of a service provider who register a service in a service directory. Then a service consumer reads the directory and finds a service which suits its needs. Finally, the consumer invokes the service. In terms of finding, for the first time, a suitable service and consuming it, SOA and our DAEM architecture are similar. Nevertheless, the advantage of our approach is the capacity of timely reaction to innovations and preference changes occurring in the business environment, which SOA cannot cope with that easily [16]. SOA is independent of the underlying technology, i.e. it survives technical changes, but not interaction changes in the business environment. An example of the advantage of our approach is given in the next section.

3.1   Supporting Adaptation: A Practical Example

We have explained in Sect. 2.1 how adaptation in supported by DAEM. We now present how adaptation in the DAEM layer is reflected on both the agency layer and the business layer making the whole organisation to react to innovations and changes. At the same time, the DAEM layer is affected by decisions taken in the business layer which triggers back more changes making the DAEM layer to adapt again. Let us see a practical example, in the automotive industry, where the three conceptual layers participate in the adaptation process.

Let us say that a company p manufactures car radios and is looking for a new CD laser unit supplier. Thus, the corresponding DAEM agent p registers a new service request to the DAEM environment, so that the latter produces marks on the virtual surface containing the new information. Eventually, DAEM agent p attracts three other DAEM agents: q, r, and s. They offer to supply the required CD laser unit. DAEM agent p evaluates the three offers and provides the corresponding feedback. Finally, DAEM agent p prefers DAEM agent q over the other two whose offers were good but not better than q's. Thus, DAEM agent p suggests to his corresponding MAS p to engage interactions with MAS q over the offered CD laser unit. (Please, refer to Fig. 1 and Fig. 2 for visualising of how agent interactions work in the DAEM layer.)

MAS p tries to interact with MAS q but it cannot due to discrepancies in the response time. Thus, MAS p informs accordingly to the corresponding user in the business layer (see Fig. 7.) Upon analysing the situation, it is pointed out that

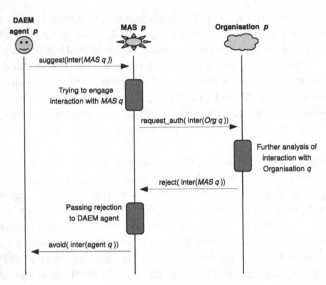

Fig. 7. Interaction suggested by the DAEM agent is rejected in the business layer

they have had response time issues when being supplied by Organisation q, even though the CD laser units are of good quality. Therefore, it is decided to avoid further commercial relationships with Organisation q. Thus, MAS p is informed about the decision and instructed to avoid further contact. Consequently, MAS p instructs DAEM agent p about the taken decision triggering preference changes which will be reflected in future interactions.

From this moment on, DAEM agent p grants a low relative evaluation (close to 0) to DAEM agent q whenever they interact. And no interactions with MAS q are suggested to the agency layer any longer. Notice that future interaction are not discouraged because no one knows when DAEM agent q will improve his service. Thus, DAEM agent p looks for the second best CD laser unit supplier instead. Immediately, DAEM agent p remembers that DAEM agent r is the second best supplier. Therefore, DAEM agent p forage for DAEM agent r to confirm part evaluations. Once they interact again and DAEM agent p confirms the quality of the offer, he grants a relative evaluation of 1.0 making his counterpart know he is the preferred supplier.

Afterwards, MAS p is informed about MAS r as a potential supplier. Thus, MAS p tries to engage an interaction with it. But then again, a conflict in the interaction shows up when arranging the minimum shipment size. Increasing slightly the price. Once again, MAS p has to ask for authorisation to the corresponding user in the business layer (see Fig. 8.) The decision reached is to carry on with the transaction. MAS p is informed accordingly and finally engages the interaction successfully. Afterwards, the user in the business layer is acknowledged about the transaction.

A business ecosystem is dynamic in the sense that changes occur highly frequent due to businesses trying to survive and dominate in their environment.

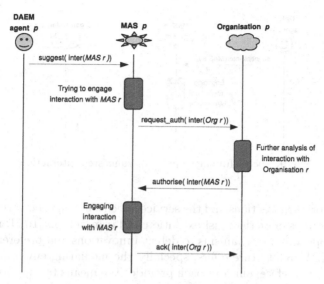

Fig. 8. Interaction suggested by the DAEM agent is authorised in the business layer

Furthermore in our example, let us say now that DAEM agent s improves the service he offers: good quality CD laser units, low price and an even better response time. DAEM agent p notices this improvement and when compared to DAEM agent r's service, it turns out that p's is better, making him the new preferred CD laser unit supplier. Thus after being suggested about it, MAS p tries to engage the transaction and succeeds (see Fig. 9.) Finally, the user in the business layer in informed about it.

Using SOA in the same example could prove difficult to make the whole system adapt to changes in the environment. For instance, when the company p is looking for a CD laser unit supplier, a web service can look for it in a service directory. Once company q's service is found, transactions could be made directly between web services from both companies. Nonetheless, there is a problem that may arise at this point: if a negotiation process is needed, services will not be able to perform it and act upon it because they are usually statically predefined [16], as opposing to MASs. This means that under the assumption of a static environment SOA works fine. A business ecosystem is not a static environment, but rather a dynamic one where changes and innovations are always happening.

Let us say that transactions between company p and q occur with no further problem. Then, company s improves its product and its willing to have a new partner. However, because services do not offer the possibility to dynamically discover either new service offers or changes in the existing ones [16], company p will find it difficult to know about it. And thus, wasting a profitable opportunity. There are two ways to cope with this situation: one is to continuously check the service registry in order to find new services; and the other one is to continuously try all service providers in order to detect innovations and determine who is better to interact with. Both solutions may prove costly and inefficient.

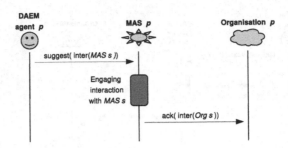

Fig. 9. Successful engagement of suggested interaction

SOA supports transactions and the service execution stage, however a business ecosystem requires more than just execution and transactions [16]. It requires negotiation support and mechanisms to detect innovations and preference changes like our DAEM architecture offers, specially the mediating environment in the DAEM layer. Therefore, our approach provides the means to support a business ecosystem better than a SOA solution.

4   Discussion and Related Work

There has been an increasing effort in the research community to explore and support environment-mediated MAS approaches (e.g. this volume.) Accordingly, some definitions have been established to uphold the movement. Thus regarding the related literature, by definition the DAEM layer constitutes a *first-class abstraction environment* [13] and functions as both resource context manager and overlay data structure according to [17]. Moreover, it reaffirms the importance of such an environment observed by others, e.g. [18], cf. common environment [19]. In general, our architecture complies with a composite configuration according to [20]: in the DAEM layer (i) we have a simulation configuration because it is mainly a virtual world where agents opportunistically find potential suppliers; and in the agency layer (ii) we have an adaptive structured information system configuration because MAS typically interact with other information systems and users.

More broadly, a *digital environment* has been loosely defined as a virtual space containing *digital species* such as software components, agents, services, business models, or rules, etc. [21]. The DAEM environment complies with this definition because it contains agents, marks, and rules of interactions. Moreover, a *digital ecosystem* has been conceptualised as a software system purposely for exploring properties of natural ecosystems in practical domains [22]. Again, the DAEM abide by this definition. Finally, a *digital business ecosystem* (DBE) is generally defined as a software platform to support business interactions similarly to natural ecosystems [22]. We do not agree with this definition because it is misleading: it does not refer in any specific way to the original business ecosystem concept defined by [1], such as competition and response to innovations.

We believe that the digital business ecosystem concept should be re-defined and consider Moore's business ecosystem properties. Thus, we extend the above definition and based on Moore's business ecosystem concept we re-define a digital business ecosystem as follows:

A *digital business ecosystem* is a software platform supporting a collection of businesses permitting them to detect and respond to innovations and market changes; it stimulates them to cooperate and form alliances; it encourages them to improve their services, and to compete for resources as they endure for survival and dominance.

Regarding other approaches to support business ecosystems, SOA is the most straightforward to use because it is already focused on business transactions. We present an example of it. In contrast, there is a work in particular we will describe that strongly criticises SOA for business ecosystem support. Additionally, we explain two other approaches using agent technology and evolutionary computation:

Customer-centric business ecosystem [14] is an approach to conceptualise and develop business ecosystems around the customer. The example they use to explain the idea is that of a car company who has to deal with many part suppliers. However, the final product is not the car itself. But the a composite product including recycling of the old car, signing up with a car insurance company, asking for a loan at the bank, etc. Thus, in this example a business model is presented where the customer is surrounded by many business ecosystems. Furthermore, a single point of interaction is proposed between the customer and many ecosystems through a single configurable platform. According to the authors, this is possible by means of SOA because complex services can be easily composed. However, as explained in Sect. 3.1, SOA struggles with dynamic service discovery and detecting new services, which our DAEM architecture can easily handle.

Ecosystem oriented architecture (EOA) [16] is a new perspective for developing business ecosystem applications. First, SOA is exposed as an inadequate technology for supporting business ecosystems due mainly to its lack of handling dynamic interactions, so essential in a business ecosystem. Then, several main mechanisms and components are described as substantial for developing an EOA, an alternative approach to SOA. Among the mechanisms, a way to search the most adequate service according to needs; publishing a reference model; and allowing adaptation. DAEM architecture permits a service search through the virtual surface which at the same time permit agents to react effectively to preference changes and innovations. Among the components enumerated, a model repository is mentioned for maintaining business models; a service registry holds references to the actual services; and a set of basic services is considered including payment and a service discovery among others. The service registry is already included in the DAEM environment; payment mechanism is handled by MASs in the agency layer; finally, service discovery is possible by means of using senses on the DAEM environment. Regardless of not mentioning any technology at all as a suitable solution for supporting business ecosystems, we believe that software agents are the most appropriate option due to their capability of autonomous problem-solving, and the simplicity of creating decentralised and distributed systems.

The Open Negotiation Environment (ONE) [21] studies adaptation and spontaneous composition of disparate services by means of Dynamic Electronic Institutions (DEIs) formed by agents. They make analogies between DEI and DBE and argue that DBEs can be constructed using DEIs. Short of presenting an architecture or model, they analogise a DEI with a DBE and propose a process to form DBEs by mean of DEIs focusing on short-term associations (cf. temporary electronic institutions) whose members align their norms and objectives "on the fly". This approach does not comply entirely with Moore's business ecosystem definition because it does not mention any means of detecting changes in the environment or supporting competition.

The Digital Business Ecosystem project [23] primarily makes extensive use of evolutionary processes to find the optimal composition of suppliers for a specific service request. They consider inter-connected nodes (called habitats) where individuals co-exist. These individuals represent services (as in SOA) and are the base unit for evolutionary processes. A population of individuals is evolved by means of a genetic algorithm to find the optimal composition of individuals to fulfil a specific composite service request. Individual composing the optimal solution create duplicates of themselves and migrate (via mobile agents) to other habitats in order to participate in other requests. Services have a tendency to remain where they are more requested making clusters cross habitats. In summary, they focus on the optimisation of one-shot service requests where supplier compositions only last until the service is fulfilled. Indeed, this approach may provide a profitable support to organisations. But falls short of entirely complying with Moore's definition of business ecosystem because it does not provide any means of detecting changes in the environment.

Contrasting with works mentioned above (except EOA [16]), DAEM and the DAEM architecture provide support to businesses in order to construct and maintain a business ecosystem as defined above. This is the novelty of our approach.

5   Conclusions

We have presented the architecture of an environment-mediated business ecosystem called Dynamic Agent-based Ecosystem Model, a novel and promising approach to model business ecosystems where the environment plays an undeniably mediating role.

Our architecture assumes the existence of an agency layer already supporting organisations. From here, we project the agency layer into an additional layer called DAEM layer where business ecosystem interactions are played out. The novelty of our conceptual architecture over other approaches is that it supports all aspects of a business ecosystem according to [1] namely, detection of changes and innovations (cf. service improvements,) creation of alliances (cf. links in a supply chain,) encouragement to innovate (through a service evaluation feedback mechanism) and competition for resources (through a service evaluation feedback as well.)

We have put forward the notion of a digital business ecosystem and extended the definition to abide by Moore's definition of a business ecosystem.

We are currently developing a DAEM layer prototype. With it, we will go through an iterative cycle to identify a set of conditions / parameters under which a business ecosystem can be maintained. For example, the environment size; amount of service offers required for the agents to gain global structure; number of agents necessary to maintain a stable system; etc. None of the projects mentioned in Sect. 4, focus on this aspect. Findings can both enhance the theoretical underpinnings of DAEM and provide valuable input into new models of business ecosystems.

We believe DAEM is a novel and promising approach for modelling business ecosystems; and the presented DAEM architecture will help to the development of applications for creating and maintaining digital business ecosystems, where the environment plays an identifiable mediating role.

References

1. Moore, J.F.: Predators and prey: a new ecology of competition. Harvard Business Review 71(3), 75–86 (1993)
2. Holland, J.: Hidden Order: How Adaptation Builds Complexity. In: Helix books. Addison-Wesley, Reading (1995)
3. Marín, C.A., Stalker, I., Mehandjiev, N.: Business ecosystem modelling: Combining natural ecosystems and multi-agent systems. In: Klusch, M., Hindriks, K.V., Papazoglou, M.P., Sterling, L. (eds.) CIA 2007. LNCS (LNAI), vol. 4676, pp. 181–195. Springer, Heidelberg (2007)
4. Mehandjiev, N.D., Stalker, I.D., Carpenter, M.R.: Activity coordination for flexible processes linking instant virtual enterprises. In: Workshops on Enabling Technologies: Infrastructure for Collaborative Enterprises. IEEE Computer Society Press, Los Alamitos (2007)
5. Green, D.G., Sadedin, S.: Interactions matter–complexity in landscapes and ecosystems. Ecological Complexity 2(2), 117–130 (2005)
6. Marín, C.A., Mehandjiev, N.: A classification framework of adaptation in mutiagent systems. In: Klusch, M., Rovatsos, M., Payne, T.R. (eds.) CIA 2006. LNCS (LNAI), vol. 4149, pp. 198–212. Springer, Heidelberg (2006)
7. Parunak, H.V.D.: Go to the ant: Engineering principles from natural mutli-agent systems. Annals of Operations Research 75, 69–101 (1997)
8. Maurer, B.A.: Statistical mechanics of complex ecological aggregates. Ecological Complexity 2(1), 71–85 (2005)
9. Levin, S.A.: Ecosystems and the biosphere as complex adaptive systems. Ecosystems 1(5), 431–436 (1998)
10. Parunak, H.V.D., Brueckner, S.A., Sauter, J.: Digital pheromones for coordination of unmanned vehicles. In: Weyns, D., Van Dyke Parunak, H., Michel, F. (eds.) E4MAS 2004. LNCS (LNAI), vol. 3374, pp. 246–263. Springer, Heidelberg (2005)
11. Mamei, M., Zambonelli, F.: Pervasive pheromone-based interaction with RFID tags. ACM Transactions on Autonomous and Adaptive Systems 2(2), 1–28 (2007)
12. Ricci, A., Omicini, A., Viroli, M., Gardelli, L., Oliva, E.: Cognitive stigmergy: Towards a framework based on agents and artifacts. In: Weyns, D., Van Dyke Parunak, H., Michel, F. (eds.) E4MAS 2006. LNCS (LNAI), vol. 4389, pp. 124–140. Springer, Heidelberg (2007)

13. Weyns, D., Omicini, A., Odell, J.: Environment as a first class abstraction in multiagent systems. Autonomous Agents and Multi-Agent Systems 14(1), 5–30 (2007)
14. Fragidis, G., Tarabanis, K., Koumpis, A.: Conceptual and business models for customer-centric business ecosystems. In: Inaugural IEEE-IES Digital EcosystemS and Technologies Conference DEST 2007, New York, IEEE-IES, February 2007, pp. 94–99 (2007)
15. Cheah, C.: The emperor's new clothes: Redressing digital business ecosystem design. In: Inaugural IEEE-IES Digital EcosystemS and Technologies Conference DEST 2007, New York, IEEE-IES, February 2007, pp. 602–606 (2007)
16. Ferronato, P.: Architecture for digital ecosystems, beyond service oriented architecture. In: Inaugural IEEE-IES Digital EcosystemS and Technologies Conference DEST 2007, New York, IEEE-IES, February 2007, pp. 660–665 (2007)
17. Platon, E., Mamei, M., Sabouret, N., Honiden, S., Parunak, H.V.D.: Mechanisms for environments in multi-agent systems: Survey and opportunities. Autonomous Agents and Multi-Agent Systems 14(1), 31–47 (2007)
18. Parunak, H.V.D., Brueckner, S., Sauter, J., Matthews, R.S.: Distinguishing environmental and agent dynamics: A case study in abstraction and alternate modeling technologies. In: Omicini, A., Tolksdorf, R., Zambonelli, F. (eds.) ESAW 2000. LNCS (LNAI), vol. 1972, pp. 19–33. Springer, Heidelberg (2000)
19. Omicini, A., Ricci, A., Viroli, M., Castelfranchi, C., Tummolini, L.: A conceptual framework for self-organising MAS. In: AI*IA/TABOO Joint Workshop Dagli oggetti agli agenti: sistemi complessi e agenti razionali (WOA 2004), Bologna, Pitagora Editrice, pp. 100–109 (2004)
20. Valckenaers, P., Sauter, J., Sierra, C., Rodriguez-Aguilar, J.A.: Applications and environments for multi-agent systems. Autonomous Agents and Multi-Agent Systems 14(1), 61–85 (2007)
21. Muntaner Perich, E., De la Rosa Esteva, J.L.: Using dynamic electronic institutions to enable digital business ecosystems. In: Noriega, P., Vázquez-Salceda, J., Boella, G., Boissier, O., Dignum, V., Fornara, N., Matson, E. (eds.) COIN 2006. LNCS (LNAI), vol. 4386, pp. 259–273. Springer, Heidelberg (2007)
22. Briscoe, G., Sadedin, S., Paperin, G.: Biology of applied digital ecosystems. In: Inaugural IEEE-IES Digital EcosystemS and Technologies Conference DEST 2007, New York, IEEE-IES, February 2007, pp. 458–463 (2007)
23. Briscoe, G., De Wilde, P.: Digital ecosystems: Evolving service-orientated architectures. In: BIONETICS 2006: Proceedings of the 1st international conference on Bio inspired models of network, information and computing systems. ACM Press, New York (2006)

Experimenting with Language Support for Proximity in Ambient-Oriented Programming

Victor Ramiro[1], Jessie Dedecker[2,*], Éric Tanter[1,**], and Peter Barron[3]

[1] PLEIAD Lab, Computer Science Department (DCC)
University of Chile, Santiago, Chile
[2] Programming Technology Lab, Vrije Universiteit Brussel, Belgium
[3] Distributed Systems Group, Trinity College, Dublin, Ireland
{vramiro,etanter}@dcc.uchile.cl, jededeck@vub.ac.be,
Peter.Barron@cs.tcd.ie

Abstract. Proximity is a key to scalable and meaningful interactions in distributed systems, both natural and artificial, and in particular in pervasive computing environments. However, proximity as such is a vague notion that can be considered both in a very factual manner (spatial distance) and in a very abstract and subjective manner (user affinity). We claim that an adequate system or programming language for ambient intelligence applications ought to support an open notion of proximity, making it possible to rely on different, possibly subjective, understandings of proximity, as well as their combinations. We explore how to extend the Ambient-Oriented Programming language AmbientTalk with language constructs that give programmers flexible control over subjective proximity definitions in both service advertising and discovery.

1 Introduction

Proximity can be defined as a *state of nearest*, the perception of *being close* to something or someone. As a concept it naturally plays a significant role in how, as humans, we interact with our environment. This can be observed in the relationships we maintain with others, or in the manner in which we interact with everyday objects around us. For instance, how we hold one friendship above another, or in the way we relate the topics of different books to each other.

The concept of proximity is also of interest to the field of pervasive computing and ambient intelligence, where the focus is on unobtrusively managing and assisting the tasks of users. In these systems the introduction of proximity allows interactions to be bounded locally. The approach aids scalability [35] as entity interaction is scoped. In addition, the application of proximity allows entities to demarcate content of interest [19] making it easier to discover services or data that are of relevance.

---

* J. Dedecker is funded by Interuniversity Attraction Poles Programme Belgian State, Belgian Science Policy.
** É. Tanter is partially financed by the Millennium Nucleus Center for Web Research, Grant P04-067-F, Mideplan, Chile, and FONDECYT Project 11060493.

D. Weyns, S.A. Brueckner, and Y. Demazeau (Eds.): EEMMAS 2007, LNAI 5049, pp. 259–283, 2008.

For example, consider a proximity defined by a geometric distance of 10 meters and a degree of separation between friends of 1. The former scopes interactions to a 10 meter radius and recognises that content exceeding the boundary is of less relevance. The later demarcates content which, in this case, are from close friends. For pervasive computing the determination of such proximities should be done at the service discovery level as this is the initial point of interaction. In this paper, we present such an approach using a broad notion of proximity that can be use in mobile ad-hoc environments.

Traditional applications of proximity have focused on the physical distance between entities. However, by providing a broader notion of proximity that incorporates a more open application of the concept it is possible to gain greater control over the interaction between entities. Unfortunately, such an open application of proximity is currently not supported by the state of the art. From this point of motivation, that *open notions of proximity should be supported by pervasive computing systems*, this paper makes the following contributions:

- a taxonomy of possible useful notions of proximity is presented in Section 2.
- from this taxonomy we present, in Section 2.4, a set of requirements capable of supporting these notions of proximity within a system.
- we propose a model that supports these requirements in Section 3.
- we present and discuss a technical implementation of this model in AmbientTalk in Sections 4 and 5.

2 What Do You Mean, "Proximity"?

"Proximity is defined as the state, quality, sense, or fact of being near or next" – The American Heritage

The above definition of proximity leads us to considering two orthogonal dimensions when it comes to analysing proximity[1]. First, being near or next depends on the notion of distance used; that is, one entity is close to another *with respect to* a given metric. Such a metric can be based on *physical* properties of the entities (*e.g.* physical location), or on a more *abstract* criteria, not related to the material world (*e.g.* nearness of relatives). We discuss physical vs. abstract proximity in Section 2.1, and then consider the interests of being able to *compose* several proximity metrics in Section 2.2.

Second, the definition mentions the word "sense" in addition to "state" or "fact", which tends to suggest a *subjective* notion of proximity, that depends on the actual perception of the subject entity. This is in contrast to *objective* criteria or metrics, for which all entities share the same understanding of what it means to be close. We elaborate on this dimension in Section 2.3

2.1 Physical vs. Abstract Proximity

Physical Proximity. In current pervasive computing and ambient intelligence systems, the proximity of entities is primarily determine by physical

---

[1] The most part of this section first appeared in [3].

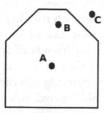

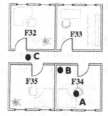

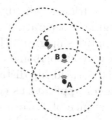

(a) Defining prox-
imity in the form a
polygon.

(b) Defining prox-
imity using a phys-
ical boundary of a
room.

(c) Defining prox-
imity using the sig-
nal propagation of
a wireless network.

Fig. 1. Different notions of physical proximity (B is "near" A, but C is not)

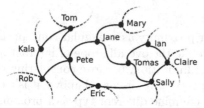

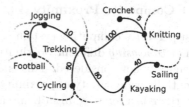

(a) Defining proximity using the relationships of users. Distance is determine by the degree of separation
between two users.

(b) Defining proximity base on
the interests or hobbies of users.
Weightings on links indicate similarity of hobbies.

Fig. 2. Different notions of abstract proximity

considerations. For example in YABS [2], a domain specific language developed for pervasive computing, interactions are limited to the local environment,
where "local" is defined by a geometric parameter (Fig. 1(a)). In Gaia [34] a
middleware framework developed for pervasive computing, proximity is admin-
istratively bound to a physical location which, in this case, is a meeting room
(Fig. 1(b)). Taking a different approach, systems such as AmbientTalk [11] implicitly define proximity based on the signal strength of wireless communications
(Fig. 1(c)): interactions can only take place when entities are in range of communication.

Abstract Proximity. Physical notions of proximity are very useful in developing pervasive computing systems [19,35], but it is also possible to extend the
benefits of proximity considerations by examining abstract notions of proximity:
an abstract proximity does not directly map to physical characteristics of the
considered entities, but rather relies on logical, domain specific criteria.

First of all, one may consider a virtual rather than physical concept of place:
e.g. although video conference participants may be in geographically different
places, they all share the same virtual meeting room. On another line, one can
define proximity based on the *relationships* of users - friends, acquaintances, or

friends of friends. The distance between two users (or entities owned by users) is the degree of separation between them, *i.e.* the length of the path relating them on a relationship graph (Fig. 2(a)). This metric can be used for instance to allow access to your personal devices to yourself, your friends, and friends of friends (that is, a friendship distance of at most 2). One can consider that present instant messenger applications consider the buddy relationship, restricting interactions to a distance of 1. In a different vain, it is possible to define proximity based on the interests or hobbies of users. The distance in this case can be described in terms of the similarity of one hobby or interest to another. For instance, jogging is arguably much more similar to trekking than to knitting (Fig. 2(b)). It is likewise possible to devise a wide number of abstract proximities, related to particular domains or applications.

2.2 Composite Proximity

Most pervasive computing systems consider proximity as a singular concept: the idea of *composing* different proximities to refine the overall scope of interactions is generally not considered. This is a strong limitation, because considering the potentially wide variety of proximity notions we have discussed above, it is clear that there is a lot to gain in being able to combine different types of proximity to express a more subtle requirement.

For example, composing a proximity based on geometric distance (Fig. 1(a)) and user hobbies (Fig. 2(b)) would first, aid scalability through the scoping of interactions within the local environment, and secondly, highlight content in the local environment that may be of interest. One could also consider spatio-temporal proximity, relating entities that are or have been, within a given time frame, in the same local environment. Another example is to combine spatial locality with network link quality, *e.g.* to aid in the development of an application disseminating multimedia content to local participants.

Alternatively, combining geometric distance (Fig. 1(a)) with the wireless signal strength (Fig. 1(c)) between nodes would define a proximity that not only scopes interactions of nodes to their physical locality but by their closeness in terms of signal strength. Such a proximity might be useful in disseminating multimedia content to local participants where link quality is important.

2.3 Objective vs. Subjective Proximity

We now turn to a crucial issue when it comes to considering different notions of proximity in the context of open networks.

Objective Proximity. Existing pervasive computing systems support a notion of proximity that can be defined as *objective* in the sense that the semantics of the proximity function are hardwired in the middleware layer. That is, all entities in the system share the same notion(s). In a system like AmbientTalk, where network connectivity is the only proximity factor, this shared understanding is obvious. In Gaia as well, proximity is defined by physical presence in an active

```
proximity(5);  // circle of radius 5
proximity(-5,-5,-10,5,-10,20,10,20,10,5,5,-5); // polygon as in Fig.1(a)
proximity(F34); // symbolic location as in Fig.1(b)
```

Fig. 3. Proximity definitions in YABS

space, *i.e.* a meeting room. In a system like YABS, each entity can define its own proximity requirement using the `proximity` function (Fig. 3). Although the actual parameters of the proximity functions are specific to each entity, the *interpretation* of the proximity function is defined in the infrastructure, and cannot be changed.

Subjective Proximity. The way systems reliant on objective proximity work implies that the different shared interpretations of proximity are installed or configured upfront in the infrastructure. Although this approach is feasible if we consider a limited and fixed number of interpretations (like in YABS), it does not fit our claim that many proximity notions are of interest, both physical and abstract, and that these notions are potentially specific to certain applications or domains. It is necessary that clients be able to define, compose and use new notions of proximity.

In other words, if a new entity joins a certain environment and looks for services of a certain type that are "close" to it, this entity ought to be able to use its *own notion* of what it means to be nearby. This means that the proximity function should possible be defined by the client itself, not predefined by the underlying infrastructure. In this case there is no globally shared understanding of the proximity, rather a *subjective view* of the client, that reflects the particular requirements of the application.

2.4   Requirements for Proximity Relationships

In order for a software system to support a notion of proximity it must be capable of defining proximity relationships. A *proximity relationship* (PR) defines when a party is considered to be in proximity of another party. The type of proximity relationship that can be expressed in a system determines its support for the notions of proximity we identified above. For example, a system will support physical proximity when it supports the proximity relationship to be expressed in terms of a physical distance.

To express the different notions of proximity we described above the underlying system needs to support evaluating proximity relationships. We distilled five requirements for these PRs, that need to be supported by the underlying system, such that they can express the identified types of proximity:

1. **Open PRs:** proximity relations should be general such that they can support both physical and abstract proximity. PRs can be defined in terms of physical location parameters (such as GPS coordinates) or application-specific parameters (such as database information).

2. **Composite PRs:** proximity relations can be constructed as a composition of a set of simpler or more comprehensible proximity relations.
3. **Idiosyncratic PRs:** proximity relations should be custom definable by both clients and servers in the network. Since a network is built from heterogeneous components, each having their own requirements, it is impossible to define a set of shared definitions of proximity. Being able to define idiosyncratic proximity relationships enables one to express subjective proximity.
4. **Distributed PR evaluation:** proximity relations are defined over a set of networked parties with the aim to reduce the number of interactions in the system. Hence, it is important that the proximity evaluation process scales and is therefore distributed over the network.
5. **Dynamic PRs:** proximity relationships should be definable with values that change in time.

A model where it is possible to define PRs with these properties provides a good basis to express the different notions of proximity we defined above. These notions ought to be supported by system software for pervasive computing. In the remainder of this paper we study how proximity can be used to scope the context in which service discovery and advertising is performed.

3   Open Proximity Model for Scoping Service Discovery

The scope of service discovery is typically defined by the broadcasting range of packets in the network. In practice this broadcasting range is limited to the subnet of the network to reduce unnecessary network traffic in other subnets. The scope of this mechanism is implicit and determined by the network configuration rather than the application requirements.

In this work, we propose to scope the service discovery based on a proximity model. In this section, we first give a brief overview of the model followed, and then discuss some of its details. We finally evaluate it in the light of the PR requirements established previously.

3.1   Overview of the Model

Service discovery is the combination of two processes: a *service query*, issued by a client, and a *service advertisement*, issued by a server. Typically, a service advertisement includes a number of attributes characterizing the service, and a service query defines constraints on these attributes, specifying what the client is looking for.

We propose to define explicit scopes based on proximity for both the query and advertising processes. This allows a server to restrict its advertisements so that they are visible only to clients within a given scope. Reciprocally, a client is able to specify the scope within which it is interested in querying services. Only if the scope of both parties intersect can the client actually see the service, check its specific characteristics according to the query, and start using it if appropriate.

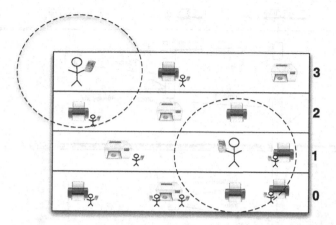

Fig. 4. Printer Scenario: Clients searching for printers around in a 10m proximity range and Printers advertise if and only if the client is in the Social scope defined by a friend network graph

The scope of a particular process is defined by a *proximity function*. Such a function is a predicate over the *properties* that characterize the other party. Properties are key-value pairs, that can include information such as the physical location and application-specific data such as a social network database from an application. The type and naming of the property information that is included should be based on an ontology shared by the involved parties.

As an example, consider the scenario depicted in Figure 4. A client application (running on a PDA) is searching for a printer server:

- The client application defines an objective and physical proximity function: it considers any printer that is in a radius of 10 meters. This proximity function defines the scope of client query.
- The printer services define an abstract and subjective proximity function based on a social network: when the owner of the PDA and the owner of the printer know each other directly (1st degree) or indirectly (until the 2nd degree) then the service considers the client to be in proximity. This proximity function defines the scope of service advertisement.

When the owner of the PDA is within the social range of the owner's printer, and the printer is located within 10 meters around the PDA, the PDA sees the printer and can run its service query to determine if the printer has the right properties (eg. resolution), and if so, use it.

3.2 Distributed Evaluation Semantics

Figure 5 illustrates the distributed evaluation process for doing service discovery. In the first phase, the client starts broadcasting in the network the requested service and its properties. In this phase the scope of service query and service

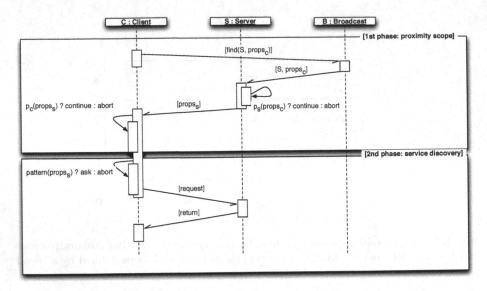

Fig. 5. Evaluation of proximity between server and client

1st phase: Proximity Scope	
$[\text{prox}_{server}(\text{props}_{client})]_{server}$	the scope of the service advertisement
$[\text{prox}_{client}(\text{props}_{server})]_{client}$	the scope of the client query
2nd phase: Service Discovery	
$[\text{query}_{client}(\text{props}_{server})]_{client}$	if a service matches client requirements

Fig. 6. Distributed evaluation of service discovery with proximity

advertisement is determined, by evaluating both the client and server proximity functions. Each function is evaluated at the site where it has been defined using the properties that characterize the other party. The second phase, the execution of the service query, is only performed when both client and server consider each other in proximity. In this stage the client considers whether the service properties match its application requirements. In the printer example, this could be the properties of the printer such as for example its printing resolution, printing speed or the number of jobs that are in its queue.

The sequence diagram intuitively describes the evaluation semantics. Figure 6 summarizes the semantics. The notation $[exp]_{site}$ denotes that the expression exp is executed on the node $site$ in the network.

3.3   Efficiency of the Model

Our objective in presenting the proximity model was simplicity in its design and usability. However, among the motivation for scoping service discovery with proximity functions is the fact of increasing scalability of the system. For this reason it is important that the model can be implemented efficiently.

Costs of Proximity. We claim that proximity relationships can reduce inter-actions among peers in the environment because a client and a service will not initiate an interaction when they are not considered to be in one another's prox-imity. In particular, the actual service query is not executed unless both client and server have agreed that they are in scope.

In the overall cost model, we have to consider *(a)* the amount of data that is transferred over the network, *(b)* the number of connections that are established, and *(c)* the computational resources used to compute the proximity.

Of course, we have to keep in mind what the cost would be if no support for proximity were provided. For obtaining the same semantics without the support of proximity relations, for instance in Jini [26], the client first retrieves all the available services that match the query, and then have to filters them according to his criteria of proximity.

So, our model implies the transmission of the properties required to compute proximity on both sides. In Jini, server properties used to compute client-defined scope would have to be passed also, after the query has succeeded. Client prop-erties are not passed over the network, but this is due to the fact that it is impossible to express server-side proximity with Jini: a published service is vis-ible to any client in reach.

So overall, the gain of our approach in terms of efficiency is that queries do not have to be evaluated against service providers that are out of scope. For this to represent a gain, the cost of evaluating a query should be higher than the cost of evaluating proximity. We believe this makes sense in most cases, where proximity is a first approximation of the range in which services should be found, while the actual service query potentially discriminates on each and every detail of the provided services. This of course depends on a design decision that the programmer has to commit to.

Staging Proximity Evaluation. If needed, it is possible to further enhance the efficiency of proximity evaluation by adopting a *staged evaluation* approach. The basic idea is as follows: since a proximity function is a predicate on the properties of a peer, it can be decomposed in smaller functions that only require a subset of these properties.

The smaller functions represent logical evaluation steps. Their composition with boolean operators allows optimization of the traffic (at the expense of con-nections). Indeed, if two functions f_1 and f_2 are composed with an *and* operator, if f_1 rejects the peer, then it is not needed to evaluate f_2 (and therefore, we avoid sending over the network the properties required by f_2).

In the worst case, all smaller functions have to be evaluated, and so all prop-erties have to be transmitted. The difference with the non-staged approach then is that more connections have been necessary (one per evaluation stage). But on average, this approach performs better.

Decomposing proximity functions in smaller functions to allow staged evalua-tion has some consequences with respect to the simplicity of the approach. First, the developer has to take special care into decomposing the proximity functions manually, to keep the desired semantics. Second, each functions must indicate the precise properties it requires for evaluation. This is crucial to allow the runtime to transmit only the required properties at each step of the evaluation. For example, as we will see in Section 5.2, our solution in AmbientTalk simply relies on a naming convention: a formal parameter of a proximity function must be the name of the property it is denoting. Finally, attention must be paid to the order of the functions because if the programmer has knowledge about the relative size of properties, he can take advantage of this fact to evaluate first the functions that require the smallest properties. We show an example of this in Section 5.2.

3.4   Discussion

Now that we have defined a model of proximity functions we can review its capabilities to express the required types of proximity relationships we distilled in Section 2.4:

1. **Open PRs:** proximity functions can express open PRs because they can be used to express both proximity based on a physical location or on application-specific information.
2. **Composite PRs:** Representing the proximity relationships as functions has the advantage that the relationships can be composed using function composition operators.
3. **Idiosyncratic PRs:** proximity functions are not predefined and both the client applications and services can define idiosyncratic PRs tailored to their requirements. As a consequence, both objective (when the functions refer to a shared library of proximity concepts) and subjective (when the functions define custom semantics for proximity) PRs be expressed in the model.
4. **Distributed PR evaluation:** In our model a PR is defined by two proximity functions, one for the client and one for the server, such that each proximity function is computed locally given the properties of each party.
5. **Dynamic PRs:** The model can support partially dynamic proximity relationships because the properties can be re-evaluated each time they are sent over the network.

The proposed model of proximity functions is capable of expressing the required proximity relationships. In order to experiment with this model, we extend the service discovery abstractions of a contemporary distributed programming language for mobile networks, called AmbientTalk [11,9]. The next section briefly explains the important programming concepts found in AmbientTalk. Section 5 then extends AmbientTalk's service discovery abstractions to support our model. If the reader is already familiar with AmbientTalk, it is safe to skip the next section and proceed to Section 5.

4   AmbientTalk in a Nutshell

The Ambient-Oriented Programming (AmOP) paradigm [10] addresses the distributed computing problems associated with the interactions of mobile devices. Interconnected mobile devices are different from traditional distributed systems:

- **Volatile Connections:** Mobile devices are communicating using wireless technology, which is subject to frequent interference such that failure is the norm rather than the exception.
- **Zero Infrastructure:** Mobile devices are expected to operate autonomously in different environments. These environments can offer infrastructure to support interactions. However, such infrastructure is not always available and a programming model should support software that does not rely on infrastructure.

The AmOP paradigm [10] has defined a number of principal criteria for distributed programming models in order to address these characteristics:

- **Time decoupling** implies that it is not necessary to have both parties of the communication connected at the same time. This criterium supports communication between mobile devices that are temporarily unavailable due to volatile connections.
- **Synchronization decoupling** means that the control flow of the communicating parties is not blocked upon sending or receiving messages. This criterium ensures that the availability of shared resources, which can be locked in a thread of control, does not depend on the availability of other resources in the network.
- **Space decoupling** implies that the communicating parties do not need to know each others addresses beforehand. This criterium is required to support communication that does not rely on infrastructure.

In order to support these AmOP criteria a distributed programming language called AmbientTalk [9] has been conceived. AmbientTalk is a distributed object-oriented programming language specifically designed for composing service objects in mobile (ad-hoc) networks. AmbientTalk inherits most of its standard language features from Scheme, Self and Smalltalk. From Scheme, it inherits the notion of lexically scoped closures. From Self and Smalltalk, it inherits an expressive block closure syntax, the representation of closures as objects and the use of block closures for the definition of control structures. The object model of AmbientTalk is derived from Self: classless, slot-based objects using delegation as a reuse mechanism. The language also supports reflection [28]. The remainder of this section will be used to summarize AmbientTalk's (distributed) object model and its syntax.

4.1   AmbientTalk Objects

AmbientTalk is a domain specific language designed to support distributed programming abstractions. Despite that, AmbientTalk remains a complete object-based language with dynamic typing support. AmbientTalk bases its object model in the prototype model from Self [39]. To explain how objects work in AmbientTalk, consider the definition of a printer object:

```
1  def Printer := object: {
2    def dpi;
3    def queue;
4    def init(dpi){
5      self.dpi := dpi;
6      self.queue := Queue.new(10);
7    };
8    def addJob(aJob) { queue.add(aJob); };
9    def getQueueSize() { queue.length(); };
10   def print() {
11     queue.foreach: { |doc|
12       doc.print();
13       queue.remove(doc);
14     };
15   };
16 };
```

In the code excerpt above we define a `Printer` object ex-nihilo [20] with the `object:` construct. This printer object has two fields: the printer resolution `dpi` and an internal `queue` to store the incoming jobs. The `init` method is used to initialize new objects when the `new` method is invoked. Rather than creating a new instance like in class based object oriented languages, the new message returns a clone of the receiver object. The `init` method initializes the object with a coherent value to all fields. There are three methods defined in the `Printer` object to manipulate the object's internal state, `addJob`, `getQueueSize` and `print`. The `print` illustrates the use of keyword syntax and closures. The `queue` object has a method `foreach:` that takes a closure[2] as its argument. The method is, unlike the other methods in the example, not of a canonical form. Instead it is based on the keyword syntax, which was first introduced in Smalltalk.

Keyword syntax can be recognized by the trailing colons after each word and can take multiple arguments. For example, an iteration is expressed as `1.to: 10 do: { |i| system.println(i); }`, where the keyword `to:do:` represents a function that take two arguments, an integer and a closure. A closure is syntactically created with `{ |arg1 ... argN| exp1; ... expN }`. In the code excerpt above a closure is used in the `print` method to iterate (using `foreach:`) over the printer's queue. The closure has one argument `doc`, it prints the document and removes the documents from the queue. In other words, the `print` method iterates over the documents in the queue and removes each document after it has been printed.

4.2   Concurrent Programming

The concurrency model of AmbientTalk is based on the communicating event loops model from the E distributed programming language [27], which is an extension of the Actors Model [1]. The E model combines actors and objects into a unified concurrency model. Unlike other actor languages such as Act1 [21], ABCL [42] and Actalk [4] an actor is a container of regular objects that can be individually sent asynchronous messages. Hence, whereas in traditional actor languages only actors can be sent asynchronous messages, regular objects can

---

[2] A closure is a nameless function that encapsulates its lexical scope.

now also be sent asynchronous messages. The container is responsible for executing these messages one at a time. To have a better understanding on how AmbientTalk actors behave, we first need to describe the fundamental concurrency properties of the event loop concurrency.

Event Loop Concurrency. The communicating event loop of the E language is an event driven concurrency model. In this model, the event loop is a thread that perpetually processes events from its event queue by invoking a corresponding event handler. In addition, an event loop can enforce three concurrency control properties:

- Serial execution: An event loop processes incoming events from its event queue one by one, i.e. in a strictly serial order.
- Non-blocking communication: An event loop never suspends its execution to wait for another event loop to finish a computation. Rather, all communications between event loops occurs by means of asynchronous event notifications.
- Exclusive state access: Event handlers and their associated state belong to a single event loop. In other words, an event loop has exclusive access to its mutable state.

Actors. In AmbientTalk concurrent event loops are created with actors. Actors represent the event queue with a message queue. This means that events are represented as messages, event notifications as asynchronous messages and events handlers are represented as methods or closures. The thread event loop of the actor is perpetually dispatching the messages of the message queue to the corresponding method in the receiver object of the message. Messages in the event queue are processed serially to avoid race conditions on shared state of objects. By default, all objects created belong to the virtual machine actor. Other actors can be created as well:

```
1 def anActor := actor: { |arg1, arg2, ... , argN|
2   ...
3 };
```

In the code above a new actor **anActor** is defined with the **actor:** constructor. An actor is isolated from its lexical scope to avoid sharing state with the actor that spawned it, a set of arguments can be given to be copied in the lexical scope of the created actor.

Communication. Each object belongs to one and only one actor. If the objects belong to different actors, the communication must be asynchronous by means of a *far reference*. A far reference is a proxy to the object belonging to another actor. Figure 7 illustrates AmbientTalk actors as communicating event loops. The dotted line represent the event loop threads of the actors which are taking messages from the actor's message queue and synchronously execute the corresponding method on the actor's owned objects. If two objects belong to the same actor, they can communicate either asynchronously or using sequential message passing.

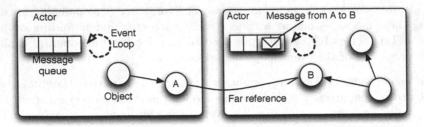

Fig. 7. AmbientTalk actors as communicating event loops

An asynchronous message is enqueued in the message queue of the actor that hosts the target object. AmbientTalk distinguishes between sequential message passing using the dot operator (`obj.m()`); and asynchronous message passing using the arrow operator (`obj<-m()`). Asynchronous messages can return futures [27], which is a placeholder for the real return value of the asynchronous call.

```
1  def printerQueueSizeFut := printer<-getQueueSize();
```

The `printerQueueSizeFut` is assigned to a future, in this case a placeholder for the queue size of the printer. After the printer has eventually processed the `getQueueSize` message the future will be resolved with the value returned by the `getQueueSize` method invocation:

```
1  when: printerQueueSizeFut becomes: { |queueSize|
2    system.print("The Queue Size is: " + queueSize);
3  }
```

The `when:becomes:` keyword takes a future and a closure as its arguments, and registers the closure as an observer of the future. If the future is resolved to a proper value, the closure is executed with the resolved value of the future as parameter.

4.3   Distributed Programming

In the previous section we discussed the AmbientTalk's concurrency model. Each actor encapsulates one thread and a collection of objects that are serially accessible by means of asynchronous message passing. From a distributed perspective traditional actor languages also employ actors as the unit of distribution and this is also the case in AmbientTalk. However, as opposed to traditional actor languages AmbientTalk's model of distribution makes it possible to remotely reference regular objects using far references as a communication channel. This means that, since far references only support asynchronous method invocations, all remote communication is asynchronous too. Hence, the concept of far references is used both for local and remote concurrent distributed computations. AmbientTalk also provides programming abstractions to deal with partial failures [9] but these are beyond the scope of this paper.

4.4 Summary

AmbientTalk is a language for distributed computing in mobile networks. Its concurrency and distribution model is based on actors and communicating event loops. This model is based on asynchronous messages exchanged between objects encapsulated in actor. The programming language features a number of language constructs, such as futures and first-class event-handlers, to marry an object-oriented distributed programming style with distributed asynchronous concurrent computations.

5 Service Discovery and Proximity in AmbientTalk

In this section we explain AmbientTalk's current service discovery abstractions and discuss its limitations. In the light of these limitations we then present an extension of AmbientTalk's service discovery language constructs based on the proximity model we proposed in Section 3.

5.1 Service Discovery in AmbientTalk

Service discovery is an important feature in ambient-oriented programming [11]. This paradigm assumes no network infrastructure such that service discovery is important to bootstrap the system and find services as users move from one location to another. Therefore an expressive and scalable manner to publish and subscribe services in the network is required.

Pattern-Based Discovery. In AmbientTalk service discovery is facilitated with a pattern matching system. A pattern has a similar structure as regular objects but differs in the interpretation of its fields. In objects, fields always refer to values (methods are also values in the form of closures) whereas a pattern's fields represent matching expressions. These matching expressions are evaluated with the service's fields. The matching expressions can be:

- **Equality:** a field must have a specific value, for instance x := 10 means that the field obj.x must be 10 in the exported service obj.
- **Wildcards:** a field may have any value, for instance x := * means that the field obj.x may have any value in the exported service obj.
- **Constraints:** a field may have any value in the range defined by the constraints, for instance x := constraint: { _ < 10} means that obj.x can be any value less than 10. Notice that "_" is bound to the runtime value of the field.

As an example, a pattern to match the printer object we defined in Section 4.1:

```
1  def printerSpecs := pattern: {
2    def type := PrinterServer;
3    def dpi := 700;
4    def queue := constraint: { _.size() < 5 };
5  };
```

In the code above, note that the pattern has a subset of the fields defined by the properties of the printer. The `printerSpecs` defines that the expected service must have exactly seven hundred dpi and less than five jobs in its queue. Furthermore, the pattern defines the field `type`, which specifies the desired type of the exported service.

Exporting and Querying Objects. An object is advertised together with a type tag using the `export:as:` construct. Since AmbientTalk is a dynamically typed language a *type tag* is used to universally identify the type of objects. In the code below, the printer service creates a `Printer` object and then exports it tagged as a `PrinterServer`.

```
1    def hp := Printer.new(Port.new("usb"), "hp9200xl");
2    export: hp as: PrinterServer;
```

On the client side we register a handler that, upon discovery of an object matches the `printerSpecs`, and sends an `addJob` message to the discovered printer object. Registering the handler, which is a closure parameterized with `printer`, is done using the `when:discovered:` function:

```
1    when: printerSpecs discovered: { |printer|
2        printer<-addJob(job);
3    }
```

This function initiates a service query based on the pattern we defined above. Note that this function does not block until a service has been found. Instead it immediately terminates and the registered handler is asynchronously invoked when a printer has been discovered.

Evaluation. AmbientTalk has an expressive pattern matching system to specify service queries. However, the programming constructs do not provide support for an evaluation of proximity prior to evaluating the queries. As a consequence, a client has to encode his proximity requirement in the query itself. But the server, like in Jini, has no means to scope his advertisement. Services are advertised in the network based on a datagram broadcasting protocol. As a consequence, service advertisements are propagated to all clients in the network broadcasting range.

5.2   Open Proximity Model in AmbientTalk

In our extension, In line with the model we presented in Section 3, we introduce two constructs to support proximity in AmbientTalk: *properties* and *proximity functions*. Their usage is explained below from the server (service advertisement) and client (service query) perspectives using the printer example introduced in Section 3.

Properties. *Properties* define the context information that is exposed to servers and clients. They are used in proximity functions for determining the scope of the service queries and advertisements.

```
1  def hp := Printer.new(Port.new("usb"), "hp9200xl");
2
3  def printerProps := properties: { |hp, gps, myAddressBook|
4    def type := PrinterServer;
5    def owner := "Jessie Dedecker"
6    def dpi := hp.getMaxDPI();
7    def queue() { hp.getQueueSize() };
8    def x() { gps.getX() };
9    def y() { gps.getY() };
10   def addressBook := myAddressBook;
11 };
```

The code above defines the printer properties. These properties are parameterized with three objects **hp**, **gps**, and **myAddressBook** that are defined in the surrounding lexical scope. These objects are encapsulated in the properties and their values are exposed through the properties via regular fields and a method invocation protocol. Fields are used to define a constant property value (such as the maximum resolution of the printer, **dpi**) whereas the method invocations are used to compute the latest value of a dynamic property (such as current printer queue size, **queue()**). Whenever the properties are requested by a server or a client all dynamic properties are computed and the results are communicated to the requesting party. Hence, only the fields are communicated and not the encapsulated objects such that this information remains hidden to the other party.

Similarly, the client also defines the properties that are needed to compute the proximity function.

```
1  def clientProps := properties:{ |gps,pda|
2    def owner := "Victor Ramiro"
3    def addressBook := pda.getAddressBook();
4    def x() { gps.getX() };
5    def y() { gps.getY() };
6  };
```

Computing the Scope of Service Advertisements. In the example in Section 3 we specified that the printer service should only advertise itself to clients whose owners are either direct or indirect (two degrees of separation) acquaintances. This type of constraints are expressed as functions that define the proximity scope in which the service is advertised to potential clients. The scope is defined by the **socialScope** function:

```
1  def socialScope(){ |client|
2    if: server.addressBook.contains(client.owner) then: {
3      true;
4    } else: {
5      def inter := server.addressBook.intersect(client.addressBook);
6      inter.length() > 0;
7    };
8  }
```

The function takes one argument, **client**, which upon invocation is bound to the client properties. The server properties are represented by the **server** object, assumed to be in the lexical scope of the function definition. The **socialScope** function checks if the owner of the client device (**client.owner**) is either a direct acquaintance or if the client's owner indirectly knows acquaintances of the server's owner. This is a case where the information transmitted over the network is heavy weight. In this specific case we need to know the friends connections graph to resolve the social scope. If we do not have information of it beforehand we need to calculate it completely. If we have information, for example using a service available in the network, the function could delegate this task to a server which knows and maintains the social graph (such as a Facebook web service).

Using Staged Evaluation. Another option to reduce network traffic is to decompose our function in stages as described in Section 3.3. For that, we need to realize that the `socialScope` function depends on the evaluation of an `if` clause, which can be divided into two smaller functions. If the first clause yields true, we do not need to evaluate the other function. We therefore reduce the `if` to the composition of two smaller functions using the `or` operator, as follows:

```
 1  def socialScopeRefined () {
 2    def f1 := { |owner|
 3      my.addressBook.contains(owner)
 4    };
 5    def f2 := { |addressBook|
 6      def inter := my.addressBook.intersect(addressBook);
 7      inter.length() > 0;
 8    };
 9    compose(or(f1,f2));
10  }
```

Although the two proposed proximity functions, the `socialScope` function and its refinement `socialScopeRefined`, have a different structure, they return the same results. Note that in order to specify which properties are needed for each function `f1` and `f2`, these functions declare their formal parameter with the actual property name (`owner` and `addressBook`). The runtime uses this information to handle the optimized staged evaluation of the proximity. In this case, if `f1` evaluates to true, we do not need to evaluate `f2`, and therefore we avoid transmitting the address book over the network.

Advertising the Service within its Scope. We have extended AmbientTalk's `export:as:` function such that the service's properties and scope function can be taken into account:

```
 1  export: hp with: printerProps in: socialScopeRefined();
```

In the code above, `export:with:in:` exports the object `hp` with its properties and the scope of the service advertisement is defined using a proximity function `socialScope`.

Computing the Scope of Service Discovery. In the example we specified that the client would restrict its service discovery scope based on a physical proximity of ten meters radius. We define a euclidean proximity function:

```
 1  def isWithinRadius(maxDistance){ |server|
 2    def d := ((client.x−server.x).expt(2) +
 3             (client.y−server.y).expt(2)).sqrt();
 4    d < maxDistance;
 5  }
```

This function is parameterized with the `server` argument that will be bound to the properties of the server. The `client` argument is bound in the lexical scope of the function. The function computes the euclidean distance based on the coordinates it finds in the client and server's properties and checks if the PDA is within the maximum radius of the server.

Initiating the Service Discovery. After we have defined the scope of service query we can register the handlers to discover a service matching our description:

```
1  when: printerSpecs discovered: { |printer|
2      printer<-addJob(job);
3      when: printer<-location() becomes: { |location|
4          gui<-showDialog("Job added to printer @ " + location);
5      }
6  } with: clientProps in: isWithinRadius(10);
```

The client registers itself with `when:discovered:with:in:` the `printerSpecs` to match services in the network and a handler to execute when a matching service is found. This handler adds the printing job in the queue of the printer server and announces where the document is being printed. It also attaches the properties of the client (`clientProps`) and scopes the service query to a circular area of ten meters of radius.

5.3 Discussion

We have extended AmbientTalk's service discovery abstractions such that both service queries and advertisements can be scoped with proximity functions. These proximity functions are used to express PRs in AmbientTalk. We evaluate our service discovery extensions to express the different PRs we defined in section 2.4:

1. **Open PRs:** functions can be defined in terms of physical location parameters or application-specific parameters. The only prerequisite is that this information is exposed in the properties such that functions can access this information.
2. **Composite PRs:** functions in AmbientTalk are first-class. Thus proximity function are first-class and can be composed. An example is shown the composition made on the `socialScope` refinement.
3. **Idiosyncratic PRs:** functions can be idiosyncratically defined. Both clients and servers can attach such a function to the service query and advertisement such that each party can define its scope based on (subjective) proximity.
4. **Distributed PR evaluation:** client and service define their own proximity function, just requiring the properties defined by the other as a parameter to locally evaluate the function. Properties are distributed in the network where each node evaluate them to determine the proximity scope. Staged evaluation further optimizes the process by avoiding evaluating superfluous conditions; this is at the cost of a manual decomposition of a proximity function into sub-functions composed by logical operators.

5. **Dynamic PRs:** the properties support dynamic fields which are re-evaluated with each transmission such that only the most recent values of the properties are used to compute the scope. The issue of how to deal with interactions that have begun based on an assumption of proximity that turns out to be invalid at some point in time is left unaddressed and represents a non-trivial challenge for future work.

6   Related Work

We focus our discussion of related work on the use of proximity in managing system interaction. In particular, we investigate the use of proximity in multi-agent systems. Also, we look at how the concept of proximity has been applied to service discovery in pervasive and ubiquitous computing.

6.1   Multi-agent Systems

The concept of proximity, or that of locality, is a technique that multi-agent systems have used to manage and coordinate agent interaction. This can be particularly seen in systems inspired by stigmergy [13], where the locality of interaction with the environment is an essential construct in determining agent behavior. For instance, Brueckner and Parunak [5] use stigmergy in a multi-agent system to find global patterns across spatially distributed real-time data. Each agent's interaction is limited spatially to the local pheromone concentrations on the individual nodes. Other applications of stigmergy can also be observed in [14,24,33,40]. In these instances, while the environment used to perform stigmergy may differ, the notion of proximity is still evident.

The application of proximity is also apparent in other multi-agent systems using different forms of swarming such as flocking and shoaling [31,37,38]. In these cases, agents coordinate their behavior based on that of neighboring agents. In [30,29], for example, De Nardi et al. control a fleet of miniature helicopters using the concept of flocking. Neighboring helicopters are determined through their physical presence or proximity to each other. In another instance, Cui and Potok [8] have developed a technique for clustering documents using a multi-agent system based on flocking. Neighbours are determined via similarities between the documents.

The use of proximity is not just limited to multi-agent systems inspired by biology. Castelli et al. [6] presents a system that allows agents to retrieve context information via a spatial proximity centered around a specific physical location. In a different approach, to aid collaboration among agents in a ubiquitous computing environment, Locatelli et al. have devised a method [23] that allows agents to perceive the physical or logical presence of other nearby agents. In [16], Hanssens et al. structures agents within societies that represent, and which also act on behalf of a user or space. Interaction is bound to agents within a society, and hence to a specific physical proximity.

Julien and Roman have developed a middleware abstraction [18] that provides agents with a *view* of the data in the system. The view, in terms of proximity, is defined using either a metric based on the geometric distance or the hop count between an agent and the data within an ad-hoc network. It is also possible for agents to define multiple views in which further access to the data can be gained using a tuple based mechanism. In a similar approach, Schelfthout et al. have developed a framework called ObjectPlaces [36]. The distance metric, in this case, is defined on a per application basis. However, in practice it would appear the metric needs also to include a hop count between nodes to ensure correct operation.

In reviewing the usage of proximity it is evident that the concept, whether it is used implicitly or explicitly, is one that is prevalent among research in multi-agent systems. This is most likely due to multi-agent systems using the environment as a primary abstraction [41] in their design. However, the extensive support that we propose for proximity, and which we have outlined in this paper, has not been fully realised in the multi-agent systems we have reviewed. As such, there is limited support for open, idiosyncratic and composite proximity relationships, as well as for their distributed evaluation.

6.2   Service Discovery

Within pervasive computing and ambient intelligence, service discovery is one of the more useful techniques for supporting spontaneous interoperability between components [19,12]. The approach facilitates the dynamic location of components that allows interaction between components to occur with little or no prior knowledge. It is a technique that has been applied successfully to a number of pervasive computing systems [32,17]. However, traditional service discovery systems such as SLP [15], Jini [26] and Salutation [7], do not fully meet the demands of pervasive systems. They tend to be designed for fixed infrastructures rather than mobile ad hoc environments which are more prevalent in pervasive computing. Also, the use of proximity to improve the discovery mechanism, as outline in Section 2.4, is not explicitly supported.

For instance, Jini [26] does service discovery based on an attribute matching system. The default matching system checks for object equality and treats null values as wildcards. The default matching process can be customized such that boolean expressions can be used to match the attribute objects. While the combination of attribute objects with a customized matching process enables one to support open proximity relationships, it does not permit dynamic relationships, because attributes cannot be changed at run time. As a result, it is not possible to manage devices with changing GPS positions or to look up a printer with a small number of documents in the queue of a printer. However, it is feasible to define composite relationships using object composition techniques such as aggregation and inheritance. It is not possible to support idiosyncratic proximity relationships because the attribute classes need to be known beforehand in order for the clients to be able to refer to the attributes of the system. Finally, while Jini does support some of the underlying system requirements of evaluating proximity relationships, it is not explicitly provided for, nor is there the ability to operate such functionality in, mobile ad hoc environment.

There is, however, a number of service discovery systems that have been designed for mobile ad hoc environments. Some of these systems have also used proximity to improve their service discovery mechanism. For instance, Meier et al. [25] have develop a system where service providers can define a proximity in which their services are available from. The definition of the proximity is limited to a geometric distance - physical proximity. The notion of abstract proximity is not supported, nor is the concept of idiosyncratic or composite PRs. Once a client registers an interest in a service they are continuously notified of any matching services as they move through the environment.

In a different approach, Yoon et al [43] have developed an overlay routing algorithm based on proximity. The approach is aimed at improving the discovery of services in mobile ad hoc networks. While the algorithm does not allow the explicit definition of a proximity, it does return the nearest service in terms of the current state of the network. This is determined periodically through measuring different aspects of the network. Liu and Issarny also use a similar approach [22] to determining proximity. In this case they use the signal strength between nodes to measure the nearness of services to a client. Open proximity relationships are not supported by these approaches, nor is the ability to compose or distribute the evaluation of these relationships.

While the use of proximity is evident among service discovery systems its application tends to be limited. In our approach we have looked to provide a verbose implementation of the concept that is both open and flexible.

7   Future Work and Conclusion

7.1   Future Work

The model we presented above has been partially implemented but there are two important open issues that require further work. First, our implementation does not explicitly consider the topology of the underlying network. This means that our protocols only consider devices within the multicasting capabilities of the network. In order to expand the range we are considering a publish-subscribe architecture where nodes are selected to act as routers. These routers link devices together that have an intersecting proximity scope. The second issue we are investigating is how to manage dynamic proximity relations once the discovery process has occurred. This implies determining an efficient way to recompute proximity conditions when required, and give programmers a way to handle the case where a proximity condition becomes false. Finally, we have to pursue empirical evidence of the benefits of the staged evaluation and property-sending mechanism described in this paper, through more complex examples and benchmarks.

7.2   Conclusion

In pervasive computing, being able to scope interactions based on a notion of proximity is important both for scalability and demarcation of content of interest. Still, proximity is a vague concept whose semantics often rely on the implicit context of its subjects. From this observation we have argued for the support of open notions of proximity in pervasive computing. We presented a taxonomy on the concept proximity from an application perspective. From this taxonomy we derived a set of requirements for defining proximity relationships between entities. This set of requirements was then used to design an open proximity model for service discovery. Our model scopes the interactions between devices by defining a scope for service query and advertisements. Hence, evaluation of service queries is scaled down to devices within this scope thus enhancing the scalability of the overall system by reducing the number of interactions. A notable difference with other discovery mechanisms is the fact that service providers can scope the advertising of services. Furthermore, since proximity is an open concept, in this model we can define the scope of interactions based on any application requirements, not only physical location. Finally, we have discussed and illustrated a first integration of this model with the service discovery abstractions of the AmbientTalk language.

References

1. Agha, G.: ACTORS: a model of concurrent computation in distributed systems. The MIT Press, Cambridge (1986)
2. Barron, P., Cahill, V.: YABS: a domain-specific language for pervasive computing based on stigmergy. In: Jarzabek, S., Schmidt, D.C., Veldhuizen, T.L. (eds.) Proceedings of the 5th ACM SIGPLAN/SIGSOFT Conference on Generative Programming and Component Engineering (GPCE 2006), Portland, Oregon, October 2006, pp. 285–294. ACM Press, New York (2006)
3. Barron, P., Dedecker, J., Tanter, É.: Proximity is in the eye of the beholder. In: Mügge, H., Tanter, É., Cherrier, P., Dedecker, J., Lopes, C., Cebulla, M. (eds.) Proceedings of the 3rd ECOOP workshop on Object Technology for Ambient Intelligence and Pervasive Computing (OT4AmI 2007), Berlin, Germany, July 2007, pp. 1–6 (2007); Technical Report 2007-12, Technische Universität Berlin
4. Briot, J.-P.: From objects to actors: study of a limited symbiosis in smalltalk-80. In: Proceedings of the 1988 ACM SIGPLAN workshop on Object-based concurrent programming, pp. 69–72. ACM Press, New York (1988)
5. Brueckner, S.A., Van Dyke Parunak, H.: Swarming agents for distributed pattern detection and classification. In: Workshop on Ubiquitous Computing, AAMAS 2002 (2002)
6. Castelli, G., Mamei, M., Zambonelli, F.: Engineering contextual information for pervasive multiagent systems. In: Conference on Engineering Environment-Mediated Multiagent Systems, EEMMAS 2007 (October 2007)
7. Salutation Consortium. Salutation architecture specification v2.0c (1999), http://www.salutation.org
8. Cui, X., Potok, T.E.: Distributed flocking approach for information stream clustering analysis. In: 7th ACIS International Conference on Software Engineering, Artificial Intelligence, Networking, and Parallel/Distributed Computing, SNPD 2006 (2007)
9. Van Cutsem, T., Mostinckx, S., Boix, E.G., Dedecker, J., De Meuter, W.: AmbientTalk: Object-oriented event-driven programming in mobile ad hoc networks. In: Astudillo, H., Tanter, É. (eds.) Proceedings of the XXVI International Conference of the Chilean Computer Science Society, Iquique, Chile, November 2007, pp. 3–12. IEEE Computer Society, Los Alamitos (2007)

10. Dedecker, J., Mostinckx, S., Van Cutsem, T., De Meuter, W., D'Hondt, T.: Ambient-oriented programming. In: OOPSLA 2005 Onward! Track (October 2005)
11. Dedecker, J., Van Cutsem, T., Mostinckx, S., D'Hondt, T., De Meuter, W.: Ambient-oriented programming in AmbientTalk. In: Thomas, D. (ed.) ECOOP 2006. LNCS, vol. 4067, pp. 230–254. Springer, Heidelberg (2006)
12. Edwards, W.K., Grinter, R.E.: At home with ubiquitous computing: Seven challenges. In: Abowd, G.D., Brumitt, B., Shafer, S. (eds.) UbiComp 2001. LNCS, vol. 2201, pp. 256–272. Springer, Heidelberg (2001)
13. Grasse, P.-P.: Le reconstruction du nid et les coordinations inter-individuelles chez bellicositermes natalensis et cubitermes sp. la theorie de la stigmergie: essai d'interpretation du comportement des termites constructeurs. Insectes Sociaux 6, 41–81 (1959)
14. Gulyas, L.: Application of stigmergy - a coordination mechanism for mobile agents. In: 1st Hungarian National Conference on Agent-Based Computing (HUNABC 1998), Budapest, pp. 143–154. Springer, Heidelberg (1998)
15. Guttman, E., Perkins, C., Veizades, J., Day, M.: Service location protocol, version 2 (1999), http://www.ietf.org/rfc/rfc2608.txt
16. Hanssens, N., Kulkarni, A., Tuchinda, R., Horton, T.: Building agent-based intelligent workspaces. In: The International Workshop on Agents for Business Automation (2002)
17. Hermann, R., Husemann, D., Moser, M., Nidd, M., Rohner, C., Schade, A.: DEAPspace: Transient ad-hoc networking of pervasive devices. In: 1st ACM international symposium on Mobile ad hoc networking and computing (2000)
18. Julien, C., Roman, G.-C.: EgoSpaces: Facilitating rapid development of context-aware mobile applications. IEEE Transactions on Software Engineering 32(5), 281–298 (2006)
19. Kindberg, T., Fox, A.: System software for ubiquitous computing. IEEE Pervasive Computing 1(1) (2002)
20. Lieberman, H.: Using prototypical objects to implement shared behavior in object-oriented systems. In: Meyrowitz, N. (ed.) Proceedings of the 1st International Conference on Object-Oriented Programming Systems, Languages and Applications (OOPSLA 1986), Portland, Oregon, USA, October 1986, vol. 21(11), pp. 214–223. ACM Press, ACM SIGPLAN Notices, New York (1986)
21. Lieberman, H.: Concurrent object-oriented programming in ACT 1. In: Yonezawa, A., Tokoro, M. (eds.) Object-Oriented Concurrent Programming, pp. 9–36. MIT Press, Cambridge (1987)
22. Liu, J., Issarny, V.: Signal strength based service discovery (s3d) in mobile ad hoc networks. In: 16th Annual IEEE International Symposium on Personal Indoor and Mobile Radio Communications (2005)
23. Locatelli, M.P., Vizzari, G.: Environment support to the management of context awareness information. In: Conference on Engineering Environment-Mediated Multiagent Systems, EEMMAS 2007 (October 2007)
24. Mamei, M., Zambonelli, F.: Spreading pheromones in everyday environments via rfid technologies. In: 2nd IEEE Symposium on Swarm Intelligence (June 2005)
25. Meier, R., Cahill, V., Nedos, A., Clarke, S.: Proximity-based service discovery in mobile ad hoc networks. In: Kutvonen, L., Alonistioti, N. (eds.) DAIS 2005. LNCS, vol. 3543, pp. 115–129. Springer, Heidelberg (2005)
26. Sun Microsystems. Jini specifications, http://www.sun.com/software/jini/specs/

27. Miller, M., Tribble, E.D., Shapiro, J.: Concurrency among strangers: Programming in E as plan coordination. In: De Nicola, R., Sangiorgi, D. (eds.) TGC 2005. LNCS, vol. 3705, pp. 195–229. Springer, Heidelberg (2005)
28. Mostinckx, S., Van Cutsem, T., Timbermont, S., Tanter, É.: Mirages: Behavioral intercession in a mirror-based architecture. In: Proceedings of the ACM Dynamic Languages Symposium (DLS 2007), Montreal, Canada, October 2007, pp. 89–100. ACM Press, New York (2007)
29. De Nardi, R., Holland, O.: Ultraswarm: A further step towards a flock of miniature helicopters. In: SAB Workshop on Swarm Robotics (2006)
30. De Nardi, R., Holland, O., Woods, J., Clark, A.: Swarmav: A swarm of miniature aerial vehicles. In: 21st International UAV Systems Conference (April 2006)
31. Olfati-Saber, R.: Flocking for multi-agent dynamic systems: algorithms and theory. IEEE Transactions on Automatic Control 51(3), 401–420 (2006)
32. Ponnekanti, S., Lee, B., Fox, A., Hanrahan, P., Winograd, T.: Icrafter: A service framework for ubiquitous computing environments. In: Abowd, G.D., Brumitt, B., Shafer, S. (eds.) UbiComp 2001. LNCS, vol. 2201, pp. 56–75. Springer, Heidelberg (2001)
33. Ricci, A., Omicini, A., Viroli, M., Gardelli, L., Oliva, E.: Cognitive stigmergy: Towards a framework based on agents and artifacts. In: Weyns, D., Van Dyke Parunak, H., Michel, F. (eds.) E4MAS 2006. LNCS (LNAI), vol. 4389, pp. 124–140. Springer, Heidelberg (2007)
34. Roman, M., Hess, C., Cerqueira, R., Ranganathan, A., Campbell, R.H., Nahrstedt, K.: Gaia: a middleware platform for active spaces. SIGMOBILE Mob. Comput. Commun. Rev. 6(4), 65–67 (2002)
35. Satyanarayanan, M.: Pervasive computing: vision and challenges. IEEE Personal Communications 8(4), 10–17 (2001)
36. Schelfthout, K., Holvoet, T., Berbers, Y.: Views: Middleware abstractions for context-aware applications in manets. In: 5th International Workshop on Software Engineering for Large-scale Multi-Agent Systems (2005)
37. Tanner, H.G., Jadbabaie, A., Pappas, G.J.: Stable flocking of mobile agents, part I: fixed topology. In: 42nd IEEE Conference on Decision and Control (December 2003)
38. Tanner, H.G., Jadbabaie, A., Pappas, G.J.: Stable flocking of mobile agents, part II: dynamic topology. In: 42nd IEEE Conference on Decision and Control (December 2003)
39. Ungar, D., Smith, R.B.: Self: The power of simplicity. In: Meyrowitz, N. (ed.) Proceedings of the 2nd International Conference on Object-Oriented Programming Systems, Languages and Applications (OOPSLA 1987), Orlando, Florida, USA, October 1987, vol. 22(12), pp. 227–241. ACM Press. ACM SIGPLAN Notices, New York (1987)
40. Valckenaers, P., Kollingbaum, M., Van Brussel, H., Bochmann, O., Zamfirescu, C.: The design of muilt-agent coordination and control systems using stigmergy. In: International Workshop on Emergent Synthesis, IWES 2001 (March 2001)
41. Weyns, D., Omicini, A., Odelli, J.: Environment as a first class abstraction in multiagent systems. Autonomous Agents and Multi-Agent Systems 14(1), 5–30 (2007)
42. Yonezawa, A., Briot, J.-P., Shibayama, E.: Object-oriented concurrent programming in ABCL/1. In: Conference proceedings on Object-oriented programming systems, languages and applications, pp. 258–268. ACM Press, New York (1986)
43. Yoon, H.-J., Lee, E.-J., Jeong, H., Kim, J.-S.: Proximity-based overlay routing for service discovery in mobile ad hoc networks. In: Aykanat, C., Dayar, T., Körpeoğlu, İ. (eds.) ISCIS 2004. LNCS, vol. 3280, pp. 176–186. Springer, Heidelberg (2004)

Environment-Supported Roles to Develop Complex Systems

Giacomo Cabri

Dipartimento di Ingegneria dell'Informazione
Università di Modena e Reggio Emilia
via Vignolese, 905
41100 Modena - ITALY
giacomo.cabri@unimore.it

Abstract. Interactions represent an important issue to be faced in the development of complex agent systems, and deserve for appropriate support. In this context, roles have been successfully exploited to design and deal with agent interactions. In this paper we explain how the role management can be supported by the environment and which the related advantages are. We will also present an infrastructure, RoleX, that can be exploited to accomplish this task.

1 Introduction

The development of today's complex systems clearly points out the need of new methodologies and tools to face the emerging requirements. Complex software systems are *very dynamic, heterogeneous*, and *unpredictable*. This requires *high adaptability, scalability, decentralization*, and *flexible interacting capability*. Traditional development approaches show their limitations, while the *agent-oriented* approach is emerging as a feasible solution. Software agents, thanks to their capability of both executing in a proactive way and reacting to environment changes, can naturally deal with dynamism, heterogeneity and unpredictability [26]. Moreover, their sociality leads to autonomy in interactions, allowing scalable decompositions of applications in terms of a decentralized multi-agent organizations [16], and enabling interactions between agents not only belonging to the same application, but also to different ones. So, agents are typically aggregated in set of interacting agents, called Multi Agent Systems (MAS). Further, we assist to an evolution toward *societies*, open sets involving agents coming from different users and acting on behalf of them, and imposing rules for their actions by means of *social norms*.

Mature but also recent work emphasizes the effectiveness of adopting *role-based approaches* for managing interactions inside MAS and in particular inside societies, since these approaches make it possible to specify security policies in terms of organisation abstractions, such as roles, role permissions and inter-role relationships [30]. One of the first and perhaps most known approaches is RBAC, where a role is properly viewed as a semantic construct around which

D. Weyns, S.A. Brueckner, and Y. Demazeau (Eds.): EEMMAS 2007, LNAI 5049, pp. 284–295, 2008.

access control policies are formulated, bringing together a particular collection of users and permissions, in a transitory way [33]. But several other approaches have been proposed and fruitfully adopted (see Section 4).

The main contribution of this paper is the discussion about the chance of supporting the agent role management by the underlying environment, sketching the advantages of this kind of approaches in general and applied to a simple application example (Section 2). To be concrete, we present also RoleX [10], an infrastructure developed inside the BRAIN framework [14]. It is reported as an example of infrastructure that can provide environment-level support for the management of agent roles (Section 3). We report some related work in the field of role-based approaches for agents (Section 4), and discuss it in connection with environment support. Before the conclusion (Section 6), we propose some open issues (Section 5), which, in our opinion, must be faced by the research community.

2   Roles and Environments

As mentioned in the introduction, roles are considered useful to develop agent systems that faces complex scenarios. In this section we give more details about roles and introduce the connection with environments, sketching the possible advantages; at the end of the section, an application example is exploited to provide concrete examples of the proposed advantages.

2.1   Roles

We can consider a role as a stereotype of behavior common to different agents in a given situation. Such a behavior is exhibited by the agent, but is also expected by other entities, mainly other agents, organizations [30,39] and environments. Biddle and Thomas defined a role as *"a set of rights and duties"*, in order to remark the twofold aspect of this concept [6]. Their work inspired the most of the role-agent approaches.

The role concept is particularly useful in managing *interactions* between agents and the related coordination and collaboration [9]. In fact, since agents live in a "social world", roles are useful to model their interactions abstracting from the actual specific agents that will perform them; moreover, this concept is useful in the different phases of the agent system development.

There are different advantages in modeling interaction by roles and, consequently, in exploiting derived infrastructures. First, it enables a separation of concerns between the algorithmic issues and the interaction issues in developing agent-based applications, leaving the former to agents and the latter to roles. Second, it enables the reuse of solutions and experiences; in fact, roles are related to an application scenario, and designers can exploit roles previously defined for similar applications. In particular, roles can also be seen as sort of design patterns [2]: a set of related roles along with the definition of the way they interact can be considered as a solution to a well-defined problem, and reused in different similar situations.

These advantages are particularly useful in developing complex systems, as mentioned in the introduction.

2.2   Environment Support

Environments represent the places where agents live, where resources are made available, where services are provided, and in general where computation takes place. They are the component often taken for granted in a system and thus less considered, but their explicit engineering as first-class citizens can provide an edge over the today's approaches [31,36]. Environments are not limited to simply host entities; conversely, they often are in charge of defining, applying and managing organizational rules for the entities they host, which play specific roles inside the organization [39]. In this paper, the term *environment* is meant as a place composed of both "truly external" entities, which are considered as "facts" by the agents, and a sort of "configurable" layer, which is not part of the agents themselves, but can be exploited to supporting agents activities in general, and interactions in particular.

With regard to the organizational point of view, strictly connected with the environments, *agent societies* are emerging as interesting and useful for agent systems. The *sociality* feature of agents empowers this paradigm by enabling the definition of *sets of agents*, where different agents can interact to carry out a global or a single goal. These sets of agents are called MAS (Multi Agent Systems), and they have evolved to *societies*. The most important feature that a society provides is to rule the interaction between members; so we can define different kinds of societies from different coordination models [17,18]. Different degrees of *openness* have been defined for societies [15], but in general we can say that open societies better model complex systems, since they are more flexible than closed ones.

In the following we identify some features that an environment should provide to effectively support the role management:

- *Role repository.* The roles available in a given environment should be maintained in an appropriate repository. An important aspect, better detailed later, is that each repository local to an environment contains the roles local to the environment itself, not only in terms of "kind", but also in terms of "implementation".
- *Role management services.* The environment should provide the basic services to manage the roles; in particular we mention services to perform a *lookup* in the role repository, services to *assume* and *discard* one or more roles, and services to actually *use* the roles (for instance, to perform role actions).
- *Policies.* The environment should provide mechanisms to *define* and to *enforce* policies; polices can be related to different aspects, from the assumption of roles to the interaction between agents playing given roles. These services are particularly relevant in the societies' context.

So, environments should provide effective "glue" between roles and agents, not limited to hosting both kinds of entities, but also actively participating in the global computation, starting from a knowledge of the situations that is wider than the one of the single entities.

In our opinion, the advantages of providing an environment-level support for roles are the following:

- *Dynamism.* If the roles are provided by the environment, along with mechanisms to assume, use and discard them, they are not statically bound to agents, enabling the dynamic discovering and exploitation of the role(s) that better suit the agents' needs.
- *Social policy.* The global view of the environment point of view enables not only the *definition* of policies that are valid for all agents present in a given environment, but also their *control* and the capability of *enforcing* them by means of roles.
- *Context dependency.* The environment can provide not only specific *kinds* of local roles, but also specific *implementations* of widely-known roles. In this way, roles become a sort of "interface" between the agents and the local resources/services [7].
- *Security.* The environment can be seen as a "trusted third party", not only in providing roles, also in managing the interactions enabled by the roles themselves.
- *Maintenance.* The maintenance of roles is made easier by the fact that they are kept in a well-defined entity (the environment) and only there their maintenance occurs, still being they available to agents living in the environment.
- *Global view.* In general, the environment can control the whole situation, so it can not only provide roles and control their use, but also "suggesting" roles to agents [12], in order to enable them better planning their actions.

2.3   An Application Example

In the following we provide readers with some concrete examples of the above-mentioned advantages. The application exploited here is an agents-based auction. Even if this could be an "abused" example, it is well-known and quite simple, not requiring a detailed explanation.

The scenario is as follows: an environment represents an auction house, where agents can attend auctions playing different roles. In particular, the *bidder*, *seller* and *auctioneer* roles are made available to agents. The system is open, so whatever agent can join, providing it can play the available roles.

The previously-mentioned advantages can be made actual as follows:

- *Dynamism.* The incoming agents can dynamically discover which roles are provided by the environment.
- *Social policy.* An example of local policy is to forbid the interactions between the bidders attending the same auction, to avoid collusion. If the interactions occur via the environment, it can actively check them, even in a more sophisticated way.

- *Context dependency.* The environment can make available "kinds" of roles useful for the local requirements; for instance, a *multiple_auction_bidder* can be provided where agents can attend multiple auctions. Moreover, the same role can be implemented in different ways according to local policies/mechanisms; for instance, the same *bidder* role can rely on message passing on an environment, while exploiting a shared dataspace on another environment.
- *Security.* The environment can grant the correct transaction after the end of the auction, for instance the payment by the bidder and the providing of the good/service by the seller.
- *Maintenance.* When the implementation of roles must be updated, the developers can act on the role repository only, without needing to know which agents has played the roles in the past, nor which agents will play them in the future.
- *Global view.* With regard to the suggestion of roles, the above-mentioned *multiple_auction_bidder* role can suggested to agents that attend different auctions by means of the "simple" *bidder* role.

This subsection did not aim at proposing a complete application example, but provided some hints to better understand the advantages in a concrete scenario.

3   RoleX

In this section we present RoleX as an example of infrastructure that can be exploited to provide environment support to the role management.

The BRAIN (Behavioural Roles for Agent INteractions) framework [1] proposes an approach where the interactions among agents are based on the concept of *role*. A role can be seen as a stereotype of behaviour, and is very useful to manage agents without knowing their details.

In the context of BRAIN, the RoleX (Role eXtension) interaction infrastructure has been implemented [8]. RoleX can easily associated to Java agent platforms by adapting the few platform-dependent classes.

In RoleX, A role is defined as a set of actions that an agent playing such role can perform to achieve its task, and a set of events that an agent is expected to manage in order to "behave" as requested by the role it plays. Interactions among agents are then represented by couples *action-event*; in particular, an *action* of an agent A is translated into an event delivered to an agent B. So, on the one hand the interaction is determined by the role-available actions and events; on the other hand, such a translation can be performed and managed by the underlying interaction system.

The meta-model of RoleX is reported in Figure 1, which shows the main entities of RoleX and their relationships.

The management of roles in RoleX is highly dynamic, since an agent can assume at runtime roles even unknown at compile time, thanks to a special class loader called `RoleLoader`. Such a high dynamism is also granted by the

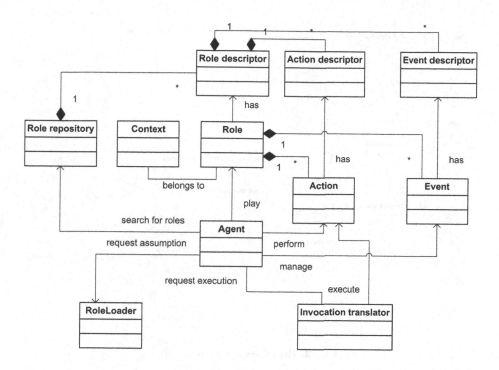

Fig. 1. RoleX meta-model

exploitation of *descriptors,* which uncouple the physical implementation of a role (i.e., the Java class) from its features.

In RoleX, the fact that an agent assumes a role means that the infrastructure, via the already-mentioned `RoleLoader`, dynamically adds each role implementation member (both methods and fields) to agent members, in order to add the set of capabilities of the role, thus modifying and extending the agent class bytecode.

The sequence of activity performed in RoleX when an agent assumes roles and perform actions is reported in Figure 2.

When an agent wants to assume one or more roles to carry out its tasks, it queries the role repository in order to find the best role(s) for its needs. Then, the agent asks the `RoleLoader` to reload itself with the new role (or, better, with the role members added to the agent's one). This step can be repeated if the found roles are more than one. If everything is right, the `RoleLoader` sends the agent an event to indicate that the agent has been reloaded. After the reload event the agent can resume its execution.

The programmers do not know anything about the role implementation but know by the descriptors, which actions can be used, and which events can occur. In the following, we focus on the action use, because the management of the events is similar and simpler. The use of descriptors means that the programmer cannot write code that invokes methods corresponding to role actions in

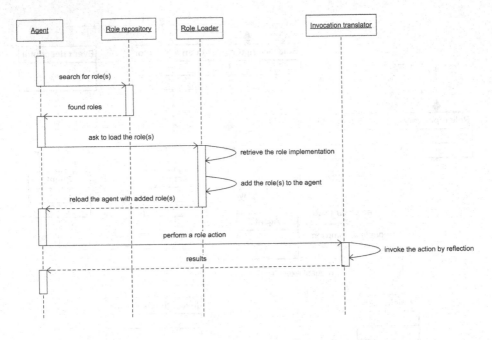

Fig. 2. RoleX sequence diagram

the usual way, because a compile-time error will occur. Therefore, there must be an *invocation translator* that does introspection on the extended agent to dynamically find which method must be call in response to an invocation on an action description. When the agent invokes a role action, it specifies to the invocation translator a descriptor of the action that wants to perform, the translator searches for a method that corresponds to the description and then invokes it using the reflection.

To release a role, the process is similar to the addition, but this time the agent is reloaded without that role.

The RoleX infrastructure can be exploited to implement the part of the environment devoted to the role management, and the previously-introduced advantages can be concretely implemented by means of the RoleX features.

As explained, RoleX enables a high degree of *dynamisms* not only in assuming, using and discarding roles, but also in finding appropriate roles for the agents' needs. The fact that the interactions are dealt with by the underlying interaction system, enforces *local policies* and *rules*. *Context dependency* relies on the availability of a local repository, but it is particularly enforced by the separation between roles' description and their implementation. *Security* is supported by JAAS-based mechanisms [11], which enable the control over the single method call. The repository is the place where the only role *maintenance* is performed, making the administrator's work easier.

4   Related Work

In this section we briefly present some role-based approaches, and in the next section we propose some related considerations.

An interesting approach is AALAADIN [21], a meta-model to define models of organizations [22]. It is based on three core concepts: *agent, group* and *role*. Fasli's proposal is based on *social agents*, and joins several concepts, such as commitments and obligations, with the powerful of roles, promoting the use of a formal notation and analysis of the applications [20]. The GAIA [38] main aim is modelling multi-agent systems as *organizations* where different roles interact; GAIA exploits roles in particular in the *analysis* phase. E. Kendall well describes the importance of modeling roles for agent systems [19], and she proposes to exploit the Aspect Oriented Programming [27] to concretely implement the concept of role in agent applications. The Role/Interaction/Communicative Action (RICA) theory [34] was born with the main aim of improving the FIPA standard with support for social concepts, which are implemented in RICA-J. The Role based Evolutionary Programming (RoleEP) treats cooperative mobile agents, which belong to the same application and that collaborate to achieve a common goal [35]. The ROPE project [3] addresses the collaboration issues and recognizes the importance of defining roles as first-class entities, which can be assumed dynamically by agents. TRANS is a multi-agent system that provides for role and group behaviors, and takes into consideration mobile agents [23]; an interesting feature of TRANS is the capability of defining rules on the role assumption by agents, such as priority, exclusivity, compatibility and the distinction between permanent and temporary roles. The Tasks and Roles in a Unified Coordination Environment (TRUCE) is a script-based language framework for the coordination of agents [25], which aims to overtake problems related to *adaptability, heterogeneity* and *concurrency*. Yu and Schmid [37] exploit roles assigned to agents to manage workflow processes; they traditionally model a role as a collection of rights (activities an agent is permitted on a set of resources) and duties (activities an agent must perform); an interesting issue of this approach is that it aims to cover different phases of the application development, proposing a *role-based analysis phase*, an *agent-oriented design phase*, and an *agent-oriented implementation phase*. In [40] Zhu and Zhou describe a role model which is tied to both the computer and human parts involved in collaborations, and in particular tries to provide help to human in computer-supported collaborations.

5   Open Issues

In the following we briefly sketch some open issues in connection with agents, roles and environments.

The first issue comes from the analysis of the reported in the previous section. The role concept is widely adopted to face collaboration and cooperation requirements, as expected. But some approaches go further, by providing some ideas of social agreement about shared norms that rule the activities not only of a single agent, but also of the whole community of interacting agents (called "society" as previously discussed). So, an "entity" that provides such social norms and enforces them is needed, and the environment is our best candidate. Even if the presented approaches do not explicitly consider the environment as a first-class entity, the most of them can be exploited in the definition of environments.

A second issue is the *gap* between *methodologies* and *infrastructures*, and concerns the development of agent systems in general. In fact, on the one hand, the development of agent-based applications requires appropriate methodologies and different ones for the analysis and design of MASs and societies have been proposed so far [5]. On the other hand, there are different emerging approaches in agent-oriented software engineering that rise from concrete application needs, and propose infrastructures to support agent development and execution; this leads to bottom-up approaches, which start from very concrete aspects such as languages, protocols, runtime supports and so on and evolve towards abstract concepts [4,24,28]. A lot of work has been done about agent methodologies and agent infrastructures, but a relevant drawback is the *separation* existing between these two aspects, which has led to a *gap* between methodologies and infrastructures, or, better, between analysis and design from the one hand, and implementation and execution from the other hand. In addition, in our opinion this separation also delays the acceptance of the agent paradigm by the industry world, which cannot fruitfully applies it to the development of software. With regard to systems where environments are considered as first-class entities, this issue is very relevant because environments often exploit infrastructures, while are disregarded by the methodologies. Some efforts in the direction of mapping methodologies and infrastructures have been made [13,29].

The third issue relates to the dynamic exploitation of the role services made available by the environment. Note that the capability of dynamically finding out and exploiting the role services can be extremely useful, because agents can then find and exploit other kind of services by means of played roles. For instance, an agent that wants to attend an auction, but does not know *a priori* the exact services of a given environment, can require the *bidder* role, which provides it all the "knowledge" to access the auction-related service (e.g., the capability of bidding, of knowing the current highest bid, and so on). In open scenarios, environments should provide "open" way for letting agents manage roles, in particular in assumption process and in operation invocation.

The fourth issue is strictly connected to the third one. An appropriate description system is required to enable agents to play the desired roles in open scenarios. In fact, we can envision an open agent world developed by different developers, for instance some focusing on agents and others on roles, not necessarily with a detailed agreement on interfaces and mechanisms. Nevertheless, if the world is open, it must enable different agents to play the needed roles. Besides the discovering and exploitation mechanisms above described, the agents need to specify *which* role is needed, or, better, *which functionalities* they need in one or more roles. We are talking about a "semantic" search for roles, which must be enabled by environments.

An approach that can be proposed to face the two previous issues is the one based on knowledge networks [32]: inspired by biology, it provides mechanisms of information crunching and re-assembly that enable to semantically find services even based on different interfaces or standards. This can be useful to face the above mentioned heterogeneity, unpredictability and high dynamism.

6   Conclusion

In this paper we have discussed about the support for agent roles provided by the environment level. We have depicted different advantages, from both the conceptual and the concrete point of view. The use of roles can significantly improve the development of agent-based systems that model complex scenarios, but their support by the environment can provide further advantages.

We proposed also different considerations, in connection with both existing approaches and the agent-role development in general.

With regard to future work, we are exploring some of the issues proposed in Section 5, proposing some research directions [13,32] that must be further evaluated by the scientific community, but in their early stage seems to be effective.

Acknowledgement

Work supported by the Italian MiUR in the frame of the PRIN project "MEnSA - Agent oriented methodologies: engineering of interactions and relationship with the infrastructures".

References

1. The AgentGroup. The BRAIN framework (2007),
   http://www.agentgroup.unimo.it/MOON/BRAIN
2. Aridor, Y., Lange, D.: Agent Design Pattern: Elements of Agent Application design. In: Proceedings of the International Conference on Autonomous Agents. ACM Press, New York (1998)
3. Becht, M., Gurzki, T., Klarmann, J., Muscholl, M.: ROPE: Role Oriented Programming Environment for Multiagent Systems. In: Proceedings of the Fourth IFCIS Conference on Cooperative Information Systems (CoopIS 1999), Edinburgh, Scotland (1999)
4. Bellifemine, F., Caire, G., Trucco, T., Rimassa, G.: JADE Programmer's Guide, JADE 2.4 (2001)
5. Bergenti, F., Gleizes, M.P., Zambonelli, F.: Methodologies and Software Engineering for Agent Systems: the Agent-oriented Software Engineering Handbook. Springer, Heidelberg (2004)
6. Biddle, B.J., Thomas, E.J.: Role Theory: Concepts and Research. R.E. Krieger Publishing Co. (1979)
7. Cabri, G.: Agent Composition via Role-based Infrastructures. Scalable Computing: Practice and Experience 7(1), 37–47 (2006)

8. Cabri, G., Ferrari, L., Leonardi, L.: Enabling mobile agents to dynamically assume roles. In: Proceedings of the 2003 ACM International Symposium on Applied Computing (SAC), Melbourne, Florida, USA, March 2003. ACM Press, New York (2003)
9. Cabri, G., Ferrari, L., Leonardi, L.: Agent role-based collaboration and coordination: a survey about existing approaches. In: Proceedings of the 2004 IEEE International Conference on Systems, Man and Cybernetics, The Hague, Netherlands (2004)
10. Cabri, G., Ferrari, L., Leonardi, L.: The RoleX Environment for Multi-Agent Cooperation. In: Klusch, M., Ossowski, S., Kashyap, V., Unland, R. (eds.) CIA 2004. LNCS (LNAI), vol. 3191, Springer, Heidelberg (2004)
11. Cabri, G., Ferrari, L., Leonardi, L.: Applying Security Policies Through Agent Roles: a JAAS Based Approach. Science of Computer Programming 59(1-2), 127–146 (2006)
12. Cabri, G., Ferrari, L., Leonardi, L., Quitadamo, R.: Role Suggestion for Agents by Overhearing. The International Journal of Intelligent Control And Systems 12(2), 179–185 (2007)
13. Cabri, G., Leonardi, L., Puviani, M.: Methodologies and Infrastructures for Agent Society Simulation: Mapping PASSI and RoleX. In: Proceedings of the 19th European Meeting on Cybernetics and Systems Research, Vienna, Austria (2008)
14. Cabri, G., Leonardi, L., Zambonelli, F.: BRAIN: a Framework for Flexible Role-based Interactions in Multiagent Systems. In: Meersman, R., Tari, Z., Schmidt, D.C. (eds.) CoopIS 2003, DOA 2003, and ODBASE 2003. LNCS, vol. 2888, pp. 145–161. Springer, Heidelberg (2003)
15. Davidsson, P.: Categories of artificial societies. In: Engineering Societies in the Agents World II, Springer, Heidelberg (2001)
16. Demazeau, Y., Rocha Costa, A.C.: Populations and Organizations in Open Multi-Agent Systems. In: Proceedings of the 1st National Symposium on Parallel and Distributed Artificial Intelligence (1996)
17. Dignum, V., Dignum, F.: Modelling agent societies: co-ordination frameworks and institutions. In: Brazdil, P.B., Jorge, A.M. (eds.) EPIA 2001. LNCS (LNAI), vol. 2258, pp. 191–204. Springer, Heidelberg (2001)
18. Dignum, V., Weigand, H.: Towards an Organization-Oriented Design Methodology for Agent Societies. In: Intelligent Agent Software Engineering, pp. 191–212 (2003)
19. Kendall, E.A.: Role Modelling for Agent Systems Analysis, Design and Implementation. IEEE Concurrency 8(2), 34–41 (2000)
20. Fasli, M.: Social Interactions in Multi-Agent Systems: A Formal Approach. In: Proceedings of the IEEE/WIC International Conference on Intelligent Agent Technology (IAT 2003), pp. 240–247. IEEE Press, Los Alamitos (2003)
21. Ferber, J., Gutknecht, O.: AALAADIN: A meta-model for the analysis and design of organizations in multi-agent systems. In: Proceedings of the Third International Conference on Multi-Agent Systems (ICMAS 1998) (1998)
22. Ferber, J., Gutknecht, O., Michel, F.: From Agents to Organizations: an Organizational View of MultiAgent Systems. In: Giorgini, P., Müller, J.P., Odell, J.J. (eds.) AOSE 2003. LNCS, vol. 2935, pp. 214–230. Springer, Heidelberg (2004)
23. Fournier, S., Brocarei, D., Devogele, T., Claramunt, C.: TRANS: A Tractable Role-based Agent Prototype for Concurrent Navigation Systems. In: Proceedings of the First European Workshop on Multi-Agent Systems (EUMAS), Oxford, UK (2003)
24. Howden, N., Ronnquist, R., Hodgson, A., Lucas, A.: JACK Intelligent Agents-Summary of an Agent Infrastructure. In: Proceedings of the 5th International Conference on Autonomous Agents, Montreal, Canada. ACM, New York (2001)

25. Jamison, W., Lea, D.: TRUCE: Agent coordination through concurrent interpretation of role-based protocols. In: Proceedings of Coordination 1999, Amsterdam, The Netherlands (1999)
26. Jennings, N.R.: An agent-based approach for building complex software systems. Communications of the ACM 44(4), 35–41 (2001)
27. Kiczales, G., Lamping, J., Mendhekar, A., Maeda, C., Lopes, C., Loingtier, J.M., Irwin, J.: Aspect-Oriented Programming. Technical report, Xerox Corporation (1997)
28. Lange, D.B., Oshima, M.: Programming and Deploying Java Mobile Agents with Aglets. Addison-Wesley, Reading (1998)
29. Molesini, A., Omicini, A., Denti, E., Ricci, A.: SODA: A roadmap to artefacts. In: Dikenelli, O., Gleizes, M.-P., Ricci, A. (eds.) ESAW 2005. LNCS (LNAI), vol. 3963, pp. 49–62. Springer, Heidelberg (2006)
30. Odell, J.J., Parunak, H.V.D., Fleischer, M.: The Role of Roles in Designing Effective Agent Organizations. In: Software Engineering for Large-scale Multi-agent Systems: Research Issues and Practical Applications, Springer, Heidelberg (2003)
31. Odell, J.J., Parunak, H.V.D., Fleischer, M., Brueckner, S.: Modeling Agents and Their Environment. In: Giunchiglia, F., Odell, J.J., Weiss, G. (eds.) AOSE 2002. LNCS, vol. 2585, Springer, Heidelberg (2003)
32. Quitadamo, R., Zambonelli, F., Cabri, G.: The Service Ecosystem: Dynamic Self-Aggregation of Pervasive Communication Services. In: Proceedings of the The First Workshop on Software Engineering of Pervasive Computing Applications, Systems and Environments (SEPCASE) at ICSE 2007, Minneapolis, MN, USA. IEEE Computer Society Press, Los Alamitos (2007)
33. Sandhu, R.S., Coyne, E.J., FeinStein, H.L., YoumanHayes-Roth, C.E.: Role-based Access Control Models. IEEE Computer 20(2), 38–47 (1996)
34. Serrano, J.M., Ossowski, S.: On the Impact of Agent Communicative Languages on the Implementation of Agent System. In: Klush, M., Ossowski, S., Kashyap, V. (eds.) Cooperative Information Agents VIII. LNCS (LNAI), Springer, Heidelberg (2004)
35. Ubayashi, N., Tamai, T.: RoleEP: role based evolutionary programming for cooperative mobile agent applications. In: Proceedings of the International Symposium on Principles of Software Evolution, Kanazawa, Japan (2000)
36. Weyns, D., Omicini, A., Odell, J.: Environment as a first class abstraction in multiagent systems. Autonomous Agents and Multi-Agent Systems 14(1), 5–30 (2007)
37. Yu, L., Schmid, B.F.: A conceptual framework for agent-oriented and role-based workflow modelling. In: Proceedings of the 1st International Workshop on Agent-Oriented Information Systems (1999)
38. Zambonelli, F., Jennings, N., Wooldridge, M.: Developing Multiagent Systems: the Gaia Methodology. ACM Transactions on Software Engineering and Methodology 12(3) (2003)
39. Zambonelli, F., Jennings, N.R., Wooldridge, M.: Organizational Rules as an Abstraction for the Analysis and Design of Multi-agent Systems. International Journal of Software Engineering and Knowledge Engineering 11(3), 303–328 (2001)
40. Zhu, H., Zhou, M.C.: Role-Based Collaborations and their Kernel Mechanisms. IEEE Transactions on Systems, Man and Cybernetics, Part C 36(4), 578–589 (2006)

Author Index

Lecture Notes in Artificial Intelligence (LNAI)

Vol. 4869: F. Botana, T. Recio (Eds.), Automated Deduction in Geometry. X, 213 pages. 2007.

Vol. 4865: K. Tuyls, A. Nowe, Z. Guessoum, D. Kudenko (Eds.), Adaptive Agents and Multi-Agent Systems III. VIII, 255 pages. 2008.

Vol. 4850: M. Lungarella, F. Iida, J.C. Bongard, R. Pfeifer (Eds.), 50 Years of Artificial Intelligence. X, 399 pages. 2007.

Vol. 4845: N. Zhong, J. Liu, Y. Yao, J. Wu, S. Lu, K. Li (Eds.), Web Intelligence Meets Brain Informatics. XI, 516 pages. 2007.

Vol. 4840: L. Paletta, E. Rome (Eds.), Attention in Cognitive Systems. XI, 497 pages. 2007.

Vol. 4830: M.A. Orgun, J. Thornton (Eds.), AI 2007: Advances in Artificial Intelligence. XIX, 841 pages. 2007.

Vol. 4828: M. Randall, H.A. Abbass, J. Wiles (Eds.), Progress in Artificial Life. XII, 402 pages. 2007.

Vol. 4827: A. Gelbukh, Á.F. Kuri Morales (Eds.), MICAI 2007: Advances in Artificial Intelligence. XXIV, 1234 pages. 2007.

Vol. 4826: P. Perner, O. Salvetti (Eds.), Advances in Mass Data Analysis of Signals and Images in Medicine, Biotechnology and Chemistry. X, 183 pages. 2007.

Vol. 4819: T. Washio, Z.-H. Zhou, J.Z. Huang, X. Hu, J. Li, C. Xie, J. He, D. Zou, K.-C. Li, M.M. Freire (Eds.), Emerging Technologies in Knowledge Discovery and Data Mining. XIV, 675 pages. 2007.

Vol. 4811: O. Nasraoui, M. Spiliopoulou, J. Srivastava, B. Mobasher, B. Masand (Eds.), Advances in Web Mining and Web Usage Analysis. XII, 247 pages. 2007.

Vol. 4798: Z. Zhang, J.H. Siekmann (Eds.), Knowledge Science, Engineering and Management. XVI, 669 pages. 2007.

Vol. 4795: F. Schilder, G. Katz, J. Pustejovsky (Eds.), Annotating, Extracting and Reasoning about Time and Events. VII, 141 pages. 2007.

Vol. 4790: N. Dershowitz, A. Voronkov (Eds.), Logic for Programming, Artificial Intelligence, and Reasoning. XIII, 562 pages. 2007.

Vol. 4788: D. Borrajo, L. Castillo, J.M. Corchado (Eds.), Current Topics in Artificial Intelligence. XI, 280 pages. 2007.

Vol. 4775: A. Esposito, M. Faundez-Zanuy, E. Keller, M. Marinaro (Eds.), Verbal and Nonverbal Communication Behaviours. XII, 325 pages. 2007.

Vol. 4772: H. Prade, V.S. Subrahmanian (Eds.), Scalable Uncertainty Management. X, 277 pages. 2007.

Vol. 4766: N. Maudet, S. Parsons, I. Rahwan (Eds.), Argumentation in Multi-Agent Systems. XII, 211 pages. 2007.

Vol. 4760: E. Rome, J. Hertzberg, G. Dorffner (Eds.), Towards Affordance-Based Robot Control. IX, 211 pages. 2008.

Vol. 4755: V. Corruble, M. Takeda, E. Suzuki (Eds.), Discovery Science. XI, 298 pages. 2007.

Vol. 4754: M. Hutter, R.A. Servedio, E. Takimoto (Eds.), Algorithmic Learning Theory. XI, 403 pages. 2007.

Vol. 4737: B. Berendt, A. Hotho, D. Mladenic, G. Semeraro (Eds.), From Web to Social Web: Discovering and Deploying User and Content Profiles. XI, 161 pages. 2007.

Vol. 4733: R. Basili, M.T. Pazienza (Eds.), AI*IA 2007: Artificial Intelligence and Human-Oriented Computing. XVII, 858 pages. 2007.

Vol. 4724: K. Mellouli (Ed.), Symbolic and Quantitative Approaches to Reasoning with Uncertainty. XV, 914 pages. 2007.

Vol. 4722: C. Pelachaud, J.-C. Martin, E. André, G. Chollet, K. Karpouzis, D. Pelé (Eds.), Intelligent Virtual Agents. XV, 425 pages. 2007.

Vol. 4720: B. Konev, F. Wolter (Eds.), Frontiers of Combining Systems. X, 283 pages. 2007.

Vol. 4702: J.N. Kok, J. Koronacki, R. Lopez de Mantaras, S. Matwin, D. Mladenič, A. Skowron (Eds.), Knowledge Discovery in Databases: PKDD 2007. XXIV, 640 pages. 2007.

Vol. 4701: J.N. Kok, J. Koronacki, R. Lopez de Mantaras, S. Matwin, D. Mladenič, A. Skowron (Eds.), Machine Learning: ECML 2007. XXII, 809 pages. 2007.

Vol. 4696: H.-D. Burkhard, G. Lindemann, R. Verbrugge, L.Z. Varga (Eds.), Multi-Agent Systems and Applications V. XIII, 350 pages. 2007.

Vol. 4694: B. Apolloni, R.J. Howlett, L. Jain (Eds.), Knowledge-Based Intelligent Information and Engineering Systems, Part III. XXIX, 1126 pages. 2007.

Vol. 4693: B. Apolloni, R.J. Howlett, L. Jain (Eds.), Knowledge-Based Intelligent Information and Engineering Systems, Part II. XXXII, 1380 pages. 2007.

Vol. 4692: B. Apolloni, R.J. Howlett, L. Jain (Eds.), Knowledge-Based Intelligent Information and Engineering Systems, Part I. LV, 882 pages. 2007.

Vol. 4687: P. Petta, J.P. Müller, M. Klusch, M. Georgeff (Eds.), Multiagent System Technologies. X, 207 pages. 2007.

Vol. 4682: D.-S. Huang, L. Heutte, M. Loog (Eds.), Advanced Intelligent Computing Theories and Applications. XXVII, 1373 pages. 2007.

Vol. 4676: M. Klusch, K.V. Hindriks, M.P. Papazoglou, L. Sterling (Eds.), Cooperative Information Agents XI. XI, 361 pages. 2007.

Vol. 4667: J. Hertzberg, M. Beetz, R. Englert (Eds.), KI 2007: Advances in Artificial Intelligence. IX, 516 pages. 2007.

Vol. 4660: S. Džeroski, L. Todorovski (Eds.), Computational Discovery of Scientific Knowledge. X, 327 pages. 2007.

Vol. 4659: V. Mařík, V. Vyatkin, A.W. Colombo (Eds.), Holonic and Multi-Agent Systems for Manufacturing. VIII, 456 pages. 2007.

Vol. 4651: F. Azevedo, P. Barahona, F. Fages, F. Rossi (Eds.), Recent Advances in Constraints. VIII, 185 pages. 2007.

Vol. 4648: F. Almeida e Costa, L.M. Rocha, E. Costa, I. Harvey, A. Coutinho (Eds.), Advances in Artificial Life. XVIII, 1215 pages. 2007.